One Family, Two Wars:

a collection of photographs, letters, diary extracts, poems, reflections and memories.

ISBN: 978-1-912728-23-7

Published and Printed by
Quacks Books
7 Grape Lane
Petergate
York YO1 7HU
01904 635967

Foreword

'The news is on, but we are fitting gas masks on the poor TB patients, whose breathing is so distressed at the best of times, that the idea of putting the masks on is almost too much, but they realize how grave the situation is, and after one or two have put them on, we have no further trouble, for the rest can see that it is possible to breathe. We have nearly finished when one of the patients tells us Mr Chamberlain, the Prime Minister, is speaking; then after a solemn speech, he tells us we are at war with Germany once more.'

The above extract from my aunt's war dairy is just one of many poignant scenes she records. As a nurse in Highgate and Lewisham Hospitals, she stayed at her post all the way through the conflict, keeping a journal of events, no doubt to help express her fear. She wrote it whenever and wherever she had time and space, often huddled under her bunk and by torchlight, after her period of duty had finished for the day. When I was working in London in the early 1980's, we went together to the Imperial War Museum to donate the original copy of the diary, which I had previously transcribed. Later it was used for research. Eight months before she died at the age of 92 in 2001, she appeared on TV in an episode called *'Forgotten Heroes'* in the series *'The Second World War in Colour'*, and she also had a mention in the accompanying book.

It seemed to me that Auntie was the only one in our family who talked of her wartime experiences, no doubt helping her, along with the diary, to come to terms with what she had gone through, as after the war was over she did in fact suffer a breakdown. Her two brothers served in the Army and the Royal Air Force: Uncle Gren was in the battle of Monte Casino during the Italian Campaign, at one point spending long hours 'hiding' in the River Volturno; Uncle Rees was 'in the desert' somewhere. There were good-humoured jokes in the family as to which uncle had had the worse time, intimating that the latter hadn't done very much. But I often think that my introverted and nervous uncle must have been terrified. My mother was a postwoman in our home town of Porthcawl in South Wales, making deliveries three times each day, and in old age suffering arthritis in her neck and spine as a result of carrying the heavy sacks on her back.

On my father's side of the family, my grandfather was a soldier in the Royal Field Artillery, serving in Belgium and gassed in one of the battles at Ypres in the Great War. When I occasionally tried to find out more details, he would give a short bark of a laugh and say:

'You don't want to hear about that! It was a rum do!'

My father, his son, was also in the Army in WW2*,* serving in a number of countries and staying on in Germany after the end of the war, to help re-build. A year after he was de-mobbed in 1947 he married my mother. Within five years he was dead of a massive coronary.

Now I need to record the part my family played in our country's history, despite my abhorrence of war itself. From what I have learned about the first global conflict, it would appear entirely pointless. Although the second has blotted the world in equal measures, fighting back to avoid a disastrous invasion would seem to be justified.

Not that it is for me to judge, of course.

The memoir is not intended to provoke debate or discussion, or indeed to provide in-depth historical data. Rather it is to pay homage to my family's stoicism and bravery, without which I wouldn't be here, enjoying the same freedom. I first started to reflect in depth upon their contribution, when I became actively involved in a 2009 exhibition at York Art Gallery called 'Reflections on War', which, much to my amazement, inspired me to write poetry on the subject. Later I was involved in a second exhibition on the same theme, which further deepened my interest, and inevitably took me to the losses I had suffered, as by then all members of that generation had died. Moreover, losing my father when I was a tiny child had left a deep hole in me, very different from the same experience in adult life. Most powerful has been the process of reading and transcribing my father's letters, where I have been able to connect with his beautiful spirit. Otherwise I have re-visited happy childhood memories of all these treasured people.

I also considered what might be the emotional and psychological impact upon my generation, of having relatives in both wars. Perhaps we are holding something in our collective unconscious which needs expression. With the loss of our parents, grandparents, and other relatives, many of us are now recognising their role in our country's history. For me, it is also an attempt to expiate my guilt at having expressed, as a rebellious teenager, absolute boredom with the whole subject of war. But maybe the same emotion drove us to fight in a different way. We were, after all, the 'Love Generation.'

I began to assemble the collection towards the end of the Great War centenary commemorations in 2018, during a new period of national and international upheaval with its own set of fears and anxieties. What my family would make of a fragmented Europe again, is hard to imagine. There must be some way, I tell myself, in which we can all try to live more peacefully together.

Susan Elliot
February 2020, York

World War One – 1914 - 1918

Grandpa: Archibald Harold Mill
1890 - 1985

Outside Liège, Belgium, 1919

Grandpa in his Military Band

I was travelling back to York by train some years ago, wanting to check on the weather:

As the Crow Flies

Glancing upwards to monitor rain,
I saw a black spot against a grey sky.
Thought at first it was a floater in my vision,
but it was too big and unwieldy,

flapping like a torn cloak, all points and edges,
like a Rorschach test: one of those blots
to find out what you're thinking. This one though
was something half-alive and inside-out,

thrashing on a wire, pasted there
by unseen currents. Higher up,
its mate balanced like a dancer, intact,
watching for worms.

As we passed the Millennium in 2000, thoughts had turned to the prospect of the centenary of the Great War in the new century, and museum staff in York subsequently started to make plans for major exhibitions. The sight of the poor crow summoned up memories of the images we have all been shown: men's broken bodies caught on barbed wire.

Grandpa served as a Bombardier in the 174th brigade of the 39th Division Royal Field Artillery: the gunners he was presumably in charge of were responsible for firing the '18 pounder' guns. Before the war he was in a military band playing the cornet in the bandstand in Battersea Park, which is where he might have met my grandmother. She also came from a very musical family: her father was Danish and a musician in the Empire Theatre Leicester Square. I still have Grandpa's cornet in my possession, along with his silver spurs and of course his medals.

I have a copy of Grandpa's army book – the history of the 39th Division - where he had marked crosses alongside comrades who were killed or wounded. His own injury is also recorded – he was gassed near Ypres on 12th May 1918. This was known as 'The Great Retreat' which had commenced in March of that year. In addition, and just as poignantly, there are crosses where horses are recorded as killed or wounded. I often wonder what happened to his.

Over the course of the war 484,000 of our horses died: one horse for every two men killed. By 1917 soldiers were told that as the animals were becoming so difficult to replace, their loss was regarded as just as serious as human casualties. In one day in March 1916 7,000 horses were killed by shellfire. Otherwise they died of disease, starvation, exhaustion, the appalling conditions, or by drowning in mud.

After the end of WW2 Grandpa bought a little blue 'baby Austin' car which he kept in a rented garage near his house. Each day, rain or shine, he would go there in the evening to wipe and polish. It was only very recently I suddenly realised that maybe he was unconsciously still wanting to groom his beloved horse, and that this ritual served as a kind of catharsis.

He and I were very close. I was his sole grandchild, my father having been an only child himself. I stayed regularly with my grandparents during school holidays, all the way through childhood and adolescence. I used to quietly wonder why his eyes watered all the time; he always had a handkerchief in his top pocket to wipe them. I didn't like to ask in case he was crying for my father: talking about that bereavement was too painful for all of us. He occasionally mentioned 'Wipers', although I had no idea where it was and what he did there:

At Ypres

So, Grandpa, what did you do at Wipers?
Was it fun? Could you swim in the sea?
Did you ride the donkeys, go to the fair?
Have parties? Joke with friends?

Drive your little car
down summer lanes smelling sweet
with wild honeysuckle, violets, bees sucking pollen,
clouds drifting gently towards England?

Why do you call it Wipers?
Is it why your eyes water? Or that
all the laughter brings tears of joy!
Sing to me again – that song - to

pack up my troubles in an old kit bag
and smile! Will you buy me one?
I would smile too, seeing you remember
the happy times, away from London grime,

a break from work, fresh air, good food,
the company of men. They'll meet you there
again someday, just like that other song!
Can I come too next time?

On wet afternoons the three of us would sometimes play cards. I remember how suddenly Grandpa's face would distort: a picture of abject misery mixed with rage. He would immediately walk out of the room and go to his shed at the bottom of the garden, for hours. Grandma would laugh and say:

"The buggers in a mood again!" - Words spoken, I guess, as much in fear as in irritation. It must have been a great trial for her (and for all the other wives) to live with such wordless unexpressed anguish, bearing her own pain as she so clearly tried to do. Grandpa's artillery brigade began recruiting in Deptford in May 1915, utilising the disused Blackheath Ironworks as its headquarters. The 174th brigade was sent to France in March 1916 and fought at both the Battle of the Somme (June – November 1916) and the third battle of Ypres (commonly called Passchendaele, July- November 1917).

In the First World War an artillery brigade was a force of 795 men commanded by a Lieutenant-Colonel. It was divided into four batteries, lettered A-D. Each battery had about 190 men and six guns. I understand that Grandpa's status as a Bombardier was the equivalent of a Corporal in the infantry. His standard equipment was the 18-pounder field gun. This was towed together with a "limber" (box for stowing ammunition), by a team of six horses. It required six men to operate, with a further four supplying the ammunition in action, so a total of ten.

Each artillery brigade was attached to a Division. There were 50 or so of these in the British Army in WW1, consisting mainly of infantry but also engineers, medics, machine gun companies, vets, cyclists, cavalry and of course artillery. At full strength (which was rare) a division numbered about 15,000 men.

By October 1917, Russia had been knocked out of the war. The German commanders therefore had thousands more troops they could transfer to the Western Front. However, by this time the United States had entered the conflict, and their forces would, the German knew, soon reach numbers which would tip the balance in the West decisively in favour of the Allies.

The Spring Offensive ("Kaiserslacht") was designed to break the stalemate before the Americans arrived by striking a massive blow at the point where the British and French armies joined, break through to the coast of France, and force Britain out of the war. For a while it looked as if it might succeed, but the Germans proved unable to break through in a series of battles all the way along the Western Front. One of these was known as the Battle of the Lys (April 1918), or Fourth battle of Ypres.

Why Worry

if it's time to get a haircut,
have my roots done, what colour
to paint the kitchen, if the washing will dry,

how many cards to send at Christmas,
if those shoes will match,
or about that noise in the car.

Your worries, unspoken:
whether your guts would be dangling
from a broken fence, like Fred's,

if the shaking would stop,
the stink of gas, the tears dry.
If you'd be at that wedding you'd planned.

But for now, there's that leaking roof,
a bill to pay, what to mix with the pasta tonight,
whether to have red wine, or white.

The Home Fire

I kept it burning. Each night, baby asleep, watched flames,
saw the waves of your hair, heaped on coals we could ill afford.
Fire and love survived, for our child, born so soon, was of a passion
I never thought to own. It seemed we three would be so happy.
In the autumn I planted bulbs. With stubby fingers he tried to help,
delighting in soil warmed by summer. He peered at worms, entranced
by the way sunshine played on leaves, the shape of clouds, the soft breath
of a garden ready for sleep. The light caught the cream of his new skin.
With winter fires, I felt desire re-kindle. Sometimes though, when the coals
hissed and wood crackled, sending sparks skywards, I thought of battle.

At last, in blue crepe and a new hat with feathers, our boy sailor-suited, his hand
clasped tight, we paced the platform, treading light. Then wheezing steam,
the train emerged through morning mist. I saw ash faces peer through smoky glass,
picked out yours. As we kissed, with a low gurgle from your throat came
strangled sentences, platitudes. We turned to our son, an excuse not to talk.
At supper, I couldn't believe the tears, mistaken for relief. On your lap,
the boy's head glistened with the drops. 'It's the gas' you said. 'I was gassed.'
As the embers sank I stared whilst your chest heaved with sobs.

It remains a mystery what my grandfather did when he eventually came home from war, or where he and his little family lived in Battersea, when my father would have been just over three years old. There is a collection of small black and white photographs dating from when my father was a child, and following him into adulthood. What struck me forcibly when first looking closely at these, was my grandfather's changed facial expression: from a proud and smiling new father to a subdued and serious young man, whose vacant gaze seems to suggest a profound emotional and psychological distance.

I assume employment was a problem for him, like all the other returning soldiers. What I do know is that eventually a relative found a job for Grandpa as an engraver at a firm called Bradbury Wilkinson and Company. The firm was first established in the city of London in the 1850s and moved to New Malden in 1917. As my father was a pupil at Battersea Boys Grammar school until he left, probably at 15 or 16, I guess my grandparents must have moved to the suburb in the Depression of the 1930's. I remember my grandfather once telling me that he paid £800 for the 3 -bedroomed terrace house. Now the equivalent is selling for over half a million. When I was (unhappily) living in rented accommodation in London in the 1970s, Grandpa gave me £5000 towards a mortgage on a little flat. Now here am I enjoying the luxury of a lovely house in York and a tiny cottage in Northumberland too. All the more reason to pay my respects to him.

In WW2 Grandpa was in the Home Guard in New Malden – as if he hadn't experienced enough stress. There were some anecdotes about unexploded bombs in back gardens, and once a strange tale about one falling through an armchair that he mended afterwards! I remember a cupboard under the stairs, in which they sometimes hid during raids. Otherwise, when the bombing was further off in the city, they used to go and watch from the new bridge over the 'Kingston Bypass', which was only a stone's throw away from their home in Woodfield Gardens. I guess there had also been an Anderson shelter in the garden, long since grassed over.

They lived frugally, although were not actually poor. I guess by comparison with the living conditions in working class Battersea as children, they were considered quite well off, owning a whole house, albeit small, in the suburbs, away from 'the Smoke'. After my father died in 1953, my grandmother developed psoriasis, what my mother called her 'nerve rash'. This meant that compared with our beautifully warm house in Wales, heated with great blazing Welsh coal fires, the house in New Malden was perishing cold, as Grandma couldn't bear any heat. She hated the idea of seeking any medical help and would dress her seeping hands and arms with old bandages, when she had exhausted herself with scratching them.

Recently this and other memories of the times I spent with them came rushing back:

Small House – a sort of prose poem

I loved to poke fingers into snapdragons to see if they would bite,
but remember only a sensation of purple velvet, the same colour
as Grandma's clothes in the wardrobe that hosted hats with long thick pins,
sturdy shoes for legs grown thick. In the hallway and up the stairs,
bleach melted with polished lino, moth balls, and the faint whiff
of spent coal. In the front parlour where no one parleyed I played
'Invitation to the Dance' on the gritty piano, daring to challenge
the unbroken spell, the silent curse. On the sofa like an open coffin
I read about Topsy and grieved for the cruel world. Grandma's old bandages
trailed from her raw fingers but in the morning sunlight of the neat garden

she would brush her long hair that cascaded down her strong back
like a silver waterfall and throw dead ends to the unsuspecting birds.
In what passed for a kitchen she ironed with the flex plugged in the light socket, scrubbed clothes with the washboard and made mouth-melting pastry on the same pine table where on a Sunday evening Grandpa would polish shoes. Milk was kept in a bowl of cold water in the sink and never curdled. The milkman came with orange juice that tasted like nectar. In the morning Grandpa would bring tea so strong as to stand your spoon. I would wait until I could pour it down the bathroom sink, not to hurt his feelings. The bed was like sleeping on molehills,

you had to curve your body around them. Grandpa grew raspberries for the pies, and peas for the lamb. He would take me to Sainsbury's in the High Street, where ladies wore white caps over their hair and you swished sawdust as you trod the floor. Cheese and sausages were wrapped carefully in greaseproof and placed gently into his old leather bag whilst he smiled with glittering eyes as he said: 'This is my granddaughter'. Then suddenly everyone was beaming - as if the sun had finally come out after a long storm. For tea we had tinned pilchards, golden syrup on white bread and butter. When no one was looking I would steal a mars bar or a bounty from the tin on the bureau. Then fart. 'You've blown orf again!' Grandma would laugh and her cheeks resume the redness I liked to see when she danced for me, albeit so ungainly, trying to kick her heavy legs heavenwards. 'Oh my poor 'ol feet. Cor blimey O'Reilly!' She and I would play rummy on the chair seat. They were square stocky folk, never kissed, held hands or even took pills, but something told me they might break like fine china if touched. In his shed next to the compost Grandpa kept old watches for repair, except no one came for collection. It was so dark I couldn't work out how he saw, but maybe it wasn't the watches that kept his gaze, maybe he was blank with memories. In the Blitz

they would cramp up together in the cupboard under the stairs, or if it was safe enough watch the bombs fall over London from the bridge over the new bypass. War for them seemed a strange mix of delight and fear. They rationed themselves for ever after, made do, never bought a fridge or a washing machine, not even a twin tub. There were occasional jaunts to brothers and sisters dispersed across the suburbs; they were a ruptured generation doomed to spend evenings watching Cilla Black and Sandie Shaw on the small screen, sleep in lumpy beds under army blankets. He was never mentioned, my Dad, his dead presence pressed down from the roof like lead. Curtains were kept drawn.

After my grandfather died in 1985 there were papers to sort out, amongst which I found a small memorial card to a soldier called Charlie Ewen, someone else's only son and probably a friend of the family. He was shot in the head in France, aged 24. A rifleman in the Queen's Westminster Rifles and on sentry duty in the trenches when he was killed, he is buried near Poperinghe in France alongside his colleagues. I wrote this to honour his memory, my 'unknown soldier' if you like. Hopefully this speaks for them all:

Charlie

Charlie is my darling, my darling, my darling,
Charlie is my darling, and soon we're to be wed.

He smothers me in kisses, he whispers lovely things,
and sometimes sends me roses, sweet love songs, often sings.

He's tall and smart and handsome, he's young and fit and funny;
he makes me laugh so much I cry. We don't have any money,

but plan to save up wages, (we don't earn very much),
to buy a little cottage. I love his tender touch,

the way he walks beside me, my sweetheart and my friend,
I think of all the times we'll have, our joy will have no end.

Yes, Charlie is my darling, my darling, my darling,
yes, Charlie is my darling, and soon we're to be wed.

I don't believe the messages that come from far away;
they make up lots of stories, he always used to say.

Your Charlie is no more, they said, you really must believe;
he isn't coming back again. My chest began to heave.

They've shot him in the head, they said, he fell back in the trench,
and now our wedding bed's the mud, my perfume is the stench

of blood and guts and gore and grime. I cannot take it in,
that he has really gone, for good, a young man free from sin.

They cannot even bring him home, for me to kiss him better,
to hold him in my loving arms. I only have one letter.

He didn't have much time to write, he hadn't been there long,
we thought they'd all be home real soon: how very, very wrong.

Poor Charlie was my darling, my darling, my darling,
poor Charlie was my darling. There's no more to be said.

✝

In Loving Memory

OF

CHARLIE,

Killed in action, in France,

January 26th, 1916.

IN HIS 24TH YEAR,

only surviving son of W. T. EWEN,
64, Victoria Rd., Clapham Common, S.W.

Rifleman CHARLES ALFRED EWEN, Queen's Westminster Rifles (T.F.), was on sentry duty in the trenches facing the German lines, when he was shot through the head and killed instantly.

Buried at north of Potijze cross roads, near Poperinghe, on January 27th, 1916, with the officers and men of his own regiment who have fallen in France.

The Great Sacrifice

"Greater love than this no man hath, that a man lay down his life for his friends."

"I am the Resurrection and the Life."

Ypres and the Comet, November 2014

We didn't die for chocolate poppies sold on street corners,
bottles of Passchendaele lager - the label prodding you
into silence before consumption; t-shirts sporting
'I'm a battlefield relic'; teddies with tin hats; supermarket adverts
with shots of men running through dead trees and trenches.
Didn't want seaside rock in this inland city; souvenir shopping bags;
long queues and traffic jams en route to cemeteries; didn't hope
for lasting peace, headstones of Portland stone. Or poetry.

Instead now, look over the fields where mustard gas fog
conceals our blood oozing from damp earth, watch
the occasional flicker of insipid light, the dogs who whimper
in certain corners, crouch and retreat. If you listen carefully
you might hear the echoes of screams which reverberate
to the metal hum of the comet holding its secrets.

This was written after listening to the Radio 4 programme *'From our own correspondent'*, broadcast on November 8th 2014, describing the scenes at Ypres commemorating the centenary of the start of the Great War. Four days later the satellite called Rosetta, in orbit for the past decade, finally landed a probe on a comet five billion miles away. It was hoped that the data collected might offer some explanation as to the birth of our planet and the genesis of the human race. The irony of this was not lost on me...

To my mind, it's a pity that we spend more time worrying where we came from and less on where we are going to....

Appendix " D "—*contd.*

RANK.	NAME.	NATURE OF CASUALTY.	DATE.
Dvr.	Vinson, H.	Killed in action	28- 3-18
Dvr.	George, J. T.	Wounded	4- 4-18
Dvr.	Quinn, F.	,,	4- 4-18
Gnr.	Longbottom, F. R.	,,	4- 4-18
Gnr.	Evans, A. J.	,,	10- 4-18
Gnr.	Slater, J.	,,	11- 4-18
Gnr.	Butcher, W.	,,	6- 4-18
Gnr.	Jackson, J.	,,	6- 4-18
Sergt.	Abraham, M., D.C.M., M.M.	,,	4- 4-18
Gnr.	Winters, H.	,,	4- 4-18
Gnr.	Collier, R.	,,	5- 4-18
Dvr.	Whiting, G. H.	,,	5- 4-18
Gnr.	Bell, J. H.	,,	9- 4-18
Corpl.	Walsh, T. M.	,,	12- 4-18
Bdr.	Davies, F.	,,	12- 4-18
Corpl.	Down, L. G.	,,	6- 4-18
Sergt.	Denison, H.	,,	6- 4-18
Dvr.	Whitehouse, F.	,,	6- 4-18
Corpl.	Penrose, J.	,,	6- 4-18
Dvr.	Wood, H.	,,	6- 4-18
Sergt.	Coleman, H.	,,	6- 4-18
Fitter	Parker, T. H. J.	,,	4- 4-18
Gnr.	Price, W.	,,	10- 4-18
Dvr.	Wade, T.	,,	10- 4-18
Gnr.	Moyle, T.	,,	12- 4-18
Gnr.	Sharp, J.	,,	4- 4-18
Bdr.	Fraser, W.	,,	4- 4-18
Dvr.	Lindsey, E. J.	Killed in action	3- 4-18
S/S.	Middleditch, E.	Wounded	10- 4-18
Dvr.	Rennie, T. W.	,,	13- 4-18
Corpl.	Medley, H.	,,	2- 5-18
Fitter	Parker, T. H. J.	Died of wounds	9- 4-18
Gnr.	Russell, J. W.	,,	18- 5-18
Gnr.	Slade, P. A.	,,	9- 5-18
Gnr.	Preece, T. W.	,,	10- 5-18
Bdr.	Edmonds, F.	Wounded (Gas)	12- 5-18
L/Bdr.	Read, J.	,,	12- 5-18
Gnr.	Crafter, H. P.	,,	12- 5-18
Sergt.	Mitchell, E. J.	,,	12- 5-18
Gnr.	Oliver, G.	,,	12- 5-18
Dvr.	Kenyon, W.	,,	12- 5-18
Gnr.	Potter, J.	,,	12- 5-18
Gnr.	Fryer, C.	,,	12- 5-18
Gnr.	Cates, A.	,,	12- 5-18
Gnr.	Latham, F. G.	,,	12- 5-18
Bdr.	Mill, A. H.	,,	12- 5-18
Gnr.	Robertson, E. J.	,,	12- 5-18
Gnr.	Mew, O. G.	,,	12- 5-18
Gnr.	Evered, W. T.	,,	12- 5-18
Dvr.	Denny, A. C.	,,	12- 5-18
Gnr.	Smith, W. G.	,,	12- 5-18
Gnr.	Owen, A.	,,	12- 5-18
Gnr.	Thompson, M.	,,	12- 5-18
Bdr.	Byott, F.	,,	12- 5-18

Appendix " D "—*contd.*

RANK.	NAME.	NATURE OF CASUALTY.	DATE.
Gnr.	Pegram, E. H.	Wounded (Gas)	12- 5-18
Gnr.	Miller, C. R.	,,	12- 5-18
Sergt.	Kieff, G. F. W.	,,	12- 5-18
L/Bdr.	Bailey, F. J.	,,	12- 5-18
Gnr.	Wilkinson, G. A.	,,	12- 5-18
Gnr.	Murray, A. J.	,,	12- 5-18
Gnr.	Pragnell, L. C., M.M.	,,	12- 5-18
Gnr.	Moore, L.	,,	12- 5-18
L/Bdr.	Welsh, W.	,,	12- 5-18
Corpl.	Stewart, J.	,,	12- 5-18
Bdr.	Smith, L.	,,	12- 5-18
Gnr.	Gillespie, J.	,,	12- 5-18
Gnr.	Cull, F.	,,	12- 5-18
Bdr.	Stokoe, J., M.M.	,,	12- 5-18
Dvr.	Maynard, G.	,,	12- 5-18
Gnr.	Sharp, J.	Wounded	12- 5-18
Gnr.	Jones, A.	,,	13- 5-18
Dvr.	Clark, J.	,,	13- 5-18
Sergt.	Halls, P. W.	,,	13- 5-18
Gnr.	Saunders, J. R.	,,	14- 5-18
Gnr.	Hunter, J.	,,	14- 5-18
Sergt.	Eccles, R.	,,	15- 5-18
Gnr.	Ruddick, G. H.	,,	15- 5-18
Gnr.	Sharp, J.	,,	15- 5-18
Sergt.	Simpson, W.	,,	4- 5-18
Sergt.	Berry, P. W.	,,	9- 5-18
Gnr.	Dunmore, A.	,,	11- 5-18
Gnr.	Ibbett, F. T.	,,	12- 5-18
Sergt.	Long, A. T.	,,	12- 5-18
Bdr.	Wetherell, A. J.	,,	12- 5-18
Gnr.	Bird, W. J.	Killed in action	28- 5-18
Gnr.	Barton, H.	,,	28- 5-18
Dvr.	Dalby, H.	,,	29- 5-18
Sergt.	Hubble, T. H.	,,	25- 5-18
Sergt.	Summerfield, P. J.	,,	26- 5-18
Dvr.	Reed, A. C.	Wounded	14- 5-18
Gnr.	Poole, H. P.	,,	25- 5-18
Gnr.	Sharpe, C., M.M.	,,	12- 5-18
Gnr.	Swain, E.	,,	14- 5-18
Gnr.	Potter, G.	,,	16- 5-18
Gnr.	Scott, C. H.	,,	29- 5-18
A/Bdr.	Varo, E.	,,	29- 5-18
Gnr.	Riggs, J.	,,	12- 5-18
Dvr.	Beckson, P.	,,	31- 5-18
Sergt.	Murray, H., M.M.	,,	4- 6-18
Dvr.	Rootham, F. C.	,,	1- 6-18
Gnr.	Darby, H.	,,	9- 6-18
Bdr.	Fraser, W.	,,	15- 6-18
Gnr.	Whatton, W.	,,	14- 6-18
B.Q.M.S.	Baggaley, H.	,,	14- 6-18
Sergt.	Denison, H.	,,	14- 6-18
Gnr.	Huddleston, A.	,,	3- 8-18
Gnr.	Noble, F.	,,	1- 8-18
Dvr.	Dunning, A. E.	Died of wounds	27- 8-18

From 'A Short History of the 39th Divisional Artillery 1915 – 1918, pub. 1923

My grandfather in military uniform and in France in 1915

My young grandparents and my father 1919/1920

My grandfather stayed on in New Malden for a while after the death of my grandmother, then went to live with my mother and aunt in Porthcawl. Very sadly and uncharacteristically, there was a quarrel, and Grandpa left to live with his sister-in-law in Hampshire. I was deeply saddened by the turn of events, but with my mother's blessing, kept in regular touch with him whilst I was working in London. He would meet me on Sundays, under the clock at Waterloo Station, take me out to lunch, then a recital at the Queen Elizabeth Hall. Afterwards we would walk down the Embankment together, the love of each other and the wonderful city, holding us tightly together.

'You're a real townie now!' he once exclaimed, his bright blue, ever-watering eyes beaming with pride.

I had no idea that he was struggling with his health, although should have guessed, of course. He was after all, in his mid-eighties. Eventually there was no alternative to residential care and I was appointed executor, which felt like a burden in addition to my hectic job as a social worker in Lewisham. At one point I was asked to arrange for him to have a spare pair of pyjamas, and to this day feel deeply guilty at having neglected to do so before it was too late. I shall never really forgive myself.

You brought out a faded photo:
your wife and son in a garden.
You asked me who they were.
Laughing, you peered blankly.
At them, at me.

'I was the child
you took to Sainsbury's
for cheese wrapped in greaseproof.
Grown up, I'd meet you under
the station clock at Waterloo.
We would stroll amongst crowds,
the chimes of Ben!'

You half-told me what I didn't want
to hear, about a pain, somewhere.

Towards the end I found you
gasping, near a window,
your vacant gaze colder
than a winter wind.

I put a single red rose on your coffin.
But it was the pyjamas I never bought,
that you had really needed.

World War Two - 1939 - 1945

My Dad:
Archibald Frederick Henry Mill

1916 - 1953

The Army photograph that my father sent to my mother.

Archibald Frederick Henry Mill
Religion: C of E
Rank: Gunner
Date of birth: 1.10.16
Date of Enlistment: 2.12.40
Period of Engagement: D/W
Trade on Enlistment: Railway Clerk
Qualifications: Signaller

Identification:

Height: 5ft. 8 ¼ ins
Weight: 125 pounds
Eyes: Blue
Hair: Brown
Girth: 34 ins.
Range of expansion: 2 ½ ins
Distinctive marks: mole, outer side, right thigh

Campaigns, medals and decorations:

1939/43 STAR
WAR MEDAL 1939/45
ITALY STAR
FRANCE AND GERMANY STAR
DEFENCE MEDAL

Testimonial: *Gnr. Mill has served with this division for two and a half years having previously served 2 ½ years in R.A. P.C. as a pay clerk. He has shown himself to be extremely patient and thorough. Under strenuous and dangerous conditions he was always unflurried and unfailingly efficient in his work. Intelligent and with a pleasant personality he uses his initiative admirably, works well without supervision and is completely reliable. Of honest and sober disposition he is a capable driver and is recommended as very suitable for high grade clerical work.*

Germany, 7th June 1946

Deceased 11.3.53

Cause of death: recurrent coronary thrombosis due to atheroma

7678301, Gnr. Mill, A. J.,
288/124 th Field Regt. RA,
c/o Army Post Office,
England.
24 th April, 1944.

Dear Doris,

Please excuse me for addressing you by your Christian name, but Alan has told me such a lot about you that I feel I know you very well already.

First, I want to thank you for taking the trouble to write (if you are!) to a mere soldier, when there are obviously plenty of fellows in more "glamorous" arms who would be delighted at the privilege. A soldier is nearly always a ~~bit of a~~

7678301, Gnr. Mill, A.F.
288/124th Field Regt., RA,
c/o Army Post Office,
England.

24th April 1944

Dear Doris,

Please excuse me for addressing you by your Christian name, but Allan has told me such a lot about you that I feel I know you very well already.
First, I want to thank you for taking the trouble to write (if you are!) to a mere soldier, when there are obviously plenty of fellows in more 'glamorous' arms who would be delighted at the privilege. A soldier is nearly always a bit of a bore, with nothing very interesting to say (quite unlike your sailors or airmen), and yet he probably appreciates letters twice as much, partly because (unlike the sailor) he knows he ***can*** *get them pretty regularly and so looks forward to them the more, and secondly because (unlike your airman), he is constantly changing his location, and hasn't the time (or opportunity) to make contacts in the nearest town, as, of course, as soon as he does make any civilian friends he is moved on.*

You will now have guessed, then, - if I haven't been rather pedantic in explaining it (and rather obvious) – that letters are most welcome to me!

There isn't much to do in the evenings at the place where we are now, so I go into the nearest town whenever I can, although I am afraid that almost the only thing to do there is to go to the 'flicks' (unless you like your 'quart pot' – a pastime which, I am afraid, doesn't interest me very much). However, there is boating (rather a grandiloquent title for it!), which makes a pleasant change, and the country round here is very beautiful, especially at this time of year.

By the way, I hope you don't think this 'business' of writing rather forward of me – I have given my excuse and my apology, so perhaps I shall be forgiven!

Of course, you know that I have known Allan for some considerable time now – since my Sicily days, in fact – where we used, (among other things) to go boating, fishing and swimming in the Mediterranean, and drink wine and eat ices, and altogether quite 'get around' and enjoy ourselves. Those ***were*** *palmy days, unfortunately passed, and ones that I think I shall always look back on! However, I hope to have some/ many more 'good times' with him, and expect I shall.*

This seems all the news for now,

Yours very sincerely,

Archie

P.S. How is Porthcawl? Very pleasant at this time of year, I should think!

This is the first of 24 letters I found stuffed in a large brown envelope, written by my father to my mother between April 1944 and December 1947, whilst he was based in West Germany, undertaking the 'high grade' clerical duties mentioned in his testimonial. There are some large gaps between dates – either letters got lost or perhaps my mother didn't actually keep them all. The other possible explanation might be that they were even more intensely personal than the others, although that is hard to imagine. Maybe they were too upsetting for her to keep after his untimely death.

My mother died in 2003, at the age of 89. During the following year, I thought about the brown envelope containing the letters, and wondered if she had meant me to read them. She hadn't anticipated dying at that point, having gone into hospital for a so-called routine procedure which went disastrously wrong: another story for another time, perhaps.

I was haunted by the big tatty envelope, and one wet afternoon, decided to take the plunge and read the letters, casting my eyes heavenwards in so doing, in some form of apology. It was a wet afternoon, inside and out. I was so moved by the sweetness of this lovely man whom I had never known, of whom I had no memory, and the great love he clearly felt for my mother, as did I.

My father was an only child, born in Battersea in 1916. His parents both came from big families living in cramped conditions, but enjoying lots of contact with each other. By all accounts my grandmother absolutely doted on him. Being highly intelligent, his teachers at Battersea Boys' Grammar wanted him to apply for a scholarship to go to university, but the story goes that my Gran wouldn't sanction this, wanting him instead to leave school to work for British Rail. Supposedly, and perhaps understandably, given that finances were no doubt stretched, this was regarded as a safer option in terms of career, although according to my mother, my father was very frustrated by the tedium of the job. Being a voracious reader, all he wanted to do was to open a bookshop.

From the letters it seems evident that my father had never had a serious girlfriend before my mother. His friend Allan, who served with him in Sicily, took pity on him and asked his fiancée Megan, who was my mother's friend, to encourage Doris to write to him.

They met, fell deeply in love, married in 1948 – the same year that Mum starred as 'Magnolia' in 'Showboat' in Porthcawl Operatic Society. They initially lived with my paternal grandparents in New Malden, Surrey. Mum saw an advert for the Royal Choral Society, auditioned, and was accepted, singing in the Royal Albert Hall under the direction of Sir Malcolm Sargent. She also had singing lessons with Professor Howard Fry in London. This was all funded by my father, who as a railway clerk earned seven pounds ten shillings a week – the lessons costing one pound ten shillings. The Professor wanted my mother to pursue a solo career, but money was short and I came along in 1949 and scuppered the plan anyway. We moved to a dilapidated Victorian terraced house in Balham in 1950. One night in March 1953 my father suddenly died from a massive coronary.

The event devastated my mother and my paternal grandparents, especially my grandmother who apart from her skin problems, became socially phobic for the rest of her life. Mum struggled on a weekly widow's pension of about two pounds ten shillings so had to go out to work. I can remember being wheeled in my pushchair to a ghastly plastic lampshade factory on Tooting Bec Common, where she worked for a while, earning a halfpenny for every lampshade covered, until the fumes began to affect her throat and of course her lovely voice. She also took in lodgers – there were two other families in the house apart from us.

Towards the latter half of the 1950's Mum's brothers suggested she come back to Wales to help in the grocery shop in New Road, and of course to be more supported by the family. She seized the opportunity, living over the next 40 years with various family members. One Sunday morning, a few years after our move, Mum felt so depressed she couldn't face going to church. Instead she spent the morning cooking all my father's favourite cakes, making so many that we couldn't eat them all. Her brother Rees took the remaining cakes to his shop to sell the following day. Customers were so impressed they asked when Mum could cook some more. The eventual outcome was that later, against all odds, she opened her own highly successful bakery, enabling her to be independent and bring me up with all the benefits I have enjoyed, including a university career.

EWHERE A VOICE IS CALLING (2).
Night and the stars are gleaming,
Tender and true;
Dearest! my heart is dreaming,
Dreaming of you!
REPRINTED BY PERMISSION OF THE PUBLISHER, J. H. LARWAY, OXFORD ST., LONDON.
BAMFORTH (COPYRIGHT).

SOMEWHERE A VOICE IS CALLING (1).
Dusk, and the shadows falling
O'er land and sea;
Somewhere a voice is calling,
Calling for me!

Postcards I found in my grandfather’s papers: the importance of letters…

7678301, Gnr. Mill, A.F.
296/74th Field Rgt., RA, BAOR

17th January 1945

My darling,

Such a nice letter that I've just received from you (dated the 12th) that I'm sure I blushed when I read it: it isn't good for my modesty, dear! And please don't thank me for the happy time we spent together (and we did have a happy time, didn't we?), for it was you that made me very happy and I did nothing at all by comparison, for I don't think there is any greater thing that a girl can give any man than her love, and I love you for it, dear.

No, I don't think you're conceited at all, for you are always in my thoughts, dear, and I shall never forget those glorious times we've spent together. Actually, I think this last leave was the best I've ever spent, in spite of the fact that we didn't go out much: we had each other and that was enough, wasn't it? Those times will come again, and as you say, the feeling that someone is thinking of you does help a lot, and with this we must be content until we see each other again…

I do hope you enjoyed the film, even though that would mean that you forgot me for a couple of hours or so; also the play-reading, although I was sorry about the bad weather. I was pleased that I came up to Irene's expectations, although of course, she doesn't know me yet! I'm no gentleman, you know, and perhaps I wouldn't if she did really know me!

I was sorry to learn about your bad weather: it's dry here, but bitterly cold and bleak, so that I long for spring to be here again: at the moment I don't know how ever the time is going to pass. However, I'm rapidly settling down to the old routine, and everything comes to an end.

And now dear, I don't seem to have any more news,

So, until next time, my sweet,

Much love from Archie xxxxxx

*

Out of respect for my parents' privacy, I will continue their story only with extracts. The correspondence continues in the same vein, recording the development of their romance, illustrating my father being head over heels in love. It emerges that he didn't keep my mother's letters to him. Initially I thought this strange, but then it became clear that in moving from one base to another he had limited room for his belongings in his pack. In the following letter I couldn't decipher some of the writing, as the paper was so thin and aged, but the message does come through, not to mention the conditions in which the men had to live:

24th January, 1945
Dear Doris,
First, I must apologise for not writing before. Actually I've just come back from an 8 – day stretch with the infantry, and, before that, on a 6 – day 'sniping' patrol with our troop of 4 guns. The latter was rather fun, as we used to come back from the O.P. ....especially as we were caught in the attack and a counter-attack, and while they.......it was just hellish. The troop commander who was with us and his 'ack'.....fell through the ice in a lake and went up to their necks in water; the roof of a room in a building where we tried to get some shelter was shattered by a direct hit by shellfire, (luckily the roof was fairly solid (concrete) and the shell burst before it could come through, so nobody was hurt, although the ack was buried under a lot of it), coming back the carrier left the road and was only prevented from toppling over a 20 feet drop down the dyke by a post in the ground, we were stranded by the aforementioned until we could get a breakdown lorry to winch us out, until about 8 o'clock at night, and altogether we were just about all-in and fed up, when we got back. We hadn't had a bath or a proper wash for over a fortnight and felt absolutely 'manky'.

However, that was last night, and after a good wash and a change of clothing, I'm beginning to feel my usual self again. They've given us quite a good billet back with the guns (a room for the three of us in a house away from the rest of the troop), and with the addition of a fire (there is a fair-sized wood close by!), and a cloth on the table, we're quite cosy!

I suppose you'll say that Allan hadn't known me very long when he introduced us, but I can tell you that being three months in action with a fellow is equivalent to knowing him for a year in ordinary circumstances!

We have just had another fall of snow here, and there is now about 6 inches of it on top of the ice. It looks very pretty when viewed from the window of a warm room, but that's about all. The roads are absolutely treacherous, especially for tracked vehicles, and to go out in anything but gum boots is absolutely asking for it. However, we survive!

27th January 1945

Please excuse this rather disjointed letter. After being back with the battery for a day and a bit we were called out again, so letter writing had to go by the board for another two days. I didn't have a bad time this time, as I managed to get a 'kip' down in with the infantry signallers at ....HR. Furthermore, things were pretty quiet (a welcome change lately), and it ***was*** *only for two days this time.*

I've just received your letter of the 21st. You were quite right about the weather out here. It's very much colder than you get anywhere in England (or Wales!), gloves and leather jerkin and I still feel it!

13th April 1945

My dear,

It seems ages since I last wrote to you: will you forgive me? Actually, I've had no mail from you since your letter of the 4th, and what with that and the fact that I've been busy (really, I have, at times up to 9 o'clock at night), I'm afraid letters to you have gone by the board. Of course, the trouble is that as well as doing the ordinary admin. duties as a troop clerk for about 40 men, I've been having to do the petrol and oil accounting (a man's job in itself), and, as this is rather a special job, I've also had the job of typing out reams of performance reports on the vehicles under different conditions. However, they've brought in another fellow for the accounting, and my work has become a little easier, so that I can breathe more freely.

I've been getting so bored these last few days – (the weather has taken a turn for the worse, with very grey skies and cold winds), that I simply had to leave my work this afternoon and get out of it – (I had to work this evening to make up for it, but that didn't matter) – so I went with another fellow to a film show that was on – 'Rebecca' – I'd seen it before, but it was worth seeing again. I like Joan Fontaine – she's so sweet and unassuming – (just like you, dear, and I dare say it!) – in fact, she reminded me of you in so many ways. Now I suppose you'll say I'm rambling. Perhaps I am: I feel very tired – (I think the height of this place and the air might have something to do with it) – so that is quite possible, and if I am, will you forgive me that too?

We are now thinking about getting ready to return to Dortmund. We haven't had a bad time here. For the fellows it's been a welcome change from life in barracks: I was all right in RHQ, but it's pretty deadly in this battery as they've gone in completely for barrack life. It's unfortunate that, although this is an independent troop, they had to billet in with 296 battery to get cover for the vehicles and guns, so, of course, they've had to fall in with their ways and ideas: otherwise things would have been vastly different. Anyway, I'm not worrying. I can stick it for a few weeks longer.

I still don't know about leave this month, but I'm not worrying unduly. If I do get some, I'll send you a telegram and perhaps they'll be room for me at 'Melrose' for a few days – (I know I've a bit of a cheek, inviting myself, but I promise you I'll cause you no trouble, apart perhaps from stopping you from working: - I have no qualms about that, because I think you do too much already!)

25th October 1945

My own little darling,

Seriously, dear, you are too good to me both in thought and deed, and I'm afraid you're sweeping me right off my feet – (or is it the girl's privilege to say that?). I don't know what gave rise to your father saying that you wanted a man to tame and make a lady out of you, for surely you're the gentlest creature alive. I don't know if you're a lady of not, as I'm not quite certain I know what they are, but I don't like them, anyway…..

I suppose that by now you've just about finished with your job, and are preparing to settle down to that brief spell as a 'lady of leisure.' As you say, giving up a job is the devil, and there's no doubt about it, you do miss the old routine – (I've been in the same position myself), but I do think it's for the best, as you would have had to have left it sometime, and what better time than now, before the bad weather starts. Besides, I want you to save yourself for me, my dear, as it would never do for you to have a cold on my leave, would it? And it will be nice for you not having to rush back (I haven't forgot the shambles we made of it last time), and for me not having to worry if I'm a day or so late arriving home, afraid that I've missed an extra day with you.

I do hope you get on all right with your singing and play-reading. As you say, it will help pass some of those long winter nights away. I wish I had something of the kind to do myself, as our clocks are going back again soon, and then it will be getting dark at about 4 o'clock; what a prospect for a winter out here! Even walking has been out for the past day or so, although I did manage to snatch a short one last night, between showers.

Still, I suppose I mustn't grumble: this time last year I was living in a stable, <u>and</u> thanking my lucky stars for it!

I'm now doing a bit of reading, by the way, and at present am on 'End of the House of Allard' by Sheila Kaye-Smith: quite good – have you read it? Of course, I'm now looking forward to the time when I can get my own library into working order again: it was one of my few pleasures before the war, and one that I think I missed most when I joined the Army. However, that's another thing to go back to, and you know what they say about pleasures deferred, don't you?

9th November 1945

My own little girl,

Four days and I still haven't written to you, and my last letter was so horrible, I know, because I wrote it when I was tired and altogether not myself. Reason (believe it or not), I have really been busy, as we've had four schemes in a row, and as we've only three wireless ops. in the section and the other two are fairly new, you can perhaps estimate exactly how busy your humble has been!

Actually I've been called out since starting this, and I'm writing it in the C.O.'s staff car while listening in at the same time. However, it's all in the day's work, and as long as I can finish this before we move off, I shall be content.

I was glad that you enjoyed your stay with Kath: actually, I've an idea that you're rather jealous (well, a bit!), and would like a whole flock of children (boys for preference, I think, or do you like little girls? I do!) of your own. Sorry to makc you blush, dear, but I don't think it's far from the truth: is it?

The other afternoon I thought I'd like a ride, so I went for a 60 mile spin with one of the fellows to collect medical stores – quite a pretty journey when once we'd left our area, even though it was rather spoiled by rain and dull weather.

Last night I saw another film – 'Sensations of 1945' – a revue, but there were some quite clever turns in it. Actually I don't really like going so often, but what else is there to do! I know you'll say that I could have written to you, but I really think that if I hadn't gone out I'd have gone mad, so perhaps you'll forgive me!

11th November 1945

My sweet,

Sunday evening, and I'm having a quiet time writing to you.

A very quiet day – I've had the day off, and I'm afraid I've just had a good lounge about. This morning I played billiards in the canteen, though the continental tables are different to ours (they're smaller, and have no pockets) and I'm not very good at it, so the other fellow beat me hollow. Afterwards we went on to darts, with a similar result – I'm afraid I'm not very good at games, and I generally get beaten, but I persevere, and am progressing gradually!

This afternoon I had a bath (a shower, unfortunately, as the water heating in the house is 'caput', and I had to go out for it) – rather draughty, but I got myself clean, and that was the main thing. Afterwards I went for a walk: there is still a wind blowing, and it was very cold and dull, but the exercise did me good, and I managed to get some of the stiffness out of my legs after the bath, and of course it gave me an appetite for tea, so it was worth it.

We had a visit by a mobile cinema yesterday evening, so we were saved the necessity of going out, and also had the advantage of the canteen easy chairs instead of the hard ones you get in cinemas. There were only about 20 of us so it was nice and cosy, and although the film was only 16mm the screen and sound were quite good (a rarity for so small a film), so it made quite a nice break……

And (when we were) coming home from the cinema, that night, when you took my arm in yours – well, I've seen Table Mountain, the Pyramids, the Blue Mosque and Mount Etna, and they left me cold in comparison! Such is the warmth of a woman's friendship!

7678301, Gnr Hill, A. F.,
RHQ., 74 th Field Regt., RA, BAOR
20 th November, 1945.

Dearest,

Such a lot of letters of yours to answer, so where shall I start?

By the way, I am sorry about my little lapse — it was a pretty awful letter, I know: anyway, you say I'm improving, so that's something! As for the waiting, keep your chin up dear: I've now reverted to 10 th on the December leave list (better than I hoped), so surely it won't be very long before I'm home again. And, if I do meet you at Paddington (I do hope that I shall be able to, and that we shan't be disappointed like we were last time), I shan't mind at all if you drop your bag, or how many people there are looking on: and I will hold you tight, and never let you go — not until we're safely home in New Malden, anyway.

The weather is awful here today: it's been very cold — much worse than you get it in England — and now a dense fog has come up: added to this, they've now turned off the central heating to put our new boiler in and I'm just about frozen — (wish you were here to keep me warm!). Your thought about the firelight, the armchair and the music on the wireless was quite a beautiful one, dear, and one that I heartily concur with, but I'm afraid that in Germany as in most European countries, the beautiful of the family fireside is noted by it's absence — you can't sit round a radiator, and gathering round a closed stove isn't very pleasant, is it?

Actually I do wish I was with you so that we could share the little joys of life together (they say that pleasures are better shared): and, of course, the trials and tribulations that all of us have, for what else is a friend for! Some day that wish will come true, and we must just have patience and wait for the day. After all, they also say that the best pleasures are deferred pleasures.

No dear, I wasn't just "being the gentleman" that first time together, for if I hadn't liked you I'd have let you know (anyway, how could anyone <u>not</u> like you!) I wasn't enjoying every minute of your company, for I hate hypocrisy in all its forms: surely it's better to be honest with a person from the start, for he (or she) always finds out the truth later on, and then the harm has been done. Being nice to a person just for the sake of being nice is all right in it's way, but it isn't the basis of true friendship, I'm afraid.

I was glad to learn that you'd put on a few pounds: a little extra weight will help keep the cold out this winter (in my absence!). Anyway I didn't think it was possible in England these days! Also that you're getting some exercise in while the weather is fine, for soon it will be too late, and soon the only thing to do will be to stay at home and sit round the fire.

Now darling, I shall have to "turn in", so I shall have to close. I haven't finished, but I do want to get this away in the morning, so I'll finish it tomorrow, so,

Until then, my dear,

Much love,

from Archie xxx xx

20th November 1945

Dearest,

Such a lot of letters of yours to answer, so where shall I start? By the way, I am sorry about my little lapse – it was a pretty awful letter, I know: anyway, you say I'm improving, so that's something! As for the waiting, keep your chin up dear: I've now reverted to 10th on the December leave list (better than I hoped), so surely it won't be very long before I'm home again. And if I do meet you at Paddington (I do hope that I shall be able to, and that we shan't be disappointed like we were last time), I shan't mind at all if you drop your bag, or how many people there are looking on: and I will hold you tight and never let you go – not until we're safely home in New Malden, anyway.

The weather is awful here today: it's been very cold, much worse than you get it in England – and now a dense fog has come up: added to this, they've now turned off the central heating to put our new boiler in and I'm just about frozen – (wish you were here to keep me warm!). Your thought about the firelight, the armchair and the music on the wireless was quite a beautiful one, dear, and one that I heartily concur with, but I'm afraid that in Germany, as in most European countries, the beautiful (scene?) of the family fireside is noted by its absence – you can't sit round a radiator, and gathering round a closed stove isn't very pleasant, is it?

Actually, I do wish I was with you so that we could share the little joys of life together (they say that pleasures are better shared): and of course, the trials and tribulations that all of us have, for what else is a friend for! Some say that wish will come true, and we must just have patience and wait for the day. After all, they also say that the best pleasures are deferred pleasures.

No dear, I wasn't just 'being the gentleman' that first time together, for if I hadn't liked you I'd have let you know (anyway, how could anyone not like you!) I wasn't enjoying every minute of your company, for I hate hypocrisy in all its forms: surely it's better to be honest with a person from the start, for he (or she) always finds out the truth later on, and then the harm has been done. Being nice to a person just for the sake of being nice is all right in its way, but it isn't the basis of true friendship, I'm afraid.

23rd November 1945

My sweet,

Many thanks for the compliment, but your letters are beautiful in my eyes too, you know. You see, I think we both write from the heart, and how could they not be so under these circumstances?

By the way, speaking of compliments (keep this to yourself, and I quote risking your wings beginning to sprout!), you were paid one or two by my mother today. I won't tell you what they were, but I would give you a hug for every one of the qualities she mentioned! Don't ever change, will you dear, for I think that the bottom would be knocked out of my world if you did.

Actually, I think your best quality is your fragility, and cuddlesome-ness…There, I suppose I'm making you blush again: it's shocking of me, I know, and I also know that I ought not to do it, but I can't help it dear, it's just how I feel, and I do hope you'll understand, for it is very lonely here and you do get fed up with men's company day after day.

It's now 1.30 in the morning, so it's really the 24th. As you will have guessed, I'm on night duty again (roll on 'civvy street', when that will be a thing of the past), and feeling pretty lonely and tired. I expect you're well into the land of nod at the moment, and I must say that I envy you sleeping there between those cool clean sheets. However, it won't be many weeks before I'm between them myself, and in the meantime I console myself with that thought.

28th January 1946

My darling,

……

The weather here has turned a bit warmer (I went out without an overcoat this morning), and I understand from civilian sources that our winter out here is over: I hope they're right, but you can never rely on them! Anyway, the finer weather and the fact that the evenings are drawing out will make life more bearable out here. When I've finished writing this letter I'm going to the pictures to see 'The Way to the Stars'. It will mean a six mile walk (three miles each way), but perhaps is will be worth it. Anyway, it will be rather warmer, and that will be something.

6th February 1946

Feeling very much 'browned off' at the moment, as things have most definitely <u>not</u> gone well today – three of our lines have gone with the recent storm, wireless communications are deadly, and altogether I've just about been worked off my feet, so I shall be very glad when I go to bed – (very soon, I hope!). Sorry to bring my troubles to you, dear, - I ought not to, I know, but I feel better for it so perhaps you'll forgive me! Incidentally, the weather is rotten – we've had continuous gales and rain for the past four days, and you can be sure, that doesn't help a bit!

Glad to hear that the time is passing quickly for you. It is for me, really, but the last two or three days have been absolutely rotten, and I've thought they would never end. However, I suppose life is a series of ups and downs, and you just have to take these things as they come. Of course, you are doing a job that you like, however busy you're kept at it: I don't dislike my job if it stops there, but we've a lot of new brooms here, and at the moment we just don't know where we are!......

I'm looking forward to seeing you in your new hat, especially as (I hope!) you'll be wearing your costume, maroon shoes and gloves (I like you best in those), and I shan't mind if I'm had up for baby snatching!

8th February 1946

Sweetheart,

First, consider yourself highly honoured, for I've managed to scrounge a pen this time! Thanks for your letter of the 3rd, more than welcome as I was really feeling 'down in the dumps' at the time that I received it. However, things are a bit easier today – some of the lines are through and we've closed down wireless communication, and I'm hoping that by tomorrow we shall be back to normal again.

Mail has been very bad again, and we had none at all yesterday: however, I had three letters today, so I'm well satisfied. The other two were from my friend John and my mother, in which she sent you her regards – (I think she likes you dear – good for you!): she says she might take you at your word and pay Porthcawl a visit in the Summer (that's what you get for inviting people!), and thanks your mother and Vic (and yourself, of course) for the invitation…..

I was glad that you enjoyed the film. I used to like going on my own, as it was the only time that I could really concentrate on what was happening, and anyway, when you're by yourself you can do exactly as you please, can't you! 'Way to the Stars' was quite good, and you should see it if you can.

Our weather here is just as bad as yours: it's been raining and we've had gales pretty continuously for the last week, so I don't go out much at nights – when I do I go by truck, and that's wet enough.

Hope you sung well in chapel, and had an enjoyable tea. Some home cooking is what I could do with at the moment, as our food is just as drab as ever: the cook does his best, but he can't achieve the impossible, I'm afraid.

11th February 1946

My dear,

I was sorry that you were so tired after Opera practice; you should take a camp stool or shooting stick with you next time! Anyway, don't they provide chairs?

I've had a day in the open air today, for after spending an hour down at the charging plant two of us got up on thc roof to clean the aerials – quite a job, as they'd rusted up with the rain and it took us about an hour to get them down. Luckily it was dry, even if it was blowing a minor gale: it isn't dry now, I'm afraid – it's started raining again, consequently I'm having an evening in.

I don't know if I told you that I'd heard from my friend John, who's now out of the army and enjoying the (doubtful) luxuries of 'civvy street'. He asked how you were – an honour, my girl, considering he's never met you!

Glad to learn that you are putting bags of money into the Post Office: what are you saving up for? Not that there's much to spend money on these days: anyone would think we'd lost the war! Anyway, we shall probably want all we can get for our holiday – (not that that is entirely necessary, for I could be happy with you even if we had no money, dear).

Since starting this I've received your letter of the 7th. You know, they are too nice for me, and I shall miss them when I come home and we probably shan't be writing so much. We've been writing to each other for a long time now, haven't we, dear, and a lot of water has flowed under the bridge since we started. I often wish now that I'd kept all your letters (and tied them round with pink ribbon!) but of course it's quite impossible to keep anything in the army except your kit: you have to think of the time when you have to start moving on and carrying it all.

9th March 1946

My darling,

Thanks for your letter of the 3rd. I can't understand why you aren't receiving my letters, for I wrote at least two last week. However, the weather out here has been terrible (and still is), so perhaps you'll have the pleasure (?) of receiving two or three at once! Anyway, don't think too badly of me dear; I do my best!

I had a very nice evening yesterday, when five of us went to a small town about 9 miles away, where there is a cinema and a Toc H canteen. We saw quite a good film – 'National Velvet', which we all enjoyed very much in spite of the fact we had cold feet because the cinema wasn't heated, and afterwards had tea and cakes (rationed to two per man) in the canteen. I expect that you will think that that wasn't much of a thrill for me, but we take our simple pleasures as they come, and manage to enjoy them too. Of course, a cosy cinema in England (or even Wales!) with you for company would have been much better, dear: however, neither of us can do anything about <u>that</u> at the moment, so we shall both just have to make the best of things.

..... I was glad to hear that Irene was a little better. Sickness is a terrible thing – (I value my health – what little I have – more than anything else I possess) – and it must be very depressing for her in this terrible weather. It's very good of you to go up and keep her company, dear, - (I've often wondered what a true Christian was, and think now that you must be the embodiment of one: - don't blush, darling, I mean it!) Let's hope that the fine weather will soon be here: that will help her a little, too.

Please excuse the writing, by the way: this is being written in bed – the best place, these days. It's now about eleven o'clock, and as I was on duty last night, you can guess that I'm not a little tired. Duties are the very devil, as there are only four of us these days (there will be only three tomorrow), and we have to have two on at a time in the mornings and afternoons, so you can guess we are busy!

16th March, 1946

Sweetheart, thanks for your lovely letter of the 12th. You don't know how much it means to me to have one from you, or how much I appreciate them: and I don't think you're forward at all for saying what is in your mind, for if you like a person surely there's no sin in telling them so; surely half the trouble in the world is caused through false pride and people not saying what is really in their minds. I love you for all of it, dear.

I really thought spring had come to this part of the world last Tuesday, when the weather was glorious: however, it was terrible on Wednesday – (dull and cold), and I came to the conclusion that I was mistaken. It hasn't been so bad today: the sun has been shining, and I went for a four-mile walk this afternoon, but it was very cold with a sharp wind, and I managed to freeze my hands <u>through</u> my gloves: it took me about an hour to thaw them out!

Saw a good film last night – Rita Hayworth and David Niven in 'Tonight and Every Night' – (the story about the Windmill Theatre, which kept open throughout the blitz). You know that they've stopped the supply of films to our regimental cinemas, and shortly I suppose those little outings will be a luxury too.

20th March 1946

Sweetheart,

... We've been very busy today, installing – (rather, beginning to install) a new exchange – a much better type, and larger and quicker, so it's a job we don't mind doing in the least! It's a beautiful job, and after some of the foreign efforts I've seen it makes me feel proud of British craftsmanship and design. So we shall all be pleased when it's finally fitted in and we can get rid of the junk that we're using now.

It's now about half past twelve at night, and I know you'll be wondering if I ever get any sleep at all. We are short-handed again – (we've just lost a chap on class B release), but I don't mind really, for as long as we're like this they can't put us on any fatigues or extra duties, and next Sunday we've a fellow coming off leave, which will make us up to four again – 24 hours on and 24 hours off. Of course, night duty is the worst thing: when I used to sit up with you until one or two o'clock in the morning I used to have a lie- in in the morning to make up for it, but even if we do sleep on the job, it isn't the same as a night off duty, for we've always got the job on our mind, and wonder if the bells are going to awaken us if we get a call, and have a thousand and one other worries: at least, I do, but I suppose that's just how I'm made! And I have to get up at the usual time in the morning or I miss my breakfast. If you miss a meal in the Army, you never make it up!

20th May 1946

Sweetheart,

… Most of the troop are away on a two or three day scheme, so today has been a day of rest for me, for, apart from spring-cleaning the office and doing a few odd jobs, we've had nothing to do. However, I was working at 11.30 last night, so perhaps I deserve it. Needless to say, I've read your letters about 12 times, and if I read them anymore, I'm afraid my wings will be sprouting… However, perhaps you'll find out all about me soon enough: - perhaps even sooner than you expect, then you can look out for yourself: James Mason is a weakling by comparison!

… Yes, the hotel does look very 'flash', and I hope I won't let you down with my uncouth 'Army' habits: I shall almost be afraid to walk about the place! Getting used to a rough soldier is going to be another of your trials! Seriously dear, I feel sure we shall enjoy ourselves: there will be so much for us to do (and enjoy) together. Sharing life's little pleasures is surely the greatest thing of all, and if we can share our lives, surely we shall be the happiest people alive.

… I do wish you had been with me last weekend, when we went to Runeburg and Celle. We did enjoy ourselves, especially as the weather was glorious – (I spent all the time with a fellow who's married and has two children, so you needn't worry about me and the Frauleins – I've successfully resisted them and their sisters in England and various other parts of the world for the past five and a half years, and think I can just about manage the last fortnight….!) They seem to do very well round here for entertainment: this Saturday we went into a nearby small town and saw 'A Thousand and One Nights' between tea and cakes in a Church of Scotland canteen. Yesterday I saw James Mason in 'They were Sisters': I had to work until 11.30 (I was exceptionally busy as the Troop Commander had been out all day on a recce, and I didn't start work until seven) to make up for it, but it was worth it.

The next and last group of letters were written from my grandparents' house in New Malden when my father had been 'demobbed', and he and my mother were beginning to make marriage plans.

4 Woodfield Gardens
New Malden, Surrey

26th November 1946

Dearest (my own!),

…So they do spoil you on occasion! Imagine not getting up until ten o'clock in the morning. Don't know what we're going to do when we're married, for if you do that then, I shall probably do likewise, and what shall we have for dinner? Am I to understand that you slept until that hour, or couldn't you pluck up enough courage to face a cold room after a warm bed. But perhaps you will be kicking me out of bed at seven o'clock on Sundays so that I can clear the place up for you; I know now that you're quite capable of bullying me into it! Anyway, it was good of Rees: suppose he thought it was his

special Sunday good turn!..

(I have a sneaking suspicion that I'm enticing you away from all your friends, and do assure you that it's the last thing that I want to do, and, when we are married, I want you to have as many as you like: for how, otherwise, are you going to manage to live with an old bore like me? I do know that you will miss your Porthcawl life terribly, more perhaps than you think, and you know the last thing I want you to be is lonely and unhappy).

...would rather you would put the money away so that we can share it after we are married, for we shall need all that we can get. However, perhaps I've hurt you again, so, if you feel that you must, get me some little inexpensive thing of your own choice. I shan't mind what it is, as long as it is from you... There was a good concert on the wireless on Sunday afternoon. I wonder what we shall do on Sundays after we are married. Shall we sit round the fire together, or will you cajole me into going out with you? I know that you cannot sit still for more than one minute at a time at most: but perhaps I shall have to be very patient with you: anyway, at first, for I know you will find me strange (and perhaps, a little dull, for I am, you know) especially after your present busy and full little life. Afterwards, when you realise what you have let yourself in for, and have come down to the habit of married life with a jerk, of course things will be vastly different; then we shall have lots of fights (each wanting our own way), but I really think that you will be the winner of most of them!

30th November 1946

Dearest,

Saturday night, and I suppose you are enjoying (or have enjoyed) yourself at Irene's, so you see that I do read your letters, and am thinking of you constantly. I do hope you have both enjoyed yourself...

Well, dear, in just over three weeks I shall (with luck) be seeing you...How I am looking forward to that time. Our pleasures don't come very often, do they, but I think we make up for that when we see each other, and when we are allowed that great gift of living with each other I think we shall both derive much more pleasure from it, knowing that it hasn't been easily come by and that we've had to strive for it. For nothing really worthwhile comes easily to us – don't you agree? - and just imagine us taking married life (and each other) and the whole circumstance of our being together for granted: can you bear the thought? I can't....

2nd February 1947

My dear,

When I wrote the date on this letter I suddenly realised that it was four weeks since I had seen you: what an age that month seems! Yet, when we are together, time simply flies: it does seem unfair, doesn't it? This business of the passage of time is rather interesting, for, at times, it seems to go past so quickly, weekend following weekend (that is how I count it) inexorably.... But I expect you don't feel the same about these things, for you are too busy to take heed of Time's passing. I don't know whether to feel compassion or congratulation at your working so hard. I only know that you do have too hard a life and that I would give the world (if it were in my power) to take you away from it. But one day I will, all this waiting will be over, and (I think) what joy will be ours for it. I mentioned congratulation at your finding so much (having so much, I suppose I ought to have said) to do: and think that a full life is to be congratulated: yet how much fuller it would be if we were in the position to share it!

This last week has seemed interminable to me, for it is very cold and bleak here and I must confess that I have been irritable and impatient at the delay in the thaw, but yesterday and today it is slightly warmer, and now it is raining heavily so that I hope that soon the snow will be washed away. I can even now see traces of our garden through it, and must confess that I feel brighter already!

I was so pleased to learn that you had enjoyed your lesson. Our pleasures don't come easily to us these days, so surely we should make the most of those few that we have. I expect you will miss your singing when you come here to live, but we have some good societies here in London (there is a good one at Wimbledon, which also boasts a symphony orchestra) and, of course, there is the Welsh Society, so perhaps you could join one of these, then you wouldn't feel so out of things: I shall have to spare you for a night or two a week! I am quite willing if it would make you happy, and I do so want that...

16th March 1947

My dear,

Of course I must apologise for not letting you have a letter sooner. I actually wrote to you a couple of days ago but I was rather pushed for time in the morning and in my haste forgot to post it, so perhaps I'll be forgiven. Anyway, what do you intend to do with me when we meet! You say that I have a way of putting you in your place: what do you mean precisely by that?

By the way, I know you will be pleased to learn that I managed to book up for our holiday... I only know that I am longing to see you and hold you in my arms again, and to feel you close to me. And I warn you that when we do meet I shall hold you so tight and hug you that I shall squeeze all the breath out of you, and you'll be fit for nothing afterwards!... I was so glad to hear about your singing, for surely you deserve some return for the efforts that you have made with regard to it in the past. And I do hope that you will get in with the B.B.C., for it will be an honour for you, as well perhaps as a little extra pocket money for yourself.

...I often wonder how we shall spend our Sundays after we are married – will you want to go to sleep in the afternoons, or shall you drag me out away from my armchair by the fire. I don't think what we do will matter very much as long as we are together, do you?

24th March 1947

My dear,

... I am so glad that you were a success, not that I don't know that you deserved it, for you worked hard enough for it: but perhaps you will say that that has made it even more worthwhile. I do wish I could have seen you (and Mum and Dad as well), but there you are! You do know, though, that I thought of you continually on Monday (and always!), and if I wasn't there in the flesh, my spirit wasn't far away....

I can't yet conceive properly that in a week's time we shall be with each other again. Oh dear, I am longing for the time when you are in my arms again, and you can depend upon it that I shall never let you go...

I drew my back pay today (about £3 extra, after Income Tax and superannuation deductions), so we should be all right for Easter and you can forget what I said about drawing some money out of the bank! The latest rumour about our other rise (although I would hate you to build up any false hopes) is that we might get 15/- of it. Do you think that we might manage on £6.10/- (gross) a week? I can tell you that I am a very small eater, but I know how you can put it away!

Much love from Archie xxxxxx

P.S. Mum has been worrying me to ask you what rations I have to take down with me, so will you let me know? I shall have no peace otherwise!

5th May 1947

My dear,

...I went for a walk yesterday with Mum and Dad, and I was agreeably surprised at the progress they had made in the bomb-damaged houses, for they seem to be working on the last of them. In fact they are building some for sale (at £1450) in quite a nice position, although they have only just started, and I don't know what they will be like inside. Anyway, I think that in a few months' time the bomb damage will be completed, and the builders will have to pull their socks up and get down to a little honest work (and competition) again. I think we can wait that long, don't you? I don't think it will be as long as I expected anyway. Isn't that good news?

I can see that I shall have to bring my old clothes with me at Whitsun. How would you like me to scrub a couple of floors for you! Just to get myself into training, you know! I do wish I could help you: you know that when we are married I shall spoil you, and look after you oh so well (anyway, as far as I can: you know that, don't you?), so I might as well get some practice in now, don't you think?

14th December 1947

Dearest,

Such a nice letter, but rather sad, too. I am sorry that you had such a bad time at your lesson, and do hope that you are now feeling a little easier in your mind about the concert, for I know that you will do well. You must always remember that we profit from our mistakes (if we've the sense to), and that will give you solace, for surely you must realise that none of us are perfect. Anyway, if nothing else, it will prevent you from having too high an opinion of yourself!

A scarf would be nice if your mother wants one. Will you take it, and I'll settle with you when I see you. I am afraid that I shall be quite embarrassed when I see your mother, especially when I ask her for your hand in marriage. How on earth does one begin!

My dear, I miss you as well, and really am just as impatient at the slow passage of time as you. But just think! Four whole days together, and I think that I might be able to afford something towards your fare: that is, if you want to come back with me this time, and wouldn't rather leave it until the spring: I leave that entirely to you.... I'm sure that I shall like the pen: was it hard to obtain? I do hope not, for I'm sure that you are very busy these days...

Life for me sometimes is its usual round – sheltered, I suppose, a trifle monotonous at the moment, but oh, with what promise for the future! Not sheltered I suppose, when I have to start worrying for both of us, but with compensations, real compensations, I am certain of that, aren't you?.... I am afraid that there isn't much of the Christmas spirit left these days, but, and I think I have said this before, things could be worse, we must be thankful for what we have, and make the best of a bad job. Don't you agree? And now I really have exhausted my stock of news. Write me soon...

Much love from Archie xxxxxx

*

And that's the last of the letters, my father's final words.

Transcribing them has enabled me in a way to 'get inside' his head and heart for a while, having a sense of the real person: gentle, kind, loving, warm, sensitive, generous, wise, principled - just a few of the adjectives that come to mind. His intelligence shines through in the way in which he expresses himself, not to mention the perfection of his punctuation, even if I take issue with too many colons, perhaps! Apparently, according to my mother, he once wrote a play and tried unsuccessfully to get it published. I wonder what it was about. Also touching is the romantic way in which he communicates – almost a kind of courtly love. Knowing what he read, which films he saw, plus his other interests, has brought me so much closer to him, helped to fill in some of the blanks.

Although he leaves out the detail of his Army experiences, there are indications of the harsh conditions and the dangers he faced, not to mention the tedium and disappointments, the sense of anti-climax after the war was over and won. Most moving and sadly ironic for me is the hope and excitement of his dreams for the future, so cruelly destroyed. The few stories my mother told me of their life in London were not entirely happy: she talked of my grandmother's jealousy and the cramped conditions in the tiny New Malden house, and how at one stage she was so desperate that she threatened to go back to Wales if my father didn't find us a house of our own. I can't imagine the pressure this must have put on him, especially after his wartime service, but I can't conceive of the pressures on my mother, either. When they finally bought a house in Balham, it was, by all accounts, in a dreadful state. They both pitched in to restore and renovate, my mother apparently even building a wall! Hopefully they had some fun in sharing the task.

Lastly in this section, a few remarks about childhood bereavement.

The loss of a parent at any stage in life is massive, but for a child can be a major trauma, whether through death, divorce or separation. In my case it left a black shadow over my life, not to mention an appalling sense of insecurity and fear. I became terrified of the dark, school phobic, and am still rather anxious and sensitive. No one talked to me about my thoughts and feelings – in the 1950's children were 'seen and not heard', and in the 1960's my mother was busy building up her business and largely 'unavailable' to me emotionally, despite our loving relationship.

There were brief anecdotes about my father, everyone describing him as 'very special', but otherwise he was rarely mentioned. His death was itself 'the elephant in the room', the only reference being my mother's regular reminders of her widowhood, not her daughter's loss of a father. This was a formula which seemed to work well to keep 'it' – maybe an overwhelming sense of responsibility for my psychological and emotional welfare - at a safe distance.

In my late 20's I had a serious psychological crisis and ended up (secretly) in therapy after I had returned to London to work, and by chance living not far from our old house in Balham. It was then that I started to grieve. On one memorable occasion, after it had at long last become obvious that I was unwell, I shared my distress with my mother. She was shocked, saying that she didn't understand how I could have such feelings as I '*had never had much of a relationship'* with my father: he had worked long hours and I was usually in bed when he got back home.

After she died I suddenly started to write poetry, feeling at last free to express myself very openly. The four poems that follow tell a little of my story. The next was in fact written as recently as 2018, indicating a life-long process of grappling with the issues. I used it for a training session on childhood bereavement for a group of Cruse Bereavement Care volunteers last year:

Party, March 1953

The child weaves her way through a forest of dark legs,
her image reflected in grandfather's shiny shoes,
grandmother's tears. There is strange noise,
not the sort that defines celebration:
mother's voice is cracked, not the same kind
that sings lullabies. China cups rattle more than usual
on their saucers, trying to secure themselves.
Outside, the smog of March curls round chimney pots,
and tries to get in.

The child coughs. Someone picks her up
in their strong arms. 'Poor little mite' they say. Their breath
smells of sherry and there are crumbs on their clothes
from the cakes her mother made last night in a frenzy of cooking.
'It will take time', says another, 'but the child will be a comfort.

The child will help.'

The child wonders how and why she must help her mother.
After all, she is never allowed in the kitchen. Undaunted,
her curiosity in permanent flow, she tugs at her grey skirt,
asks if it's someone's birthday. She is hushed and shushed,
the wheezing sounds like the cold draught under the door.
Already in her tiny mind she senses an unclear transgression,
worse than the worms she dug up in the garden, or the coal
she smeared over her white dress one Sunday morning.

She will bury this time at the back of her garden
where nothing but weeds grow under the pear tree.
The other time too, that long dark night
when her screaming parent squeezed her so tight
she couldn't breathe, will lie in stagnant water after rain.
Instead she will search endlessly: in the arms of lovers,
in the notes of a Nocturne, in poems and stories,
in the sea, in the sunset, in the smell of a tweed jacket.
She will stare at the photographs, daring him to speak;
scrutinise his face for any message, good or bad;
feel desire at his slim body, the way he holds
a cigarette, the calm with which he stands like a star,
gazing into some distant space. She will devour his books,
knowing he has held the pages in his gentle hands,
occasionally delighting in the faint scribbles
written hastily in a margin, with which she agrees.

Otherwise all she has is a lock of hair,
a brown leather wallet with the last train ticket,
a crumpled ten shilling note, unspent.

Everything afterwards will be un - something:
unlived, unloved, unheard, unfelt, unshared.
Even his resting place is unmarked.

All leavings, partings and endings will make her breath uneven,
dig an ache in her side, sending her back somewhere
into that tangled undergrowth of black suits, grey skirts,
the shiny shoes of her grandfather.

But in these moments
she will endeavour to remember
the sight of that rainbow
arching over the graves,
when she once searched fruitlessly for his.

Mary

A sudden memory of wheeling my doll
on a summer morning,
silently wishing for a frilly sunshade.
But maybe we couldn't quite stretch to it.

Then after you died, leaving her out in the rain
so that her body rotted: the head hairless,
one eye blue, the other purple, a fractured eyelid.

I put stones in the pram.

An old arthritic aunt restored her to life
with stuffed fabric: arms, legs, torso.
She's in the attic gathering dust
in her torn pink dress.

Occasionally I go up to say hello.

Maybe

I saw you reading
in a corner, under yellow lamplight,
hair still damp from November smog,
or smelt the tweed of your cheap jacket:
stale smoke, a father's sweat. Maybe
heard you whistling in spring
as you upturned soil ready for flowers.
No doubt tasted love in your gaze
as you tucked up sheets, read stories,
full of hope for a future not to be yours

or mine.

An Unlived Life

So I'm to die now, like this, not in the heat of battle with guns blazing,
but in a bed in Balham, listening to the gentle snores of my small wife.

I'm not one to talk - prefer to read, anything I can get my hands on.
Now that's all finished. I'm a shy man, given to quiet introspection.

Had to join up, with a father scarred by the trench, and other unsung heroes.
I've never told her the full story, how sleeping under a lorry with dead animals

made me vomit, how each day I longed for suburbia and apple blossom.
It's been a strange life, growing up in the shadow of war: my silent father,

puzzled mother, our little lives. I did my best out there, observed the enemy,
then a job that's brought a living but boredom. Each day

a journey in crowded trains with pale office boys, seeing them dream
in smoky tunnels. We found a place we could call our own, cheap and rotten

from bombs and neglect. Worked like crazy to restore; took in lodgers,
built walls, dug the garden. We were ready to plant. Last Christmas

I made paper lanterns, hung them over banisters and stairs, bright paper chains
from light fittings. But now in the smog of March a clot of blood

winds its rogue way through the terrace of veins. I won't see daylight,
watch my child grow. Remember me and my unlived life.

My parents' wedding, May 1948

With my Dad in Porthcawl, 1951

My Mother:
Doris Mill (née Thomas)
1913 - 2003

Top row: Elwyn, Grenville, Rees
Middle row: Doris, Grandpa Ebenezer Thomas, Grandma Elizabeth Thomas, Victoria
Bottom row: Gwyneth, Margaret

My mother as 'Magnolia' in 'Showboat', Porthcawl Operatic Society

My mother was born in a little village outside the seaside town of Porthcawl on the South Wales coast, the youngest of seven children. She had happy memories of her childhood by the sea, but when the family's finances became stretched in the 1930's Depression and the Miners' Strike, they took in visitors to make ends meet. Mum described a house always full of people, everyone thriving on the company and the fun. As the youngest, she had responsibility for a lot of housework, and at school developed talents in a number of practical skills, winning a prize for pastry-making at the age of 14. Her ambition though, was to be a children's nurse, but as her sister Gwyneth was already training away from home, and Victoria developing a career as a music teacher, Margaret married and living in the Welsh valleys, Elwyn and Rees in the grocery business, Grenville a carpenter, she had to stay at home.

On leaving school she worked as a dressmaker and upholsterer. This income enabled her to take singing lessons under the Professor of Music at Cardiff University. She joined Porthcawl Operatic Society where she took many leading roles over the years. In 1938 her beloved father had a stroke. Mum gave up the sewing to stay at home to look after him and her ailing mother. She was devastated by his death, to the extent that she became ill with nervous exhaustion. On recovery in 1941 she was employed as a postwoman, also helping her mother to look after the Dutch soldiers who were billeted in the house. A strong connection with one Dutch family, and which was to last for many years, developed from this. Towards the end of the war Mum worked for the Refuge Assurance Company; she didn't much like the selling part of the job, but being very sociable, loved meeting people.

The following account was prepared by her for a presentation at the 50th anniversary of the end of WW2 at the Porthcawl Pavilion in 1995.

'Home Guard was formed by the older men – these were responsible for getting the people off the streets in the event of a raid warning, and to remain indoors until the 'All Clear' was sounded. Later air raid shelters were dug in the back gardens. Everyone cultivated what gardens they had, for vegetables. Black curtains were made for every window, and kept tight closed at night so that no light should be seen. Canvas bags were filled with sand, to build up against important buildings. These were done by men who were either too old to go to War, or those not considered fit.

Food was rationed and clothing coupons issued. Beaches were barricaded in the form of heavy wire netting all along the coast. All young men joined the Army, Air Force or Navy. Most volunteered. Women were drafted to the Arsenal in Bridgend, making bombs. A yellow powder was used which gave their faces and hands a yellow colour. Others joined the forces or Land Army, the latter sent to work on farms etc. Some who had elderly or sick parents to care for were sent to work in the local Post Office, also men who were in the older grade – late 30's, who had not yet been called up. As my mother was ill, I was allocated to the Post office, so was my eldest brother (Elwyn) who had volunteered to join the Army, but was rejected, due to having had a cataract operation. My other two brothers volunteered and were accepted – one for the Air Force (Rees) and the other the Army (Gren).

Evacuees came from London. Each household had to take in two or more, according to the number of rooms available. On arrival they were first sent to the Pavilion, where their hosts welcomed them. Next came the Welsh Regiment who were stationed in camps on Coney Beach Dunes. I was on duty at the Post Office at 7 a.m. The Dutch camped at Newton, the Americans in the Seabank Hotel, so you can imagine the thousands of letters to be sorted, and then delivered, plus heavy parcels. These we put into a large haversack, and we carried them on our shoulders. Then home for breakfast, then back to more sorting and delivery. In the afternoon parcels came to the railway station in Dock Street, and then wheeled in a large truck – this was heavy work. Churches opened to allow any Army, Navy or Air Force personnel to use for entertainments – billiards, table tennis etc. Many of the Dutchmen used to come to our house. Mother loved to welcome them – most of these could not speak a word of English, so between the help of dictionaries which they always had with them, and the spoken word in the churches, and our home, it was amazing how quickly they learned to speak sufficient English to be understood.

Gradually the soldiers were drafted abroad or transferred to various parts of Britain in camps or offices, but wherever the Dutch went, they came back to Porthcawl when on leave, several came back to our house throughout the War. After the War in 1957 my sister Gwen and I were invited to visit the family of one of the Dutchmen, Jan, and his wife Tina and daughters. They gave us the most wonderful fortnight's holiday. We travelled throughout Holland the first week, then spent the second week in their houseboat, to which was attached a large yacht, so we spent the time on the water. The Salt Lake, where the inhabitants of Porthcawl sailed their small boats, held swimming galas and so on, was filled in during the early part of the War. The Americans helped us to do this, to enable the military vehicles to be parked there.

My brother Elwyn still had his grocery shop. The family used any damaged goods to boost the rations. The Dutch soldiers brought their rations with them. German Prisoners of War were held in a camp just between Bridgend and Porthcawl Many escaped only to be captured out in the country or on roads, in various parts of Mid Glamorgan etc. We were terrified, and told to be alert.

The Dunkirk soldiers – many came to Porthcawl and were accommodated at the Baptist Church which was then in South Road, where they laid on the floor on blankets. Mother saw three of them pass the house so she called them in, told them to have a bath, they were flea infested and dirty. Then she gave them something to eat before they joined the rest in the Church, and were later taken away to their various camps. We were spared heavy bombing, just a few were dropped on Stormy Down on the return from the bombing in Cardiff and Swansea. We thanked God when this terrible War came to an end, and my brothers returned. Grenville who had been in the front line during the battle of Monte Casino in Italy, had been wounded there and paralysed for a time, but fully recovered by the time he came home.'

Photographs Mum sent to my father during the war

Auntie Gwen:
Miss Gwyneth Thomas S.R.N., R.F.N., S.C.M.
1908 – 2001

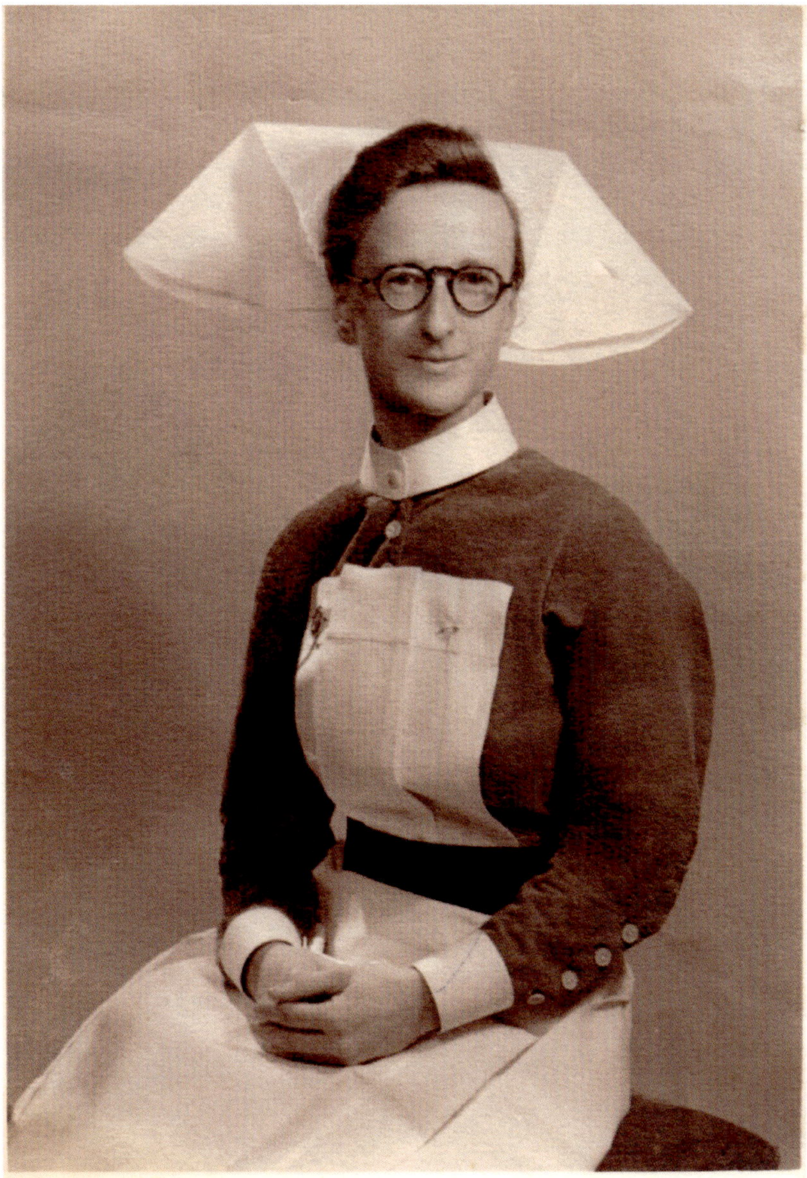

Auntie Gwen – as I called her – was my favourite in our large Welsh family. As a child in the 1950's, whilst staying with my grandparents in New Malden, I enjoyed time with her too at her hospital flat in Clapham. She introduced me to the glittering city, still of course in the throes of recovery from the aftermath of war. I remember her as kind and gentle, interesting and interested, with a fantastic sense of humour, despite many setbacks in her personal life. She was entirely dedicated to her profession. Each night in preparation for duty the following day, I would watch her darning black stockings and sewing newly-starched bleached-white collars and frilly cuffs onto her immaculate grey uniform. In my introduction to her war diary, I describe how she would greet me on arrival, remembering:

'the unique smell that engulfed me for a moment - a delicious blend of carbolic, light eau–de-cologne, and the crisp pure whiff of clothes kept perpetually clean.. an antiseptic-ism that successfully blended cold hygiene and warm affection'.

One of our many treats was to go to the Brasserie in Lyons Corner House, Trafalgar Square (long since vanished), before trips to the Royal Festival Hall to watch ballet, or go to the cinema. Much to her well-hidden dismay, I would order the most expensive dish on the menu – chicken in the basket at twelve shillings and sixpence. As it was early, the restaurant would be comparatively empty, so the little band of musicians used to serenade us. I thought I was in heaven:

Dining Out with Auntie Gwen, 1959

What was really interesting
was the way the lettuce stayed crisp
under the chicken and chips;
how the basket never got soggy,
the napkins matched
the red check of the tablecloth,
the fiddlers' waistcoats.

Then with her after-dinner cigarette
fitted neatly into ivory, inlaid,
looking as cool as that mountain spring,
she drew gently. Mesmerised,
I watched the ribbons of chiffon
drift skywards, then licked the salt
from my greased fingers.

Trafalgar Square, 1958

In Appreciation

(written when I was 16)

I don't profess to be a poet,
Not a patch on my Auntie Gwen,
For this is one of many talents
To flow straight from her pen.

I'm very sure of one thing though,
She's kind to me and I love her so.
She'll take me out and give me a treat,
Although sometimes she must feel dead beat.

There is always a welcome waiting for me
When to the flat I climb,
And we always go up the West End
Where we have such a marvellous time.

Please don't think I'm ungrateful
Or don't realise how lucky I am
If I can't think of words to express myself
To give all the thanks I can.

So let this be a little token
Of my thanks and admiration
And in all the years that are to come
I will look back in appreciation.

Auntie commenced nurse training in 1927 in a small isolation (fever) hospital in Chippenham, Wiltshire. She went on to work at St. Mary Abbotts in Kensington, the Brook in Woolwich, Highgate and Lewisham Hospitals, ending her career as a Home Sister in the South London Hospital for Women and Children in Clapham.

During WW2, by which time she had been promoted to Sister, she stayed at her post, like so many others, continuing to nurse in Highgate (1935 – 42) and Lewisham (1942 – 47) – all the way through the Blitz.

Here are some extracts from the diary:

WAR DIARY

AUGUST 28th 1939: ...It was almost dark when I reached the hospital, and it was as I entered the hall that I realised that preparations had been made for air raids, etc. The hall was in semi -darkness, the corridors looked like badly lit tunnels, black curtains shut out what daylight was left. At last I reached my corridor, there meeting several other sisters and I learned that all who were still on holiday had been sent for; those who were ready to go that day were told to unpack. Every one of them did so readily.

29th AUGUST 1939:..Returning to Isolation I find most of the cubicles empty, only five children left, and they are to be evacuated on Monday. I have been instructed to paste paper in strips on all the cubicle glass, and windows, and pack up in readiness to close the block. It seems impossible to realise that Isolation, where I have been so very happy in my work, is to be idle. What type of lunatic is this man Hitler to cause such an upheaval in our lives? So my staff help me to collect every article and pack them for storage......During our off duty, we are preparing strips of cardboard for the sides of the windows, thousands of strips are cut and nailed up.

30th AUGUST 1939: The morning is spent in packing again and preparing to send the sick children off tomorrow morning. During our off duty, we help to put gas masks together. Hundreds of these are dealt with every hour throughout the days following, during our off duty time. We are just living from day to day, waiting for the fatal moment, which we all realise must come, since Hitler has invaded Czechoslovakia, slaughtering thousands of innocent people.

31st AUGUST 1939: ...Papering of windows is still going on in all parts of the hospital, while day and night the lorry loads of sand pass through the gates. Everyone is giving a helping hand with the sand bags, even our Medical Superintendant is working as hard as anyone, so are doctors, sisters, nurses, clerks and porters; outside people have also come in to help, ...

At night it is so strange, the streets which are usually so brightly lit are now in darkness, and it is so dark in the buses that you can only make out the forms of people. We are allowed to use torches, the bulbs of which must be covered with two layers of tissue paper. The drivers of buses, cars, etc., must have eyes like cats and nerves of steel. I admire them more every time I have occasion to travel by night.

So the end of the week sees Isolation deserted; I feel heartbroken at leaving it. ...Thousands of children have been evacuated, tearful parents have parted with them because they know it is the best, some have been able to go with them. This great evacuation has been going on all the week, and so smoothly has it been run that there has not been one hitch, every child reached their destination safely. Splendid work!

SUNDAY, 3rd SEPTEMBER: Arrangements have been made for about ¾ of the nurses to leave tomorrow for "base hospitals". Ten sisters are included, but I am not one of them. My destination is Ward 13, a female Pulmonary Tuberculosis ward, mainly all advanced cases..... Hitler has now marched into Poland, so war is inevitable...Some of the patients are crying bitterly but quietly - others with brave voices try to cheer them. I have difficulty in restraining my tears but the realization that these people - so very helpless -.will look to the staff for comfort, makes me pull myself together. Then, before we had time to get over the first shock, the sirens go… MONDAY - 3 a.m.: Was awakened by the shrieking sirens again; never in my life have I jumped out of bed as quickly, or dressed so quickly; most of the staff were at their posts in seven minutes. When I reached my ward, I could hear some of them sobbing. I walked from bed to bed trying to console them, while only heaven knew how sick with fear I really felt. Still, when I heard a few say - "Is that you, sister?", and to my reply - "Oh, we are so glad we have you nurses with us," - this gave me courage again…

April 1940: Isolation is still closed, so are many of our wards; the hospital is so changed. Most of my patients who became so much worse soon after war broke out, during the severe cold and snow, and the "black-out" at night, have since died…

In March I collapsed when setting the AP dressing trolley for Dr Back. I was warded for 3 weeks with "vertigo" due to over- strain on the nervous system, and still felt very weary when I returned from my fortnight's sick leave at home… as I went on duty, I thought how little my health meant to these people, that I should be put on the TB ward again after working like a slave throughout the winter…

MAY 24th 1940: During this past week, the Germans have got so far as Boulogne but I feel they are walking into a net; the next few days will prove whether I am right or not…9 p.m. The King spoke to the Empire…

MAY 26th: The King has expressed a wish that this should be a day devoted to prayer by all people. I went to service at the hospital at 10 a.m. and to an outside church at 11 a.m. The Queen of the Netherlands accompanied our King and Queen to Westminster Cathedral for service. The Germans are near the French coast, now we know they are very near us, but even so, I cannot feel that we are doomed, far from it, my faith in our own defence is too strong.. parents of children now in towns on the East Coast are asked to be prepared to send their children to places of safety suggested by the Government tonight. So this brute Hitler is tearing up homes, not by bombs, but by separating loved ones from each other.

27th MAY: TB ward has just taken another young girl, 21 years old... Gladys never uttered one word of complaint, and she must have had terrible pain for the past three months. So while the "boys" are fighting so gallantly in France for freedom, so these girls go on fighting against TB, which has attacked them just as brutally as Hitler has attacked the small countries. Today we each had 4 ounces of sugar - our allowance for a week. Tomorrow we have our butter. Up to the present, it has been put on our tables daily.

28th MAY: The King of Belgium, King Leopold, has capitulated. Everyone is very surprised, but his government still insists on fighting. We shall perhaps understand his move better later on. Our position is extremely grave, but the spirit of' the people is undaunted. There have been air raids off the East Coast during the past week, several people have been wounded. An American hospital at Ostend has been bombed by the

Germans, killing all patients, doctors and nurses.

29th MAY: Everyone talks of the King of Belgium; most feel we cannot criticize until we know the full facts…

30th MAY: They are endeavouring to bring our soldiers out of Boulogne, where they were when the King of Belgium capitulated, leaving them surrounded by Germans.

3lst MAY: Thousands of soldiers have been brought home safely, some badly wounded.

1st JUNE: …two sisters are leaving to nurse the wounded; it is very true that we live only from day to day. Who knows less than we shall soon all be nursing the soldiers.

2nd JUNE: On duty 7.30 a.m. to find they had taken another nurse, leaving me with one for the morning and two probationers alone from 3.30 p.m…

3rd JUNE: The fighting is still going on in the North of France, Paris has been bombed. Had a new filter attached to my gas mask today, so did the rest of the staff.
Matron saw all the staff in the recreation room today, to tell us that the Ministry of Health wish all nurses to do 58 hours a week instead of 48 hours, the night staff 60 hours. We are all prepared to do what we can…

6th JUNE: So Clarke and Hopkins must leave for a base hospital on Monday. Whose turn next? I hope it's mine. Terrific fighting going on in France.

9th JUNE: Sister Jenny and Corrigan back for the evening. Both seem to enjoy nursing the soldiers who fought in such a splendid way at Dunkirk. The news tonight is very grave, there is every possibility that German troops will try to land here on the British Isles, but I feel sure we are prepared for them, both from a defence and spiritual standpoint. I hope if such a thing happens I shall not be a coward, but be able to think and act quickly. Received snaps of the boys at home, I hope they will all come out of this safely…

10th JUNE: Italy joined the Germans. Clarke and Hopkins left for base hospital 11 a.m. Very few of us left now.

15th JUNE: Chest X - ray report N.A.D., that's a relief. It looks as if I shall be nursing the TB's for duration; it will please me as long as my health will stand it. Cleared most of dispensary from Isolation which, by the way, looks desolate, all the cubicles are so thick with dust, everything up there looks so cheerless.

17th JUNE: Very bad news from France today. We have been informed that they have had to give in. Everyone really does feel depressed, most of my patients though still have faith and believe as I do that we shall win this battle on our own land...

19th JUNE: Went to an A.R.P. practice tonight. Everything went off well.

20th JUNE: Very busy with outpatients. Poor little Lilian Crowden so very ill tonight, thought she would die this afternoon, remained with her for most of the early evening. Off duty 6.30, went to Auntie Cissie's to fetch more posies which she sells in aid of Red Cross...

21st JUNE: 10.30p.m. Very, very weary. Just came off duty. Tonight, of all nights, two TB patients decided to quarrel, and they did it with a vengeance, regardless of all the ill patients in the ward. Mrs K hit Mrs J in the face; nurse managed to get a glass out of Mrs J's hand before she threw it at Mrs K, but not before she had thrown the water over her. Meanwhile, I managed to pull Mrs J away from Mrs K's bed; heaven knows how I did it or where I had the strength from, as she is 11 stone while I am 6 stone 13 lbs. Then Doctor came and again we had to listen to the one patient accusing the other. So at last Doctor managed to persuade Mrs J to stay in the side ward for the night. So ended my nursing of TB patients. Poor things, I am so sorry for them; it is only a few behave like this, and then I believe it is their long illness and the monotony of each other's company that nearly drives them mad. Such a pity that my last night on duty should have been spoiled by such an upheaval.

22nd JUNE: Commenced duty on the casualty ward.

23rd, 24th: Liking my change of work very much. No change in war news

25th: Pleasant surprise - saw someone I am very fond of.

26th – 30th: No news except that matron saw all the sisters and informed us that the most rigid economy must be exercised in the use of electricity, gas, water and materials for cleaning purposes.

1st JULY: ...Germans have invaded the Channel Islands.

2nd JULY: Still no letter from home, wonder why? If only they would write a postcard. Surely there must be something wrong, or they would not keep me in such suspense. Matron and Nurse Watts, who live near me have heard from their people, so I cannot imagine what has happened.

3rd JULY: Still not a word from home. ..Stretcher practice - 8 p.m. - very satisfactory.

6th JULY: Heard from home; just said they were sorry to have kept me so long without a letter.

13th JULY: Uneventful week in London. No raids. Numerous raids in Wales, but cannot get any details, hope all is well at home. Some of the soldiers from Dunkirk came in during the week as outpatients. It is impossible to relate their experiences here; if they never fight again, they have done their share.

10th AUGUST: Commence holidays... Mother looks pale but appears quite happy. It's grand to be back again. Elwyn looks ill.

11th AUGUST: Elwyn in bed. Very ill? Nursed him all week… Went to see Doctor about having Elwyn's eyesight attended. Raids every night. We stayed in bed, even though the Germans were overhead. Two Dutch sergeants, Laurence and Jan, coming to the house for meals, very grateful to Mother when she told them they could make it their home.. They have no idea if their wives and children (who are still in Holland) are alive or dead, and what they dread most is that they may be starving or tortured under Hitler's rule, since he invaded Holland.

12th AUGUST: Glorious time haymaking on Phyllis and Ray's farm near home the night before I returned to London. On our way home that night, we were caught in a raid. We saw a car in the distance, but on approaching it, discovered the occupants had no petrol, so we suggested that we should push it. We were six, including the two Dutchmen, so we pushed it for about 11/2 miles, at last reached the petrol station, where we had to leave them in hopes of obtaining a little. So we trudged on - the raid made no difference to us - it was a glorious night. We were soon overtaken by a bus. Crowded though it was, we got in and so my holiday ended.

24th AUGUST: I was very upset when I had to say goodbye to all the family, knowing full well that all kinds of things may happen before I was able to visit home again. Rees was waiting to be called up, poor boy, he is so loveable. I hope he will come through it fit and well.

Mother is nearly 70 years - too old to have all this grief of parting with her sons, but she is very brave A splendid example of British motherhood. For the first time since I first left home did I have to turn back, my eyes too full of tears to say goodbye to Mother. At last I got a grip on myself and kissed her a hurried goodbye. I know she understood.

25th AUGUST..12 midnight; Air raid. Out of bed dressed in full uniform on Ward 19, which is full of Spanish refugee children from Gibraltar. They have been in the thick of air raids for the past three months. Very lovely children, mostly all with scurvy, pneumonia, skin infections.

26th AUGUST: 5 hour air raid at night. Bombs dropped, four fires seen, very tired but I will go to sleep during my off duty today for 2 hours.

27th AUGUST: Slept while off duty. Feel refreshed. Air raids again at night.

28th AUGUST: Out in the afternoon, caught in an air raid. Luckily I was in a shop, took shelter there. Air raids at night.

29th AUGUST: If only I could speak Spanish, it would be so much easier to nurse these children.

30th AUGUST: Raid at night. But what joy - a whole night in bed. Three raids during the day, did not hear any bombs drop. Feel so fresh again after a night's sleep. Baby Delipani much better. Seems all so strange to be working so hard to save these little mites' lives while the planes overhead are doing all in their power to destroy them. Dreadful raid at night - 6 hours, during which time bombs dropped very close, what a noise. I remained on the ward from 11 a.m. on 30th to 4 a.m. on 31st, except half an hour for dinner and half an hour for tea. The eldest child in the ward, aged 5, screamed with terror as the bombs dropped. What a night!

<u>31st AUGUST:</u> Six raids up to 10.30 p.m., each one lasting approximately one hour. No damage near us so far... 10.30 p.m. Letter from home, they are all very cheerful, despite the raids they are having, but the nearest in Cardiff and Swansea. 11 p.m. - Air raid. German planes overhead; just got into bed, up and on the ward; this time went into empty ward next to my own. Slept between various all clears and warnings and of course the bombs disturbed nurse and I. No damage to hospital. Over to my room at 7 a.m., heaven knows when the last all clear went - too tired to look at my watch.

<u>1st SEPTEMBER:</u> Raid at 11 a.m... Another raid about 3 p.m., again a short one. Did not hear the planes. ..Undisturbed night as far as raids are concerned, but dreamt there was one, and it was so very real that I wakened with a start and could not make up my mind if it was only a dream or a real one - this was at 5.30 a.m. So to reassure myself, I got out of bed to see if there was anyone in the cover points. Was pleased to see there was no one there, so went back to bed saying quite a few words about my dream! To think that for a week we had been up every night, and the only peaceful night we get, I must have such a dream.

<u>2nd SEPTEMBER:</u> Well, today has been fairly quiet, one short raid in the morning, and one in the evening, lasting about two hours - no damage near us. At 11 p.m. they had us out of bed again. I went over to my ward and remained there, at least in the empty ward next to it, until 6.30 a.m. I slept on and off throughout the night, roused only when the bombs dropped, not so near us as before and when the "all clear" went. Came over to my room, had a bath - how one appreciates it these days...

<u>5th SEPTEMBER:</u> 9 a.m. - a phone call from Jan Bawalda, the Dutchman - lovely surprise. Met Jan and a friend of his at 6.30 p.m., so brought them up to see the Matron, and also took them round the wards. I think they enjoyed it very much. At 8 p.m. we went to the city to have dinner. How very much I enjoyed the evening. Alas, at 9.30 p.m., the air raid warning went, so I had to return. For the rest of the night, I had to sleep on the corridor. It was at least 5 a.m. before the "all clear" went. Then at 5.30 a.m. the sirens started again; this time too tired to go down to the corridor.

<u>6th SEPTEMBER:</u> Very busy on the ward, but all the Spanish children improving. G. taken off the danger list but still the parents insist on remaining in the hospital, so that they will be near their child during an air raid; wonder what kind of panic there would be if each Spanish child's parents insisted on staying with their child. So I was compelled to send the father to the medical superintendent, who was firm and refused to allow more than one parent to remain in the hospital, as he says that if a bomb struck and all these parents were with their children, the Government would have something to say. The L.C.C. have not racked their brains to arrange the visiting hours so that only a few people are visiting every day, instead of all twice a week, to have all these rules broken by refugees.

7th SEPTEMBER: *Quiet up to 5 p.m., then what a raid! Bombs seem to have been dropping all round us, but we saw that they were near the Thames. A few moments later, we saw huge fires, then the Germans went, only to return at 8.30 p.m., and remain until 5 a.m. What a night – we knew they could see so well by the aid of the fires. Several people killed, and 1,000 injured. Oh, how I thank God that so far we are alive.*

8th SEPTEMBER: *Raid at 10 a.m. - far away this time. Spanish visitors very hysterical about their babies being away from them - I am very sorry for them all. ...Raid all night, nearer this time, but we are all unhurt.*

9th - l0th SEPTEMBER: *I still sleep near the babies every night; the raids are more severe. We are beginning to receive some of the casualties, women and children, of course, are amongst Hitler's victims. As we hear the bombs (some of the whistling ones) it seems they must fall on the hospital, they are so near. All the staff are very splendid and I cannot praise the adult patients enough. Five raids on 9th.*

11th SEPTEMBER: *Still sorting things out in the ward - too busy to stop work during a raid - one at 11.30 a.m. and 5 p.m. A "time bomb" exploded near the Palace, fortunately doing little damage, no one hurt. 8.30 p.m. another raid which lasted until 5.30 a.m. I slept for short periods only; our anti - aircraft gunfire was in action with a vengeance; the planes seem to come over our heads every half hour but even though the noise was deafening, we all felt our boys were putting all the fury they could into the action of their big guns. The hospital shook each time they went off, which was every minute while the raiders were overhead. Last night I had hoped to go to town, but it was not safe, so back to my room at 6.30 a.m., to get ready for another day; it's surprising how well one feels with such broken sleep. Heard last night all's well in South Wales, but why don't they write oftener, how little they know what we are going through, or surely they would write to me, not keep me a whole week.*

12th SEPTEMBER: ...9 p.m. air raid, just finished supper; lasted until 6 a.m. Terrific noise of our guns, but so reassuring that I was able to get off to sleep about 11 p.m., near the babies, after seeing that their cots were well covered in case the windows were smashed. All were sleeping.

13th SEPTEMBER: *Returned to my bedroom at 6.45 a.m. As I passed some corridors, I saw that some staff were still huddled up on their mattresses on the floor, sleeping. For a week now, some of us have not slept for one moment in our beds, and we don't seem very much the worse for it. It has been raining, the air is so fresh.*

How blissfully ignorant the little babies are, they seem happier than ever, little do they realise how much sunshine they bring into the nurses' lives by their happy laughter. Today we have had one long raid, and one short. Buckingham Palace has been hit but our King and Queen are unhurt. Beautiful churches are down to the ground. Downing Street, Regent Street and Belgrave Square have also had their share of the damage. It is 6.30 p.m. I have tried to get in touch with my friend in Bedfordshire, but failed. I hope the letter which I have written will reach her.

<u>14th SEPTEMBER:</u> Letter from home… They have warnings, but no raids. Rees is in the Air Force. Could not meet my friends because I could not get in touch with them. This staying in is the hardest part of this war. You feel you dare not go far from the hospital in case you will be unable to return should there be a raid, and as all my friends are a distance away, my off duty is no use. If only I could know whether they are safe, but we have been asked not to use phones unless it is an emergency. The walks round here are also limited as there have been time bombs dropped in the district. So except for a walk to the shops in the morning, my day was again spent indoors. Up to 9.30 p.m. we have had six raids over London. The Palace was hit again, and a time bomb has gone off near the Queen Victoria Statue, but this did very little damage as they had covered it with sandbags. 'Our Lady of Victories', a beautiful Roman Catholic Church in Kensington, has been destroyed. They have dropped bombs on every part of London, but have gained very little. Went to sleep in the 'cover point' in the sisters' home, which meant sleeping on a mattress in the corridor; no siren heard until about 1.30 a.m., when the Germans had been overhead for about two hours and our guns going off with such a fury, it was surely like hell let loose. The hospital shook but not a window cracked. The 'All clear' went about 3.30 a.m. Most of us were asleep, we seem to be getting used to these battles. There is no doubt about our guns being successful, and no doubt about us winning.

<u>15th SEPTEMBER - Sunday morning:</u> The air is fresh, the sun bright. How I should love a walk over the 'Heath', but no, they have dropped time bombs there also, so it seems one must be patient until the war is over. I will go to Church, as I am not on duty until 12.30 p.m…Several raids again; it seems as soon as I order the blinds and curtains to be drawn, the sirens go again, so it goes on all day, but everything goes on in the hospital as usual between the heavy gunfire. We still have our meals, and food is not short. Several of the babes will be going out soon, tomorrow maybe. I shall miss them. Darkness again, what of the night ahead of us? The siren has gone, I must fetch my blanket and pillows, my little case too, in which I have packed my valuable papers. I have my weekend case packed with clothing all in readiness in case we will have to leave our hospital hurriedly. I think it is well to be prepared. 6.30 a.m. I slept very well regardless of the raid, which played havoc in some districts. Oh, I was very very tired.

<u>16th SEPTEMBER – Monday:</u> Four raids up to 6 p.m., my training school has been hit, (St Mary Abbotts, Kensington), many staff killed, part of nurses' home destroyed, and it is only one of the many hospitals. Gallant men have removed a time bomb outside St Paul's. All the London papers are ringing their praises. The Queen's private sitting room at the Palace has been damaged. The Royal couple were not in residence. 9p.m. Another warning. All the sisters sat in the sitting room until about 11 p.m., then the gunfire was getting too hot for us, and owing to the numerous panes of glass in this room, we thought we had better get cover. Heavens, what a din! I did not sleep until the all clear sounded at 3.30 a.m. Then I went to sleep and did not waken until about 4, when the chatter of my night nurse and day nurse who slept on the ward with me, wakened me. It seemed that a screaming bomb passed the ward window, breaking one of ours, and the wards above, but on investigating it was just another piece of shrapnel. So we need not have sat there waiting and wondering if either of us would be alive in the morning; strange how indifferent we were, I suppose we just know if our name is on it, we will get it, but I don't feel that Hitler will ever get to know mine.

17th SEPTEMBER: St Pancras and St Bernards hospital was hit in last night's raids. Parts of Mayfair and the city also suffered, but as I do not go out to see these various places that are bombed, I cannot give full details; I think as long as I can keep my nerve, I will. I fear if I saw too much havoc, I would lose it, and become a coward. I cannot understand why people go out of their way to see this havoc, and come back with all the tales of destruction, such as "Oh, I saw bodies underneath the debris".. …Sisters are relating their experiences when they try to go out. One has to go into a shelter, where the children cry…now do their mothers realize that the Government was right when they implored them to send them away.

18th SEPTEMBER: What a night. Nearer and nearer they seem each night, how hot it seemed in the cover point, sleeping in uniform does not help. The bombs dropped very near, three fireman were badly hurt; two were stationed at this hospital up to a month ago. Bill (as everyone knows him) was one; a piece of shrapnel went into his back across his shoulders. The other two were badly wounded also. Gives you a cold feeling when someone you know has been hit. Three of the big stores hit last night. The people who were there at the time were safe in the basement. Today we have had five raids so far up to 3 p.m…

19th SEPTEMBER: …a lad was brought in to have his leg amputated - now we are beginning to see the results of Hitler's madness…woken by a terrific crash… The bomb dropped in the road near a doctor's house and a few others near a church at the bottom of the hill… The guns are terrific. All the sisters are listening to the news, bombs or no bombs! …soon we shall have to go to cover points; the noise is getting pretty close, even so, some of them are wondering if they could risk a bath..9.40 p.m. On the way to my ward, greeted with - "The children's block is being evacuated - they think a time bomb has dropped just outside your ward". On turning to the block, was met by the cots being wheeled to a safer part of the building from the two wards above me. Matron was down on my ward. So I began to wrap up my babies who slept soundly through it all. Two had been taken when a message came to say it wasn't a time bomb; they are safe - it was a shell which had certainly fallen as near the hospital as a yard or two.

2Oth SEPTEMBER: All the nurses had to leave their home on the top of Highgate Hill in the earlier hours of the morning. A time bomb has landed in their grounds…

21st SEPTEMBER - 9 a.m.:. It is my day off, but time hangs, because we cannot get away from hospital, or at least only a short distance. 5 p.m. Went to the Church. Very pretty wedding. No raid until we arrived back at the flat. So pleased they were able to be married. Raids during the night but they seemed to keep away from us for longer periods.

22nd SEPTEMBER: …Spent the time up to 6.15 p.m. sorting out more things to pack in readiness for evacuation, and the remainder of my property I have packed in my trunk - these I shall have to leave behind and hope for the best.

23rd SEPTEMBER: Time bombs dropped in several streets near the hospital during the night, each one seemed to be coming on us. The Archway hospital was hit but no one injured…

24th SEPTEMBER: …At first a bomb dropped very near, then the second time the smell of fire which was thought to be in some part of the hospital, but again God deemed it otherwise, and the incendiaries had dropped in the park grounds, which is next door to this hospital. As it only caused a smouldering, it did not light us up enough to help the Germans make sure of their target. So at 6.30 a.m., we are wakened by the ward night nurse to greet another dawn, and to find the hospital intact once more, but other people were not to see the dawn again. Two young girls who were sisters, aged 15 and 17, were brought in dead. They had escaped from their own home which had been bombed, and had gone to spend the night with a friend of theirs, and so were found dead after the friend's house had been bombed. They had done their hair up in curlers, so sure they would be going to work in the morning.

25th SEPTEMBER: …St Pancras Hospital has been bombed again - today we have taken in some of their patients... Last night we sisters had a sing - song to brighten things up.

26th SEPTEMBER: ..it is only by the grace of God that we did not have a land mine on the hospital. It fell a distance away, a block of flats falling like a pack of cards. Several of the injured were brought in here: one poor man had his eyes smashed, they were taken out in the theatre later; in the afternoon he died. And now the night is approaching again with all the terror it brings.

27th SEPTEMBER: ... Two raids during the morning. During one, there was a terrific fight between the German planes and our Spitfires but very soon these drove them away. Went down to the city by Underground. Even as early as 2 p.m. children were sitting on rugs and old blankets - keeping a place for the family in readiness for the night. Heavens, what a sight. Went to New Bond Street and Regent Street. Some of the buildings are down like a pack of cards, and those that remain have no windows. …there was fierce fighting overhead, but I was in a shop so heard nothing of it…To look at the people in the street, one would never think that every day may be their last. Most just getting their shopping done as usual, the only difference being that everyone is so much friendlier toward one another. It was with difficulty that I eventually got into a train, by now the platforms were crowded with all the people who had come to sleep for the night. Some reading, (or trying to), others knitting, sewing, eating, babies and children laughing, crying, playing. What are they going to be like at the end of the winter with so little fresh air, and such cold? No toilet facilities - the air is foul. I was glad to get back to hospital, where even though several of us have to sleep in a small space, it is at least clean, and warm… one of the sick babies cried so much it was impossible to go to sleep, so I had the babe brought to our cover point and there I held it close to me to try to comfort it… The following day….only one nurse on with me. Six bottle babies… In the afternoon, during nurses off duty, I was alone, and during the evening, when I should have been off duty, I had to return to help nurse with the feeds. I was glad I went back, as a new baby became worse…. I remained with it until 11 p.m., when I could see some improvement. Then I lay down on my mattress, so very tired, slept all night. They say several bombs dropped, and the gunfire terrific, but I was too dead asleep to hear.

30th SEPTEMBER: Several of our non - resident staff have lost their homes, and quite a number their relatives... At 5.30 p.m., one sister and I were in the sitting room when suddenly a plane seemed to dive down from nowhere, drop a bomb... the room shook, and we really thought it must be coming down on us. Well, if it had, I would not be writing this now. I often wonder if I shall be spared to the end of the war to finish this diary. If not, I would like my mother to have this book, and then after her days, my little niece, Margaret - it may help her a little in her History. It's been great fun writing this, and a great relaxation. Please overlook the mistakes, it is all done so hurriedly.

5th OCTOBER: Almost a week, and no writing been done, but I fear I have been sleeping during what off duty I have had. Only two nurses on the ward with me... More sick babies again. Raids continue, but again we have been lucky.

6th OCTOBER: Taken off my baby ward to relieve on the casualty ward. Very upset about leaving them, but we have to do what we are told.

8th OCTOBER: 5 p.m. The news is on while all the sisters, including myself, sit knitting, writing or reading;... Oh, there goes another bomb, now the plane is overhead, yet each sister goes on with her respective hobby as if there was no war.

15th OCTOBER: ...The remaining days of last week found me busy in the casualty ward.... I could tell many tragic stories, but one is enough for an example of what we meet with every day now. A bomb dropped one night on some houses near here: the occupants - man, wife (about 55 years old) and daughter (aged 17 years) were in their Anderson shelter, in which they were all buried for about four hours. The mother was admitted, rather badly hurt, the father was still in the casualty ward when I went on the following morning. There he sat, still dazed, otherwise not injured, wondering where his daughter was. He could not remember whether she was rescued or not. 9 a.m., still no news, then at 10.30 a.m., a girl rushed into the ward, the relief on her face when she saw it was her father sitting there! I shall never forget these scenes as long as I live. Needless to say, they both broke down completely. It is difficult not to be just like them at times, and relieve my feelings with a good cry. Last night was, I believe, the worst night. Bombs fell all around us, closer than ever. Several people were injured, one little girl of 7 was brought in dead. God knows when all this will end! .... The enemy planes are right overhead, our guns are crashing furiously; windows are rattling. It seems to be coming lower. The drone alone is apt to get on one's nerves. In the room where I write, there are other sisters, one sewing, one writing, four talking about patients. In the dining room next door, there are about 26 of the night nursing staff having their meal before going on to the wards for the night. So life goes on as usual. Heavens, what a crash! It seemed just then that the guns were just outside the window.

19th OCTOBER: ... Today, I ventured as far as Paddington to see John before he went home to spend the weekend at Mother's where there is peace... After 7 p.m. I went upstairs to change into uniform for the night. I had only taken my coat and skirt off when suddenly a bomb came whistling towards the hospital. Never have I run so quickly down the stairs to cover point. Luckily it missed us again, but I found myself shaking from head to foot afterwards... another bomb has just dropped. I have a very uneasy feeling tonight. During my journey this morning, I have seen some terrible destruction - perhaps this has unnerved me a bit. Thank heavens we have water once more - for several days people have been walking miles to get a bucket of water. We have been unable to wash properly, our aprons have to be worn dirty. Little water to drink. The planes are over again. I must wait until they are a little further away. 8.50 p.m. - Casualties have been brought in - one woman, 38 years, dead…

22nd OCTOBER: … There is no need to listen in to Health & Beauty talks about knees bend, etc., we get plenty of practice getting flat on the floor every time a bomb comes whistling by. If you are the last one down, you see the funny side of it…
Last night was the worst…Six incendiary bombs dropped on our hospital, and the wonder of it all is that not a soul was hurt. Our staff of men were grand - each one was put out before they started a serious fire. The home I live in had one, two fell on the female block. Three on the night nurses quarters. I cannot describe the awful fear that a fire would start and so light up our hospital and enable the plane to make a hit at us again. This happened at 7.30 p.m. The night was young. Once again they have struck the houses nearby, several bombs dropped on the park next door. Now again, another night is here, soon, I suppose, the Germans will be here again. What is in store for us? Today I had a letter from my brother, Rees. It is well they still think I am in a safe area. If they only knew what we are going through, I believe Mother would die with worry. I hope the people who are leaving London will not enlighten them.

- -

So many weeks have passed since I have written in this book - there has been so much knitting to do for the forces...

NOVEMBER 25th 1940: Tonight I feel that it is a Godsend that I started this log book, for I feel it is such a relief to write, it takes my mind off the feeling of imprisonment that we are all feeling here just now. The shops close at 5.30 p.m. - of course, there is no point in them keeping open, as very few people are out in London at that time of night. One cannot go far in the afternoons in case the return journey will be difficult…
I had such a restful holiday at my sister's in Wales...The Sunday night before I returned on the Monday, a high explosive bomb dropped into the garden path just outside my ward. The damp earth prevented it from doing more damage than cracking the wall of the children's block and blowing the windows to pieces. The children were moved that night, but on my arrival the next day, my first duty was to take them back again after all the repairs had been completed. The nurse on duty had a fearful shock, but the children were too young to realise what was happening. Not a single person had even as much as a scratch. The mackintosh covering which I had instructed the nurses to put over the cots during each raid afforded ample protection. Now the block which was built in recent years for the children is considered unfit for use. We are very grieved about this, it was the pride of the hospital…

JANUARY 26th 1941: … Everyone thought Christmas would be a very sad one, but at the last moment we realized that we should try to make it one of the happiest, and I think we all succeeded….. I still had my little children, so that speaks for itself. I packed their stockings the night before but tied them at the back of the cots so they would be unable to see them first thing when they wakened… There was one little English girl,

Julie, aged 5 years, and being a little chatterbox and the type that showed such great pleasure when she was pleased, we all looked forward to some fun. We were not disappointed. When she saw me she called - "Sister, Daddy Christmas forgot us", to which I replied, "Oh no, Julie, that could not be possible, I am sure he came into the hospital, so he must have hidden them somewhere. I think you had better get out of bed and look for them". To this she readily agreed... She looked in all the other babies' lockers, but no, at last she gave up and came to me very disgusted. So I suggested she should call up the chimney and ask him where he had put her toys. She did so, but got all mixed up and called on Hitler instead. So I told her it was no good asking him... It was certainly a jolly Christmas... The next week it was nothing but dinners and dancing, then on 4th January, I went down to Lacock in Wiltshire to spend the weekend with Hilda and her two boys, Peter and Alan, who have lived down there from London since the heavy raids began. It was on the Sunday of this weekend that London had one of its heaviest raids, during which terrific fires were started. I was lucky to be away, although our hospital did not suffer. So the time since Christmas has gone on until 3 weeks ago...when ...I went to the casualty ward where I was kept busy. The next move was just what I expected - in the Matron's office, doing Home Sister's duties...

26th FEBRUARY: Well, this week I have been told that I must take on the head dietician's work, or at least part of it - so what next? I told someone the other day that the next thing they will be asking me to do will be the Electrician's work! This morning, strange as it may seem, the engineer came to me saying that the stoker had not come in. I said "Now don't tell me you want me to turn into a stoker!' "Well now, that would be a good idea, Sister," he said, "but as it happens, all I want is a breakfast for the one who has been on all night, and is likely to be on for the next 16 hours if relief doesn't come."

20th MARCH: ...It is almost a month since I have made an entry. I have since been home for a week, which I thoroughly enjoyed, but for the fact that Mother was not well...

27th MARCH: ...I visited a friend of mine today whom I have not seen since before Christmas... it is impossible to visit any of my friends in the evening. In any case, we are not off duty until 6.30 p.m. since we have commenced working 56 hours a week. ...One little girl of 5 years has been very difficult to nurse. She has been very ill; now she is better she is a little more friendly, yet I have felt all along that she has been frightened by someone, and since last night I think I know what it is...I had to leave the ward about 7.30 p.m. to take my report to Matron's office. One of my little patients, a boy aged 4 years, called Freddie, was still awake, and so was this little girl, Maureen. Freddie wanted to know where I was going. I told him and promised I would not be long, and that nurse was still there to look after them. On my return, Freddie said, "Now here's sister, you won't be afraid, will you?" "No", replied Maureen, "I ain't afraid. My mufer said I aren't to be afraid when she leaves me in our house at night when the bombs drop. So I ain't afraid, 'cos my mufer said I musn't be, see". *So this child has been left alone at night when the Mother goes out, and it seems her Mother must threaten her if she tells anyone she's afraid. Poor little mite, no wonder she goes about as though everyone would punish her. I must find out what truth there is in this and have it rectified.*

As I write this, it is 10.15 p.m. I can hear a German plane overhead but there has been no warning - perhaps I am mistaken, a few moments will tell… I begin to wonder how much more we can stand… I can still hear the drone of the plane so it must be ours, because no siren has gone and no bombs dropped. Yesterday, Yugoslavia signed the Pact with Germany, but today, King Peter, 17 years old, has formed a Government against this pact, and all the people are with him. So Hitler is going to see what power a 17 year-old boy has. Good for King Peter! There is great rejoicing in his country and ours. We have won some great battle in Egypt also today.

3rd APRIL: Back to office duties again.

16th APRIL: Was listening in to a Welsh story, and such glorious singing, when the warning went about 9.35 p.m...– it seems there is an endless stream of German planes overhead…I came to bed about 10 p.m., but sleep is out of the question, the noise is far too terrifying… . I find I am in a cold sweat - I am frightened tonight. I lie on my tummy, put a pillow over my back, also a pillow over my head, but it is no use, I must get up, I cannot stay alone…

I heard voices coming from the direction of the ground floor… so I went down to find I wasn't the only one who had been too frightened to stay in bed… some went to each other's bedrooms, five of us sat in chairs in the cover point on the ground floor. So we sat until 4.45 a.m. telling stories of our training days, etc. while the almost ceaseless bombing and bursting of shells went on. Once we looked out across London; we could see ten huge fires raging from one window, and then the most fearful and yet most beautiful sight of the chandelier flares which remain suspended (by means of a parachute arrangement) in the air for about three quarters of an hour, just like a chandelier of bright fires lighting up the city. They drop these from the German planes to light up their target. Many were killed, landmines were dropped. Every part of London was affected…

19th APRIL: 9.15 p.m… I suppose they are here for the night again. Quite a number are overhead, guns are making a hectic noise. Some of the sisters have decided to go to bed, a few of us have made up our minds to go to the cover point. Miss Jones, the assistant Matron is in one corner knitting. The rest of us are sitting on a mattress, namely, Miss Watson, kitchen superintendent, then there is Pickford, the Theatre Sister, Carter, the Home Sister, Corrigan, Ward 10, Reinhard, Ward 1. Now two bombs have dropped near, and the plane is still overhead…casualties will be with us in a moment…

24th APRIL: Today I have had my first injection of T.A.B. - for immunisation against typhoid.

10th MAY:… I managed to have a little sleep, but was soon roused by someone saying "Casualties are coming in." Sister Pickford came for me, so since about 1 a.m. (and now it is 4.30 a.m.) I have been very much awake, helping in the wards.
Mr P. is badly shocked; Mrs P. was B.I.D. - brought in dead, Ivy P. was B.I.D. Leslie, aged 8 years, not too badly injured, also her little sister. There are still two children of this family somewhere...at 4.30 a.m. we returned to the home. We just peeped out, and to our horror, it looks as if the whole city is on fire. ..When will it all end?....- there are numberless without homes, and many without a soul left out of their families. Hundreds

are buried in their shelters, while I wonder how great a figure of wounded. I need to thank God that our hospital was spared again tonight. 9 a.m. The maid wakens me for my breakfast. Then she says "What a night, Sister, we are lucky to be alive." It is a glorious morning, the sun is shining through my window. I can hear the birds singing, and if I do not look over London, I could even pretend for a while that everything is just as it was before the war… The other two children (the P. family) are alive, but are injured, not too badly, and are in Hampstead Hospital. The father has been told of his wife's and child's death. The two little ones brought in here keep calling for Mummy and Daddy.

MAY I94I: Great excitement everywhere, except Germany. Hess has come over to England, or rather Scotland. A farm labourer captured him, at least he went out to the plane that had crashed near his home, and saw who he thought was just another German airman, but it proved to be Rudolf Hess, Hitler's Deputy. Now why has he come over here, right in the thick of the enemy? It still remains to be seen. He is no good either way: if he has flown from his leader, he is a traitor, otherwise it is another piece of treachery on their part, to try to trap us.

7th OCTOBER: So very many developments have taken place since my last entry, but I fear I have been too lazy to write. Russia is with us now, and they have fought well. We have had no further raids in London. A reunion was held at St Mary Abbotts Hospital on 11th September… Dr Edith Summerskill presented the prizes and made a very excellent speech. The Medical Superintendent also spoke very highly of the bravery of his staff during the time when they had heavy bombing on their hospital, how the staff worked ceaselessly day and night, and while parts of the building were falling, fought hard to rescue the injured. One night C2 block was bombed. Sister Skinner and eight patients were killed. The nurses and, in fact, all the staff, porters included, and the maids, fought their way through broken glass, heedless of the danger of suddenly dropping several feet into a bomb crater…

On 27th September, I went for a fortnight's holiday, first to Monmouthshire to my sister's, then home to Wales, which I love so well. The thing that struck me most was the empty streets in the mining villages. Before the war, they were always crowded with young men out of work, and children with ragged clothes. Even the war brings some good - all the men are working now, so the children are no longer ragged. Despite what Hitler says, there is no shortage of food…

8th OCTOBER: … The Germans have decided not to release our prisoners over there in exchange for theirs. How many relatives broken-hearted tonight? The prisoners were all ready to sail. This surely is one of Hitler's most terrible acts… There is a terrific battle on about 150 miles away from Moscow... Had a letter from my brother, Rees, today. He wrote it before the news came through about cancelling the exchange of prisoners - he was so pleased about it saying he hopes some of his pals will be amongst the lads to return. I guess he feels sad tonight.

25th OCTOBER: Tonight I feel as if I have entered a cage from which there is no escape… winter is upon us once again with the war raging in Russia. ..it's not often I feel depressed, but the very thought of being unable to go out at night after coming off duty, at least with any peace of mind, seems to have gripped me in its full reality. I know I should be happy with the thought of having all the comforts we have here. I am very grateful for it all, but it's the monotony of being with the same people every night. They all feel the same about it: here we have five such months to live through. If only I was looking after the wounded, but no, we cannot be released. So we must carry on...I think I will try writing some letters. I feel sure it will help. I feel a little better already, having written this.

22nd NOVEMBER: Last Tuesday, I had to go to a cinema in indoor uniform to distribute pamphlets to recruit nurses. How I hated walking through the street - how different I should have felt had I been a new probationer. I well remember how proud I used to feel when out in uniform. Well, I got through the afternoon very well, ended up by having tea with the managers. A hospital film was shown during the afternoon. I feel if the girls of today wished to become nurses, they would do so without all this propaganda. Then Thursday, I went to a lecture by a very eminent psychiatrist. He lectured on "Psychology of the Sick"; it was extremely interesting.

The rest of the week has been very difficult; I feel more than ever that I must get back to the nursing and children at that. I must go to a war nursery or something. I can't go on day after day looking after bedrooms, writing or running errands. I finish each day with the same thought, "What have I done today?" It may be necessary to be a Home Sister before being a Matron, but I just want to go on being a Ward Sister, so that I can be with the children…

20th FEBRUARY, 1942: …this book has closed for nearly three months. I must try to recollect the interesting times since my last entry...I remember how weary I felt about this life, then preparations for Christmas began. We arranged to make up a concert party for the patients, we practised old songs and new songs. The greatest difficulty was the dress. The Assistant Matron solved that by producing yards and yards of red, white and blue material used for draping the balcony over the main entrance of the hospital for the Coronation of Queen Elizabeth and King George 5th in 1937. Well, we cut this up and made pretty pleated skirts, and wore white silk blouses. They were quite a success. So was the concert, for which a few sisters and about 14 nurses practised after duty 8.30 p.m. Then Christmas Eve, the carol singing. It has been done at this hospital for many years. As many of the nursing staff as possible walk round the wards in crocodile fashion. The only lighting is supplied by lanterns held by the individuals. Most impressive! Christmas Day and Boxing Day is the patients'. They had turkey and all that goes with it, and oh such splendid Christmas pudding…

*Then, January 14th, holiday for 10 days. What a relief Rees my brother was home. … Then Lawrence and Mr De Ruyscher arrived on Tuesday, 17th. My cousin was staying with us, as she had been sent to my home town to teach evacuated children. Tori was billeted at my home, he was in the Air Force, and then Edna, who was a child of 12 years, was our evacuee. So, we were a merry crowd; can't say I had a rest, but it was a grand change and I loved the crowd… So I returned to hospital to a task I had never attempted before - organise a dance… Now it is midnight of 20th February… The Russians are doing well against the Germans. The Japs have got Singapore - a terrible blow to us… we feel all the more determined to win in the end…*today is 27th

April... *Bath was heavily bombed last week; one of our student nurses lost her father in that raid.*

SUNDAY, 10th MAY: *Mona (sister-in-law), arrived at hospital 1.30 p.m. We left at 1.45 p.m., and arrived at Austin Friars where the Dutch church had been before the blitz. The Dutch choir sang amidst the ruins, then we took Lawrence to see the Tower, Houses of Parliament, Westminster Abbey, then to Buckingham Palace by St James and Green Park, next up the Mall, past the Admiralty into Trafalgar Square, then went to the Royal Hotel where the choir were staying while they were in London. There we met many Dutchmen, heard them sing again, and had a very enjoyable evening...*

20th JANUARY 1943: *Over six months have passed since my last entry, so much has happened during that time...On 9th of the month I had a letter from brother, Rees that he is being sent overseas. I trust that he will come through it safely. During the first week of December, I had instructions to attend County Hall for an interview re promotion, and to my amazement, I went up on 17th December and was successful, commencing duties at Lewisham on January 3lst as Administrative Sister...I visited Lewisham a week ago. I feel the Matron and her staff are very nice, but to my horror was told that* **I** *should be going on night duty, which may mean for a year, and was told several things that are enough to put the stoutest heart off this new venture of mine, but I will give it a trial....Last Sunday, 18th January, we had our first raid for such a long time, during the evening, ..Wednesday - heavy raid over S.E. London, many children killed in a school. A train was machine - gunned, shops and houses down. The Park Hospital near Lewisham was hit by a bomb but not a soul killed, which is a miracle.*

28th JULY: *On July 26th, Mussolini disappeared. Everyone is on tiptoe wondering when the news will come through that Italy has capitulated, but here we are two days later. The King of Italy has formed a new Government, but they still intend to fight on. My brother Rees is in Egypt, Grenville waiting to go abroad any moment; wonder where all this fighting and loss of life will bring us this time, back to the old England? I, like many other ordinary people, hope not, not the England where only the rich lived, while the rest of us just existed, but let us hope that the ordinary man will have the courage to stamp out all that we knew of England before this war. We see relics of it even now. A lad of 18 years is sick with TB, strong and healthy before he did 'his bit" in this war. He has only a mild attack and he will be sent to a ward where each patient has virulent TB - he is poor. Now if he had an officer for a brother, instead of a porter, he would have every chance of a side ward, and would be in a sanatorium in no time, but he has no position in this life, so no one who could do anything for him. This class distinction must be wiped out.*

NOVEMBER: *Again, I open my book - first time for four months...I have been here at Lewisham Hospital nearly 10 months... Rees my brother is still in Egypt. Grenville is in North Africa or Italy. For many months we had no raids, but for these past few weeks, we have had one almost every day.*

FEBRUARY 19th 1944: *...my brother, Grenville, has been wounded in Italy... now the guns are firing overhead. There seem to be many planes, and many rockets are being sent up. I am sitting outside my sitting room on a bunk writing this. Six of the staff are* *on the roof, fire - watching. Matron… has just been consoling me about Grenville, but now I am over the shock, I realise he is out of it for a while. There is a terrific battle of planes and guns overhead - strange how we no longer feel that awful dread, and I don't think any of us fear death, but we do fear being buried… I should so like to be spared, life is so very sweet. Now there is a hush, just a rumble in the distance. I think I will go up to the roof to see what the result is. Incendiaries have been dropped around us, but really quite a distance away… the all clear has gone at 10.30 p.m.*

JUNE 6th: We have invaded France. Many incidents have occurred since my last entry, which I wrote while sitting on a bunk in the corridor, and my pen was dry, hence the pencil. Last Saturday quadruplets were born in this hospital, a very great event. The mother and her 3 girls and 1 boy are doing as well as can be expected - but greater news than even this came through on the wireless on June 4th - our fighting men have entered Rome, the whole of Europe is delirious with joy. And yet there was more inspiring news at 9.45 a.m. today. The invasion commenced during the night, and by this morning our troops, with all the allied troops, have landed in Normandy. I have been sitting in my room listening to the great men speaking of it on the wireless. The King, General De Gaulle, General Eisenhower, General Montgomery and several war correspondents. It is difficult to realise so much fighting is now going on, because here in London everything is quiet. Grenville is out of the fighting - just now he has been graded B6 since he was wounded. Wonder if his hearing has improved. Rees is in Italy also now but as he is on the R.A.F. ground staff, at least he does not have to kill…

8th JUNE: …I can hear the birds singing - their notes seem clearer. Perhaps it is because the air is so fresh after the rain we have had this evening, or maybe we hear them more clearly because our hearts feel lighter now that news is coming through that all goes well in France so far; they have secured the "beach heads' where they landed and have gone some way inland. We listen anxiously for all the news we can get.

15th JUNE: 12 midnight, suddenly a plane dived, it seemed to come from nowhere. A load of incendiaries or bombs were dropped, then complete silence. It was all over in a moment; everyone thought it was a stray plane, but in 20 minutes the same thing happened again, and so it went on all through the night. Now it is 7.30 a.m. and still the guns are going, and the 'phantom' planes still come, unload and then silence. Several of the victims have been brought in here. 2 p.m.: Three more rockets over during the morning, the last one came while four of us were in the dining room about to eat our dinner, when the warning went, and at the same time this terrific noise, then crash came all the glass that was left in the dining hall windows. I still do not know how we escaped, none of us had a scratch, the medical superintendent had a small cut, the block of houses just a stone's throw from my window have been very badly blasted… Warnings through the night, little sleep.

17th JUNE: Quiet morning, tired. Raids commenced again, six from 4 p.m. to 7 p.m. Did not hit us, but casualties are coming in. 9.15 p.m. - just finished listening to the news, in two seconds another one coming over in our direction - Heavens, what a near miss! Thought our last hour had surely come…

18th JUNE: No sleep last night - all through the night bombs from the pilotless planes dropping. Casualties being brought in. Off duty until 2 p.m., when managed to get half an hour's sleep, now with the casualties who came in during the night. These are the ones who are considered fit to go to the base hospitals. We have detained some head cases; the eye cases have been sent to Moorfields; one a little girl of 9 years with both eyes cut by glass…now back to the casualty ward to clean up and prepare it in readiness for the next lot…Sunday night I slept in my bed, but fully clothed still. How uncomfortable it is to sleep with a uniform dress on…

Monday: Our men on the coast are getting most of these "bumble bombs" down before they reach us. 10 p.m. - Now I have dared to come to my room, so have all the staff, but we are all ready to spring out to our bunks, if necessary.12.30 - a.m. Once again out of bed, the bumble bombs are over again, so throughout the night, sometimes with an interval of' five minutes. Then we all slept until the next lot in about an hour's time.

Tuesday: …They started coming over 10.30 p.m.

21st JUNE: …Casualties in last night. Little sleep, no fresh air on the corridors.

22nd JUNE: … they are coming over again. I hear them dropping approximately every 10 minutes, only one has come very near. It is such a lovely morning, but it is hopeless to think of going out. Casualties again during the night.

23rd JUNE: I think Hitler celebrated last night. It was just a week ago that he commenced sending these pilotless planes over… I counted 22. At times, though, he sent 3 or 4 at once, so had we been able to see them, I am very sure the actual number of planes during that time was over 30, then from 5 a.m. we had peace. 7 a.m. he sent another, then at 7.15 a.m. yet another. We seem to be encircled by the results, but only God knows why we have been missed by a few hundred yards more than once. The last two dropped just behind the trees I can see across the road… Friday, 9.30 p.m.: … about 3 bombs all day, but casualties came in during the morning, all ages, 28 in all. 20 went off to base hospital, the others were too badly injured…I feel if only I could scream, but that would be fatal. I dread this night again.

Saturday, 24th JUNE: … At night, it was quiet until 12.30 a.m., two or three came over then. I was so tired I went to sleep and did not hear the 'all clear'.

25th JUNE:.. I prepared my bunk but decided to try to sleep in my room, so hence hoping for some rest, but the clouds are low, too favourable for these wretched planes. So far, there are over 1000 homeless in this area alone.

26th JUNE - 3.30 p.m.: …it was a terrible night. The sky has been cloudy so all in favour for these bombs to do their work. (9 have been over since 12.50 p.m.) I am on my bed, having just completed my letters home, after 6 dives into the corridor. You hear the low rumble in the distance, then it comes nearer, nearer, nearer! Then it seems to come right into the building, but really it is over the top. Then you just wait, that's all, just wait; you are helpless to do anything about it. My head feels heavy with the din of bombs, ambulances, and fire engines. This perpetual straining your ears so that you shall not miss hearing the "plane" in time for you to get under cover.

<u>TUESDAY, 27th JUNE:</u> Cherbourg has been captured at last in Italy. .. At last, when there was a lull, I went off to sleep, awakened only when the bombs dropped very near. There is nothing we can do about them, but … try to get as much sleep as possible… with only short periods of rest, we are becoming 'edgy'. Today, just to help matters, we had a heavy thunderstorm. I was on duty, sitting in my office at 3 p.m. - doors which have been blasted so that they will not close, began to slam, cardboard which serves as a window pane became loose, and began to flap to and fro with each gust of wind. The trams running past my office window seemed to make more noise than ever, and there was a raid on. I thought I should go mad… What keeps us going in times like these? It is no use getting into bed tonight… The evening sun is bright, but the low clouds still persist. The rain has ceased, we needed it for the ground, but it has also been the last straw to people who have had their houses blasted so badly that the rain has done damage to the rooms. They too have gone past caring about houses and furniture: the latter they have tried to pack in rooms on the ground floors, knowing all too well that is all they can do, and hope that the 'thieves', of which there are many, will not take it away while they are at work, or in the shelters at night. 9.10 p.m. - another warning…From my window, I see the people running into the shelters…Now I will get ready for the night. I have my two cases packed near my door. I also have a leather shopping bag in which I keep a few necessities. This I have on my bunk, and then under my pillow, I keep my spectacle case in which there are a few phone numbers of friends and my home address. My torch is also there. I change my frock for my night one, I keep a whistle in my pocket, just in case I should be buried, maybe I would have a chance of getting at it. Maybe I, with many others, will laugh as I read this book long after the war is over, but there is not much to laugh at now. True, when you are with other people, you keep a grip on your nerves, and carry on at least with a pleasant face. But when you are alone, you are full of fear. You want to cry, but you dare not least someone should catch you… How soon it becomes dark these nights…

<u>Thursday, 29th JUNE:</u> …One of the most terrible nights. All 'A' block was blasted, patients taken into corridors, about one hour of sleep, if that. My head throbs, my eardrums seem to be bulging with the result of the almost continual noise. I get into my own bed at 7 a.m. hoping to have some sleep. The sky is clear - 11.30 a.m., no hope for sleep, they still come over. I try to cover my head with pillows to keep out the noise but I gave it up... I take a hurried bath (about two inches of water allowed) and dress.12 noon - another alert. Just finished dressing, so rush out to corridor as the bomb passes over once again…

<u>Saturday, 30th JUNE:</u> Thursday night …I only heard 4 pass over but the night sister reported one almost every half-hour. Throughout the day, with only a few short intervals, they came over. Casualties came in from one morning raid. People go to the shelters more quickly now. Friday night - very little sleep again… two bombs have dropped while I have been writing for 10 minutes. I can see the main road from here, trains and buses are still running, people cycling to their work. If you can close your eyes to the damage, it is a peaceful scene. I think the engine of these bomb planes must be silent altogether now, or at least very faint. The last two dropped and no one heard them coming.

Sunday, 1st JULY: ...spent it shelling beans and peas in the kitchen - short of domestic staff, so we help anywhere we are needed... bombs throughout the day, always just missing us... 9.30 p.m. There is an eerie stillness everywhere since the last bomb dropped at 12.40 p.m. "Now what is he up to?" is on everyone's lips. I thought of going into my own bed, but guess it's wiser to go on the bunk.

Monday, 2nd JULY: ...casualties rolling in. I go in to help, it was just like a battlefield - old people, young, and infants, moans and groans, babies screaming, faces cut, limbs broken, blood everywhere. Relatives who had escaped searching for their loved ones. Strange that you see few people cry, everyone looks stunned. One poor man could not be convinced that his daughter-in-law had not been brought in; he was sure he saw them putting her in an ambulance. Her face was badly cut, she could not see - but she did not come in here. Maybe she has been taken to another hospital as we were full up. No, although I had been through all the records of admissions, he would not believe; he felt if he could look around the casualties he would find her. So I took him to each bed, I went to the operating theatre, and even the mortuary. I wonder where he found her, and if she was alive...

Thursday, 5th JULY: ...have such a cold, guess it is the draughts in the corridors at night. In Mr. Churchill's speech on the "Flying Bombs", he advised all the people who had children to take them out of the areas involved, others to stick to their posts. Well, I don't suppose for a moment that we would desert.

Saturday, 7th JULY: Glorious day, no 'alerts'. Evacuation of children today...

Wednesday, 11th JULY: Last night was the first night's complete sleep for a month. Not one alert, not one bomb, the silence seems eerie. Then between 3.15 p.m. and 8 p.m., 23 bombs have dropped, the respite was not long...

Friday: Slept in my bed for the first time for a month...

Saturday: Perhaps this terror is nearly over now, for we had yet another quiet night and up to 2.30 p.m.

Sunday: Alas, they have come again.

Saturday, 29th JULY: How little we knew this time last week that we should go through such hours of terror....

THE EVENING NEWS, F

)LICE WILL SEE LONDON D

HITLER Passed This Way—No.

LEWISHAM- HIGH STREET

As there was no military target within miles, Hitler made what he would probably consider a lucky hit with a flying bomb in High-street, Lewisham, on a Friday morning in July, 1944. 18th.

Without warning from sirens, it fell about 9.45 on a shelter in front of Lewisham's street market, wrecked the stalls, many large stores and shops on both sides of the highway, and a public house, the Albion.

The stores and shops were crowded and there were queues at the market stalls. Nearly 60 people were killed—some were never found at all—and well over 100 were badly injured. The King and Queen visited the scene afterwards. It was one of the worst of the flying-bomb incidents.

Lewisham's familiar clock tower, commemorating Queen Victoria's diamond jubilee, is in the centre of the pictures: it had its four faces blown out for the second time that grim morning. It still keeps good time, on new faces. Market stalls, too, are doing business again on the old site.

On 26th July we had a direct hit, on the medical block, next to our nurses' home where we were sleeping. The corridor walls next to the one I was in, caved in, yet no one screamed, everyone was out of their bunks and various cubby - holes in a split second, all making for the wards that were by now blazing. The dispensary nearby was like a furnace, the medical superintendent's office next to it, the linen store, and sewing room, plus a room where there were thousands of records of patients, the Ration Book office, all blazing like fury. I had to stop on my way to the ward to attend to a maid who had been on the corridor (the walls of the corridor where the maids slept had collapsed on them). She had a deep laceration on her scalp. We packed her up with hot water bottles, covered her wounds, and then, after making sure she would be alright, left her in the charge of two nurses and the other maids who had escaped. I then got over to the wards. God only knows how we got 200 patients out of that furnace; two were trapped, but were rescued just in time. A visitor was burned to death in the waiting room, and one nurse was buried, or rather, shut off by the fallen masonry, where they found her 4 hours later - she was, of course, dead. Then we started on the next block with another 120 - odd patients. This block was not yet alight, but we knew it was possible any moment if a piece of broken timber came over. I could not fully describe the scene: by now patients were first put on blankets on the ground, (on the drive) then later, when we were sure all had been rescued, we brought them over to the nurses' home, lined them up in lecture rooms, sitting rooms, corridors - many old people, some paralysed, some dying from their various ills, not many injured. Three nurses were among those who were; one nurse had worked through it all with a severed artery which she had had bound, the others with deep lacerations of legs, one with a head wound...I should tell of many heroic deeds that morning: nursing staff trying to fight through to the patients they thought were trapped. Matron was marvellous as a head, she let her staff use their common sense, and they did. I had always wondered how we would all react if we did get a direct hit. God gave us superhuman courage and with it strength to lift the helpless. So from dawn to dusk that day, we worked, and not until we stopped to get into our bunks at night did we feel the effects. No sleep that night, bombs were coming over frequently, and by now we felt that each one was for us. This was the first night I had shivered from head to foot, my heart thumping against my ribs. We all felt the same that night, then came the blessed dawn. What a relief. How pleased we are to get up and go on duty these mornings. We worked again all day, salvaging as much as we could, evacuating patients, sorting linen to be sent out to be washed, as our laundry was also burned out. The grounds were just crowded with rescue squads, soldiers, firemen, police, priests and ministers, W.V.S. vans, ambulances inside and lining the streets, mobile canteens; men on top of the wrecked buildings, demolition squads. A grand and comforting sight. Above all, I take my hat off to the firemen. In no time, men of the press were here. By the end of Thursday, I could hardly lift my feet off the floor, and when I did get my shoes off, there were blisters on my toes, my nails bruised, feet bleeding - they felt as though they were on fire...I could not enjoy the relief for long because bombs came again, so I struggled into my shoes again. So during the short hour I had hoped to rest, I spent under the bunk. Then night time again, I went down to a bunk in the basement, just couldn't face another night up on the 2nd floor...

Friday, 28th JULY 1944: Matron made me take a day off, so I plucked up courage and decided if only I could get out of this area for one day, I should feel at least rested. So I was on my way out at 10.30 a.m., when I met a sister who was also going out

- she carried a case, so I asked her how long she was off. When she said "Oh, just taking a few things to my friends", I turned back to my room and packed a few things to take to my friends for safety. Just that little act saved me from either being killed or injured; when I did get out by the bus stop, a bus was just leaving so I missed it. There was no warning, but a bomb passed over, and dropped on the market place, about 2 minutes ride in the bus in the direction I was going. I got on the second bus, not knowing then that the bomb had blocked the road, so when we reached Lewisham shopping centre, it was to be met with such a sight I shall never forget, or wish to see again. Marks & Spencer's was ablaze, people trapped, screaming, dead, lying in the roadway, girls with hair and clothes alight, could be seen running wildly in the blazing building, a girl with half her scalp off, an old lady lying naked in the roadway, people running everywhere, shouting, screaming, dying, burning. This was hell with all its fury let loose, no battlefield could be worse, or more bloody. Suddenly, as if out of the air, ambulances, vans of all descriptions, fire services, rescue squads, all working like fury I just felt sick, but got out of the bus. (The one before it was caught and all its occupants injured). So I thanked God I had met the sister, and turned back, so missed it. Eventually I reached the station. Never have I had a bigger fight to keep from screaming, so at last I reached my friends, and there broke down. I suppose I knew there was no need to fight anymore - I collapsed and screamed and Hilda gave me brandy…

13th AUGUST: Nearly 3 weeks since we were hit, and if we did not see the results of it as we walk in and out of the nurses' home, it would seem just like a nightmare, and perhaps just as easily forgotten. After the first week, I can go out again, fear has left me once more… I went to Luton last weekend…It was a good break away from bombs, into the peaceful country. Now we are having quieter nights, so let it be.

17th AUGUST: …they are coming over day and night again…spent my half day in my room, the weary hours passed very slowly. I was glad to be on duty yesterday… tiredness is a better state to be in than depression… Quiet night until the early hours; I …was kept awake by the fear that someone was trying to find the door of the basement, and as I was the nearest to that particular door, I was in a terrible state of nerves. The Germans had at last come? I took a grip on myself and realised it was the effect of the wind moving the waterproof sheeting which had fallen from the windows. I dare not put my torch on in case I should disturb the other 50 nursing staff. I put the bedclothes close to my ear so that I should not catch the sound, but then I was too hot, I could not breathe, then someone in a bunk nearby stirred - this gave me confidence. Also, eventually I dropped off to sleep, to be wakened next by the siren and bombs bursting. This morning they are over again. From my window, I see the laundry women sorting the hospital laundry on the lawn as there is no other place, and then the other side of the wall, workmen are working on a bombed building putting up supports, they stand on the scaffolding. The siren has gone, a bomb is coming over. I feel braver this morning, so I watch these people to see what they will do as the bomb comes nearer, nearer: now it is over the hospital. The women run for cover; one doesn't wish to leave her work, but the superintendent makes her. The men put their coats on, but make no attempt to get down. True, they stop working just as it is over, but it passes on, and they resume their work…

We had several casualties yesterday, and there have been two cases where young men have suddenly gone raving mad, one in a shelter and one in the pictures; little wonder! .. I just cannot face another day in this place, surrounded by the destruction of the incident. Eight wards demolished, eight out of action, laundry, dispensary, medical superintendent's office, case paper office, ration book and identity card office, visitors' waiting room, electro-cardiogram room, linen room and linen stock all went; main kitchen, Doctors' house, approximately 100 rooms, matron's office, assistant matron's room, my office, telephone room, uniform room, X-ray and massage, all badly blasted. One corridor in the nurses' home, the rest of the home walls cracked, window frames out, and all the new building blasted, but that is still in use, at least 9 wards and one maternity ward. The outpatients', the pathological department out of use, almoner's office and steward's office, all blasted. In one split second, all this happened.

5th SEPTEMBER: Nearly three weeks have passed since my last entry and what amazing things have happened during that time. As far as the flying bombs are concerned, they are past history, things have moved so quickly in the battle area that even the experts have found it extremely difficult to keep pace with the news. It seems that every hour our troops have travelled miles. Last week they reached Paris, Sunday they were in Belgium, yesterday they had entered Holland. The news is so amazing that it is like a dream. I am grieved that our Dutch friends will be returning to their country. We know them so well now, but soon they will visit England again, when happier days will be here.

16th SEPTEMBFR: ...I mentioned bombs were past history; alas, I was too optimistic; they started again three days ago, about 7 a.m. each morning.

20th SEPTEMBER: I have been off since 2 p.m., sitting in Green Park, lovely sunshine, everything so peaceful. Returned to hospital 8.30 p.m., to hear that a rocket had dropped in a street nearby, several badly injured... surely we are not going through all these fearful experiences again.

12th DECEMBER: We have lived through many more weary months of war since my last entry. The rockets have played havoc round here in South East London. Sometimes I think I shall not enter another word in this book until I can write 'final' to this war, but here again I have taken it up to add a few words... .As I write, the horrors of this war become too vivid, it brings back the agony I have seen in the eyes of the victims of the bombs and rockets, so I will close this book and read a pleasant tale before going to sleep.

20th JANUARY1945: It is no use writing often in this book now, for there is much the same day after day, monotony, a daily fight against tempers, wrought by overstrained nerves, but we must keep heart, for victory will come soon.

30th JANUARY: 10 p.m. The 12th anniversary of Hitler's power. Tonight he is broadcasting to his people. This, I feel sure, is his last broadcast, what has he to tell them now, after 12 years of slaughter, he has failed. By the help of God, we are near the end of this fearful war. How weird it has been these past few nights as we pass the bombed wards on the way from hospital to the nurses' home. This last week the weather has been extremely cold, temperatures below zero, heavy falls of snow, roads in some districts impassable, people huddled up in their bombed houses to keep warm, some round a fire if they are lucky enough to have one. Tonight thaw has set in. As you come down the main drive - about 5 minutes' walk - you hear a sudden thud followed by a soft patter as if someone was treading softly behind. How silly you feel when you have run a few steps and then realise that it is the sound of the snow falling in the bombed wards. Even so, you hurry on, your mind travels back to that early morning in July when you fought against time and fire to get those patients out of this building that is now just a shambles; you think of the visitor who was burned alive, the nurse who died up there on the second floor, all the terrible things are brought back, so quickly and so vividly when your nerves have been overstrained for years. But ...as we near the end, there is so much more work to do.

FEBRUARY 15th: ...each waking moment filled with the fear of the next rocket, so many have dropped, around us, bringing death and unbelievable destruction.

I think and think of last Sunday evening, which was just the same as every other Sunday evening, families gathered together around the fireside, the men smoking and reading, the women knitting or maybe washing up the supper dishes, some having their bath, for it was about 9.30 p.m. I can still picture the one family, one of the women worked here, we knew her as a happy soul. Her father, 85 years, sits in his own armchair, his son, aged 50, next to him, one of his daughters, 32 years, sits opposite. They have had a little party, for it was Anne's birthday, she is 43 years old and worked here. Anne has just come out of the kitchen with a tea towel over her arm, the old gentleman no doubt thinking how lucky he was to still have his children with him. 10 p.m. - There was no sound until it dropped, no hope of taking cover, not even time to get under a table, nothing - the family circle is broken up. No laughter will come from Anne's lips again, she is dead, the old gentleman need have no further fear of age, the kindly son is also dead. The other daughter is pinned down by the debris and calls out in the darkness to the rest of the family to no avail. She is eventually reached and rescued, and is brought to us, still thinking that her relatives were alive somewhere. The next day she was told. That's all, it's just like that - living here, knowing in a split second you may be crushed beneath the building you are in. There are three floors above me, so I guess if one fell on this Nurses' Home we may hope for instant death. We had 26 in that night, all seriously injured; 5 are still in the casualty ward, too ill to move. One girl of 20 odd years has four fractures in her spine and a crushed arm.

4th MARCH: So a week has passed since my return from holiday - a week away from this world, or so it seemed. What a different outlook one has on life when fear has left, the weary mind is at rest, one can eat, walk and sleep in peace. I felt rested on my return, but now very weary again after a week of V2's and VI's which have begun again. We had little sleep the last 2 nights. Our only hope is that this is his last lot. Eight casualties - most of them have been buried for 5 hours. A V2 bomb dropped at 3.30 a.m., and they were brought in at 8 a.m. One lad, aged l4 years, left side crushed, paralysed; his sister, 4 years, in the next bed died one hour after admission. Mother and father killed. A nearby hospital took most of the casualties as it was not in our area. The V2 fell on a block of flats, 5 storeys high - over 100 killed, many will die in the next few days.

8th MARCH: V2's every night, more casualties, today 32, this one fell in Blackheath village at 12 noon - caught people shopping…

11th MARCH:.. I was on my way to see night superintendent when crash! - a V2 near enough to shake the whole building. Casualties began to arrive at 8.30 p.m., went back on duty to help. One poor man nearly distracted, only one laceration near right eye, but he knew his wife and 2 day-old baby were in bed with a little boy aged 3 years in a cot in the same room - all buried…10.54 p.m. - Came back to the home, police came with message to say the rest are buried and it will take some time before they can be dug out. The father of the little boy in bed has come back to say that his wife is dead, the two sisters in beds 23 and 26 are eagerly waiting to hear if their elderly father has been found….

6th APRIL: …now at last we are very near the end of this war, at least. No raids, V1's or V2's for 10 days, in fact, we have had peace since our troops crossed the Rhine a week last Sunday, what news! Now they are well into Germany and Northern Holland, where the Dutch are dying in the streets of starvation. Now we are counting in days instead of months and years, it seems too good to be true…

FRIDAY 13th APRIL: President Roosevelt died 10.30 p.m. last night. We, the very ordinary British working class, feel his loss deeply, he has been such a loyal friend to us in all our troubles. Poor America, how deeply they must mourn the loss of so great a leader.

23rd APRIL: Blackout curtains can be left undrawn for the first time. It seems strange to see the naked lights again: it's difficult to find words to express our gratitude to God for guiding us in these past 5 years.

7th MAY: News came through …that tomorrow will be V.E. day (Victory in Europe). 12 midnight - wakened by fireworks, flashes in the sky - thought the war had commenced again, then the glorious knowledge that it was a few impatient people who could not wait until today to celebrate.

8th MAY: 7.05 a.m. Slept after the noise had stopped about 1 a.m. - there will be little sleep for the next few nights if last night was any example. Strange how I feel I would like to be quiet and just thank God for our deliverance.

9th MAY: Most of the staff went out last night, the rest of us went on the nurses' home roof. From here we had a grand view of all the bonfires, floodlights, the grand display of searchlights. It seemed rather difficult to associate fires, rockets and guns with peace, they had for 5 years and a half meant nothing but disaster to us, so I think it was easy to understand our mixed feelings of joy and sad memories. It was good to hear the children's voices again, laughing and screaming with joy as the squibs, etc. were set off. They used all the instruments that had been forbidden throughout the war in Europe - whistles, rattles, etc. At 1.30 a.m. we came to bed. This afternoon, we …met in town and were lucky enough to see Mr Churchill, the King, Queen and two princesses. The crowds were happy but orderly.. The most impressive scene was the two van loads of our prisoners of war which followed the Prime Minister's car. They had been recently freed from Stalag 3. We also went into St Martin's in the Fields Church to thank God for our deliverance. So ends the last chapter of my book of war in Europe.

Now what of the war in Japan?

MAY, JUNE, JULY: Japan still at war.

GLAMORGAN GAZETTE, NOVEMBER 16, 2000

Gwyneth's diary of the London Blitz

BY DEBORAH REES

PEN PICTURE: Pam Morgan and Doreen Owen of the Porthcawl Museum and Historical Society examine the hand-written diary.

WARTIME memories of a Porthcawl woman take centre stage on ITV tonight (Thursday).

Britain at War in Colour, broadcast at 10pm, tells the story of the Blitz as seen through the eyes of former nurse Gwyneth Thomas.

The keen writer, now aged 92, spent hours keeping a daily diary of her experiences as a nurse in London at the height of World War II.

The unique document, scribbled in a mixture of pencil and ink pen, is safely under lock and key at the Imperial War Museum in London.

Miss Thomas lived for many years at the family home in New Road, Porthcawl, where her sister also ran a cake shop called Elizabeth's.

Now a resident of Poole in Dorset, Miss Thomas has vivid memories of the war years.

"It was an exciting time but we were continually frightened," she said.

"We hardly had a night's sleep in four years.

"We all wore our uniforms to bed in case we had to rush to the casualty ward after a bombing raid.

"We were constantly aware we might not be alive the next day."

She recalls the day war was declared.

"I was on duty at Highgate Hospital and saw the balloons go up," she said.

"And I was working at Lewisham Hospital when it was bombed and an entire block came down."

She remembers rushing to help serving maids when their room took a direct hit from a bomb blast.

"My shoes were hurting me so much my feet were bleeding – but you had no time to worry about it," she said.

"There is some humour in the diary too, though. I can remember watching a tutor sprinting down the stairs with an incendiary bomb following close behind her."

After the war, Miss Thomas came back to Porthcawl for a break. She worked at the Rest Convalescent Home in Rest Bay.

"I was very much a nervous wreck," she said.

"I ended up as deputy matron in the Rest Home for four years before heading back to London.

"I have devoted my life completely to nursing."

WARTIME ANGEL: Gwyneth Thomas as a nurse at South London Hospital

London of Old — ST. CLEMENT'S DANE, STRAND

War 1939 - 1945

LONDON OF OLD—

our fathers loved it well!
But words can never tell
How dear to all our hearts is London now,
As, wounded sore, but undismayed,
Battered, and threatened yet, but unafraid,
The ancient city proudly lifts its brow.
Our London cannot perish ! All in vain
The foe pours out his hell of bombs and fire ;
Brave hearts fight now that hell, and do not tire;
Brave hearts shall build the ruins up again,
But build them fairer still,
And this great city, victor over ill,
With glorious memories on every side,
Shall be, as ne'er before,
Even in the bravest days of yore,
The Nation's throbbing heart, the Empire's pride !

N.A.H.

(Uncle) Grenville Thomas
1910 - 1995

Taken in Salerno Italy, 1944. Uncle Gren on the left with two young soldiers, both of whom were killed in the battle of Monte Cassino.

See (X) my brother Grenville Thomas. advancing army towards the Casino Monastery which the Germans occupied, Italy.

THE DAILY TELEGRAPH AND MORNING POST, FRIDAY, OCTOBER 22, 1943

AIL

SCENES ON THE VOLTURNO: FIFTH ARMY CROSS THE RIVER. 5th Army was American under General Mark Clark.

...res from the Volturno River showing how the ...Army crossed after the night attack of Oct. 14-15. ... British infantry cross a pontoon bridge built ...ited States Engineers. Centre and right: In the morning light, supplies are carried ashore on the bank and a small assault boat loaded with troops is paddled over.

Uncle Gren, or Grenville, as he was christened, would have been 29 at the outset of war. He joined the Army in 1943 and served in the Italian Campaign in the 5th battalion of the Hampshire Regiment. My family were shocked when they saw the photo of him in this newspaper cutting, crossing the River Volturno in October 1943. There was a dramatic story told by my aunt, that he had spent 24 hours in the river, although I am unsure how accurate this is. His only story of the episode, told to us with a chuckle, was of seeing, as he emerged from the river, and much to his apparent surprise:

'A Jew-Boy on a 'orse!'

Another find amongst family memorabilia, was a tiny diary of his, not more than two inches by three, containing scrawled and faded entries of his experiences as a soldier between January and December 1944. My curiosity prompted me to read an account of the Hampshire Regiment in WW2, courtesy of the museum archives. I also watched the original horrific footage of the campaign from the archives of the Imperial War Museum. Uncle Gren's battalion was clearly at the front line, experiencing the most appalling and dangerous conditions, including the difficulties imposed by the rugged terrain.

After the Allied landing at Salerno and the fall of Naples, the Germans retreated behind the River Volturno. The 2nd battalion established a position 2500 yards along the river and were then joined by the 5th. Under heavy fire both battalions crossed the first canal where they held position despite frequent shelling and air attacks. Then the weather broke: heavy rain fell on already swampy ground which quickly turned to deep mud. Soldiers were then plagued by mosquitos. They moved east to Capua where they crossed the river there and advanced to the Massico Ridge south-west of Cascano. Civilians turned out in the now liberated villages, to welcome the troops and offer them food and wine. Maybe the 'Jew-boy' was one such grateful civilian.

The battalions had fought continuously for two months with no respite. Between September and the end of October there were 1100 Allied losses.

The Germans withdrew to the River Garigliano where the Hampshires defeated them in January 1944. It was then that the Germans headed for the abbey on Monte Cassino, which was reduced to rubble in February with an air assault by 254 bombers. Conditions became so appalling that they were likened to WW1 trench warfare: Allied tanks became stuck in bomb craters filled with muddy water. It must have been here that Uncle Gren was wounded with shrapnel to his arms, chest and shoulder. He was then – according to the diary - sent back home to Wales for surgery. At one point he records his sympathy for a young German soldier with both legs shot off, who must have been a patient on the same ward. He might have been one of the prisoners in the camp situated between Bridgend and Porthcawl, which my mother alludes to in her account. Uncle Gren's empathic approach says it all.

Uncle was sent back to his battalion, but after his injuries it seems that he was given lighter duties, using his skills as a carpenter.

The Germans had retreated north after the fall of Rome in June 1944, followed by Florence in August. That month the Allies closed on the so-called 'Gothic Line' which extended from Pisa across to the Adriatic – the last defensive position. Operation 'Olive' in August produced no significant breakthrough but as there were by now two governments in existence in Italy, one pro-British and the other pro-German, there was much partisan activity, almost like a civil war, in addition to the world war. After a final offensive in April 1945 hostilities ended in May. It would have been doubly interesting to find a similar diary for 1945, but sadly no such thing exists.

As a child I had been told that some of the shrapnel in Uncle Gren's body was too deep to extract. I guess as no one else in the family had sustained injuries, he was therefore something of a war 'hero', and justifiably so, considering the ferocity of the campaign. He was therefore a great curiosity: I used to stare at his shoulder, trying to imagine what it looked like inside. Even more interesting, was Auntie Gwen's account of how she had woken up in the middle of the night with a pain in her shoulder. The news of Uncle Gren's injury came the next morning. She reckoned that the dream coincided exactly with the moment when he was shot.

But then, we Welsh are rather prone to dramatise!

She was in fact very proud of him, always describing him as a 'master carpenter'. He was certainly talented, fitting out people's houses, building all sorts of furniture in our little home town of Porthcawl. I still have a three-legged stool he made out of oddments of wood. Much like his brother Rees, he wasn't a communicative man. They were both mainly prone to short bursts of conversation, interspersed with grunting and laughing, leaving the main responsibility for small talk to the women, the latter group having no problem there. He seemed fond of me – always called me Suze – and 'gave me away' (awful phrase) on my wedding day, given that there were no other men around in the family by that time. This was a month after he had lost his own wife: I well remember his struggle to hold the tears at bay.
On the inside cover of the diary, much to my surprise (as I had never thought of my uncle as poetic), I found scrawled a little poem:

Dawn 1944

This the dawn of a new unknown year
And 'ere it comes, I hope it brings victorious cheer
The lot I play, it seems so small,
Yet I hope to return to Melrose after all.

His longing for home and family haunts the diary. Melrose, the family home where he lived from childhood to his late 70's, is frequently referred to, and usually underlined or written in bold type. I shall try to give a feel of what he went through in the extracts I have chosen. As with all such diaries, inevitably there is a lot of repetition and (understandably) little attention to punctuation. I thought long and hard about how to transcribe, or if I should even edit such a rough document.

January was clearly a very stormy month:

What a day, gale, at house without a roof. Keep smiling, it will end one day. Then Melrose ***.....The day (Sunday) I loved so much. Sunshine. 7 o'clock received 3 Xmas cards...shall be thinking of Highfield*** (the family church) *at half six tonight...No mail today. Still cold little frost. Drink of chocolate 10.30. What a night...cold, dark, 3 hours on 3 hours off...glad when dawn broke again....*

Wind cold, no mail, R.A. all day and air bombing .....moonlight but what a wind, R.A. all night, looking forward to a hot cup of tea in the morning...Still a gale, tea was bon 1 ½ bars chocolate and of course the V air bombing all day. Midday meal was good tho only bis(cuits) with cheese good cook....

Sunshine, air bombing, little news for today. Tired of this war, of living, still the end will come one day. Let's hope it will be soon....The day I loved so much and HATE so much in the Army life...... (Sunday) *Mist this morning, out of front line for a few days rest before the river cross(ing). What a march uphill....Good sun, C.O. parade 10 o'clock. Eye treatment. Maybe we will have a good sleep tonight, do the lads good...Sunshine. Good night's sleep. Concert at 10. Inoculation today. Also bath much needed little to report...Transport to Volturno river crossing back at half 9...Inspection morning back into line. Left camp ...what a march up ?Mocho Hill. What a night. Sleep in field...cold mist. 12 months today what a day joined the Army life hard graft...march to ?Camento? Up at 5 o'clock to move to front lines. pack all kit...Shelling on right of house...Bombing all night*

February:

Bath which was much needed move back up line....what a march 5 o'clock to 4 next morning...little sleep... - to Gen. Hospital X-ray to shoulder, thought it was my last.... At least it is a rest in hospital after 12 hours on stretcher....Train journey to Barry hosp. ...Had shrapnel taken out of my arm. Chest and back not too good...^{h} – two eggs for tea. News of our 5th army still on the march....house to house fighting ...My ear sore. Still must not complain. Enjoyed corned beef for supper....Shrove Tuesday – but no pancakes....must not complain that poor German lad with legs off what a war...

The diary then becomes even more difficult to decipher, but my uncle continues to record his longing for home – '*Yet another Sunday in this country*' (July). He talks about working in the Y.M.C.A. and in a shop, and clearly values being occupied. At one point he is able to meet up with his brother Rees, recording this as *'the best day of my life'*. As with my father's letters to my mother, weather plays a large part in either raising or lowering his spirits. By July the news of the war seems to have improved. Sundays continue to be an important reminder of home and presumably the comfort of his religion. He gradually becomes more active working as a carpenter: '*hanging doors in the Indian wing.*' At one point he makes six pairs of doors at the wireless station. He enjoys evening shows and ENSA.

He continues to suffer pain from his injuries. On Friday 21st July he records '*another attempt on Hitler's life*'. The diary, although incomparable with Auntie Gwen's more detailed notes, is clearly important to him, recording his mood, news of the war and reminders of little pleasures such as '*egg for breakfast*'. On Sunday 3rd August: '*today 5 yrs war. Time it comes to an end.*' He keeps busy now '*making tables for the Mess.*' In October he is making racks for the cookhouse. Towards the end of the year he is with his battalion in Florence.

On Christmas Day he says: '*What a Christmas, hope it is the last overseas*' .... '*should be home this time next year all being well. Will have to wait and see...the end of another year of war. How much longer will it last...* '

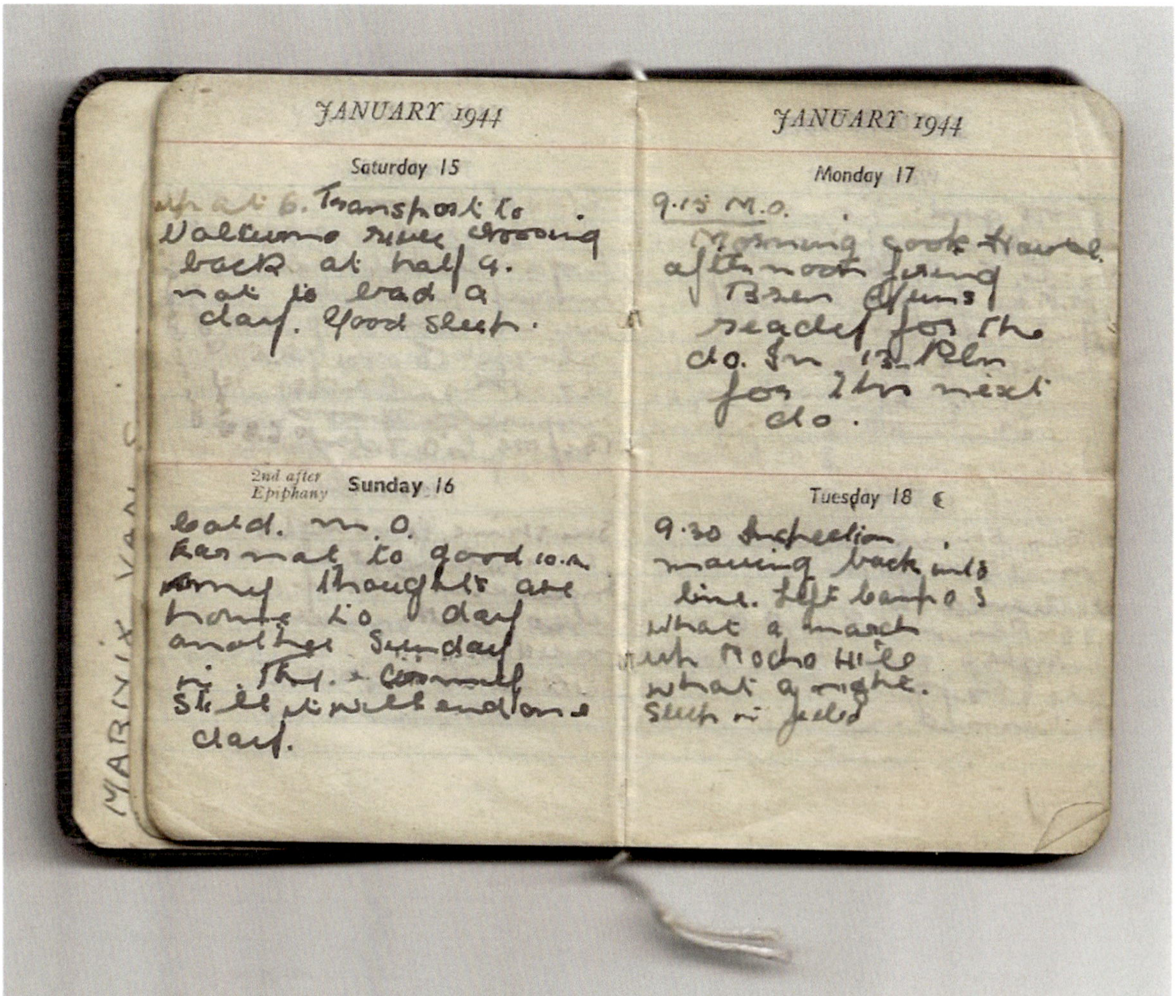

Uncle Rees and Uncle Elwyn

Uncle Rees was, as I have described, in the Royal Air Force at the same time as Uncle Gren was serving in the Army. One surprise to me on reading through the diary, was to learn that Uncle Gren and Uncle Rees were so close. Such brotherly love didn't really manifest itself to me as a child, but then they were men...All I heard of Uncle Rees' experience in the Air Force was that he was *in the desert somewhere.* My first cousin Margaret, the daughter of my mother's eldest sister, is 20 years older than me and was the only child in the large family of aunts and uncles before I came along. Her memories of the war are understandably hazy, being nine years old at the outbreak, but what she remembers of Uncle Rees was that he seemed to be frequently on leave! Maybe, as I have suspected, his nervous disposition was looked upon sympathetically by his superior officers.

His older brother Elwyn had taken over his father's grocery store in the town. He was rejected for war service on medical grounds, having significant sight problems. Later he suffered a slipped disc. He is a very sad figure in our family, developing mental health problems in the form of severe depression, for which he was treated with ECT. In later life he was agoraphobic. By the time I was in my twenties, he rarely left the house, and even then, only for short distances. I often wonder if his depression was partially, if not wholly due, to a profound sense of failure. Maybe there were many men like him whose story has never been told. .

Uncle Ben

Uncle Ben was my cousin's father, married to my mother's eldest sister, Margaret. When my mother and I first moved back to Porthcawl after the death of my own father, we lived in a small house in the same cul-de-sac. As a little girl, with my mother working in her brother's shop, I would go after school to sit with this uncle. My memory is of a tall white-haired man, sitting back in his chair, smoking his pipe quietly. He had coloured 'spills' for lighting the pipe in a Toby jug on the mantelpiece, with which he allowed me to play on the floor at his feet. He rarely spoke, perhaps never, just puffed away in silence, staring at me. I never felt frightened, I suspect I was glad of a bit of peace myself. Years later I learned that he had been in the trenches of WW1 and had come out with shell shock. According to my mother, he suffered thereafter with fits, so violent that the *'whole house shook from top to bottom.'*

'I am no longer an artist….I am a messenger who will bring back word from the men who are fighting to those who want the war to go on forever'… Paul Nash

In 2016 I was involved, with a group of fellow writers, in producing work inspired by paintings on the subject of the Great War in a new exhibition at York Art Gallery called 'Truth and Memory:'

View from the Trench

The claimed land swelters. Do you feel summer?
Hear the crickets tick, marking spent seconds, feel the faint breeze
tug at the trench, saying 'Hush,' to the echoes of men's sighs,
'It's time to rest'.

I took a stroll over rolling land, to where the crosses spot the hill.
The mud is caked, baked dry, slips through your fingers
like sugar. In places the grass rusts, timbers like fractured ribs
delve downwards.

I mixed a palette, resplendent with colour: green, brown,
red and yellow, whereas in fact the air was thick with white.
Fluttering wings patted my face, as if mistaking tears and sweat
for nectar.

I did not brush them away. If you look closely enough,
there's a few dotted around. 'Almost Turner-esque'
I heard someone say. Well, maybe. Another grew excited
at the line of blue.

There was argument about accuracy. The river? The sea?
'Can't be!' As for me, I needed the water, whether it was there
or not, craved some kind of baptism. I stayed all day.
The grey clouds

drifted in, casting shadows; the butterflies melted
in the sunset. I packed up my paints, jacked up
my easel, wiped my stained fingers on leaves,
on unearthly earth.

The silence held me, made me look again.
I could have sworn the crosses walked
like lame men on sticks, holding hands
in a strange connection.

After the painting 'View from the Old British Trenches, looking towards La Boiselle', William Orpen, 1917)

Youth Mourning

In half-light the girl, like a curved shell, weeps blue tears
into brown soil. Blades of grass struggle through pebbles,
rock pools wait for the night with an indifferent sea.
Her white form bends towards an unnamed cross:
she tries not to see the guts on a foreign fence,
dangling like torn flags.

Her body stiffens, sobs the only sound
in the bird-less air. No curlews here,
no herons stalking the water,
no gulls that circle and dive,
no clouds in a dull sky,
no children playing in the waves.

Nothing moves save her chest that heaves,
save the grass in a faint breeze.

The cross sends a shadow over her bent back,
speaks to her of something,
lest she forget why she is here.

She will sleep until dawn.

(After the painting 'Youth Mourning' by George Clausen, 1916)

At the factory

Women with new lives, wondering if they'll last.
I carry his child. Sometimes feel him move,
as if he's turning East, and hearing the distant
crack of a rifle, shell fire, already itches for war.

I hold on, one memory: that last night. Meantime
I stuff bombs. The cold steel pierces my warm skin,
a different caress, while Charlie maybe smiles,
if only for an instant, hidden deep in the trench:

music and kisses by the fire may come to mind.
Time was stretched out then, long summers.
We would stroll through the park, listen to the band
with the light catching the cornets, the buttons

that gleamed on uniforms, the French horns,
trumpets, oboes and clarinets. Elsie and me
spotted the ones that were ours, flirted outrageously
in our long skirts on Sundays. Now here we are,
linking arms, our feet like dancers poised for pirouettes.

But we don't feel like dancing.

(After the painting 'Women's Canteen at the Phoenix Works, Bradford' by Flora Lion, 1918.)

I have continued to write about war, trying to use my imagination to express thoughts and feelings, make some kind of contribution of my own:

Goodbye and God Bless

We had said our goodbyes and our blessings,
holding back on the sobs and the tears –
we had hoped for a quick resolution,
that in months you'd be home, not in years.
I had trusted that God would protect you,
that our faith would enfold you in love –
that nothing could wrench you from safety.
How we trusted the good Lord above!

Whilst I kept the home fire brightly burning,
and our baby grew stronger each day,
I continued to pray and send blessings
as all of you went your sad way.
The news wasn't good – there was Charlie –
he was shot in the head, so they said.
It was hard to take in, a young man free from sin,
who'd been found in a trench, stone cold dead.

As I watched embers glow in the evening,
I thought of you lying in mud.
When the wood sent bright sparks flying skywards,
I saw bodies that fell with a thud.
I wondered to whom I was praying,
what we meant by those blessings we sought.
But still I stood firm, though now seeing
the image of thousands who fought.

It seemed like a lifetime I waited.
I thanked God for the man he had spared.
As I stood by to greet you in autumn,
I blessed Him for showing He cared.
When I saw those blue eyes, my heart melted,
but my smile grew quite faint as I saw
that instead of their warmth there was coldness,
sensed a pain which had left your soul raw.

'Like lambs to the slaughter.' The headlines
proclaimed the dread truth. We felt numb.
But still every night I kept praying
that those blessings towards us would come.
That they'd help you to tell me your story,
find the words that would paint and describe
how the children of Man waved 'Goodbye,
God bless', with a smile, and a wave, and then died.

Tulips in winter

standing aft
the boat throws a road onto the water
later towards port
carves marble in mud where
the reds blues and dusty browns of cranes
dot the reclaimed land
all is sea sunshine and seagull

we cross the bridge at Arnhem
it's hard to picture them assembling
where now unlittered paths and tall trees
divide up rows of neat houses
impossible to imagine tulips in winter

I eat only half the Dutch pannini
served by flaxen girls with butter cheeks

The Empty Synagogue

A village near the border: canals with ducks too relaxed
to come begging for bread. Swept streets, neat gardens
with polished leaves, rain on petals. We come upon a place
marked by time. In the square tourists stroll, looking for cards,
gaze at church towers, peer at guides. Arms entwined, lovers
amble aimlessly down sun-streaked cobbles to the chimes of bells.

But I hear men with strident voices barking orders, cries
of people being rounded up, driven like cows for milking;
the clash of steel on stone, a gunshot, a cry, a body in slow motion
thumps on a thoroughfare. Blood runs in a gutter, people gape,
children hide behind long skirts as a cold wind rounds a corner.

Now just names on a plaque: we stand, stare, mumble.
Then, the tour over, pile into long coaches, our rich lives
lived long, theirs lost in chambers, naked flesh piled.
In my dreams I see gold letters on slate.

(The above two poems written after a trip to Belgium and Holland, the latter after a day spent in Lochem, near the German Border).

Image

One of so many bad dreams in a year:
small boy, grubby clothes
caked in mud, blood and dust,
perched on a high chair of hard pink plastic.

He is soundless and alone against the
droning of statistics, doesn't even
swing his short legs; they hang limp.

Suddenly in slow motion a left hand
moves to the side of his head. He holds it
for a moment. A shock of once dark hair

is streaked white, brown and red.
He draws down the hand, rests it
gently in his lap. The camera stills.

Huge tearless eyes, tarn-black, stare
at the upturned palm, read there
the strange mix of substance and colour.

He does not see the lens, which is fixed

on the hand,
the pink chair,
the gap between
legs and ground,
empty room,
bare walls,
the space
between the boy
and the rest of us.

The image freezes into his story.

For the children of Syria

Afterword

And now, hopes for universal peace since the end of the last world war have been shattered by yet more hostilities in many countries, and the sinister 'war on terror' that has blighted communities. It seems endless. I think of my family and what they all went through, how they would feel now, given the sacrifices they made and how hard they worked to restore stability. I consider too my own generation of 'Baby Boomers' – how optimistic we all were, all those messages and prayers for peace and love in the 60's and beyond. *'We are the Champions'* sang Freddie Mercury. *'All you need is Love'* sang the Beatles...

Putting together this collection has been no easy task, bringing up so many memories of my family and trying to reconcile my sense of loss and sadness, with awe and admiration. It is impossible to analyse the impact of this dark period of world history and how it will continue to shape the future. In the run-up to the end of the centenary of the Great War, we were fed a daily diet of TV and radio programmes and discussions, documentaries and films, not to mention new history books, novels, art installations, all of which offer new insights and knowledge. I have become increasingly aware of my own ignorance. Having recently watched a programme about the Home Guard, for example, I was shocked to realise what a dangerous role this was; what guts Grandpa had, to put himself in such a situation again.

There are so many stories yet to be told.

Reflecting on the whole subject inevitably gave rise to new unanswerable questions. One for me was how my father made sense of his own father's experiences; what it was like, growing up, to have a battle-weary parent. Given that I occasionally witnessed Grandpa's 'moods' in the 1950's, I would imagine these to have been much worse earlier on. Knowing Grandpa as I did, though, his resistance to talk, his capacity for containment, was perhaps also governed by his instinct to protect his son, in the same way that he protected me. Yet another wonder is how my grandparents kept some kind of faith, scarred as they were by two horrific wars, and then suddenly losing their only child in their early 60's.

Auntie Gwen's life haunts me too. The nervous breakdown she suffered after the end of the war was not just related to her physical and psychological exhaustion, the trauma of such close brushes with death, but was also the result of a broken relationship and dashed hopes for marriage and security. She had fallen deeply in love with the Dutch officer Laurence, whom she mentions in the diary. His wife had been pronounced *'missing, presumed dead'*, but as they were making marriage plans she was suddenly found alive. After Auntie died I discovered some unopened engagement presents in her chest of drawers, together with Laurence's photograph. Also a shock was to find a little pistol. I assume that, like many others, she kept it ready in case of capture, but it's a very dark thought indeed.

There were several occasions later in her life which indicated she was still suffering from what we now know as post-traumatic stress. The worst of these was when she accidentally got trapped on her own in a (locked) parked car and the alarm went off. I had always known her as such a dignified woman and was upset now to see her so terrified and inconsolable. The ghastly noise must have sounded like a siren, and the fear of being buried alive had clearly never gone away.

Another insight dawned when I realised how mistaken I had been to think that family members left at home in Wales were rather removed from the action. I had not fully considered how frightening it must have been, sandwiched in a small coastal town between the two major cities of Cardiff and Swansea, both of which, being major ports, were badly bombed. In the 'Cardiff Blitz' a total of 2100 bombs fell over a period of four years. Swansea too was a major target, having a huge oil refinery. During one three-night raid, 230 people were killed. One Porthcawl resident was recorded as remembering the latter attacks all too vividly, when *'The German aircraft were circling the area above Porthcawl...preparing to dive on Swansea. The few anti- aircraft guns were doing all they could and shrapnel was falling all around. Swansea looked like a giant sea of flame.'*

Porthcawl in fact, like many towns across the country, was fully involved in the war effort. According to one local historian it welcomed thousands of British, French, Dutch, Canadian, Polish and American service men and women who trained at the nearby RAF airfield or amongst the sand dunes and on the beaches. There was an Air Sea Rescue base in the harbour, residents were enlisted as ARP wardens, everyone took in evacuees. No one escaped untouched. They had the additional anxiety about family members serving on the front line.

I am very lucky that none of my close relatives were killed or seriously disabled in either conflict. Their positive outlook, especially Auntie Gwen's, and their innate sense of fun, coloured my childhood with many hues. They were miraculously capable of putting the past behind them and 'moving on'. Despite my grandmother's anguish at the death of her only son, and having her young marriage blighted by war, for example, she could at times re-visit happy memories of music hall days. To entertain me as a child, she would often try to do a 'knees up' on her old legs. My mother too was helped by music (as I have been). So many songs she sang come to mind:

'Walk on through the storm with hope in your heart, and you'll never walk alone.'

Moreover, forgiveness, particularly after WW2, clearly played a part in the healing process. In retirement my Mum and Auntie Gwen joined a choir in a town twinned with Ulm in Germany. They went there to sing in the cathedral and became very good friends of the German family with whom they stayed, and who later made a reciprocal visit to Wales. No doubt one of many such attempts at reconciliation.

New connections and perspectives will keep emerging alongside deeper knowledge, as long as we all keep our hearts and minds open. Lest we forget.

Susan Elliot
February 2020

Acknowledgements

James, for his comments and advice on historical facts, and his tireless love.

My close friends, especially Wendy for proofreading, positive feedback and encouragement, and for Julie's ongoing interest in and support for my endeavours.

My writing group, for their literary advice.

My family, for everything.

Sources:

Wikipedia

'Porthcawl at War 1939 – 1945' - Mansley. M (1994, Harris Printers)

My background:

I read English at Royal Holloway College, London University, between 1968 and 1971, after which I returned to Wales to train as a teacher. I taught English at Tonypandy Grammar School in the Rhondda Valley, then in a language school in Sweden. On my return home to Wales I decided on a change of career and trained in social work at Chelsea College, London. I was a social worker in two London Boroughs, specialising in mental health. In 1990 my husband and I moved to York with his work in the British Library. I took early retirement in 2005 since which time, in addition to undertaking work in various charities, I obtained a Master's Degree in Creative Writing at St. John's University in York in 2012. Subsequently I have been involved in writing workshops and in exhibitions at York Art Gallery, and in 2016 self-published my first collection of poetry, *'Walking the Waves'*. A second collection, *From a Picasso Head,* was published in 2019. My writing group has to date published two anthologies: *'A Pattern of Words'* and *'A Harvest of Words'*.

This is my first attempt at writing a memoir.

Oxford
KS3 Science

Activate 1

Question • Progress • Succeed

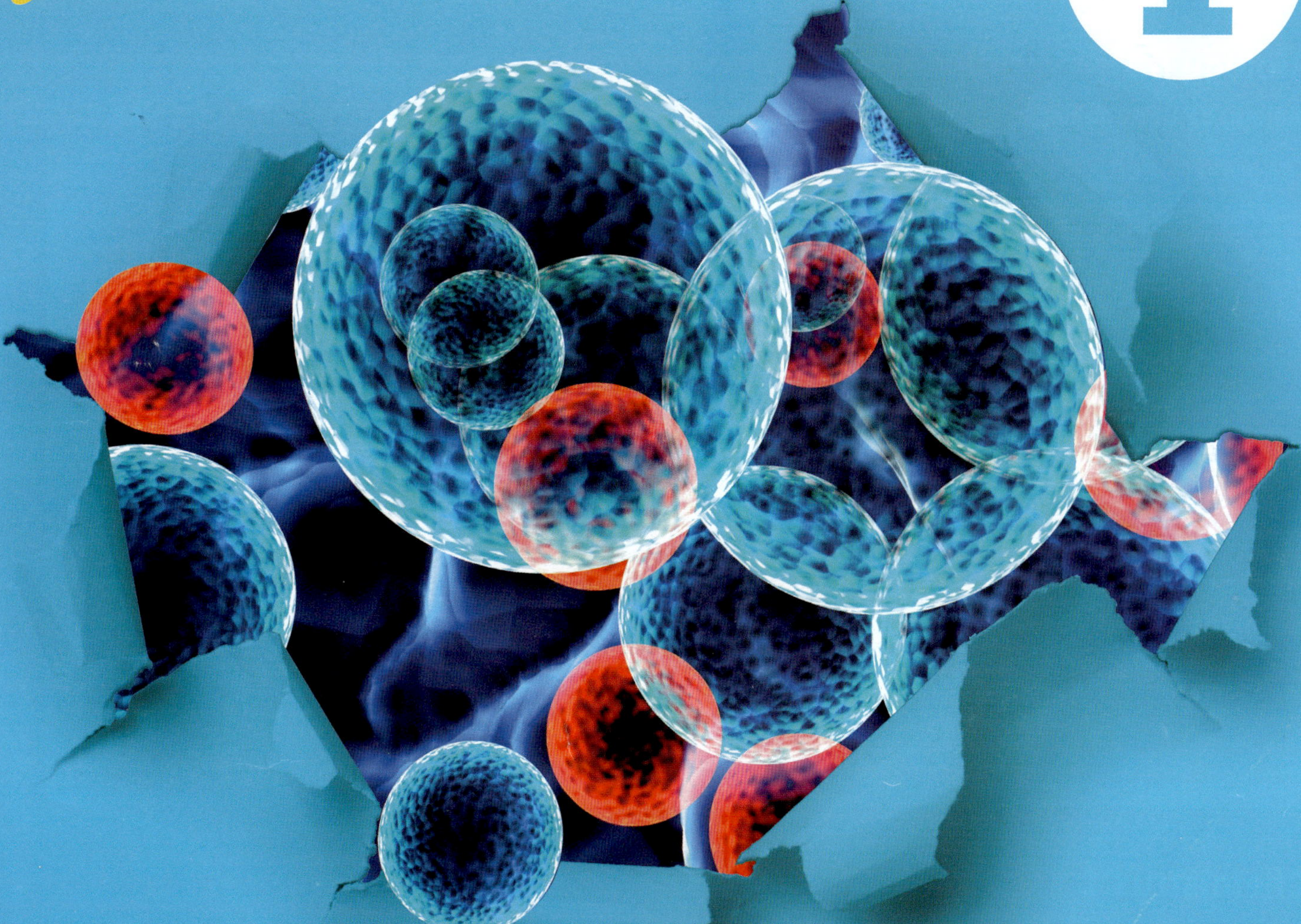

Philippa Gardom Hulme
Jo Locke
Helen Reynolds

Assessment Editor
Dr Andrew Chandler-Grevatt

OXFORD
UNIVERSITY PRESS

Contents

Introduction

Learning objectives

Each spread has a set of learning objectives. These tell you what you will be able to do by the end of the lesson.

Welcome to your *Activate* Student Book.
This introduction shows you all the different features *Activate* has to support you on your journey through Key Stage 3 Science.

Being a scientist is great fun. As you work through this Student Book, you'll learn how to work like a scientist, and get answers to questions that science can answer.

This book is packed full of fantastic (and foul!) facts, as well as plenty of activities to help build your confidence and skills in science.

Key Words

The key words in each spread are highlighted in bold and summarised in the key-word box. They can also be found in the Glossary.

Q These boxes contain short questions. They will help you check that you have understood the text.

Link

Links show you where you can learn more about something mentioned in the topic.

Maths skills

Scientists use maths to help them solve problems and carry out their investigations. These boxes contain activities to help you practise the maths you need for science. They also contain useful hints and tips.

Literacy skills

Scientists need to be able to communicate their ideas clearly. These boxes contain activities and hints to help you build your reading, writing, listening, and speaking skills.

Working scientifically

Scientists work in a particular way to carry out fair and scientific investigations. These boxes contain activities and hints to help you build these skills and understand the process so that you can work scientifically.

Summary Questions

1. Questions with one conical-flask symbol are the easiest.
2. The questions get harder as you move down the list.
3. The question with three conical-flask symbols is the hardest. In these questions you need to think about how to present your answer.

Fantastic Fact!

These interesting facts relate to something in the topic.

Opener

Each unit begins with an opener spread. This introduces you to some of the key topics that you will cover in the unit.

Picture Puzzlers

These puzzles relate to something in the unit – can you work out the answers?

You already know

This lists things you've already learnt that will come up again in the unit. Check through them to see if there is anything you need to recap on.

Big questions

These are some of the important questions in science that the unit will help you to answer.

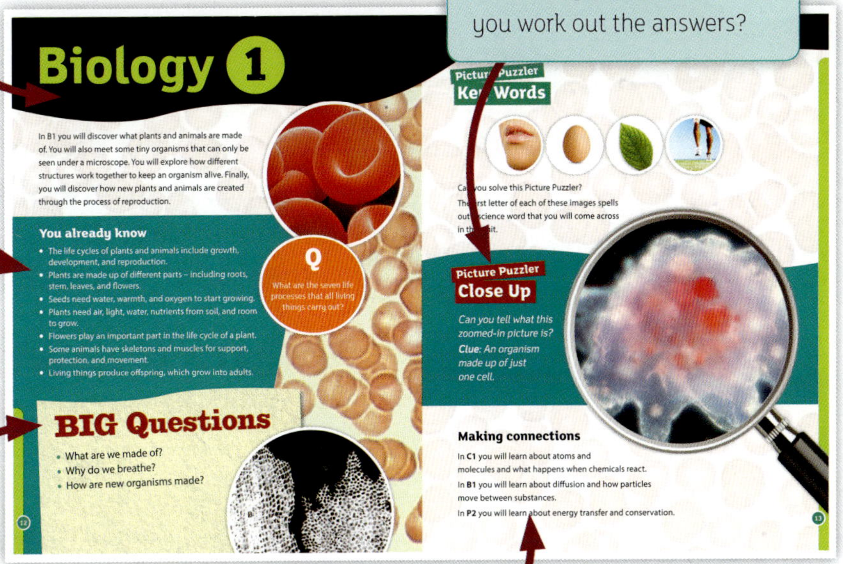

Making connections

This shows how what you will learn in the unit links up with the science that you will learn in other parts of the course..

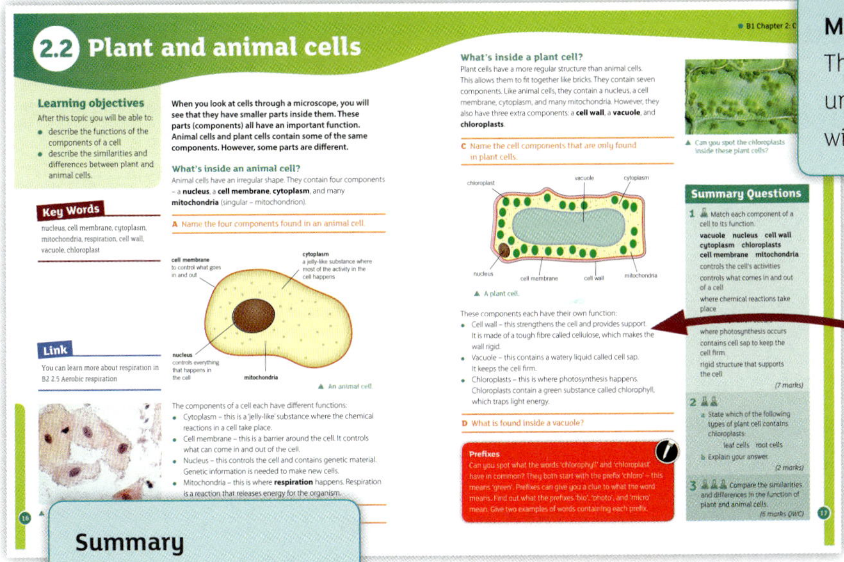

Topic spreads

Each topic in the chapter has a double-page spread containing learning objectives, practice questions, key words, and task boxes to help you work through the chapter.

Summary

This is a summary of the chapter. You can use it to check that you have understood the main ideas in the chapter and as a starting point for revision.

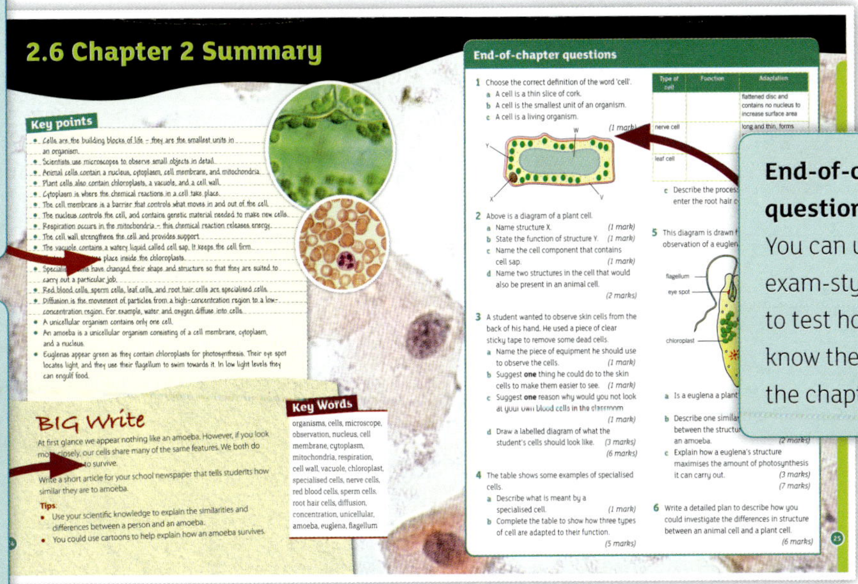

End-of-chapter questions

You can use these exam-style questions to test how well you know the topics in the chapter.

Big write/Maths challenge/Case study

This is an activity that you can do at the end of the chapter. It will help you to practise using your scientific skills and knowledge.

1.1 Asking scientific questions

Learning objectives

After this topic you will be able to:

- describe how scientists develop an idea into a question that can be investigated
- identify independent, dependent, and control variables.

▲ What affects the battery life of your mobile phone?

▲ The balls are changed every seven or nine games during a tennis match.

Why does the battery last longer in some mobile phones than others? What might mobile phones be like in the future? We can ask lots of different questions about the world. Some are questions that science can answer.

What's the question?

Scientists make **observations** of the world, and ask questions such as, 'How do fossil fuels form?' or 'Why are there are so many different animals on Earth?' These are scientific questions.

Scientists do **investigations**. They collect **data** to try to answer their questions.

Suggesting ideas

Tom and Katie are talking about balls used in sport.

The football doesn't bounce as high as the tennis ball. Maybe size affects the bounce.

Katie makes an observation about footballs and tennis balls. An observation can give you an idea that you can test in an investigation.

Developing ideas into questions

Tom watches a tennis match. New tennis balls are brought out from a refrigerator during the match.

Here are some questions that Katie and Tom might investigate:

- How does the size of a ball affect how high it bounces?
- How does the temperature of a ball affect how high it bounces?

What's a variable?

The size and temperature of the ball are not the only things that might affect the height of the bounce.

Let's investigate how the temperature of the ball affects how high it bounces.

In science, anything that might affect the outcome of an investigation is called a **variable**. The thing that is affected as a result of the change is also a variable.

The temperature is the **independent variable**. It is independent because you change it. How high the ball bounces is the **dependent variable**. It is dependent because it changes when you change the temperature.

A State the two types of variable that you can change in an investigation.

Other variables

Katie and Tom think about all the other variables that might affect the bounce height. Here is their list:

- the height you drop the ball from
- the type of ball
- the surface that you drop it onto
- the size of the ball

Katie and Tom need to keep these variables the same during their investigation so that they do not affect the bounce. These are called **control variables**.

B Name the type of variables that you keep the same in an investigation.

Making a prediction

Katie makes a **prediction** about what might happen. This is only part of the prediction. Katie should use her scientific knowledge to explain *why* she thinks that the ball will bounce higher.

I think that if the temperature of the ball is higher it will bounce higher.

Name those variables!

Imagine that you are going to investigate whether the size of a ball affects how high it bounces.

a State your dependent and indepedent variables.

b List all the variables that you would need to control.

Key Words

observation, investigation, data, variable, independent variable, dependent variable, control variable, prediction

Fantastic Fact!

Over 50 000 tennis balls are used during the Wimbledon tennis championship each year.

Summary Questions

1 Copy the sentences below, choosing the correct bold word.

You can turn an **idea/question** into an **idea/question** that you can investigate. You can answer some scientific **ideas/questions** by doing an investigation. You collect **data/observations** or make **data/observations**. Things that can change in an investigation are called **predictions/variables**. Science can answer **all/some** questions. *(7 marks)*

2 A student is looking at an ice cube melting in a glass of water.

a Suggest a question that she could answer by doing an investigation. *(1 mark)*

b Explain why this is a question that science can answer. *(2 marks)*

3 Suggest three questions that scientists could investigate about food, and three that they could not. Explain your choices. *(6 marks)*

1.2 Planning investigations

Learning objectives

After this topic you will be able to:

- describe how to write a plan for an investigation
- recognise what makes data accurate and precise
- describe a risk assessment.

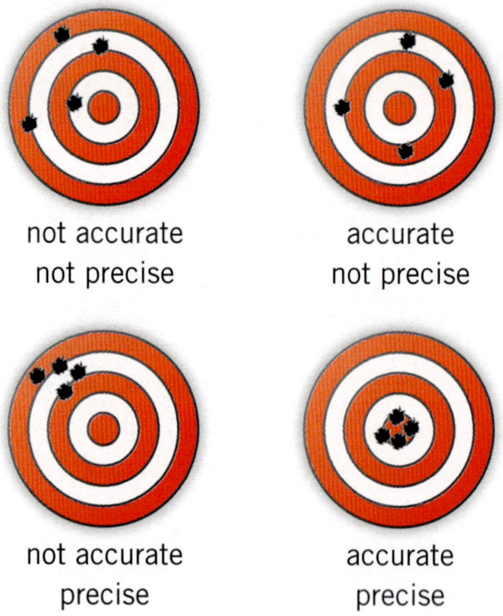

▲ Readings can be precise but not accurate.

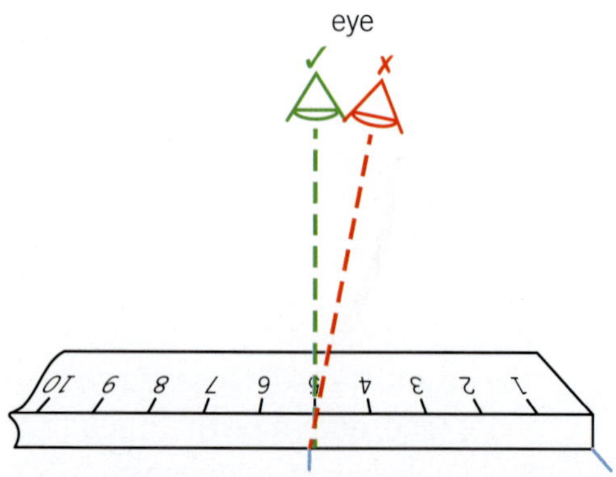

▲ You should look straight at a scale to make an accurate measurement.

Have you ever cooked from a recipe? Did it turn out the way you wanted? The plan for an investigation or experiment is a bit like a recipe. It says what equipment and materials you are going to use, and what you are going to do with them.

Make a plan

Katie and Tom need to write a **plan** for their investigation. They need to think about how they will collect data to test their ideas. Their plan should include:

- what equipment they are going to use, and why
- what method they are going to use, and why.

We will need to use balls at different temperatures.
We will need a metre ruler to measure how high the ball bounces.

A State two things that you need to include in an investigation plan.

Accurate and precise data

The measurements you make in an investigation are called data. It is important to collect data that is **accurate** and **precise**.

Accurate data is close to the true value of what you are trying to measure. For example, Tom needs to look directly at the ruler to get an accurate reading.

Precise data gives similar results if you repeat the measurement. Scientists talk about the **spread** of their sets of repeat data. Precise data has a very small spread when measurements are repeated. The repeat measurements in each set are grouped closely together.

B State how to use a ruler accurately to measure length.

Uncertainty

If you look at a thermometer it might be hard to tell whether the temperature is 21.5 °C, 22.0 °C, or 22.5 °C. There is an **uncertainty** in your measurement because of the measuring instrument that you are using.

Repeatability and reproducibility

If Katie and Tom do the same investigation several times, or repeat a measurement in an investigation, the data should be similar. It is **repeatable**.

If other students do the same investigation they should get data similar to Katie and Tom. The data is **reproducible**.

Types of data

The data you collect might be words or numbers. Data can be:

- **continuous** – it can have any value, such as length or temperature
- **discrete** – it can have only whole-number values, such as number of paperclips or woodlice
- **categoric** – the value is a word, such as 'blue' or 'hot'.

How many measurements?

Katie and Tom need to plan what temperatures to test. They need to decide:

- the biggest and smallest temperatures – this is the **range**
- how many different temperatures they will test.

Is it safe?

A plan should also include a **risk assessment** . This explains how you will reduce the chance of damage to equipment, or injury to people.

What should a plan include?

Katie and Tom write a plan for their investigation. They include:

- the scientific question that they are trying to answer
- the independent and dependent variables
- a list of variables to control and how they will do it
- a prediction: what they think will happen and why
- a list of the equipment they will need
- a risk assessment
- how they will use the equipment to collect accurate and precise data.

Key Words

plan, accurate, precise, spread, uncertainty, repeatable, reproducible, continuous, discrete, categoric, range, risk assessment

Investigating dissolving

Does the temperature of water affect the mass of salt that dissolves in the water?

Write a plan to investigate this.

Summary Questions

1 Copy and complete the sentences below.

The plan for an investigation includes a list of the ______ that you will use and how you will use it. It shows how you will collect data that is ______, ______, ______, and ______. To make your investigation as safe as possible you need to do a ______ ______.

(6 marks)

2 A student investigates whether the type of surface affects the bounce of a ball.

a Explain why she should read the scale on the ruler by looking straight at it. *(2 marks)*

b Explain why the readings are not exactly the same when she repeats them. *(2 marks)*

c State and explain whether she needs to do a risk assessment. *(2 marks)*

3 Explain in detail why Katie and Tom's is a good plan.

(6 marks)

1.3 Recording data

Learning objectives

After this topic you will be able to:

- describe how to make and record observations and measurements
- calculate a mean from repeat measurements
- present data appropriately in tables and graphs.

You usually collect data in a table. It is easier to see patterns in the data if you then draw a graph or chart.

Collecting data

Each time Katie and Tom change their independent variable they should take repeat measurements of their dependent variable.

Recording data

Katie and Tom make a table for their results. They need to record their measurements as they go, including all the repeat measurements.

A results table helps you to organise your data. This is Katie and Tom's results table:

Temperature	Height of bounce (cm)			
	1st Measurement	2nd Measurement	3rd Measurement	Mean
cold	45	40	35	40
warm	50	60	20	55
hot	65	75	70	70

A State the best way of recording data collected during an investigation.

Repeat readings

You should check your data for **outliers**. An outlier, or anomalous result, is a result that is very different to the others. You should repeat the measurement to replace an outlier.

In the table above, the third measurement for the warm temperature, 0.20 m, is an outlier. Katie and Tom do not include it when they work out the **mean**.

The mean is a type of average. You add up all the results and divide by the number of results. For example, the mean of the heights measured at the cold temperature in the table above is:

$$0.45 \text{ m} + 0.40 \text{ m} + 0.35 \text{ m} = 1.2 \text{ m}$$

then divide by 3 as there were 3 results:

$$\frac{1.2}{3} = 0.40 \text{ m}$$

B State how to calculate the mean of a set of numbers.

Fantastic Fact!

The first ever tennis balls were hand stitched, so no two ever bounced in the same way.

Key Words

outlier, mean, line graph, bar chart, pie chart

Which graph?

The values of the independent variable are words. That means we need to plot a bar chart.

Tom and Katie have collected lots of data. They want to present their results in a graph or chart. To work out which graph or chart to plot you need to look at the variables in your investigation.

- If both your independent and your dependent variables are continuous, then you should plot a **line graph**.
- If your independent variable is categoric, you should plot a **bar chart**. In some cases you might want to display discrete or categoric data in a **pie chart**.
- For both line graphs and bar charts, you plot the independent variable on the *x* axis and the dependent variable on the *y* axis.

Temperature (°C)	Time to dissolve (s)
30	75
40	60

Surface	Height of bounce (cm)
Carpet	25
Floor	45

You plot a line graph:

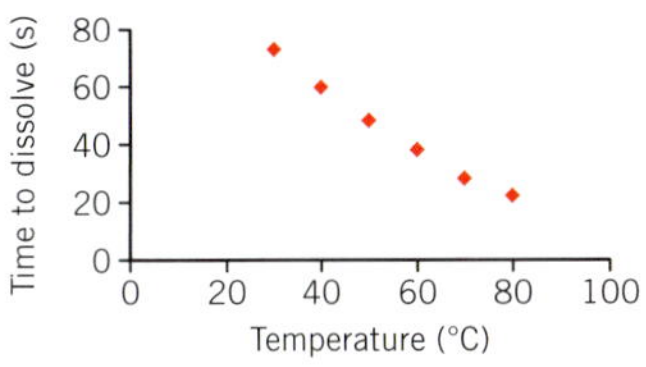

You plot a bar chart:

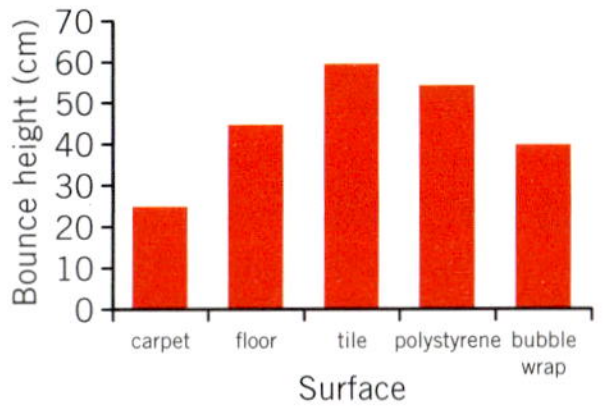

… or a pie chart

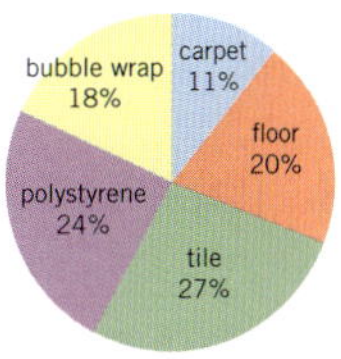

C State what type of graph or chart you should plot if one of your variables is discrete.

When you draw a chart or plot a graph you should do the following:

- Choose scales for your axes so that your graph is as big as possible.
- Use a pencil and a ruler.
- Label the axes with the quantity and the unit, such as 'time (s)'.
- Write a title for your graph.

Dealing with results

A student investigated how fertiliser affects how high plants grow. Copy it and complete the final column of the table.

Mass of fertiliser (g)	Height of plant after 10 days (cm)			
	1st Measurement	2nd Measurement	3rd Measurement	Mean
2	3.2	3.7	3.6	
4	4.7	7.3	5.0	
6	5.1	5.5	5.3	

Summary Questions

1 Copy and complete the sentences below.

When you are collecting data you need to make sure that you are using ______ ______ correctly. You need to make ______ measurements to check that your data is repeatable. You need to look for ______, which are readings that are very different to the others. Then you calculate the ______.

(5 marks)

2 A student is investigating how the temperature of water affects how long it takes sugar to dissolve.

a Describe two things that he should do when collecting data. *(2 marks)*

b Draw a table that he could use for his results. *(2 marks)*

c State and explain the type of graph that he should draw. *(2 marks)*

3 Design a hint sheet for students carrying out investigations. *(6 marks)*

1.4 Analysing data

Learning objectives

After this topic you will be able to:

- find a pattern in data using a graph or chart
- interpret data to draw conclusions.

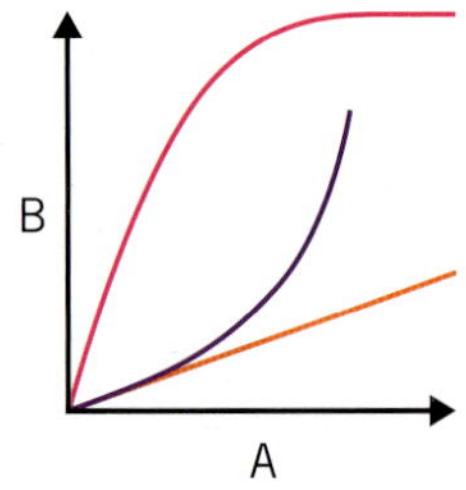

In these graphs, if A increases then B increases.

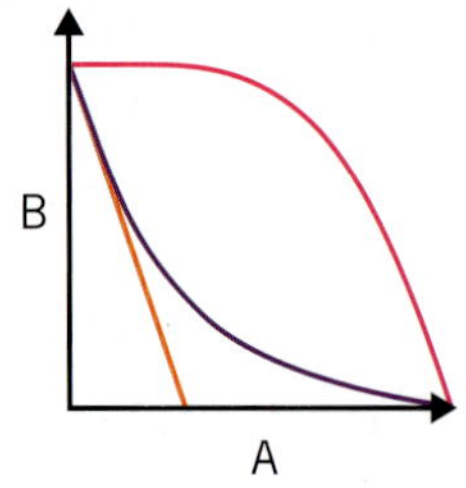

In these graphs, if A increases then B decreases.

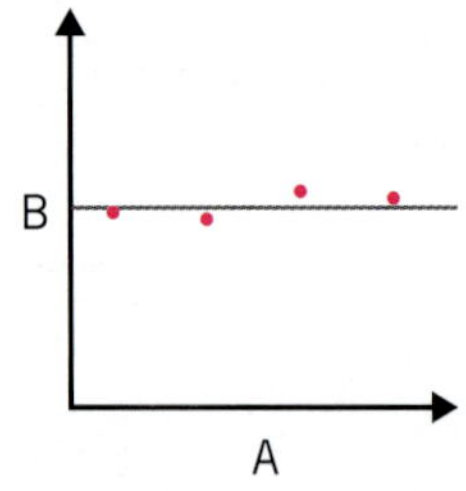

In this graph, if A increases B does not change.

Katie and Tom have collected data and plotted a bar chart. Now they need to:

- work out what their graph tells them
- write a conclusion
- compare what they found out with their prediction.

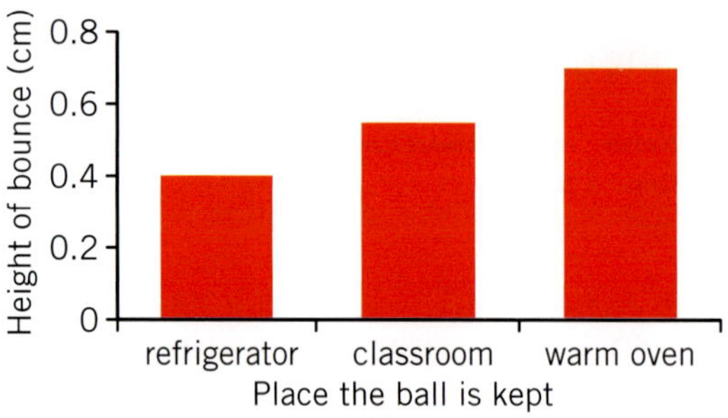

▲ Katie and Tom's bar chart.

Using graphs or charts

When you **analyse** your data, plotting a line graph or chart helps you to spot a pattern. It shows how the dependent variable depends on the independent variable.

Your scientific knowledge will help you suggest why the independent variable affects the dependent variable in this way.

Find a pattern on a line graph

Once you have plotted a line graph you need to draw a **line of best fit**. This is a line that goes through as many points as possible, with equal numbers of points above and below the line. If there are any outliers, you should ignore these when you draw your line of best fit.

A State what is meant by a line of best fit.

Writing a conclusion

Once you have analysed your graph you can write a **conclusion**.

State what you have found out

Start by saying what the investigation shows. Then describe any relationship you can see between the two variables. Use your graph to support your conclusion.

B State two things to include in your conclusion.

Key Words

analyse, line of best fit, conclusion

Tom and Katie look at their bar chart and start to write a conclusion:

When the ball is warmer it bounces higher.

Link

You can learn more about why balls bounce in P1 1.1 Introduction to forces

Explain what you found out

Saying what your results show is only part of analysing results. You also need to use scientific knowledge to explain the pattern.

The ball bounces higher when it is warmer because the ball is softer.

Tom begins to explain the relationship between temperature and the height of the bounce. However, to come up with a good explanation he needs to understand why balls bounce.

Comparing results with predictions

Finally, you can compare your results with your prediction.

What's the relationship?

A student plots a graph of water temperature and the time that it takes sugar to dissolve in the water.

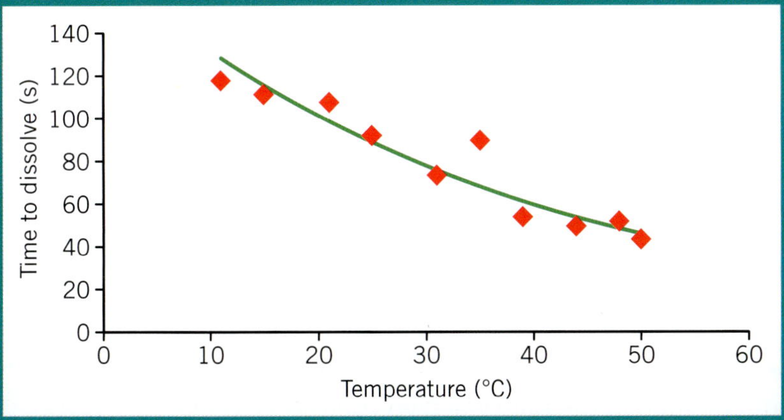

Use information from the graph to describe what happens when you double the temperature of the water.

Summary Questions

1 Copy and complete the sentences below.

To analyse your data you plot a graph or chart and work out the _______ between the variables. Then you write a _______ that includes what you have found out, and explains why, using _______ _______. Finally you compare your results with your _______.

(5 marks)

2

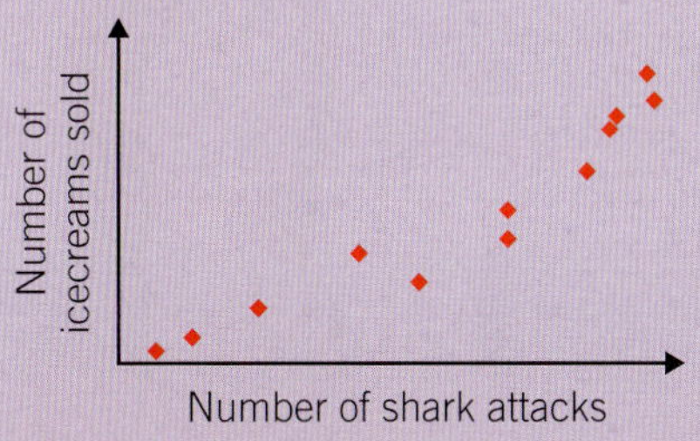

A student has drawn a graph for an investigation into the relationship between the number of icecreams sold and the number of shark attacks in a certain period. Draw a flow chart to show how he should complete the analysis of his data and draw conclusions.

(4 marks)

3 Look at the graph in Question 2. Describe and explain in detail what the graph shows and suggest a conclusion that you can draw from the data.

(6 marks)

1.5 Evaluating data

Learning objectives

After this topic you will be able to:

- describe the stages in evaluating data
- suggest ways to improve a practical investigation.

Katie and Tom have collected data and analysed it by plotting a bar chart. Now they need to evaluate their data and their methods.

How do you think our investigation went?
I think there are things we could improve if we did it again.

▲ Evaluating means working out what is good and what is not so good.

There are two ways to **evaluate** your investigation. You should:

- discuss the quality of the data that you have collected
- suggest and explain improvements to your method so you can collect data of better quality if you did it again.

Your suggested improvements should increase the **confidence** that you have in your conclusion.

There was only one outlier in our experiment, and the spreads do not overlap.

The number of outliers and the spread of the measurements do not affect how confident we are in our conclusion.

Evaluating the data

Katie and Tom look at their data. They had only one outlier in their experiment – the third measurement for 'warm'. If there were lots of outliers then they would have less confidence in their conclusion.

What's the spread?

The spread of data tells you how precise the data is. The spread is the difference between the highest and the lowest readings in a set of repeat measurements.

A State what is meant by the spread of a set of measurements.

In their experiment the measurements for one temperature do not overlap with the measurements for another. That makes the data very precise.

A small spread in the data will give you more confidence in your conclusion. You should discuss this in your evaluation.

Key Words

evaluate, confidence, random error, systematic error

Errors and uncertainty

There is uncertainty in any measurement that you make. This is one of the reasons why there is usually a spread in experimental data.

There are two types of error that can affect scientific measurements. These are:

- **random error** – this can affect the spread, or cause outliers. An example is the temperature of the room suddenly changing because someone opens a door.
- **systematic error** – this can make your measurements less accurate. An example is a newtonmeter reading 1 N even when there is nothing attached to it.

You should think about possible errors as well as the outliers and spread to help you to decide how confident you are in your conclusion.

Range and number of results

Tom and Katie only measured at three different temperatures. They cover a wide range, but it would be better to test more different temperatures within this range.

B State whether it is better to measure a wide range or a narrow range of values.

Suggesting improvements

You might get better data by:

- including a bigger range, or taking more readings
- using different apparatus – giving a smaller spread and fewer outliers.

Evaluating data

Ali and Emma do the same tennis-ball investigation as Katie and Tom. They produce this data:

Temperature (°C)	Height of bounce (cm)			
	1st Measurement	2nd Measurement	3rd Measurement	Mean
–4	25	27	45	
4	30	26	25	
20	42	59	49	
40	54	59	61	
60	65	42	71	

a Identify the outliers.

b Calculate the mean bounce height for each value of temperature.

c Comment on the spread of data for each value of temperature.

Improving data

Use your data to decide if your method was good, or could be improved. You should say how any improvements would make the data better.

Summary Questions

1 Copy and complete the sentences below.

When you evaluate your data you need to look at how many ______ you had. Then you need to look at the spread, which is the difference between the ______ and ______ reading within each set of repeat measurements. You need to look at the ______ and ______ of values. Finally, you can propose how to improve the ______ if you did it again.

(6 marks)

2

a State two ways that Katie and Tom could improve their data. *(2 marks)*

b Suggest one other way that they could improve the quality of their data. *(3 marks)*

3 Explain how using a video camera could improve the quality of Katie and Tom's data. *(6 marks)*

Biology 1

In B1 you will discover what plants and animals are made of. You will also meet some tiny organisms that can only be seen under a microscope. You will explore how different structures work together to keep an organism alive. Finally, you will discover how new plants and animals are created through the process of reproduction.

You already know

- The life cycles of plants and animals include growth, development, and reproduction.
- Plants are made up of different parts – including roots, stem, leaves, and flowers.
- Seeds need water, warmth, and oxygen to start growing.
- Plants need air, light, water, nutrients from soil, and room to grow.
- Flowers play an important part in the life cycle of a plant.
- Some animals have skeletons and muscles for support, protection, and movement.
- Living things produce offspring, which grow into adults.

Q

What are the seven life processes that all living things carry out?

BIG Questions

- What are we made of?
- Why do we breathe?
- How are new organisms made?

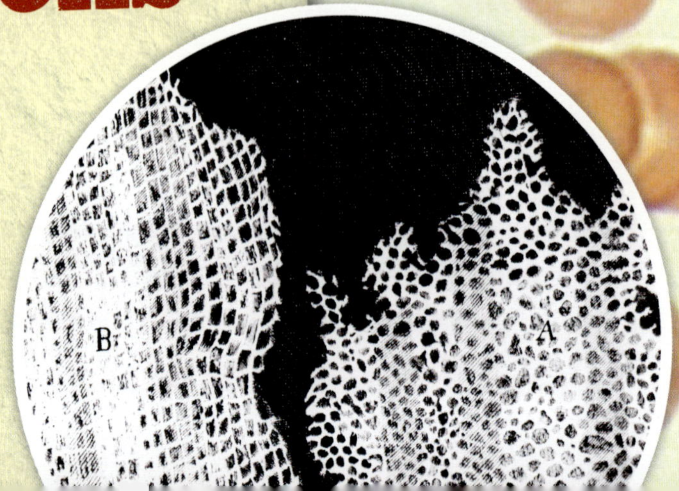

Picture Puzzler

Key Words

Can you solve this Picture Puzzler?

The first letter of each of these images spells out a science word that you will come across in this unit.

Picture Puzzler

Close Up

Can you tell what this zoomed-in picture is?

***Clue**: An organism made up of just one cell.*

Making connections

In **C1** you will learn about atoms and molecules and what happens when chemicals react.

In **B1** you will learn about diffusion and how particles move between substances.

In **P2** you will learn about energy transfer and conservation.

1.1 Observing cells

Learning objectives

After this topic you will be able to:

- describe what a cell is
- explain how to use a microscope to observe a cell.

Fantastic Fact!

Cells are so small that about 100 animal cells would fit across the width of this tiny full stop.

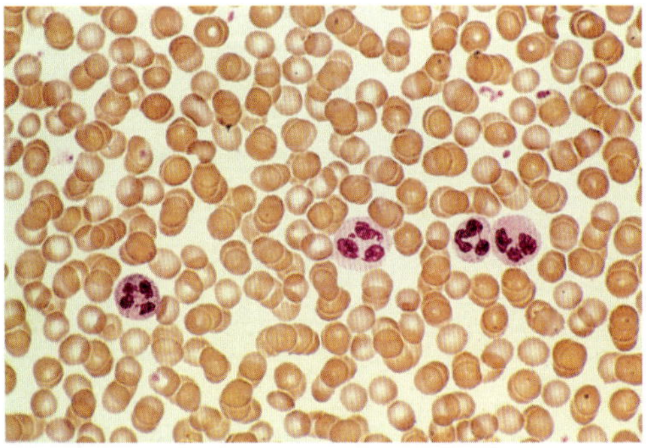

▲ There are different types of cells in your blood.

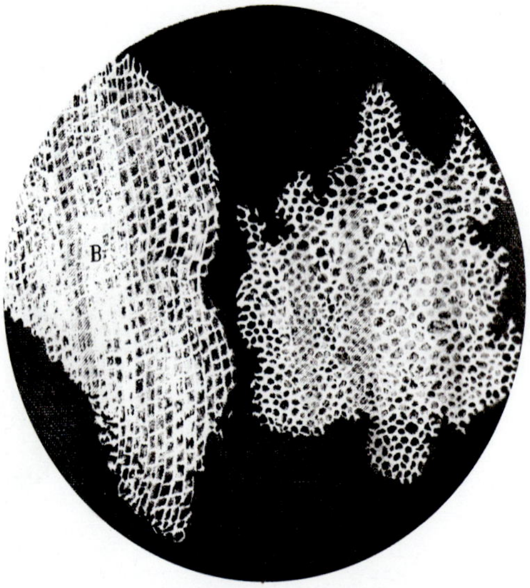

▲ This is the drawing that Hooke made of cork cells.

Look around you. Can you see any dust? Most household dust is actually dead cells. These come from anything living in your house. To see the cells, you need to look through a microscope.

What are living organisms made of?

All living **organisms** (things) are made of **cells**. Cells are the building blocks of life. They are the smallest units found in an organism. Organisms such as bacteria can be formed from a single cell. Millions of cells can join together to form a person, like you.

A State what all living organisms are made up of.

Seeing cells

Cells were first seen about 350 years ago when Robert Hooke, a scientist, looked down a **microscope** at a thin slice of cork. He saw tiny roomlike structures, which he called cells. These were plant cells; cork is a type of tree bark.

B Write down what Robert Hooke saw when he looked at cork using a microscope.

Making an observation

To see a very small object in detail, you need to use a microscope. This magnifies the image using lenses. Looking carefully and in detail at an object is called making an **observation**.

To make an observation, the object you wish to observe needs to be very thin so that light can travel through it. You might need to add coloured dye to make the object easier to see.

C State what is meant by a scientific observation.

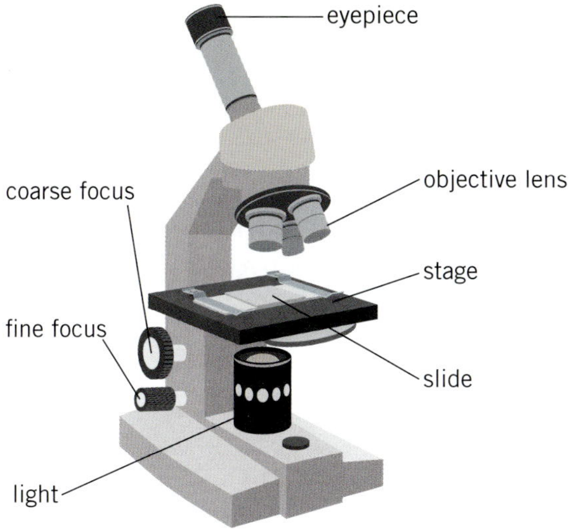

Parts of a microscope

Follow the steps below to observe an object using a microscope.

1. Move the stage to its lowest position.
2. Place the object you want to observe on the stage.
3. Select the objective lens with the lowest magnification.
4. Look through the eyepiece and turn the coarse-focus knob slowly until you see your object.
5. Turn the fine-focus knob until your object comes into focus.
6. Repeat Steps 1 to 6 using an objective lens with a higher magnification to see the object in greater detail.

D Name the part of a microscope you look through.

Magnification

The eyepiece lens and objective lens in a microscope have different magnifications. Together they magnify the object.

For example, if you have an eyepiece lens of ×10 and an objective lens of ×20 the object would be magnified 200 times.

Total magnification = eyepiece lens magnification × objective lens magnification

= 10 × 20

= 200

Magnification

You are asked to observe an onion cell using a microscope. The eyepiece lens has a ×10 magnification and the objective lens has a ×50 magnification. What is the total magnification?

Microscope observations

When recording your observations from a microscope, you should always note down the magnification you used. Use a sharp pencil to draw diagrams, and use a ruler to draw label lines.

Key Words

organism, cell, microscope, observation

Summary Questions

1 Copy and complete the sentences below.

All living organisms are made up of ______ – these are the ______ blocks of life. To ______ cells in detail you need to use a ______. This ______ the object.

(5 marks)

2 Describe what the following parts of a microscope do:

a lenses *(1 mark)*

b stage *(1 mark)*

c focusing knobs *(1 mark)*

3 Describe in detail the method you would use to observe the cells within a white flower petal.

(6 marks)

1.2 Plant and animal cells

Learning objectives

After this topic you will be able to:

- describe the functions of the components of a cell
- describe the similarities and differences between plant and animal cells.

Key Words

nucleus, cell membrane, cytoplasm, mitochondria, respiration, cell wall, vacuole, chloroplast

Link

You can learn more about respiration in B2 2.5 Aerobic respiration

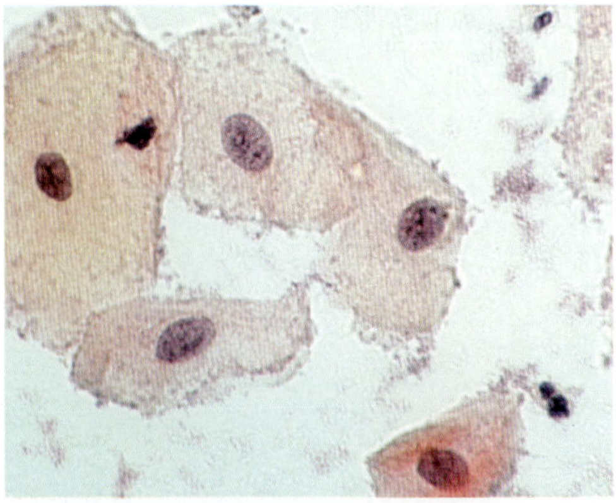

▲ Can you spot the nucleus inside these cheek cells?

When you look at cells through a microscope, you will see that they have smaller parts inside them. These parts (components) all have an important function. Animal cells and plant cells contain some of the same components. However, some parts are different.

What's inside an animal cell?

Animal cells have an irregular shape. They contain four components – a **nucleus**, a **cell membrane**, **cytoplasm**, and many **mitochondria** (singular – mitochondrion).

A Name the four components found in an animal cell.

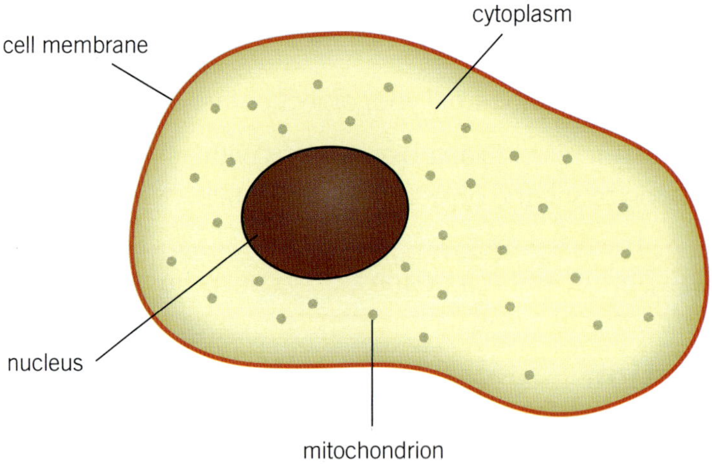

▲ An animal cell.

The components of a cell each have different functions:

- Cytoplasm – this is a 'jelly-like' substance where the chemical reactions in a cell take place.
- Cell membrane – this is a barrier around the cell. It controls what can come in and out of the cell.
- Nucleus – this controls the cell and contains genetic material. Genetic information is needed to make new cells.
- Mitochondria – this is where **respiration** happens. Respiration is a reaction that transfers energy for the organism.

B State the function of a cell nucleus.

What's inside a plant cell?

Plant cells have a more regular structure than animal cells. This allows them to fit together like bricks. They contain seven components. Like animal cells, they contain a nucleus, a cell membrane, cytoplasm, and many mitochondria. However, they also have three extra components: a **cell wall**, a **vacuole**, and **chloroplasts**.

C Name the cell components that are only found in plant cells.

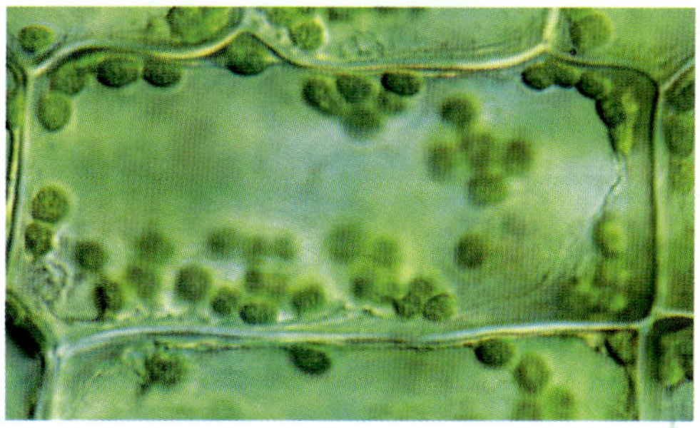

▲ Can you spot the chloroplasts inside these plant cells?

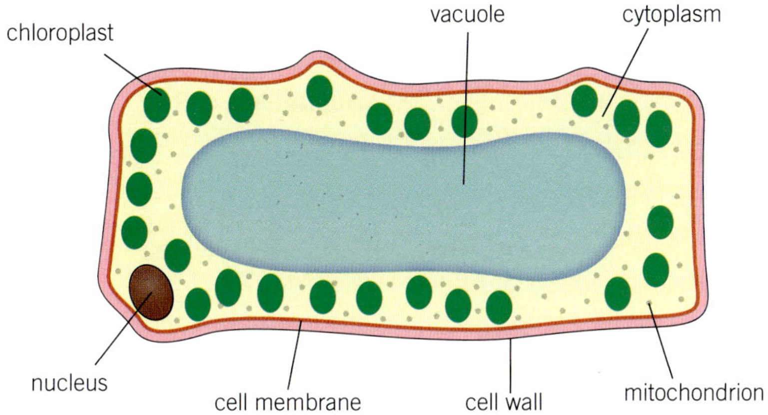

▲ A plant cell.

These components each have their own function:

- Cell wall – this strengthens the cell and provides support. It is made of a tough fibre called cellulose, which makes the wall rigid.
- Vacuole – this contains a watery liquid called cell sap. It keeps the cell firm.
- Chloroplasts – this is where photosynthesis happens. Chloroplasts contain a green substance called chlorophyll, which traps energy transferred from the Sun.

D What is found inside a vacuole?

Prefixes

Can you spot what the words 'chlorophyll' and 'chloroplast' have in common? They both start with the prefix 'chloro' – this means 'green'. Prefixes can give you a clue to what the word means. Find out what the prefixes 'bio', 'photo', and 'micro' mean. Give **two** examples of words containing each prefix.

Summary Questions

1 Match each component of a cell to its function.

vacuole **nucleus** **cell wall** **cytoplasm** **chloroplasts** **cell membrane** **mitochondria**

controls the cell's activities

controls what comes in and out of a cell

where chemical reactions take place

where respiration occurs

where photosynthesis occurs

contains cell sap to keep the cell firm

rigid structure that supports the cell

(7 marks)

2

a State which of the following types of plant cell contains chloroplasts: *(1 mark)*

leaf cells **root cells**

b Explain your answer. *(1 mark)*

3 Compare the similarities and differences in the function of plant and animal cells. *(6 marks)*

1.3 Specialised cells

Learning objectives

After this topic you will be able to:

- describe examples of specialised animal cells
- describe examples of specialised plant cells.

As you are reading this, your body is doing many different things. Each function carried out in the body is performed by different cells. Each type of cell has slightly different features.

Fantastic Fact!

The sciatic nerve is the largest and longest nerve in the body. It is as wide as a thumb at its largest point. It starts in the bottom of your spine and extends all the way down the back of your leg to your toes.

Key Words

specialised cell, nerve cell, red blood cell, sperm cell, leaf cell, root hair cell

Detailed descriptions

Use the description below to draw a diagram of a type of cell called a ciliated cell.

Ciliated cells are found in your airways. They are rectangular-shaped cells and each contains a nucleus. They are arranged in a single layer, like bricks standing upright. On their top surface they have lots of little hairs called cilia. These cilia sweep a sticky substance called mucus away from your lungs.

How do animal cells differ?

Most cells in your body contain a nucleus, cell membrane, cytoplasm, and mitochondria. However, many cells have changed their shape and structure so that they are suited to carry out a particular job. These cells are called **specialised cells**.

If you look carefully at a specialised cell, its shape and special features can provide clues about what it does.

A Write down what specialised cell means.

Nerve cell

Nerve cells carry electrical impulses around your body.

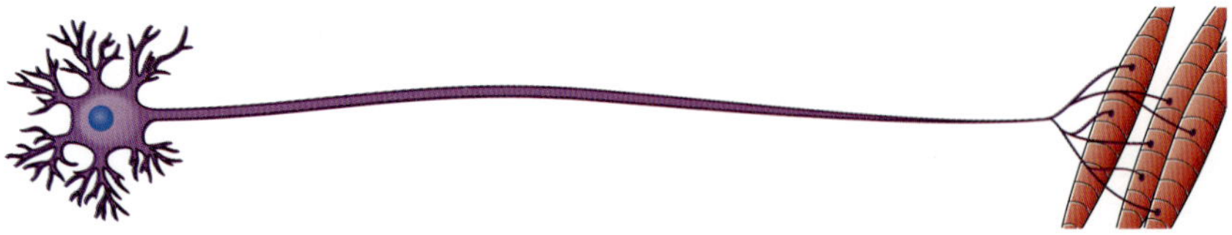

▲ A nerve cell. Its scientific name is a neurone.

They are long and thin and have connections at each end where they can join to other nerve cells. This allows them to transmit messages around the body.

B State the function of a nerve cell.

Red blood cell

Red blood cells transport oxygen around the body. They contain haemoglobin, a red pigment that joins to oxygen. Unlike most animal cells they have no nucleus. They also have a disc-like shape. This increases their surface area for carrying oxygen.

C Name the component, normally found in animal cells, that is missing in a red blood cell.

Sperm cell

Sperm cells carry male genetic material. They have a streamlined head and a long tail. This allows the cell to move through a liquid. They contain lots of mitochondria to transfer energy. This allows the tail to 'swim'. When the sperm cell meets an egg cell, the head of the sperm burrows into the egg.

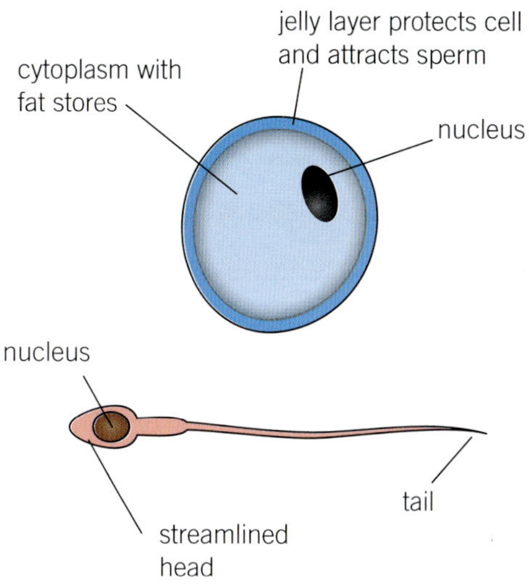

▲ An egg cell and a sperm cell.

D Name two features that help a sperm cell to do its job.

How do plant cells differ?

Not all plant cells are the same. Cells in different parts of a plant are specialised to perform their job.

Leaf cell

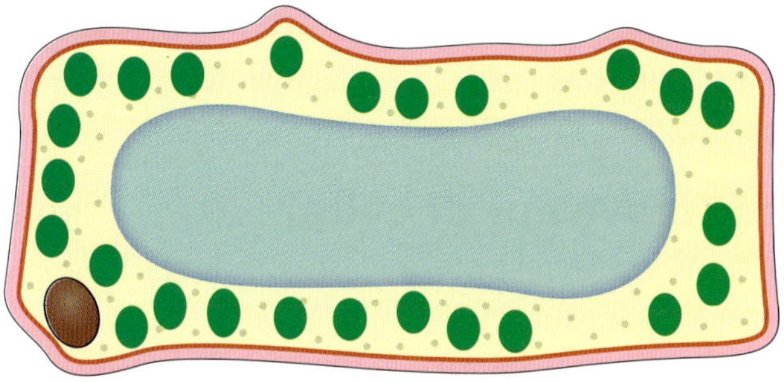

◀ A cell from the top of a leaf. Its scientific name is a palisade cell.

The **leaf cells** found near the top of a leaf carry out photosynthesis. The cells are long and thin and packed with chloroplasts. This means they have a large surface area for absorbing energy transferred from the Sun.

E Name two special features that help a leaf cell to carry out photosynthesis.

Root hair cell

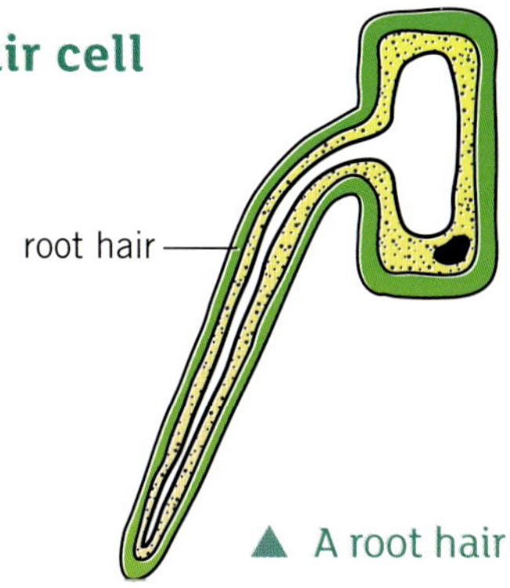

▲ A root hair cell.

Root hair cells absorb water and nutrients from soil. The root hair creates a large surface area for absorbing water and nutrients. They have no chloroplasts as there is no light underground, so these cells do not carry out photosynthesis.

Summary Questions

1 Copy and complete the sentences below.

_______ cells have special features to allow them to carry out their _______. Red blood cells carry _______ around the body. Leaf cells are packed full of _______ to carry out _______.

(5 marks)

2 Choose an animal or plant cell from this page and describe the features that make it specialised.

(2 marks)

3 Draw a labelled diagram of a sperm cell. Explain how each feature enables the sperm cell to perform its function.

(6 marks)

1.4 Movement of substances

Learning objectives

After this topic you will be able to:

- name some substances that move into and out of cells
- describe the process of diffusion.

How do you know when someone is cooking? The chances are that you will smell the food before you see it. A scientific process is taking place. It is the same process that moves substances into and out of your cells.

Can substances move into cells?

All the cells inside your body need glucose (a substance gained from food) and oxygen for respiration. During respiration energy is transferred. Glucose and oxygen are carried around your body in the blood. They then pass into the cells that need them.

A Name two substances that move into a body cell.

Can substances move out of cells?

Some chemical reactions inside cells make waste products. For example, carbon dioxide is produced during respiration. It passes out of the cell into the blood. The blood then transports the carbon dioxide to the lungs, where you breathe it out.

B Name one substance that moves out of a body cell.

How do substances move in and out of cells?

Substances move in and out of cells by **diffusion**. Diffusion is the movement of particles from a place where they are in a high **concentration** to a place where they are in a low concentration. The concentration of a substance means the number of particles of a substance present in an area.

Think about what happens when someone burns toast.

The particles that make up the smell of burnt toast move from a place of high concentration (the kitchen) to one of low concentration (the rest of the house). At first, you may only be able to smell the burnt toast in the kitchen. A short time later, you may be able to smell the burnt toast in the living room. Diffusion continues until there is the same concentration of the particles everywhere.

Link

You can learn more about diffusion in C1 1.6 Diffusion

Key Words

diffusion, concentration

Stink-bomb alert!

Imagine you work for a company that makes stink bombs. A toy shop is interested in selling your stink bombs but wants to know how they work. Using ideas about diffusion, write a reply to the toy shop that explains simply how stink bombs work.

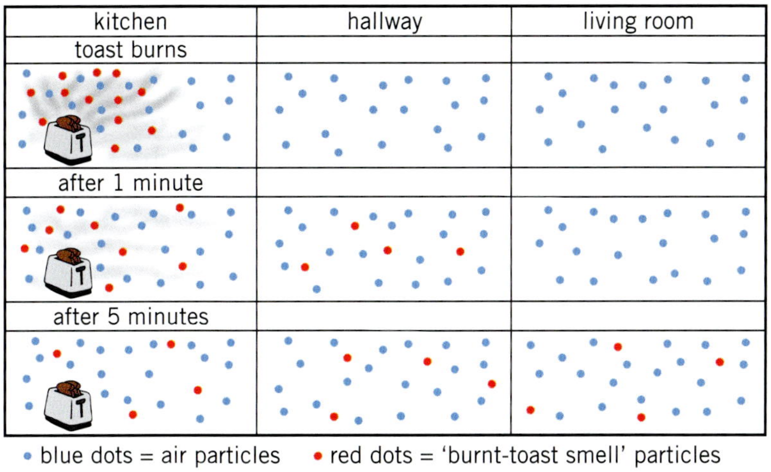

▲ This diagram shows how you smell burnt toast in another room.

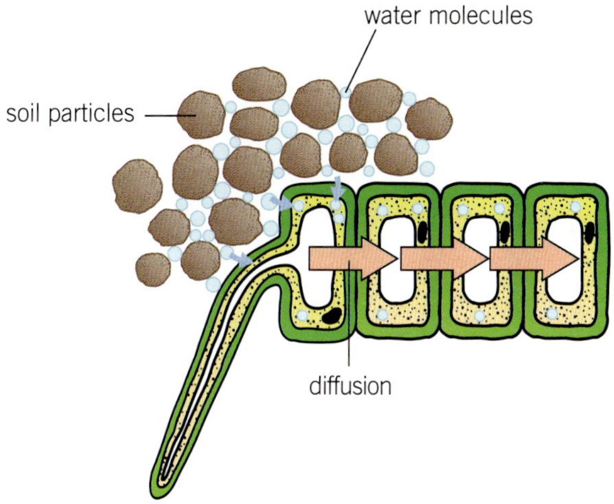

▲ The diffusion of water is known as osmosis.

Diffusion in plant cells

Plants need a constant supply of water for photosynthesis. Water diffuses into the plant through the root hair cells. The water molecules move from the soil (high water concentration) into the root hair cell (low water concentration). Water then travels from the root hair cells to other cells in the plant by diffusion.

Why do plants wilt?

If plants are not watered regularly they will wilt and eventually die. Inside the cells, water fills up the vacuole. This pushes outwards on the cell wall and makes the cell rigid. This helps the plant to stand upright.

If the plant does not have enough water, the vacuole shrinks. The cells then become floppy and the plant wilts.

▲ If a plant does not have enough water it will wilt.

Link

You can learn more about molecules in C1 2.3 Compounds

Summary Questions

1 Copy and complete the sentences below.

Substances move from an area where they are in a ________ concentration to an area where they are in a ________ concentration. This process is called ________ .

(3 marks)

2 Explain how the smell of perfume can move throughout a room.

(3 marks)

3 Draw a visual summary of the key ideas on this page about cells and diffusion, including diagrams.

(6 marks)

1.5 Unicellular organisms

Learning objectives

After this topic you will be able to:

- describe what a unicellular organism is
- describe the structure of an amoeba
- describe the structure of a euglena.

Not all living organisms are as complicated as you are. The first organisms that existed on Earth were made up of just a single cell. There are still many organisms alive today that consist of only one cell.

What is a unicellular organism?

A **unicellular** organism is an organism that is made up of just one cell. It is not a plant or an animal, as these are made up of lots of cells.

A State what unicellular means.

Unicellular organisms

Working in small groups, produce a presentation to introduce an amoeba and a euglena to another group. What are they? What do they look like? How are they similar, and how do they differ?

Amoeba

An **amoeba** is a unicellular organism that has no fixed shape. Amoebas look a bit like a blob of jelly. They can be found in fresh water, salt water, wet soil, and even inside animals.

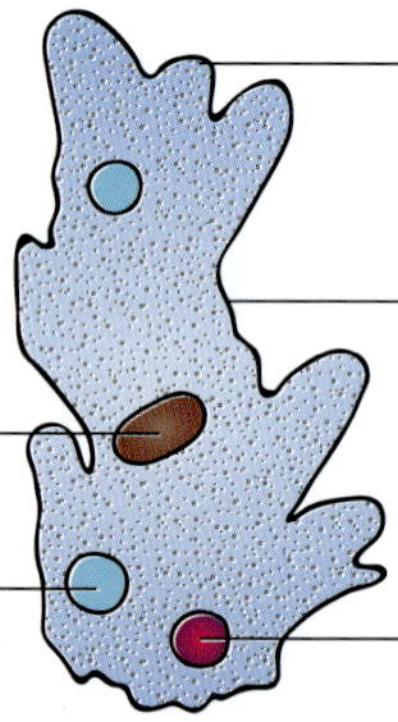

▲ Parts of an amoeba.

Key Words

unicellular, amoeba, euglena, flagellum

Just like an animal cell, an amoeba consists of a cell membrane filled with cytoplasm. Inside the cell there is also a nucleus, which controls growth and reproduction.

Amoebas move by changing the shape of their body. They can make part of their body move in the direction they want to travel. The rest of the cell then slowly follows.

Foul Fact!

The amoeba naegleria is known as the brain-eating amoeba. It is found in warm fresh water. Very occasionally it infects people. It attacks the nervous system and slowly destroys the brain tissue, almost always resulting in death.

B Name two structures found in both an animal cell and an amoeba.

What do they eat?

Amoebas eat algae, bacteria, and plant cells. They eat by surrounding tiny particles of food and forming a food vacuole. This is known as engulfing. The food vacuole then digests the food.

How do they reproduce?

To reproduce, an amoeba splits itself into two cells. This is known as binary fission. First, the nucleus in the cell divides. Then the cytoplasm divides, producing two identical cells.

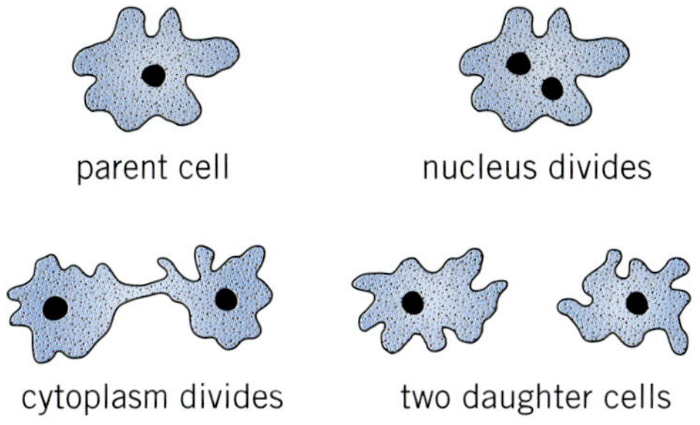

▲ Amoebas divide by binary fission.

Euglena

A **euglena** is a microscopic unicellular organism, found in fresh water.

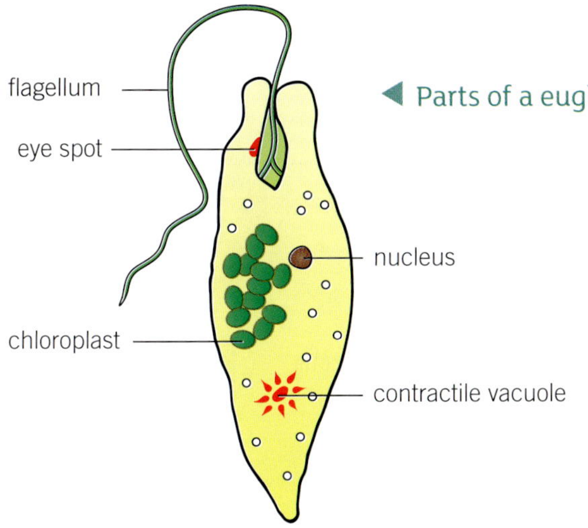

◀ Parts of a euglena.

Like amoebas, euglenas contain cytoplasm and a nucleus. However, they also have chloroplasts, which make them look green. The chloroplasts trap energy transferred from the Sun so that the euglena can make food by photosynthesis.

Euglenas also have an eye spot, which detects light, and a **flagellum**. This tail-like structure spins like a propeller, causing the euglena to 'swim' towards the light. This allows the euglena to maximise the amount of food it makes.

C Name one way in which a euglena is different to an amoeba.

What do they eat?

When a euglena doesn't have enough light to make its own food, it looks for other things to eat. They eat other microorganisms, such as bacteria and algae, by surrounding and engulfing them.

How do they reproduce?

Like amoebas, euglenas reproduce by binary fission.

Link

You can find out more about photosynthesis in B2 2.1 Photosynthesis

Summary Questions

1 Copy and complete the sentences below.

Amoebas and euglenas are examples of ______ organisms. This means that they are only made up of ______ cell. Both organisms reproduce by ______ ______. Amoebas have to ______ food to survive but euglenas can carry out ______ to produce their own food.

(6 marks)

2 Describe how amoebas and euglenas reproduce.

(3 marks)

3 Compare the structures of euglenas and amoebas. In what ways are the organisms similar and in what ways are they different?

(6 marks)

B1 Chapter 1 Summary

Key Points

- Cells are the building blocks of life – they are the smallest units in an organism.
- Scientists use microscopes to observe small objects in detail.
- Animal cells contain a nucleus, cytoplasm, cell membrane, and mitochondria.
- Plant cells also contain chloroplasts, a vacuole, and a cell wall.
- Cytoplasm is where the chemical reactions in a cell take place.
- The cell membrane is a barrier that controls what moves in and out of the cell.
- The nucleus controls the cell, and contains genetic material needed to make new cells.
- Respiration occurs in the mitochondria – this chemical reaction transfers energy.
- The cell wall strengthens the cell and provides support.
- The vacuole contains a watery liquid called cell sap. It keeps the cell firm.
- Photosynthesis takes place inside the chloroplasts.
- Specialised cells have changed their shape and structure so that they are suited to carry out a particular job.
- Nerve cells, red blood cells, sperm cells, leaf cells, and root hair cells are specialised cells.
- Diffusion is the movement of particles from a high-concentration area to a low-concentration area. For example, water and oxygen diffuse into cells.
- A unicellular organism contains only one cell.
- An amoeba is a unicellular organism consisting of a cell membrane, cytoplasm, and a nucleus.
- Euglenas appear green as they contain chloroplasts for photosynthesis. Their eye spot locates light, and they use their flagellum to swim towards it. In low light levels they can engulf food.

BIG Write

Amoeba and me

At first glance we appear nothing like an amoeba. However, if you look more closely, our cells share many of the same features. We both do similar things to survive.

Task

Write a short article for your school newspaper that tells students how similar they are to amoeba.

Tips

- Use your scientific knowledge to explain the similarities and differences between a person and an amoeba.
- You could use cartoons to help explain how an amoeba survives.

Key Words

organism, cell, microscope, observation, nucleus, cell membrane, cytoplasm, mitochondria, respiration, cell wall, vacuole, chloroplast, specialised cell, nerve cell, red blood cell, sperm cell, root hair cell, diffusion, concentration, unicellular, amoeba, euglena, flagellum

End-of-chapter questions

1 Choose the correct definition of the word 'cell'.

A A cell is a thin slice of cork.

B A cell is the smallest unit of an organism.

C A cell is a living organism.

*(**1 mark**)*

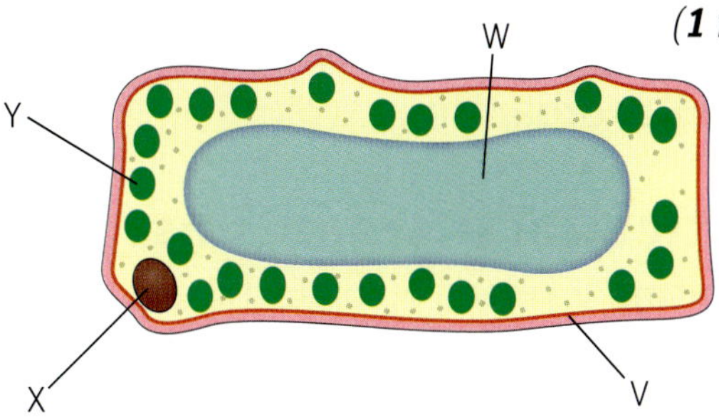

2 Above is a diagram of a plant cell.

a Name structure X. *(1 mark)*

b State the function of structure Y. *(1 mark)*

c Name the cell component that contains cell sap. *(1 mark)*

d Name **two** structures in the cell that would also be present in an animal cell. *(2 marks)*

*(**5 marks**)*

3 A student wanted to observe skin cells from the back of his hand. He used a piece of clear sticky tape to remove some dead cells.

a Name the piece of equipment he should use to observe the cells. *(1 mark)*

b Suggest **one** thing he could do to the skin cells to make them easier to see. *(1 mark)*

c Suggest **one** reason why you would not look at your own blood cells in the classroom. *(1 mark)*

d Draw a labelled diagram of what the student's cells should look like. *(3 marks)*

*(**6 marks**)*

4 The table shows some examples of specialised cells.

a Describe what is meant by a specialised cell. *(1 mark)*

b Complete the table to show how **three** types of cell are adapted to their function. *(5 marks)*

Type of cell	Function	Adaptation
		flattened disc and contains no nucleus to increase surface area
nerve cell		long and thin, forms connections with many nerves
leaf cell		

c Describe the process that causes water to enter the root hair cell. *(3 marks)*

*(**9 marks**)*

5 This diagram is drawn from a microscope observation of a euglena.

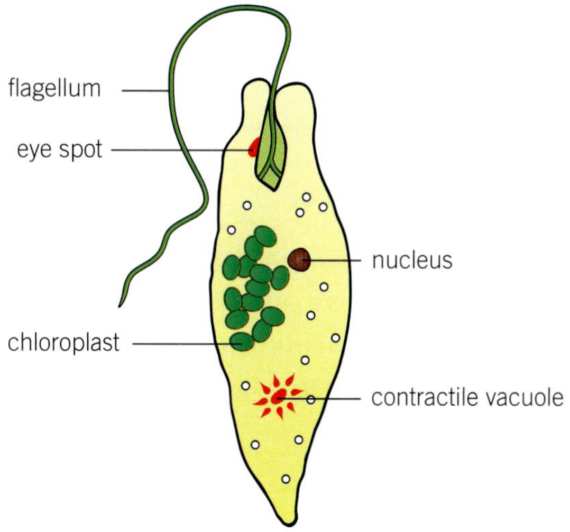

a Is a euglena a plant? Explain your answer. *(2 marks)*

b Describe **one** similarity and **one** difference between the structure of a euglena and an amoeba. *(2 marks)*

c Explain how a euglena's structure maximises the amount of photosynthesis it can carry out. *(3 marks)*

*(**7 marks**)*

6 Write a detailed plan to describe how you could investigate the differences in structure between an animal cell and a plant cell. *(**6 marks**)*

2.1 Levels of organisation

Learning objectives

After this topic you will be able to:

- define and state examples of tissues, organs, and organ systems
- explain the hierarchy of organisation in a multicellular organism.

Link

You can find out more about plant and animal cells in B1 1.2 Plant and animal cells

Fantastic Fact!

Your skin is your largest organ. It covers your entire body and has a surface area of about 2 m^2. The skin on the bottom of your feet is the thickest. The thinnest skin is found on your eyelids.

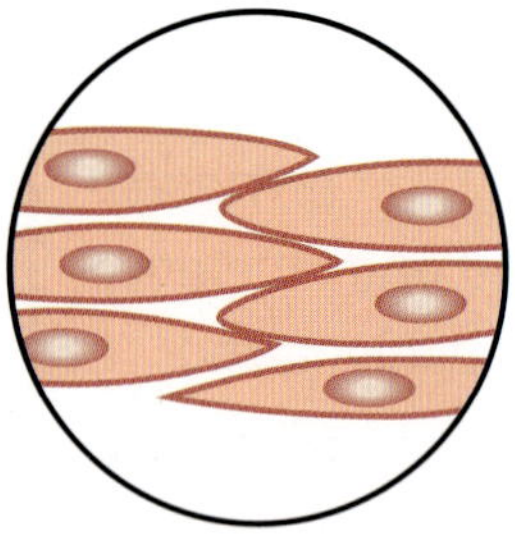

◀ Muscle tissue is a type of animal tissue.

Organise this

Organise these terms into a hierarchy. Start at the bottom level.

nervous tissue, chimpanzee, brain, nervous system, nerve cell

Do the trees outside look like a euglena? No, not really! As well as being much larger, they are much more complicated. They consist of many cells working together to form a multicellular organism.

What are multicellular organisms?

Multicellular organisms are made up of many cells. They contain organ systems to perform their life processes.

Multicellular organisms have five layers of organisation. This is called a hierarchy. Cells are the building blocks of life. They are the first level of organisation. Nerve, muscle, and red blood cells are examples of animal cells. Root hair and leaf cells are examples of plant cells.

A State the first level of organisation in a multicellular organism.

What is a tissue?

The second level of organisation is a **tissue**. A tissue is a group of similar cells that work together to perform a certain function.

An example of an animal tissue is muscle tissue. Muscle cells contract together to make the body move. Another example is nervous tissue – nerve cells work together to transmit messages around the body.

An example of a plant tissue is the xylem – these are tubes that carry water around the plant.

B State one example of an animal tissue.

What is an organ?

The third level of organisation is an **organ**. An organ is made up of a group of different tissues that work together to perform a certain function. The main organs in a plant and animal are shown below.

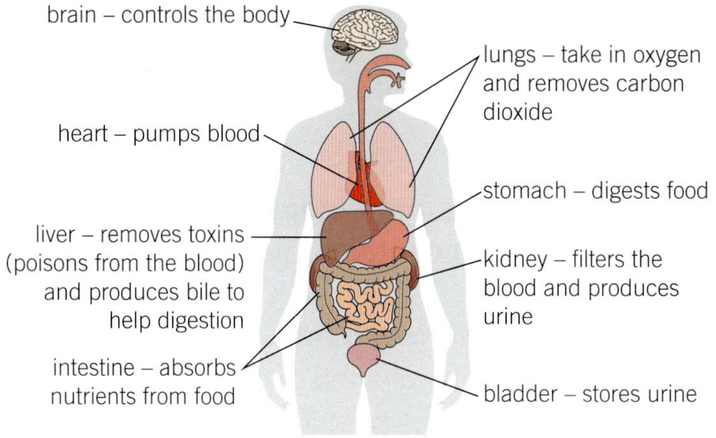

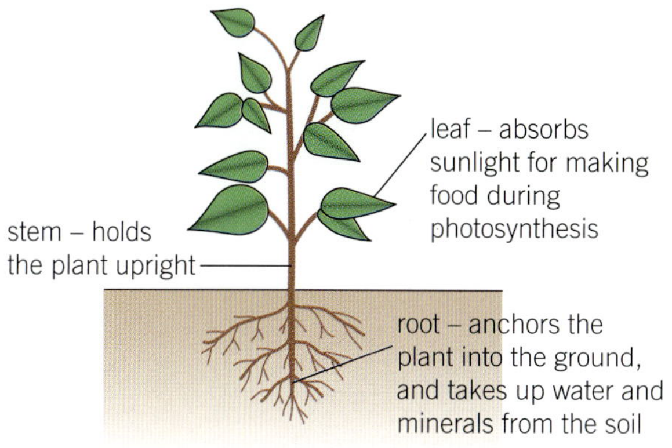

▲ These are the main organs in plants and animals.

C State one example of an organ.

What is an organ system?

The fourth level of organisation is an **organ system**. An organ system is a group of different organs that work together to perform a certain function. Some examples of organ systems are:

- circulatory system – transports materials around the body in the blood
- respiratory system – takes in oxygen and removes carbon dioxide
- reproductive system – produces new organisms

Plant structure is mainly organised into organs or tissues. However, flowers are an organ system. They usually contain both male and female sex organs, which form the reproductive system.

D State one example of an organ system.

The fifth level of organisation is a multicellular organism. A multicellular organism is made up of several organ systems working together to perform all the processes needed to stay alive. The diagram below shows how the human body is organised into different levels.

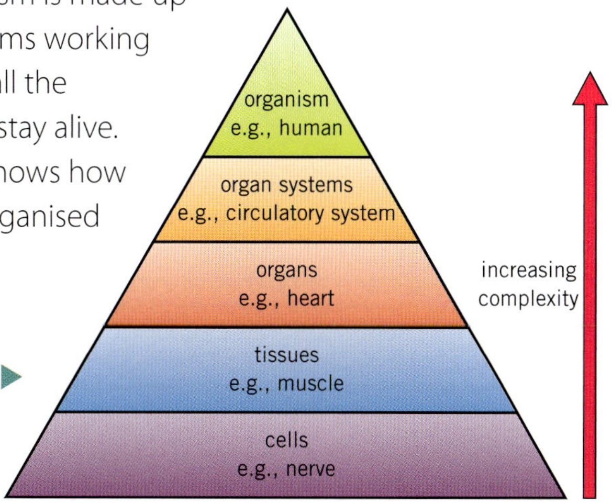

This is the hierarchy of organisation in the human body. ▶

Key Words

multicellular organism, tissue, organ, organ system

Summary Questions

1 Match the level of organisation to its function.

cell group of organs working together

tissue group of tissues working together

organ group of similar cells working together

organ system group of organ systems working together

organism building blocks of life

(5 marks)

2 Describe an example of an organ system and describe the organs it is made up of.

(2 marks)

3 Draw a diagram that shows the levels of organisation within an organism – choose either a plant or an animal and give an example for each level of organisation.

(6 marks)

2.2 Gas exchange

Learning objectives

After this topic you will be able to:

- describe the structure of the gas exchange system
- describe how parts of the gas exchange system are adapted to their function.

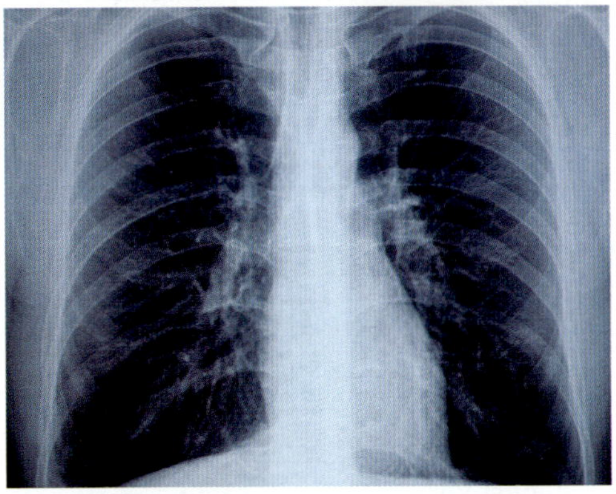

▲ You can see the lungs on a chest X-ray.

Link

You can learn more about why you breathe in B2 2.5 Aerobic respiration

Key Words

gas exchange, lungs, ribcage, respiratory system, trachea, alveolus, inhale, respiration, exhale, condense

Fantastic Fact!

Your lungs are not the same size. The left lung is normally smaller than the right lung, which leaves space for your heart to fit in.

If you are travelling on a bus, the windows may sometimes steam up. This is because it contains lots of water vapour.

What happens when we breathe?

When you breathe, you take in oxygen and give out carbon dioxide. This is called **gas exchange**. It takes place inside your **lungs**. They are made of elastic tissue that can expand when you breathe in – this allows you to take in lots of oxygen. However, your lungs are delicate, so they are protected by the hard and strong bones that make up your **ribcage**.

A Name the structure that protects your lungs.

The diagram below shows the main components of your **respiratory system** (gas exchange system). Follow the arrows with your finger to see how air travels through your mouth and nose and ends up in the blood around your lungs. The blood then takes the oxygen to all cells in your body.

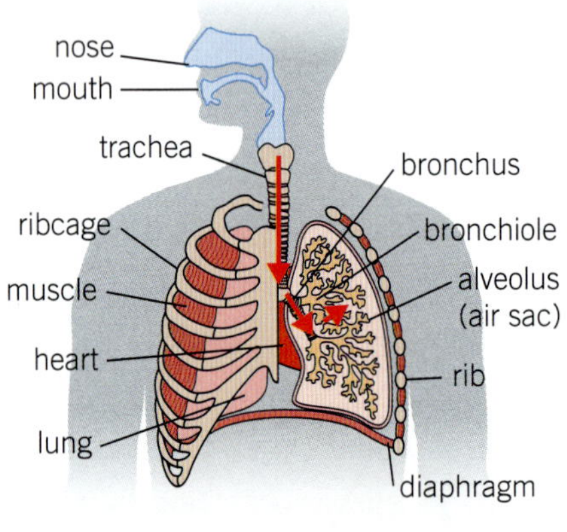

Air enters your body through your mouth and nose.

↓

Air moves down the **trachea** (windpipe) – a large tube.

↓

Air moves down a bronchus – a smaller tube.

↓

Air moves through a bronchiole – a tiny tube.

↓

Air moves into an **alveolus** – an air sac.

↓

Oxygen then diffuses into the blood.

There are millions of alveoli (plural of alveolus) in your lungs. They create a large surface area. They also have thin walls that are only one cell thick. This means that gas exchange can occur quickly and easily.

B State the scientific name for an air sac.

Why do we breathe in and out?

When we breathe in we **inhale** to take in oxygen. The oxygen is used in **respiration** to transfer energy. Respiration produces carbon dioxide, which needs to be removed from the body. When we breathe out we **exhale** to remove carbon dioxide.

The pie charts below show how much of the different gases are present in inhaled and exhaled air. This is called the composition of the air.

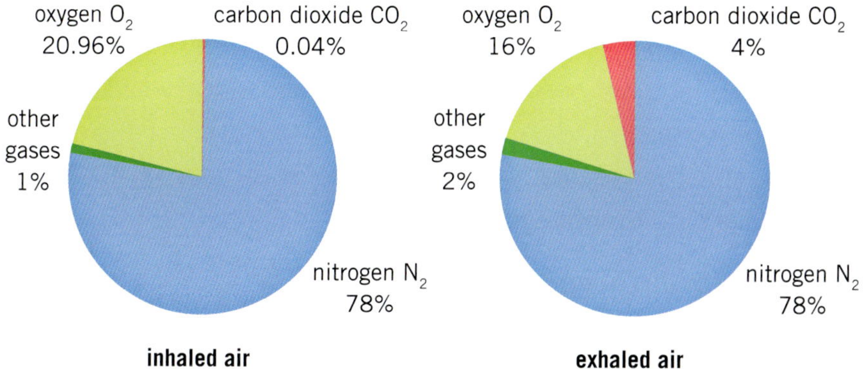

▲ These pie charts show the amount of each gas in inhaled and exhaled air.

Why can you see your breath on a cold mirror?

If you breathe onto a cold mirror, it steams up. This is because the air you breathe out contains water vapour. Water is a waste product of respiration. When the warm exhaled water vapour hits the mirror it **condenses**, turning it back into a liquid. This is what you see on the mirror.

C State which gas, present in air, is not used by the body.

▲ Water vapour in the air you breathe out condenses on cold surfaces.

Which chart?

The composition of inhaled and exhaled gases is shown in a pie chart. Why is this the best chart to use? Would another type of graph be better?

Link

You can find out more about condensing in C1 1.5 More changes of state

Summary Questions

1 Copy and complete the following table to show the differences between inhaled and exhaled air. Use the words **less**, **more**, **same**, **hotter**, **colder**. Words can be used once, more than once, or not at all.

	inhaled	exhaled
oxygen		
carbon dioxide		
temperature		
water vapour		

(4 marks)

2 Draw a diagram of the gas exchange system and label how each structure is adapted to its function.

(3 marks)

3 Describe, step by step, the journey that carbon dioxide takes from the alveolus out of the body.

(6 marks)

2.3 Breathing

Learning objectives

After this topic you will be able to:

- describe the processes of inhaling and exhaling
- describe how a bell jar can be used to model what happens during breathing
- explain how to measure lung volume.

Even when you are sitting still, your ribcage is moving. This allows your lungs to fill with oxygen. This is essential for you to stay alive.

How do you breathe?

When you breathe, muscles in your chest tighten or **contract**.

A bell-jar model can show you what is happening inside your lungs when you breathe in and out. The jar represents your chest, the balloons represent your lungs, and the rubber sheet represents a muscle called the **diaphragm**.

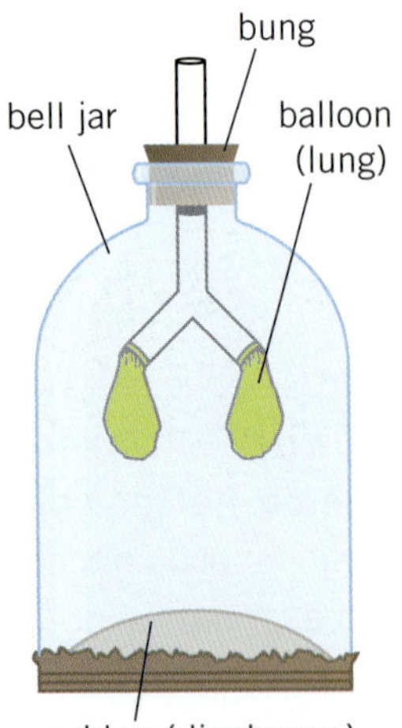

▲ A bell-jar model shows what happens inside the lungs when we breathe in and out.

Inhaling (breathing in)

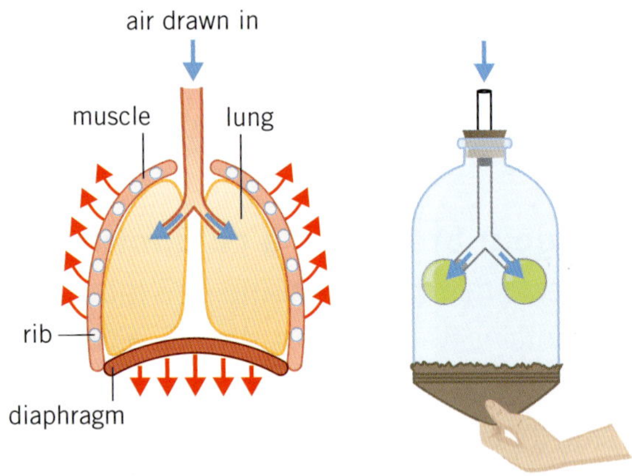

▲ Inhaling in the lungs and in the bell-jar model.

This is what happens in the body when we inhale:

- The muscles between your ribs contract – this pulls your ribcage up and out.
- The diaphragm contracts – it moves down.
- The volume inside your chest increases.
- The pressure inside your chest decreases – this draws air into your lungs.

A State what happens to your ribcage when you breathe in.

To show inhaling, this is what happens in the bell-jar model:

- The rubber sheet is pulled down.
- The volume inside the jar increases.
- The pressure inside the jar decreases – air rushes into the jar.
- The balloons inflate.

Link

You can find out more about gas pressure in C1 1.7 Gas pressure

Key Words

contract, diaphragm, lung volume, asthma

Exhaling (breathing out)

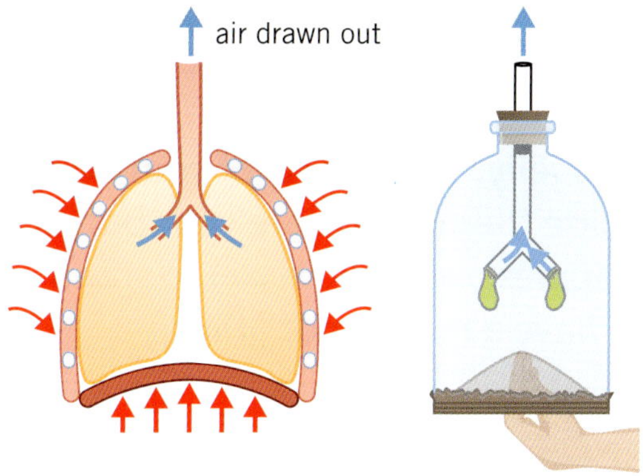

Exhaling in the lungs and in the bell-jar model.

This is what happens in the body when we exhale:

- The muscles between your ribs relax – this pulls your ribcage down and in.
- The diaphragm relaxes – it moves up.
- The volume inside your chest decreases.
- The pressure inside your chest increases – this pushes air out of your lungs.

To show exhaling, this is what happens in the bell-jar model:

- The rubber sheet is pushed up.
- The volume inside the jar decreases.
- The pressure inside the jar increases – this makes air rush out of the jar and the balloons.
- The balloons deflate.

B State what happens to your diaphragm when you breathe out.

How can we measure lung volume?

You can measure your **lung volume** using a plastic bottle.

As you breathe out into the plastic tube, air from your lungs takes the place of the water in the bottle. If you breathe out fully, the volume of water pushed out of the bottle is equal to how much air your lungs can hold.

Lung volume can be increased with regular exercise. A large lung volume means that more oxygen can enter your body. Smoking, diseases such as **asthma**, and old age can reduce lung volume.

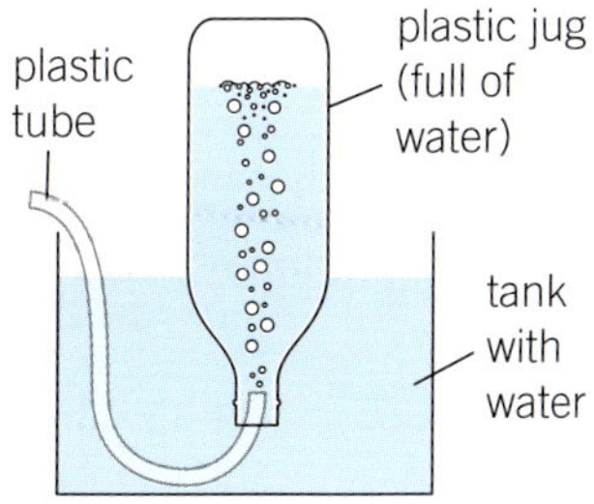

You can measure your lung volume by breathing into a bottle.

Lung volume

How big are your lungs? Calculate your own lung volume by breathing as hard as you can into a 3-litre bottle of water. Suggest why your doctor would not use this as an accurate measurement of your lung volume.

Summary Questions

1 Copy and complete the table using the following words:

up and out **down and in** **down** **up** **decreases** **increases**

	Inhaling	Exhaling
ribs move		
diaphragm moves		
chest volume		

(3 marks)

2 Name two factors that can reduce lung volume. *(2 marks)*

3 Imagine that you are an athletics coach at the Olympics. Describe how you would measure the lung volume of Usain Bolt. *(3 marks)*

4 Describe how a bell-jar model can be used to represent inhalation. Include a diagram and suggest at least one problem with the model. *(6 marks)*

2.4 Skeleton

Learning objectives

After this topic you will be able to:

- describe the structure of the skeleton
- describe the functions of the skeletal system.

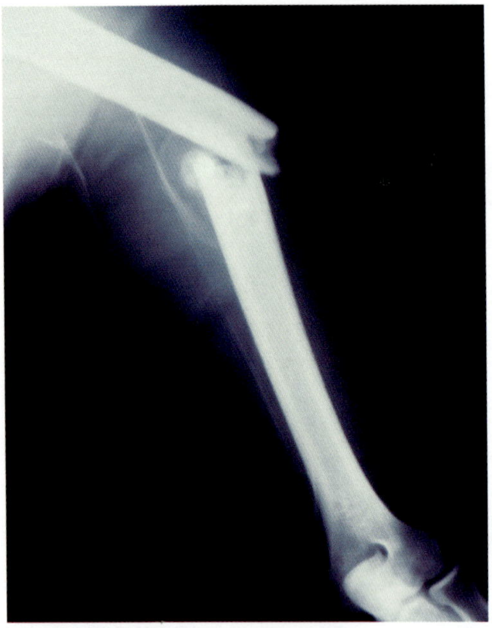

▲ Doctors use X-rays to check if a bone is broken.

Naming bones

Find out the scientific names for these parts of the body: kneecap, shoulder blade, jaw

Link

You can learn more about how your body moves in B1 2.5 Movement: joints

Why are you not a blob of jelly? Most parts of your body have hard structures inside them. These are your bones. They stop you being shapeless, and allow you to stand up and move. They also have a number of other important roles.

What are bones?

Although **bones** in a museum are old and dry, the bones in your body are different. Bone is a living tissue with a blood supply. It is growing and changing all the time. Just like other parts of your body, it can repair itself when damaged. Calcium and other minerals make the bone strong but slightly flexible. Exercise and a balanced diet are important to keep your bones healthy.

A State what a bone is.

What is a skeleton?

Together all the bones in your body make up your **skeleton**. They are joined together to form a framework. The average adult human skeleton consists of 206 bones.

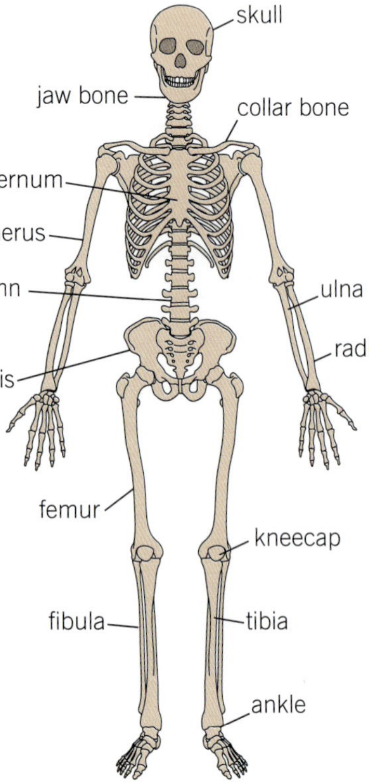

◀ The main bones of the human body.

Why do we have a skeleton?

The skeleton has four main functions:

- support the body
- protect vital organs
- help the body move
- make blood cells

B State four functions of the skeleton.

Support

The skeleton provides **support** for your body and holds your internal organs in place. Without bones the body would be floppy, like a jellyfish. The bones create a framework for your muscles and organs to connect to. Your vertebral column (backbone) holds the body upright.

Protect

Bones are hard and strong so they can **protect** vital organs from being damaged. For example:

- Your skull protects your brain.
- Your ribcage protects your heart and lungs.
- Your backbone protects your spinal cord.

Move

Muscles are attached to bones. If a muscle pulls on a bone, it will cause the bone to move. The skeleton moves at joints, such as your knee. The movement of bones about joints allows the body to move.

C Name the tissue that causes your skeleton to move.

Making blood cells

Some bones inside your body, such as the long ones in your arms and legs, are not solid. In the middle of these bones is a soft tissue called **bone marrow**. The bone marrow produces red and white blood cells. Red blood cells are needed to carry oxygen around the body, and white blood cells are used to protect against infection.

D Name the tissue that produces red and white blood cells.

Fantastic Fact!

Around 2.5 million red blood cells are produced each second by bone marrow.

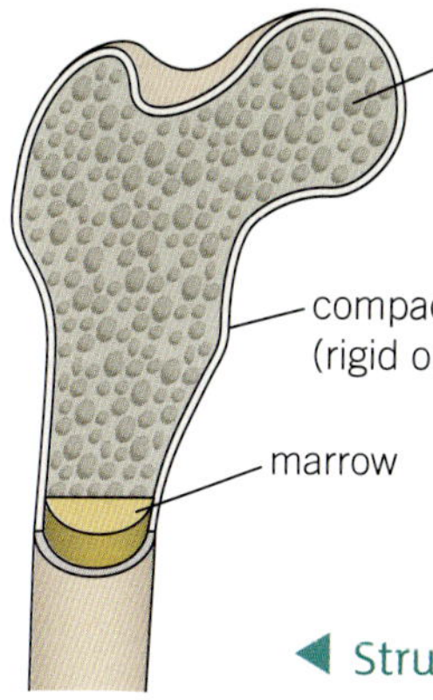

Structure of a bone.

Key Words

bone, skeleton, support, protect, bone marrow

Summary Questions

1 Copy and complete the sentences below.

Your skeleton is made up of ______. The skeleton has four important functions – to ______ the body, to ______ organs, to help the body move, and to make ______. Red and white blood cells are produced in bone ______, which is found in the centre of some bones.

(5 marks)

2 Describe the structure and function of one of the long bones in your leg.

(3 marks)

3 Write a summary of the skeletal system, including the structure and function of the bones on this page.

(6 marks)

2.5 Movement: joints

Learning objectives

After this topic you will be able to:

- describe the role of joints in movement
- explain how to measure the force exerted by different muscles.

Without muscles and joints, we would all look like statues. Muscles move bones, and joints allow the skeleton to bend. This combination is called biomechanics.

What are joints?

Joints occur where two or more bones join together. Most joints are flexible. However, some bones in your skeleton are joined rigidly together and cannot move.

A State where joints are found.

How do joints allow you to move?

Your joints need to be strong enough to hold your bones together but flexible enough to let them move. Different types of joint allow movement in different directions. Three types of joint are:

- hinge joints – for movement backwards and forwards, for example, the knee and elbow
- ball-and-socket joints – for movement in all directions, for example, the hip and shoulder
- fixed joints – do not allow any movement, for example, the skull.

B Name two types of hinge joint.

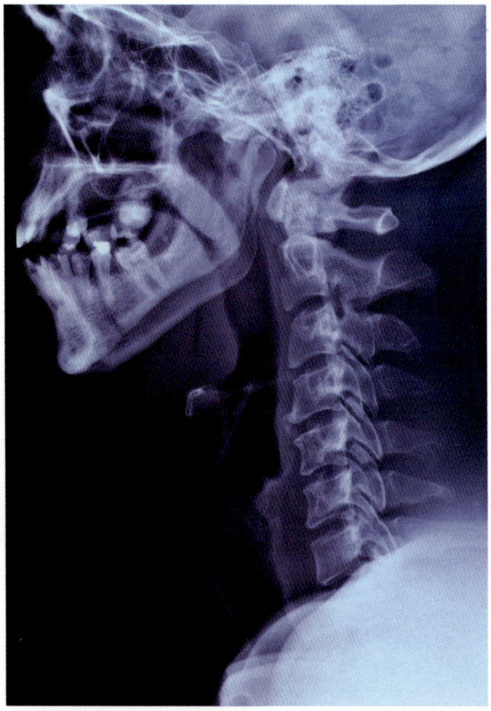

▲ Pivot joints allow movement around a point. Your neck is a pivot joint. It allows you to rotate your head from side to side.

What does a joint look like?

If your bones moved against each other, they would rub, causing lots of pain. Eventually, the bone would wear away. To stop this happening, the ends of bones in a joint are covered with **cartilage**, a strong, smooth tissue. It is kept slippery by fluid in the joint. This allows the bones to move without rubbing together. The two bones are held together by **ligaments**.

Structure of a hip joint and a knee joint. ▶

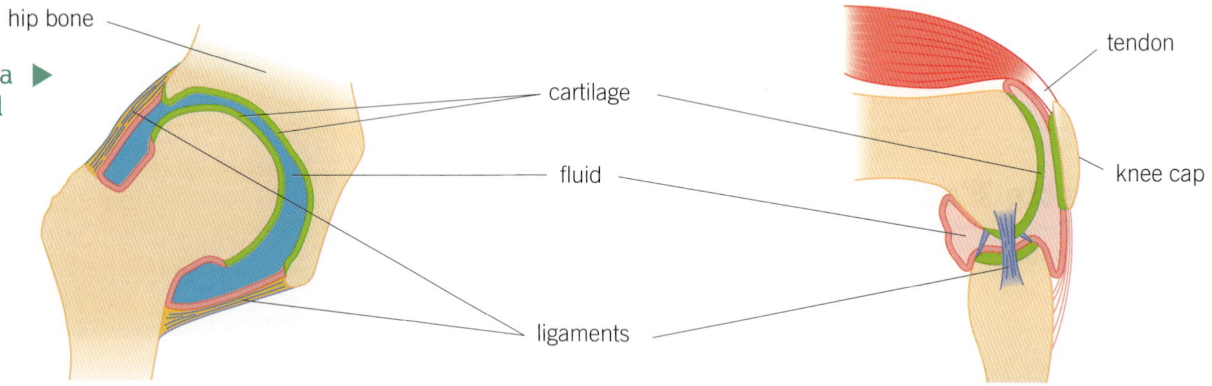

How can you measure muscle strength?

Different muscles in your body have different strengths. For example, arm muscles are much stronger than the muscles in skin that make body hair stand up when it is cold.

The strength of a muscle can be measured by how much force it exerts. You can measure the strength of your muscles using a Newton scale. The harder you can push on the scale, the greater the force exerted. Force is measured in **newtons** (N).

C State the unit of force.

You can use a newton scale to measure the strength of many different muscles. For example:

- to measure the strength of your triceps (muscles in the back of your upper arms) – push down as hard as you can on the scales
- to measure the strength of your biceps (muscles in the front of your upper arms) – put the scales under the table and push up as hard as you can (ask another student to sit on the table to ensure it doesn't move)
- to measure the strength of your forearms – hold the scales in the air and squeeze together as hard as you can, without using your thumbs.

In each technique you or your partner should read the force you exerted, in newtons, from the scale.

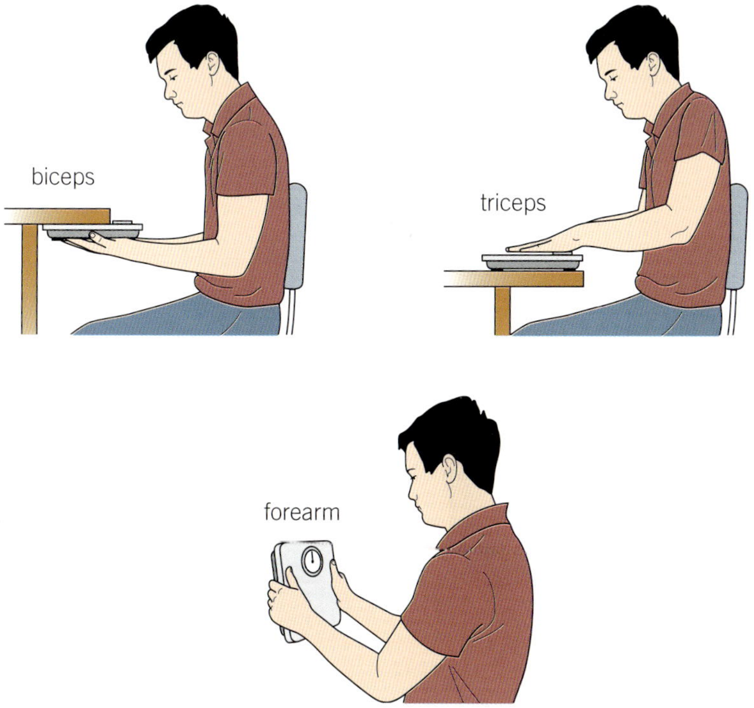

▲ Measuring your muscle strength using scales.

Health and safety

Many people go to the gym and lift dumbbells to improve the strength of their muscles. What are the risks of trying to lift the heaviest dumbbell?

Key Words

biomechanics, joint, cartilage, ligament, newtons

Summary Questions

1 Copy and complete the sentences below.

Joints occur where two or more _______ join together.

Different types of joint allow _______ in different directions. For example, ball-and-socket joints in the _______ allow movement in all directions. _______ covers the end of the bones in joints to stop them _______ together.

(5 marks)

2 Draw a diagram of a joint in the body, labelling the key structures.

(3 marks)

3 Imagine you are a fitness trainer at a gym. Write a set of instructions for gym users on how they can measure their muscle strength using a set of newton scales.

(6 marks)

2.6 Movement: muscles

Learning objectives

After this topic you will be able to:

- describe the function of major muscle groups
- explain how antagonistic muscles cause movement.

Can you feel the muscle in the front of your arm working as you bend it? The muscle is pulling on one of the bones in your forearm, causing it to move upwards.

Muscles in the body

Muscles are found all over your body. They are a type of tissue – lots of muscle cells work together to cause movement.

A State why muscle is a tissue.

There are many types of muscle in your body. For example, your heart is a muscle made of cardiac muscle tissue. This muscle pumps blood around the body. Other muscles are found in your gut to help squeeze the food along. The diagram below shows the major muscle groups in your body that are used for movement.

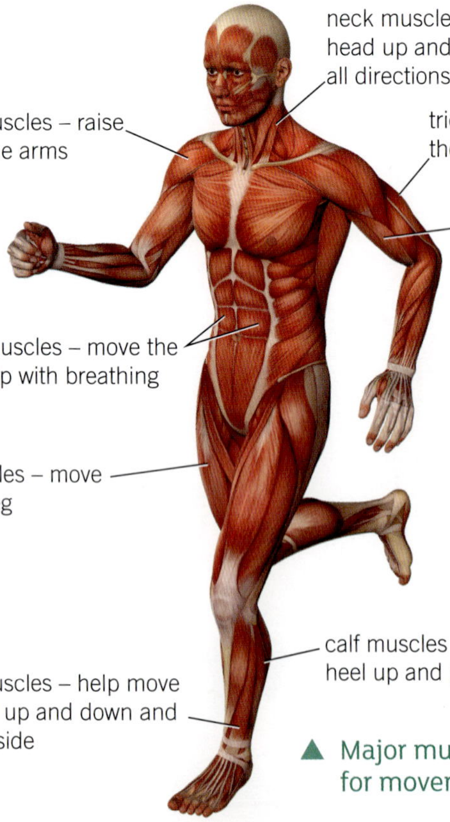

▲ Major muscle groups used for movement.

B Name three groups of muscles in the body used for movement.

Model limb

Design a model to show how antagonistic muscles allow your leg to move. Present your model to a partner, explaining how it represents antagonistic muscles.

How do muscles work?

To make you move, muscles work by getting shorter – they contract.

Muscles are attached to bones by **tendons**. When a muscle contracts, it pulls on a bone. If the bone is part of a joint, the bone will move.

C State what happens to the length of a muscle when it contracts.

How do pairs of muscles work together?

Muscles can only pull. They cannot push. This means that two muscles have to work together at a joint. If you only had one muscle in your arm, you may be able to bend your arm but you would not be able to straighten it again.

At each joint a pair of muscles work together to cause movement. These are known as antagonistic muscles. When one muscle contracts, the other muscle relaxes.

The biceps and triceps are an example of a pair of **antagonistic muscles**. These are used to bend and straighten the arm at the elbow joint.

To bend the arm:

- the biceps muscle (on the front of the upper arm) contracts
- the triceps muscle (on the back of the upper arm) relaxes.

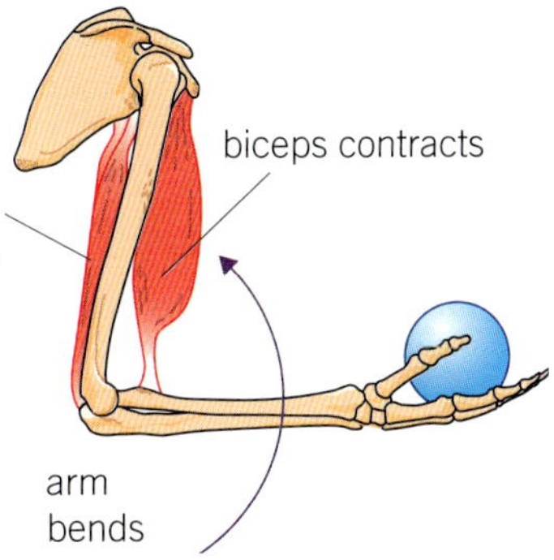

The biceps muscle contracts to bend the arm. ▶

To straighten the arm:

- the biceps muscle relaxes
- the triceps muscle contracts.

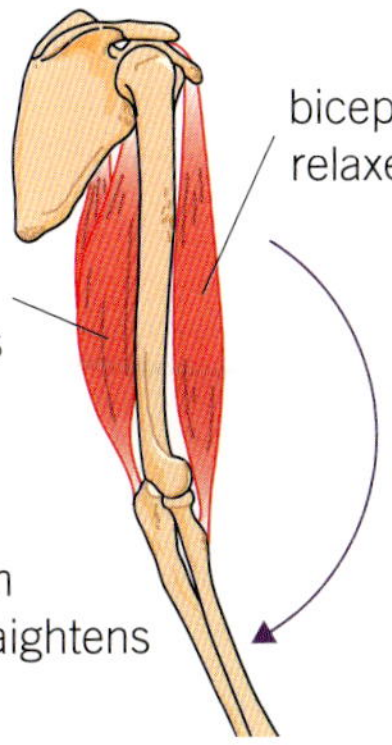

The triceps muscle contracts to straighten the arm. ▶

Key Words

tendon, antagonistic muscles

Summary Questions

1 Copy and complete the sentences below.

Muscles are attached to bones by ________. When a muscle ________ it shortens and ________ on a bone. If the bone is part of a ________ this will cause the bone to move. Pairs of muscles work together to control movement at a joint. They are called ________ muscles.

(5 marks)

2 Describe the difference between a tendon and a ligament.

(2 marks)

3 Explain in detail why two muscles are needed to bend and straighten a joint. Draw diagrams to help explain your answer.

(6 marks)

B1 Chapter 2 Summary

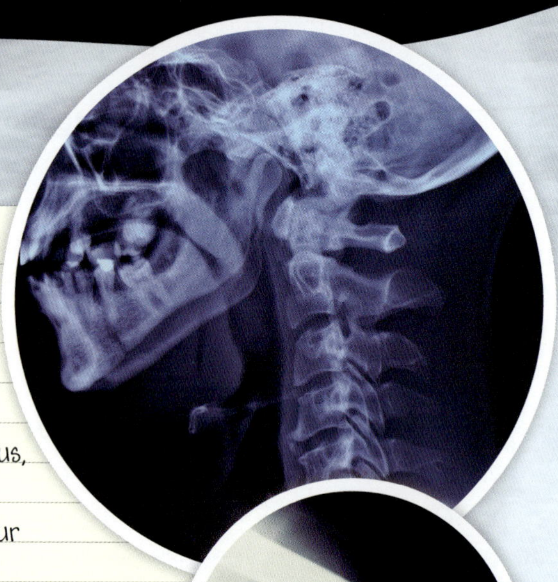

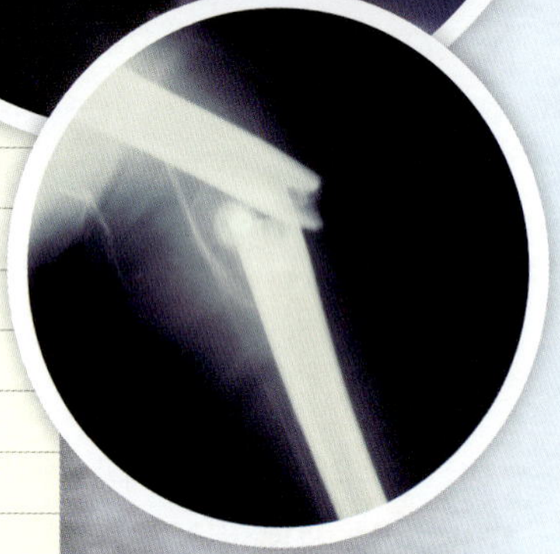

Key Points

- Multicellular organisms are made of many cells. They are organised into layers: cells → tissues → organs → organ systems → organisms
- Gas exchange takes place inside the lungs – oxygen is taken in and carbon dioxide is given out.
- Oxygen enters the body through the mouth and nose. It then travels down the windpipe, through a bronchus, then a bronchiole, into an alveolus, and diffuses into the blood.
- Exhaled air is warmer and contains more carbon dioxide and water vapour than inhaled air, but less oxygen.
- When you inhale, muscles between your ribs and the diaphragm contract. This increases the volume inside your chest. The pressure decreases and air is drawn into the lungs.
- When you exhale, muscles between your ribs and the diaphragm relax. This decreases the volume inside your chest. The pressure increases and air is forced out of your lungs.
- The skeleton is made up of bones. It has four important functions – support the body, protect the organs, allow movement, and make blood.
- Red and white blood cells are produced in bone marrow found in the centre of some bones.
- Joints occur where two or more bones join together.
- Cartilage in joints stop bones rubbing together.
- Bones are held together by ligaments. Muscles are attached to bones by tendons.
- Antagonistic muscles are pairs of muscles that work together at a joint. When one muscle contracts, the other muscle relaxes.

BIG Write

How do you toss a pancake?

Everyone enjoys tossing pancakes but which parts of your body are needed to do this?

Task

Produce an A4 cartoon strip showing how your muscles and skeleton work to make your body move when you are tossing a pancake.

Tips

- Include labelled diagrams to show the structures inside your body.
- Use speech bubbles to explain what is happening during each part of the cartoon strip.

Key Words

multicellular organism, tissue, organ, organ system, gas exchange, lungs, ribcage, respiratory system, trachea, alveolus, inhale, respiration, exhale, condense, contract, diaphragm, lung volume, bone, skeleton, support, protect, bone marrow, biomechanics, joint, cartilage, ligament, newtons, tendon, antagonistic muscles

End-of-chapter questions

1 Draw a line to match each organ system to its function in the cell.

reproductive system	takes in oxygen and removes carbon dioxide
digestive system	transports materials around the body
respiratory system	produces new organisms
circulatory system	breaks down food so it can be absorbed into the body

(4 marks)

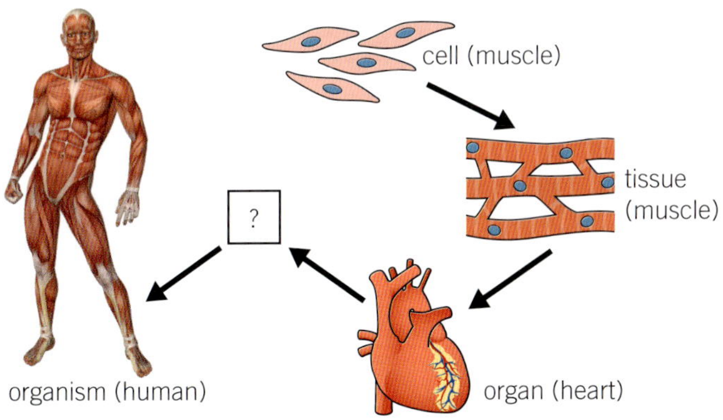

2 The diagram shows how the body is organised into levels.

a Name the type of cell shown in the diagram above. *(1 mark)*

b State the function of this cell. *(1 mark)*

c State what is meant by a tissue. *(1 mark)*

d Name the level of organisation that is missing from the diagram above. *(1 mark)*

e State and describe the function of **two** organs. *(4 marks)*

(8 marks)

3 A student wanted to measure the strength of his biceps muscle.

a Name a piece of equipment he could use. *(1 mark)*

b State the unit of force that he should use. *(1 mark)*

c Explain why the student should repeat each measurement that he takes. *(1 mark)*

d Describe the experimental procedure the student should follow to measure the strength of his biceps muscle. *(3 marks)*

(6 marks)

4 This diagram shows the main structures in the respiratory system.

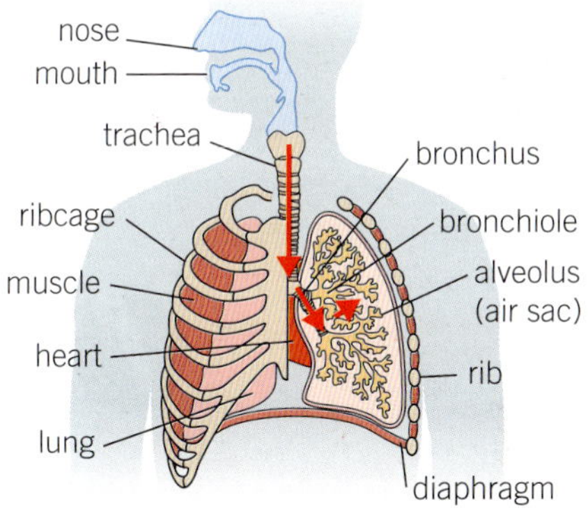

a Name the bones that protect the lungs. *(1 mark)*

b Name the process that occurs in the alveolus. *(1 mark)*

c State what the diaphragm is made of. *(1 mark)*

d Describe what happens in the lungs when you exhale. *(3 marks)*

(6 marks)

5 Compare the main differences in the composition of inhaled and exhaled air.

(6 marks)

3.1 Adolescence

Learning objectives

After this topic you will be able to:

- state the difference between adolescence and puberty
- describe the main changes that take place during puberty.

▲ Most teenagers get spots or acne. This is caused by hormones.

Problem pages

Imagine you are the editor of a magazine for teenagers, called Teen Mag. You receive the letter below from a 12-year-old boy.

Dear Teen Mag,
In the past few months my voice has started making funny squeaky sounds and my body is changing shape. What is happening to me, and can I do anything to make it stop?
Thanks,
Kyle

Write a reply to Kyle that will be published in the next issue of the magazine.

Think about yourself and your friends. Do you think of yourselves as children or adults? Everyone in your year group is at a different stage of their emotional and physical development. The time during which you change from a child to an adult is known as adolescence.

What happens during adolescence?

Adolescence involves both emotional and physical changes. These can cause you to become moody, self-conscious, and angry. Some adolescents' behaviour may also change – they want to experiment with new and risky activities, such as smoking, alcohol, and sex.

During adolescence your body goes through physical changes; this is called **puberty**.

A State what is meant by adolescence.

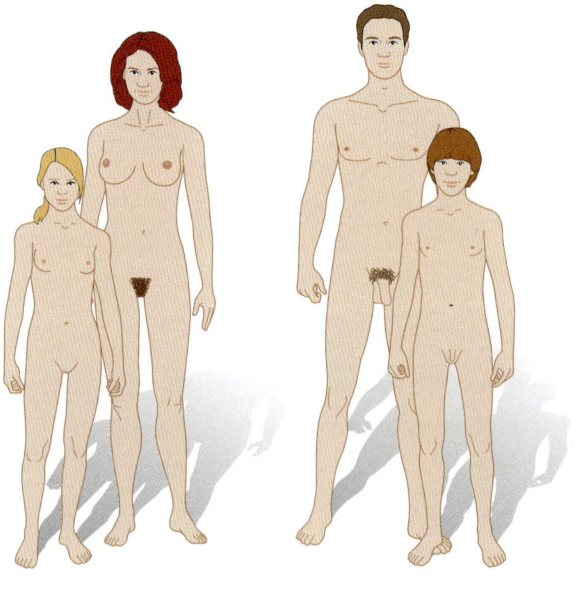

▲ Physical changes take place during puberty.

Puberty takes place between the ages of about 9 and 14 in most people. Generally girls start puberty before boys but it differs for everyone. Most of the changes take place in your reproductive system. The system needs to develop so that you can have children if you choose to when you are older.

B State what is meant by puberty.

What happens during puberty?

There are a number of changes that happen to both girls and boys during puberty. These include:

- your pubic hair and underarm hair grows
- your body smell becomes stronger – this is often called body odour
- you experience emotional changes
- you have a growth spurt (get taller).

What happens to a girl during puberty?

Some changes only happen to girls. These include:

- breasts develop
- ovaries start to release egg cells
- periods start
- hips widen.

C State two changes during puberty that only happen to girls.

What happens to a boy during puberty?

Some changes only happen to boys. These include:

- voice breaks – it gets deeper
- testes and penis get bigger
- testes start to produce sperm
- shoulders widen
- hair grows on the face and chest.

D State two changes during puberty that only happen to boys.

What causes puberty?

All of the changes that take place in your body during puberty are caused by **sex hormones**. These are chemical messengers that travel around your body in the blood. Female sex hormones are made in the ovaries. Male sex hormones are made in the testes.

These chemicals trigger different processes, such as egg release in females and pubic-hair growth in both males and females.

Link

You can learn more about periods in B1 3.5 The menstrual cycle

Key Words

adolescence, puberty, sex hormones

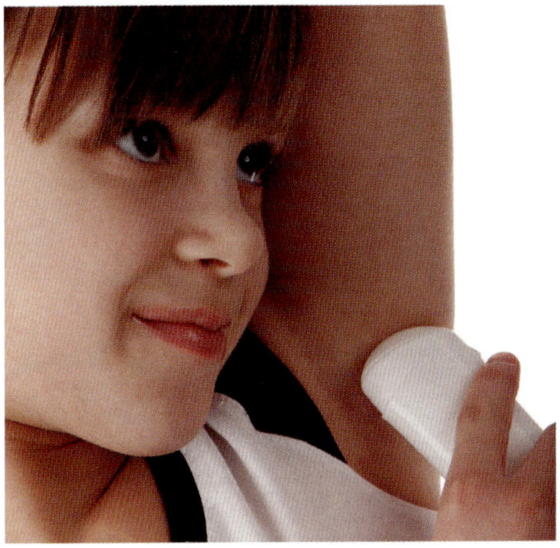

▲ To reduce unwanted body odour, you should wash regularly and use deodorant.

Summary Questions

1. Copy and complete the sentences below.
   The period of time when a person develops from a child into an adult is known as ________.
   The ________ changes that take place are known as ________.
   These changes are caused by ________.
   (4 marks)

2. State **three** physical changes that occur to both boys and girls during adolescence. *(3 marks)*

3. A boy in Year 6 has noticed that his body is changing. Write the text for an information leaflet that details all the changes that will happen to him and explain why they occur. *(6 marks)*

3.2 Reproductive systems

Learning objectives

After this topic you will be able to:

- describe the main structures in the male and female reproductive systems
- describe the function of the main structures in the male and female reproductive systems.

You have known since you were very small that males and females look different. They look different because their bodies have to perform different jobs, or functions. Their reproductive systems need to work together to produce a baby.

The male reproductive system

The function of the male reproductive system is to produce **sperm cells** (the male sex cells) and release them inside a female.

A State the function of the male reproductive system.

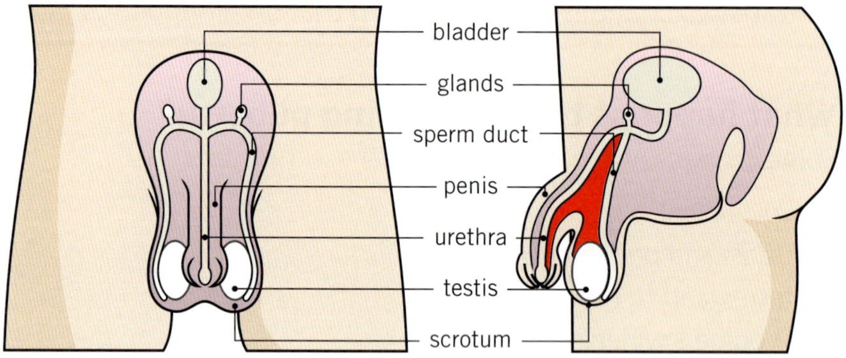

▲ The male reproductive system.

The main parts of the male reproductive system are:

- **testes** – the two testes are contained in a bag of skin called the **scrotum**. The testes produce sperm cells and the male sex hormones.
- glands – they produce nutrients that help to keep sperm alive. The mixture of sperm and fluid is called **semen**.
- **sperm ducts** – these are tubes that carry sperm from the testes to the penis.
- **urethra** – a tube that carries urine from the bladder out of the body or sperm from the sperm duct.
- **penis** – this carries urine or semen out of the body. The penis swells with blood and stiffens. This is known as an erection, and allows the male to release sperm into a female during **sexual intercourse**. The bladder cannot empty when the penis is erect, so semen and urine are never released at the same time.

Glossary

A glossary provides a definition of key words used in a book. There are many new words on these pages. Produce a glossary of the terms you have learnt so far.

Link

You can learn more about sexual intercourse in B1 3.3 Fertilisation and implantation

B State where sperm are produced.

The female reproductive system

The job of the female reproductive system is to produce **egg cells** (the female sex cells), and then grow a baby for long enough that it can be born and survive.

C State the function of the female reproductive system.

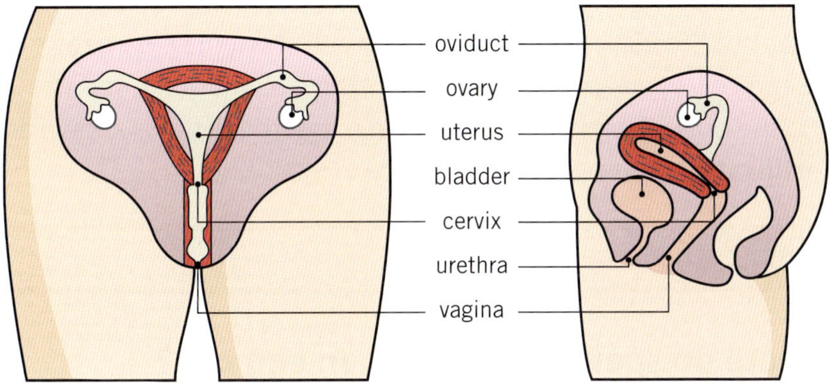

▲ The female reproductive system.

The main parts of the female reproductive system are:

- **ovaries** – they contain egg cells. One egg is released each month.
- **oviducts** (egg tubes) – they carry an egg to the uterus.
- **uterus** (womb) – this is where a baby develops until it is born.
- **cervix** – a ring of muscle at the entrance to the uterus. It keeps the baby in place while the woman is pregnant.
- **vagina** – receives the sperm during sexual intercourse. This is where the man's penis enters the female's body.
- **urethra** – a tube that carries urine from the bladder out of the body.

D State where an unborn baby develops inside its mother.

Key Words

sperm cell, testes, scrotum, semen, sperm duct, urethra, penis, sexual intercourse, egg cell, ovary, oviduct, uterus, cervix, vagina

Summary Questions

1 Match each structure to its function.

penis	contains eggs
vagina	produces sperm
sperm duct	carries an egg to the uterus
oviduct	carries sperm out of the body
testes	carries sperm to the penis
ovaries	receives sperm during sexual intercourse

(6 marks)

2 Describe the difference between sperm and semen. *(2 marks)*

3 Draw a flow chart to show the structures a sperm cell would pass through on its way out of the male and into the female's body. *(6 marks)*

3.3 Fertilisation and implantation

Learning objectives

After this topic you will be able to:

- describe the structure and function of gametes
- describe the processes of fertilisation.

Link

You can learn more about the structure of a sperm cell in B1 1.3 Specialised cells

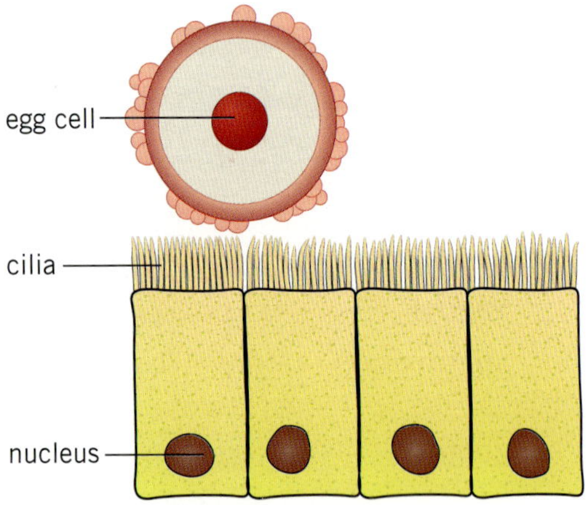

▲ Cilia in the oviduct waft the egg towards the uterus.

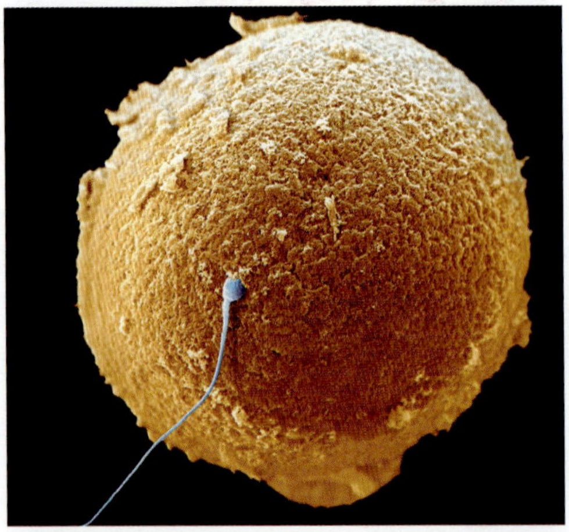

▲ During fertilisation, the head of the sperm burrows into the egg.

How are you made? Babies are made by a mother and a father but how does this actually happen? During adolescence, your body becomes able to create a baby with someone of the opposite sex.

What are gametes?

Gametes are reproductive cells. They join together to create a new organism. The male gamete is a sperm cell. The female gamete is an egg cell. To create a new organism, the nucleus of the sperm and the nucleus of the egg have to join together – this is known as **fertilisation**. This process takes place in most animals.

A State what a gamete is.

Where do sperm cells meet an egg cell?

Each ovary is connected to the uterus by an oviduct. An egg cell cannot move by itself. However, the oviduct is lined with **cilia** – these are tiny hairs on the surface of cells. Every month, an egg is released from an ovary. The cilia then waft the egg along the inside of the oviduct towards the uterus.

The sperm are released into the vagina in semen during sexual intercourse. They then swim towards the egg in the oviduct.

B Describe how an egg cell travels along the oviduct.

What happens during sexual intercourse?

When people 'have sex' or 'make love', semen is released into the vagina. People do this to make a baby or to show how much they care for each other. It is a very intimate act that gives many people a lot of pleasure.

When a male becomes sexually aroused, his penis fills with blood and becomes erect. When a woman becomes sexually aroused her vagina becomes moist. This allows the penis to enter her vagina.

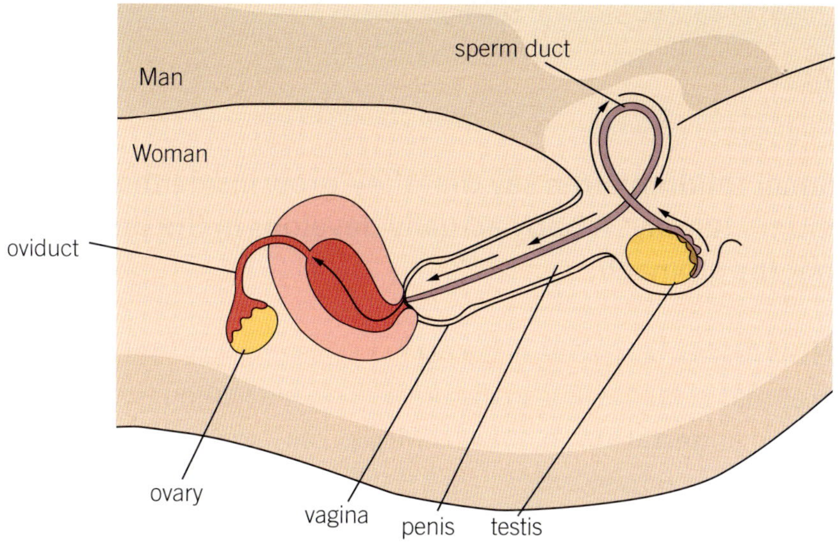

▲ During sexual intercourse, sperm are released into the vagina.

During intercourse, the male moves his penis backwards and forwards. This increases the pleasure and stimulates the release of semen into the vagina. This is known as **ejaculation**.

C State what happens during sexual intercourse.

How do sperm cells reach the egg cell?

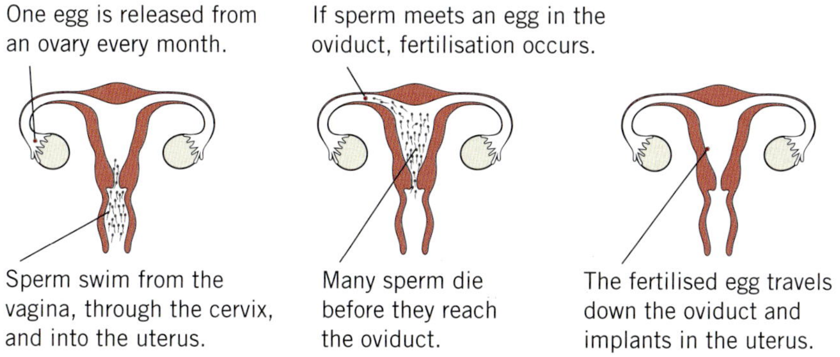

One egg is released from an ovary every month.
If sperm meets an egg in the oviduct, fertilisation occurs.
Sperm swim from the vagina, through the cervix, and into the uterus.
Many sperm die before they reach the oviduct.
The fertilised egg travels down the oviduct and implants in the uterus.

▲ Sperm cells swim from the vagina to meet the egg cell.

Sperm cells swim from the vagina to the uterus. They enter the uterus through the cervix and travel to the oviduct. If a sperm cell meets an egg cell there, fertilisation can happen.

The fertilised egg divides several times to form a ball of cells called an embryo. The **embryo** attaches to the lining of the uterus and begins to develop into a baby. This is called **implantation**.

D State what happens during implantation.

Fantastic Fact!

In each ejaculation, up to 500 million sperm are released.

Key Words

gamete, fertilisation, cilia, ejaculation, embryo, implantation

Summary Questions

1 Match each word to its meaning.

fertilisation	the fertilised egg attaches to the lining of the uterus
ejaculation	the nuclei of the sperm and egg cell join together
implantation	the little hairs that move the egg cell along the oviduct
cilia	semen is released into the vagina
gametes	reproductive cells

(5 marks)

2 Describe what happens during sexual intercourse. *(3 marks)*

3 Draw and complete a table to compare the structure of sperm and eggs and how they are produced. *(6 marks)*

3.4 Development of a fetus

Learning objectives

After this topic you will be able to:

- describe what happens during gestation
- describe what happens during birth.

Link

You can learn more about the harmful effects of smoking in B2 1.8 Smoking

In elephants, gestation lasts for around 22 months. Calculate how may weeks this is, and compare it to gestation in humans.

Key Words

gestation, fetus, placenta, umbilical cord, fluid sac

Small children often say that they 'grow inside their mum's tummy'. A baby actually develops in the uterus, not the stomach.

How long to grow a baby?

In all mammals the time in the uterus from fertilisation until birth is known as **gestation**. In humans we also call it pregnancy. It takes around 9 months (40 weeks) for a fertilised egg to develop into a baby.

During pregnancy a woman has regular check-ups with a midwife to check her health and her developing baby's health. The midwife will advise the woman to eat a healthy diet, not to smoke, and to avoid alcohol. Smoking can cause babies to be born early, when they are not fully developed. Alcohol can cause problems in the development of the baby's brain.

A State how long gestation lasts in humans.

Where does a baby grow?

During the early stages of pregnancy, cells in the embryo divide and specialise. After eight weeks of growth the embryo is called a **fetus**.

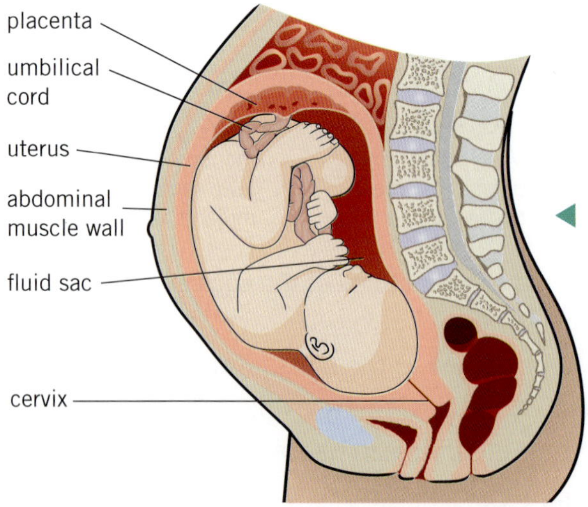

A baby develops inside the uterus.

To grow, a fetus needs nutrients and oxygen. It receives these from its mother, through her blood.

B State what a fetus needs in order to grow.

There are three important structures inside the uterus:
- **placenta** – an organ where substances pass between the mother's blood and the fetus's blood. It acts as a barrier, which stops infections and harmful substances from reaching the fetus.
- **umbilical cord** – this connects the fetus to the placenta.
- **fluid sac** – this acts as a shock absorber, protecting the fetus from any bumps.

Inside the placenta the blood of the mother and the blood of the fetus flow very close to each other. They do not mix. Oxygen and nutrients diffuse across the placenta from the mother to the fetus. Waste substances, such as carbon dioxide, diffuse from the fetus to the mother.

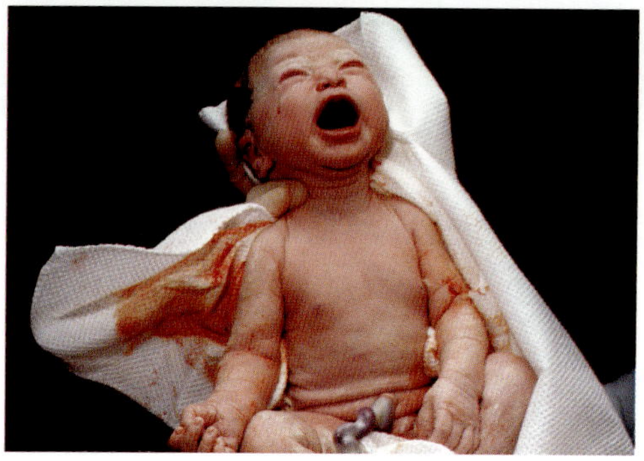

▲ This baby has just been born – the umbilical cord still needs to be cut.

How does a baby develop?

The diagram below shows the main steps in a baby's development.

Just a dot	○	1 week – cells beginning to specialise
3 mm long		4 weeks – spine and brain forming, heart beating
3 cm long		9 weeks – tiny movements, lips and cheeks sense touch, eyes and ears forming
7 cm long		12 weeks – fetus uses its muscles to kick, suck, swallow and practise breathing

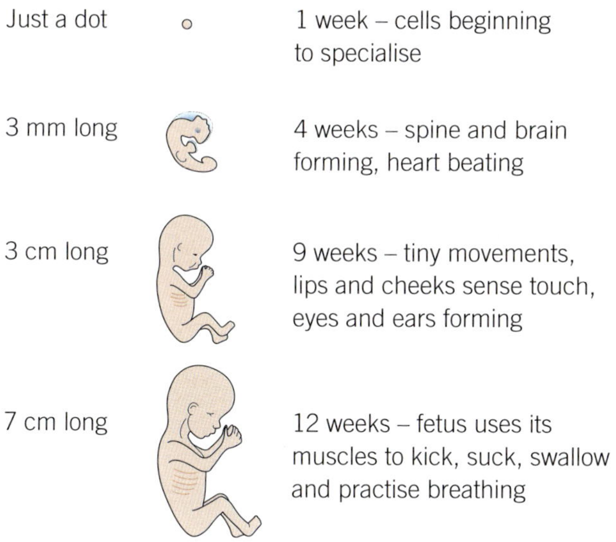

▲ Steps in development.

C State when the baby's heart starts to beat.

What happens during birth?

After around 40 weeks the baby is ready to be born. The mother's cervix relaxes, and muscles in the wall of the uterus contract. This gradually pushes the baby out through the vagina.

When the baby is born it is still joined to its mother by the umbilical cord. This needs to be cut. The placenta is then pushed out.

D Describe how a baby is born.

Link
You can learn more about diffusion in C1 1.6 Diffusion

Summary Questions

1. Copy and complete the sentences below.
A _____ develops in the _____. This is known as _____. The _____ protects the fetus from bumps. The fetus is attached to the placenta by the _____. Substances transfer between the mother and baby through their _____ in the placenta. After _____ weeks the baby is ready to be born.
(7 marks)

2. Describe how substances are transferred between a mother and her fetus.
(3 marks)

3. Explain how the uterus supports the development of a baby during gestation.
(6 marks)

3.5 The menstrual cycle

Learning objectives

After this topic you will be able to:

- state what the menstrual cycle is
- describe the main stages in the menstrual cycle.

Key Words

period, menstrual cycle, ovulation, contraception, condom , contraceptive pill

You may have heard your classmates talking about periods. You may know that only girls have them, but what are they and why do they happen?

What are periods?

During puberty a girl will start her **periods**. Around once a month, blood from the lining of the uterus leaves the body through the vagina. Each period normally lasts between three and seven days.

A State how often a period occurs.

The female reproductive system works in a sequence called the **menstrual cycle**. This lasts about 28 days, though the length and timing of each stage in the cycle is different for each female. The cycle is controlled by hormones.

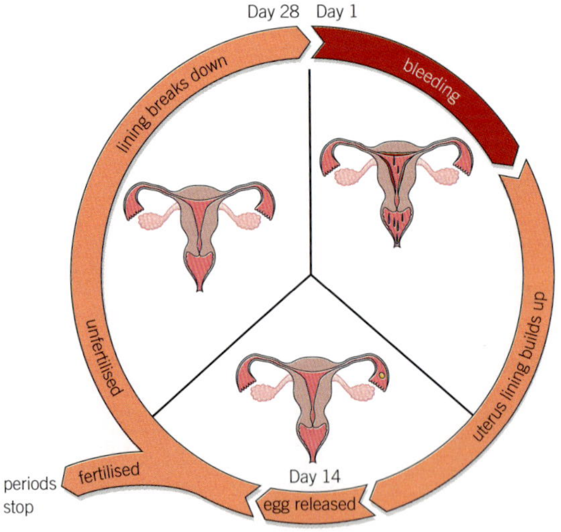

The menstrual cycle.

The stages in the cycle are:

- Day 1 – blood from the uterus lining leaves the body through the vagina.
- Day 5 – bleeding stops. The lining of the uterus begins to re-grow. The lining is spongy and filled with blood. This will provide a deep layer for implantation if an egg cell is fertilised.
- Day 14 – an egg cell is released from one of the ovaries. This is called **ovulation**. The egg cell travels through the oviduct towards the uterus.

B State what is meant by ovulation.

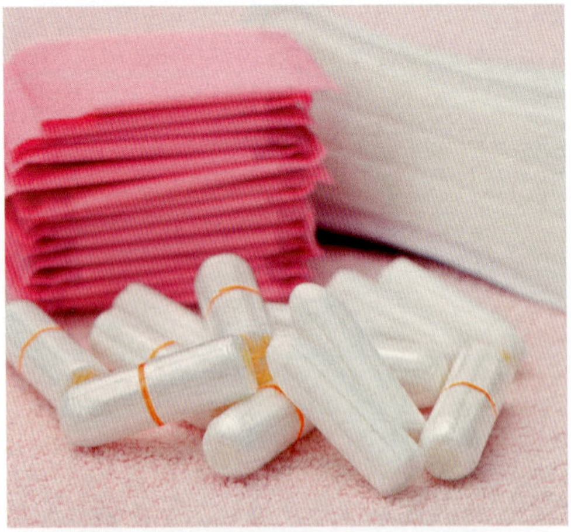

Girls can choose to use sanitary towels or tampons to absorb the blood during her period.

If the egg cell does not meet with a sperm cell, the lining of the uterus break downs and the cycle starts again from Day 1.

However, if the egg is fertilised, it attaches to the lining of the uterus and the woman is pregnant. During pregnancy a woman does not have any periods.

What is contraception?

Pregnancy is a result of sexual intercourse. Until you decide to have a baby, you should take steps to avoid pregnancy. This is called **contraception**. Two of the most common forms of contraception are **condoms** and the **contraceptive pill**.

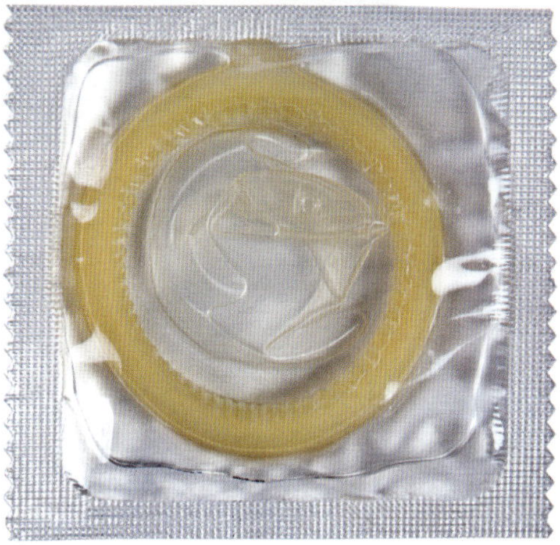

▲ Condoms are a barrier method of contraception.

C Name two different methods of contraception.

How do condoms work?

A condom is a thin layer of latex rubber that fits over an erect penis. It is called a 'barrier' method of contraception. It prevents semen from being released into a woman's vagina.

When used correctly, condoms are a very effective method of contraception. Condoms also prevent the transfer of sexually transmitted infections (STIs), such as HIV and syphilis.

D State what method of contraception a condom is.

How does the pill work?

The contraceptive pill ('the pill') is a tablet that a female must take daily in order for it to work. The tablet contains hormones, which can prevent pregnancy by stopping ovulation.

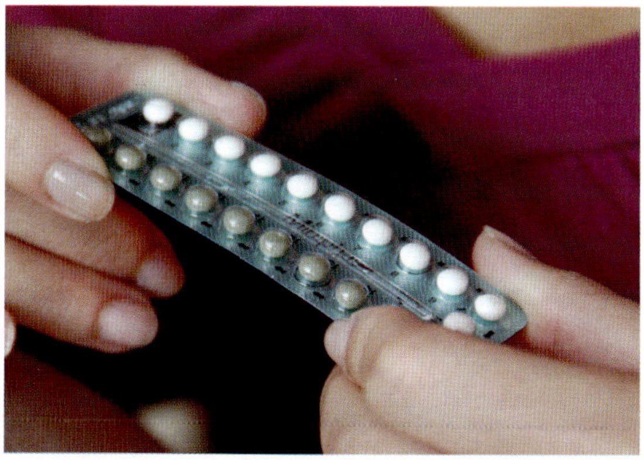

◀ The contraceptive pill is very effective at preventing pregnancy.

When used correctly, the contraceptive pill is a very effective method of contraception. However, it provides no protection against the transfer of STIs.

Summary Questions

1. Copy and complete the sentences below.
   The female reproductive system works in a cycle called the ________. An egg is released each month.
   If the egg is not fertilised then the ________ of the uterus breaks down and leaves the body through the ________. This is called a ________. The contraceptive pill and ________ can be used to prevent ________.
   (6 marks)

2. Describe the key stages that take place during the menstrual cycle.
   (4 marks)

3. To avoid pregnancy, people use contraception. Compare the use of condoms and the contraceptive pill as methods of contraception.
   (6 marks)

3.6 Flowers and pollination

Learning objectives

After this topic you will be able to:

- identify the main structures of a flower
- describe the process of pollination
- describe the differences between wind-pollinated and insect-pollinated plants.

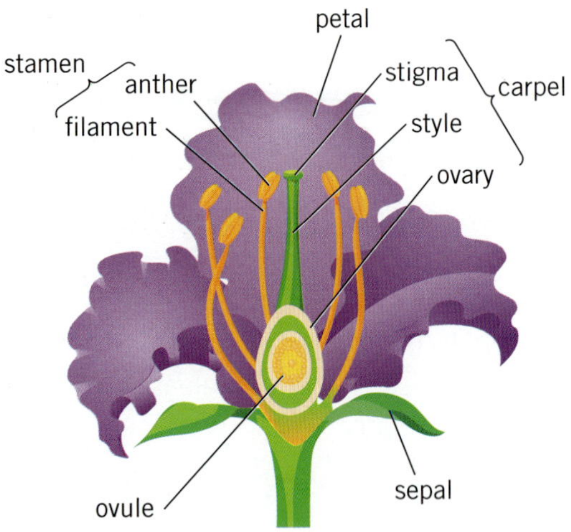

▲ Parts of a flower.

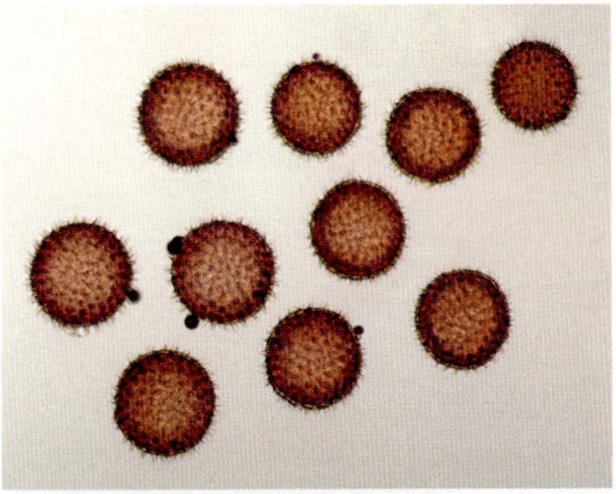

▲ These are pollen grains. If you suffer from hayfever you may be allergic to some types of pollen grain.

When looking at a flower, you often just notice its colour or its smell. But what is inside a flower and why are flowers important?

What's inside a flower?

If you look carefully inside a flower you will see different structures. The **petals** of a flower are normally brightly coloured to attract insects. Underneath the flower are the **sepals** – these are special leaves that protect unopened buds.

A State why flowers have petals.

Inside the flower there are both male and female parts.

The **stamen** is the male reproductive part – it contains:

- **anther** – produces **pollen**, the male gamete
- **filament** – holds up the anther.

The **carpel** is the female reproductive part – it contains:

- **stigma** – this is sticky to 'catch' grains of pollen
- **style** – holds up the stigma
- **ovary** – contains **ovules**, the female gamete.

B State where pollen is made.

How are new plants made?

Just like people, the formation of a new plant begins with fertilisation. The pollen grain needs to fertilise the ovule. For this to happen, pollen from the anther needs to transfer to the stigma. This is called **pollination** and is caused by insects or the wind.

Pollination can occur between two different plants (cross-pollination) or between the male and female parts of the same plant (self-pollination).

C State what happens during pollination.

How does pollination happen?

There are two ways that pollen can be transferred to the stigma – by the wind or by insects.

Insect-pollinated plants

Features of insect-pollinated plants include:

- brightly coloured and sweet-smelling petals to attract insects
- often contain nectar, a sweet, sugary fluid; bees use nectar to make honey
- smaller quantities of pollen produced
- pollen is often sticky or spiky, to stick to insects
- anthers and stigma are held firmly inside the flower, so insects can brush against them
- stigma has a sticky coating, so pollen sticks to it.

When insects visit the flower, pollen gets stuck to them. When they move to the flowers of another plant, the pollen from the first flower rubs off on to the stigma of the next flower.

Insect pollination is very important in food production. Foods such as fruit, vegetables, and nuts are pollinated by insects.

D State what nectar is.

▲ An insect-pollinated plant.

▲ A wind-pollinated plant.

Wind-pollinated plants

The features of wind-pollinated plants include:

- small petals, often brown or dull green
- no nectar
- pollen produced in large quantities to increase the chances of it reaching another plant
- pollen has a very low mass so it is very light; it can be blown easily by the wind
- anthers are loosely attached and dangle out of the flower, to make it easier to release pollen into the wind
- stigma hangs outside the flower, to make it easier to catch pollen blown by the wind.

The pollen from the flower of one plant is blown by the wind and might land on the stigma of another plant's flower.

Cartoon strip

Produce a cartoon strip showing how a plant is insect pollinated. Each frame should contain a caption explaining what is happening.

Key Words

petal, sepal, stamen, anther, pollen, filament, carpel, stigma, style, ovary, ovule, pollination

Summary Questions

1 Match each part of a flower to its function.

anther	holds up the anther
filament	brightly coloured to attract insects
stigma	produces pollen
style	contains ovules
ovary	this is sticky to 'catch' pollen grains
petal	holds up the stigma

(6 marks)

2 Pollination can occur in a number of ways.

a Describe what pollination is. *(2 marks)*

b Describe the differences between cross-pollination and self-pollination. *(2 marks)*

3 Explain in detail the difference in structure between an insect-pollinated plant and a wind-pollinated plant. *(6 marks)*

3.7 Fertilisation and germination

Learning objectives

After this topic you will be able to:

- describe the process of fertilisation in plants
- describe how seeds and fruits are formed.

Have you ever grown a plant from a seed? Seeds need water, oxygen, and a warm enough temperature to start to grow. A plant only needs light once it has grown its first leaf. All the nutrients a seed needs are stored inside the seed.

Key Words

fertilisation, fruit, seed, germination

How do plants make seeds?

Carried by either the wind or an insect, a pollen grain lands on a stigma. If the stigma is the correct species, it grows a pollen tube down the style until it reaches an ovule inside the ovary. The nucleus of the pollen grain then travels down the pollen tube. The nucleus of the pollen grain joins with the nucleus of the ovule. This process is called **fertilisation**.

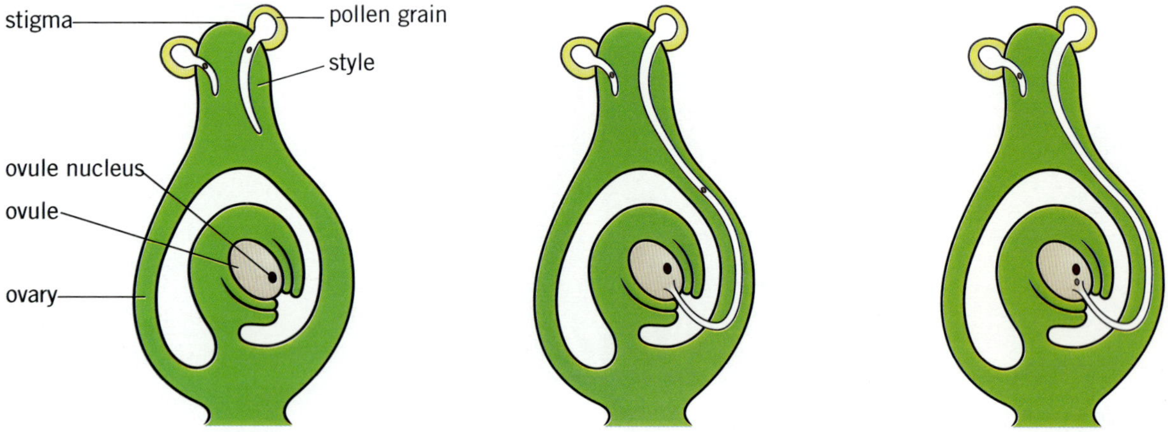

The tube grows out of the pollen grain and down through the style.

The pollen nucleus moves down the tube.

The pollen nucleus joins with the ovule nucleus. Fertilisation takes place and a seed will form.

▲ Fertilisation of a plant.

A State what happens during fertilisation in plants.

After fertilisation the ovary develops into the **fruit**, and the ovules become **seeds**. A fruit is normally the sweet and fleshy product of a plant that can be eaten as food. All fruits contain seeds.

B Name the part of the flower that becomes the fruit.

▲ Fruits contain seeds.

What's inside a seed?

Most seeds have a similar structure but they vary in shape, size, and colour. Seeds have three important structures:

- a seed coat – a tough, protective outer covering
- an embryo – the young root and shoot that will develop into the adult plant
- a food store – a store of food (starch) that the young plant uses until it can make its own food by photosynthesis.

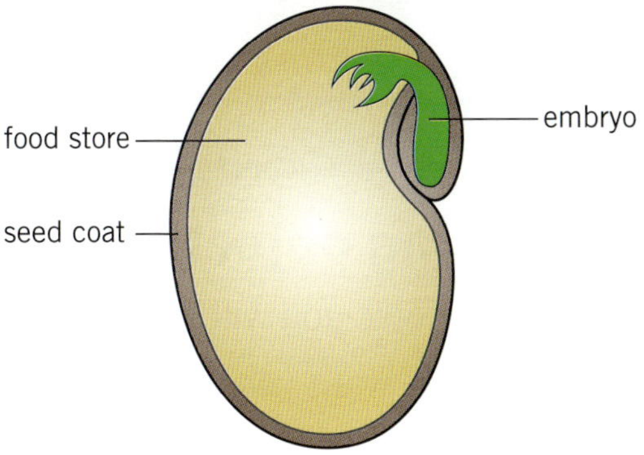

▲ The structure of a seed.

What do seeds need for growth?

When a seed starts to grow, it is called **germination**. A seed needs three things to germinate:

- water – this allows the seed to swell up and the embryo to start growing
- oxygen – this is used for respiration, transferring energy for germination
- warmth – this speeds up reactions in the plant, speeding up germination.

Link

You can learn more about respiration in B2 2.5 Aerobic respiration

C State the three things needed for germination.

How does a plant grow?

The diagram below shows the main steps in germination.

The seed absorbs water rapidly, causing it to swell. This causes the hard seed coat to split.
The root grows downwards.
The shoot starts to grow upwards.
The first leaf starts to appear – the plant starts to make its own food by photosynthesis (using light from the Sun).
More leaves start to appear – the plant now uses photosynthesis to produce all the food it needs.

Investigating germination

Design an investigation to test the hypothesis that warmth, oxygen, and water are required for germination. What equipment will you need? What method will you use? What variables will you keep the same, change, and control? How will you know if the hypothesis is correct?

Summary Questions

1. Copy and complete the sentences below.

   During ________ the nucleus of the ________ grain and the nucleus of the ________ join together.

   The ovary then develops into the ________ , and the ovules become ________.

   To ________ ,the seed needs ________ water and oxygen.

   (7 marks)

2. Describe what happens after the ovule is fertilised.

   (2 marks)

3. To produce new plants, the seeds have to germinate. Describe in detail what happens during germination.

   (6 marks)

3.8 Seed dispersal

Learning objectives

After this topic you will be able to:

- state the ways seeds can be dispersed
- describe how a seed is adapted to its method of dispersal.

▲ Dandelion seeds being dispersed by the wind.

Sometimes on a summer's day you can see lots of things blowing in the air. Many people think this is pollen but pollen grains are tiny and hard to see. You are probably looking at seeds being moved away from the parent plant. This is known as seed dispersal.

How are seeds dispersed?

Seeds are dispersed away from each other and from the parent plant. This is so they have space to grow and do not compete for resources such as nutrients. Nearly all seeds are found inside fruits. This increases the number of ways they can be dispersed. The main methods of **seed dispersal** are:

- wind
- animal
- water
- explosive.

A Name four methods of seed dispersal.

Wind dispersal

The wind is very useful for dispersing seeds and fruits. To help them catch the wind, some fruits and seeds have a small mass and extensions that act as parachutes or wings. Examples include dandelion and sycamore seeds.

Animal dispersal

Animals can disperse fruits and seeds in two ways:

- internally – animals eat lots of fruit, including tomatoes, blackberries, and strawberries. Fruits are normally brightly coloured and taste sweet, which attracts animals to them. These fruits contain seeds with hard coats. This means the seeds pass through the animal without being damaged. When they reach the ground in animal droppings, the seeds might be able to germinate. They are surrounded by waste material, which provides nutrients and helps the plant to grow.

Key Words

seed dispersal

- externally – some fruits have hooks on them, which help them stick to animals. As an animal brushes past a plant such as goose grass or burdock, the seeds get caught in their fur. They get carried away from the parent plant. The seeds drop off the animal's fur and reach the ground, where they might be able to germinate.

▲ Burdock seeds have little hooks on them to help them stick to animals' fur.

B Name two types of seed that are dispersed by animals.

Water dispersal

Many plants that live near water, such as willow trees, produce seeds with a small mass that float on water. The seeds are transported away from the parent plant in streams and rivers. They might germinate if they get washed up onto land. Other trees, such as the coconut, produce woody fruits that are waterproof. They are carried away by the sea and might germinate if they reach another shore.

C Describe the structure of a seed that can be transported by water.

Explosive dispersal

Some fruits burst open when they are ripe, throwing the seeds in all directions. Peapods and gorse disperse seeds in this way.

▲ Peapods burst open when ripe, dispersing the seeds away from the parent plant.

D Name a plant that disperses its seeds by explosion.

Summary Questions

1 Copy and complete the sentences below.

Seeds are ________ away from the parent plant and other seeds to reduce ________. This increases their chances of having enough space and ________ to grow.

Seeds can be dispersed by the ________, water, ________, and explosion.

(5 marks)

2 Describe the two ways that animals can disperse seeds.

(4 marks)

3 Explain in detail how different seed types are adapted to their method of seed dispersal.

(6 marks)

B1 Chapter 3 Summary

Key Points

- Adolescence is the time when you change from a child to an adult.
- The physical changes that your body goes through during adolescence is called puberty. Puberty is caused by hormones.
- Boys and girls both have a growth spurt, and grow pubic and underarm hair.
- Girls develop breasts, the ovaries release egg cells, and the hips widen.
- Girls begin the menstrual cycle. Periods occur when the lining of the uterus breaks down. This happens once a month.
- Boys' voices break, the testes and penis get bigger, the testes start to produce sperm, shoulders widen, and hair grows on the face and chest.
- Fertilisation in animals occurs when the nucleus of a sperm joins with the nucleus of an egg.
- The fertilised egg divides several times to form a ball of cells called an embryo. This implants in the lining of the uterus and begins to develop into a baby.
- The fetus receives nutrients and oxygen from the mother through the placenta.
- Pollination occurs when pollen from the anther is transferred to the stigma.
- Fertilisation in plants occurs when the nucleus of a pollen grain joins with the nucleus of an ovule.
- The ovary becomes a fruit and the ovules turn into seeds. The seeds are dispersed by either the wind, water, animals, or explosion.
- A seed requires warmth, oxygen, and water to germinate.

Case Study

Seed-dispersal investigation

The shape and mass of a seed plays an important role in its method of dispersal.

Task

Plan an investigation to see how far different types of seed can be dispersed.

Tips

- Think about the variables. What will you change, measure, and control?
- How will you measure how far the seeds travel?
- How will you make the investigation repeatable and reproducible?

Key Words

adolescence, puberty, sex hormones, sperm cell, testes, scrotum, semen, sperm duct, urethra, penis, sexual intercourse, egg cell, ovary, oviduct, uterus, cervix, vagina, gamete, fertilisation, cilia, ejaculation, embryo, implantation, gestation, fetus, placenta, umbilical cord, fluid sac, period, menstrual cycle, ovulation, contraception, condom, contraceptive pill, petal, sepal, stamen, anther, pollen, filament, carpel, stigma, style, ovary, ovule, pollination, fertilisation, fruit, seed, germination, seed dispersal

End-of-chapter questions

1 a Sort the physical changes that take place during adolescence into those that happen to boys, those that happen to girls, and those that happen to both.

breasts develop **voice deepens**
testes produce sperm **growth spurt**
pubic hair grows **periods start**

Boys	Girls	Both

(6 marks)

b State the name given to the physical changes that take place during adolescence.
(1 mark)

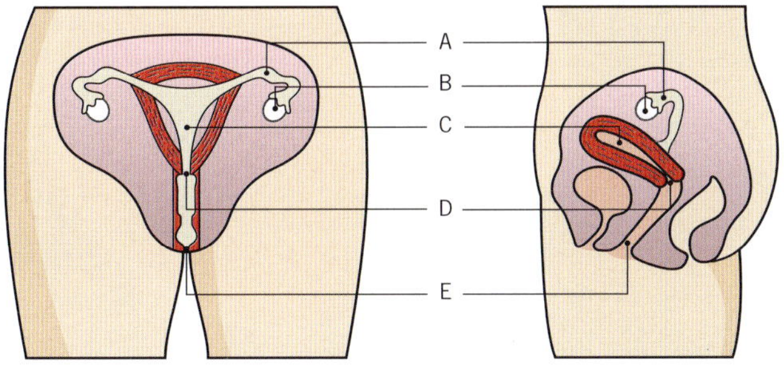

2 The diagram shows the main structures in the female reproductive system.

a Name structures A and D. *(2 marks)*
b State where sperm are released during sexual intercourse. *(1 mark)*
c State where the baby develops during pregnancy. *(1 mark)*
d Describe what happens during ovulation. *(2 marks)*
(6 marks)

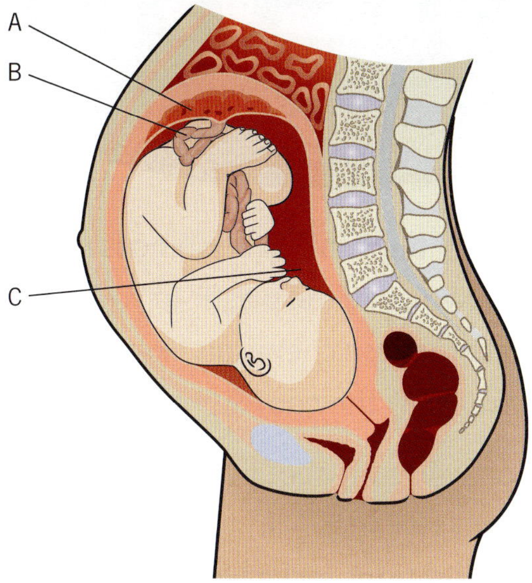

3 A fetus develops inside the uterus. During this time it depends on the mother for its growth and development.

a Name structure B. *(1 mark)*
b State how the fetus is protected from bumps. *(1 mark)*
c Describe what happens during birth. *(3 marks)*
d Explain the role of the placenta. *(3 marks)*
(8 marks)

4 Plants can be pollinated by insects or the wind.

a State **two** features of a wind-pollinated plant. *(2 marks)*
b State **two** ways that an insect-pollinated plant is different. *(2 marks)*
c Describe what happens during pollination. *(2 marks)*
d Describe how a seed is formed after pollination has taken place. *(4 marks)*
(10 marks)

5 Describe in detail the structure and function of the main parts of a flower.
(6 marks)

Chemistry 1

What is stuff made of? Everything is made up of chemicals – the food you eat, the plastic in your phone…and you! But what are these chemicals like inside, and why do they behave the way they do?

In C1 you will learn about the atoms that make up everything on Earth… and beyond. You will explore how chemical reactions make vital materials, and transfer energy for almost everything we do.

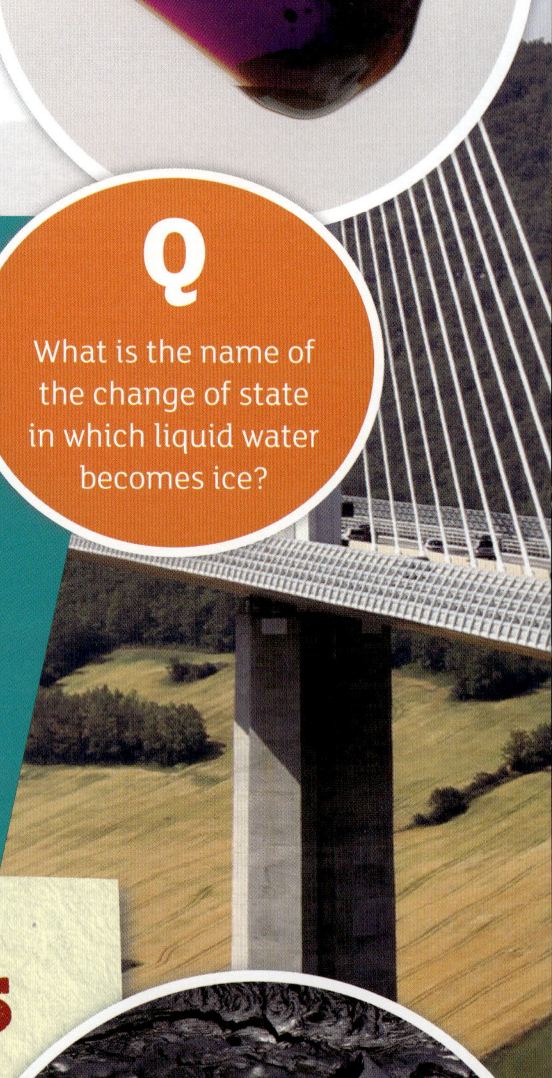

Q

What is the name of the change of state in which liquid water becomes ice?

You already know

- Different materials have different properties.
- The different properties of different materials make them suitable for different uses.
- Many materials can exist in the solid, liquid, and gas states.
- The state of a material depends on the temperature.
- Changes of state are reversible.
- Melting, freezing, evaporating, boiling, and condensing are changes of state.
- Changes that form new materials are not reversible.
- Changes that are not reversible include burning, oxidation, and reactions of acid.

BIG Questions

- What are materials like inside and why do they behave as they do?
- What are atoms and elements?
- How do scientists make new materials?

Picture Puzzler
Key Words

Can you solve this Picture Puzzler?

The first letter of each of these images spells out a science word that you will come across in this book.

Picture Puzzler
Close Up

Can you tell what this zoomed-in picture is?

***Clue**: It's a cold and frosty morning.*

Making connections

In **C1** you will learn about atoms and molecules and what happens when chemicals react.

In **B1** you will learn about diffusion and how particles move between substances.

In **P2** you will learn about energy transfer and energy conservation.

1.1 The particle model

Learning objectives

After this topic you will be able to:

- describe how materials are made up of particles
- use the particle model to explain why different materials have different properties.

▲ Gold is a single substance. All of its particles are the same.

Fantastic Fact!

If people were the same size as gold particles, the world's population would fit into a ball less than a thousandth of a millimetre across.

Look around you. Can you see things made of wood, plastic, or steel? The different types of stuff that things are made from are called materials. There are millions of materials.

What's in a material?

Materials are made up of tiny **particles**. You cannot see the particles. They are too small. There are about 8 400 000 000 000 000 000 000 000 particles in a glass of water.

A State what materials are made up of.

Are all particles the same?

Many materials are **mixtures**. Wood is a mixture. So is milk, and the air. But some materials are not mixtures. They consist of just one substance. A **substance** is made of just one type of material. Substances include gold, water, and oxygen.

▲ The bridge cables are made from steel. Steel is a mixture.

In a substance, every particle is the same. One gold particle is the same as all other gold particles. One water particle is the same as all other water particles. In the air, all oxygen particles are identical.

But gold particles are not the same as oxygen particles. Oxygen particles are not the same as water particles. Every substance has its own type of particle.

B State what is meant by a substance.

What gives a substance its properties?

The **properties** of a substance describe what it looks like and how it behaves. Every substance has its own properties. The properties of a substance depend on its particles.

The table shows data for gold and water.

Substance	Relative mass of particle	Mass of 1 cm^3 of the substance (g)
gold	197	19
water	18	1

A gold particle has a greater mass than a water particle. This helps to explain why 1 cm^3 of gold weighs more than 1 cm^3 of water.

In liquid water, particles slide over each other. In an ice cube, the particles do not move around. This explains why you can pour water from a glass but you cannot pour water from an ice cube.

The properties of a substance depend on three things, or factors:

- what its particles are like
- how its particles are arranged
- how its particles move around.

C List three factors that give a substance its properties.

Vital vocab

Plan how to explain the meanings of the key words on this page. Present your explanations to a partner.

Key Words

material, particle, mixture, substance, property

Link

You can learn more about the arrangement and movement of particles in C1 1.2 States of matter

Summary Questions

1 Copy the sentences below, choosing the correct bold words.

There are **hundreds/millions** of materials. Materials are made up of **practicals/particles**. A substance has **the same/different** properties all the way through. In a substance, all the particles are **the same/different**. The particles of different substances are **the same/different**. The properties of a substance describe its **behaviour/particles**.

(6 marks)

2 Use the data to estimate which is heavier, 10 cm^3 of water or 10 cm^3 of mercury. Show how you decided.

Data: relative mass of water particle = 18; relative mass of mercury particle = 201.

(2 marks)

3 Using all the key words, draw a visual summary to summarise and organise the information on this page.

(6 marks)

1.2 States of matter

Learning objectives

After this topic you will be able to:

- describe the properties of a substance in its three states
- use ideas about particles to explain the properties of a substance in its three states.

▲ Ice is water in the solid state.

Do you like ice in cold drinks? An ice cube is made up of water particles. Ice is water in the solid state. Now imagine a steaming kettle. Steam is also made up of water particles. It is water in the gas state.

Water can exist in three states, as a **solid**, a **liquid**, or a **gas**. These are the **states of matter**. The particles of water in its three states are identical. But the properties of ice, liquid water, and steam are different. These pages explain why.

A Name the three states of matter.

How does state affect properties?

Most substances can exist in three states. The state of a substance depends on temperature. At room temperature, gold is solid. But if you make it hot enough, gold exists as a liquid or gas.

The table compares the properties of a substance in its three states.

State	Can you compress (squash) the substance in this state?	Does the substance flow?	Shape
solid	no	no	fixed, unless you apply a force
liquid	no	yes	takes the shape of the bottom of its container
gas	yes	yes	takes the shape of the whole container

B Identify three differences between a substance in the solid and liquid states.

How do particles explain properties?

The particles of a substance do not change. All water particles are the same, in all three states. But the arrangement and movement of particles are different in each state.

The solid state

When a substance is in the solid state, its particles touch their neighbours. This explains why you cannot compress a solid. In the solid state, a substance's particles are arranged in a pattern.

In the solid state, particles do not move around. They vibrate on the spot. This explains why solids cannot flow.

The particles of a substance in the solid state.

The liquid state

When a substance is in the liquid state, its particles touch their neighbours. This is why you cannot compress a liquid. The particles move from place to place, sliding over each other. This explains why liquids flow and why they have no fixed shape.

The particles of a substance in the liquid state.

C State why you cannot compress a liquid.

The gas state

In the gas state, particles spread out. So it is easy to compress a gas. The particles move throughout the whole container. This explains why gases flow.

The particles of a substance in the gas state.

Express particle?

In 2010 a Chinese train became the world's fastest passenger train. It reached a speed of 486 km/h (0.135 km/s). In the air, oxygen particles travel at about 500 m/s. Calculate which is faster – the train or the particles.

Key Words

solid, liquid, gas, states of matter

Summary Questions

1. Each sentence in the paragraph below has one or more mistakes. Write corrected versions of the sentences.

   There are two states of matter. You can compress a substance in the solid state because the particles touch each other. In the liquid and gas states, a substance flows because the particles cannot move from place to place. You cannot compress a gas because the particles are spread out.

   (4 marks)

2. Compare the properties of a substance in the liquid and gas states.

   (3 marks)

3. Use the particle model to explain in detail why the properties of water are different in its three states.

   (6 marks)

1.3 Melting and freezing

Learning objectives

After this topic you will be able to:

- use the particle model to explain changes of state involving solids and liquids
- interpret data about melting points.

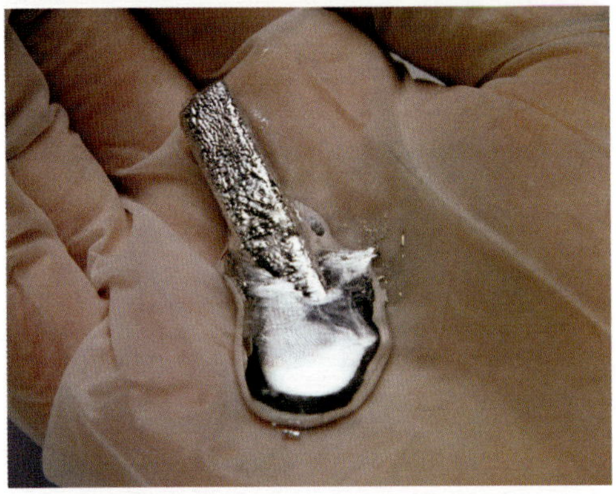

▲ Gallium metal is solid at room temperature. On a warm hand, it melts.

▲ Lava cools and freezes. This forms rock.

Key Words

melting, change of state, freezing, melting point

Imagine an ice cube in your hand. What happens?

When a substance changes from the solid to liquid state, it melts. **Melting** is a **change of state**. **Freezing** is the change of state from liquid to solid. Liquid gold freezes if cooled to 1063 °C.

A Name the two states involved in freezing.

Explaining melting and freezing

What happens when an ice cube melts? The surroundings transfer energy to the ice, so its particles vibrate faster. Particles move away from their places in the pattern. They continue to move around. As more particles leave the pattern, more ice melts.

When a liquid starts to freeze, its particles move more slowly as they transfer energy to the surroundings. The particles get into a pattern, and vibrate on the spot. Eventually, all the liquid freezes. The mass does not change when a substance melts or freezes. This is because no particles have been added or removed.

B Describe how particle movement changes when a substance melts.

What is a melting point?

The temperature at which a substance melts is its **melting point**.

Substance	Melting point (°C)
gallium	30
gold	1063
oxygen	–218
water	0

Melting points give information about the states of substances at different temperatures. The melting points of gallium and gold are above 20 °C. So at 20 °C, gallium and gold are solid. You cannot work out the state of oxygen from the data in the table.

C List the substances in the table in order of increasing melting point.

Using melting points

Identifying substances

Jackson and Marcus are at university. They have three painkillers – paracetamol, aspirin, and ibuprofen. They do not know which is which. They use the Internet to find out their melting points. They record the data in the table shown on the right.

The students measure the melting point of one painkiller. It is 136 °C. They conclude that it is aspirin.

Substance	Melting point (°C)
paracetamol	169
aspirin	136
ibuprofen	76

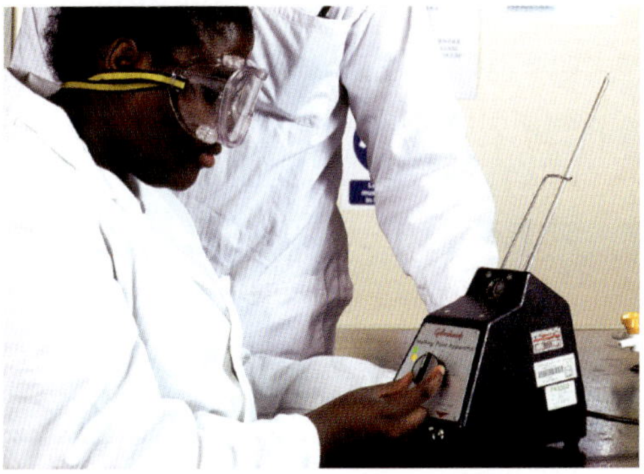

▲ Apparatus used to measure melting points.

Checking purity

A single substance has a sharp melting point. Stearic acid is solid at 20 °C. If you heat the acid, it stays solid up to 70 °C. Then it starts to melt. It stays at 70 °C until it has all melted. Then the liquid warms up.

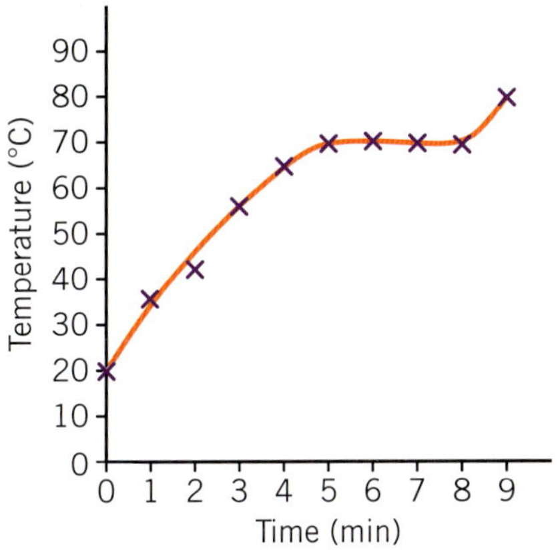

▲ The graph shows the temperature of stearic acid as it is heated.

A material that is a mixture of substances does not have a sharp melting point. Chocolate melts between 30 °C and 32 °C. This shows that it is a mixture.

Butter wouldn't melt...

Look at the graph. Is butter a single substance or a mixture? Explain your decision.

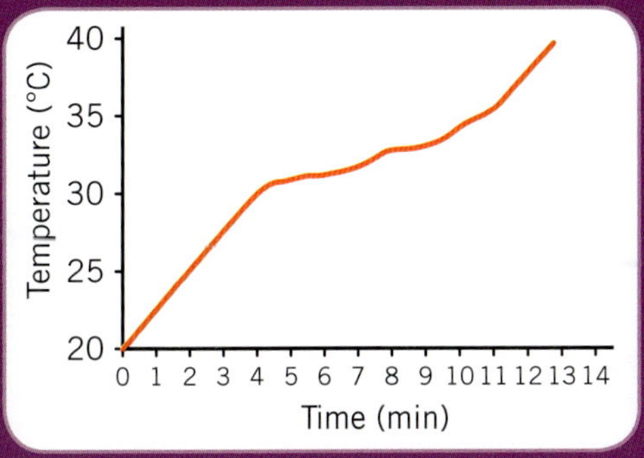

Summary Questions

1 Copy the sentences below, choosing the correct bold words.

The change of state from solid to liquid is **freezing/melting**. As a substance melts, its particles vibrate **slower/faster**. The particles start moving **around/upwards**. The substance is now in the **liquid/solid** state. The melting point of a substance is the **speed/temperature** it melts at.

(5 marks)

2 A substance has a melting point of -7 °C. Tom says the substance is liquid at 20 °C. Ben says it could be liquid or gas. Explain who is correct. Use evidence to support your answer.

(3 marks)

3 Use the particle theory to explain in detail the difference between melting and freezing.

(6 marks)

1.4 Boiling

Learning objectives

After this topic you will be able to:

- use the particle model to explain boiling
- interpret data about changes of state.

Link

You can learn more about evaporation in C2 2.5 Evaporation and distillation

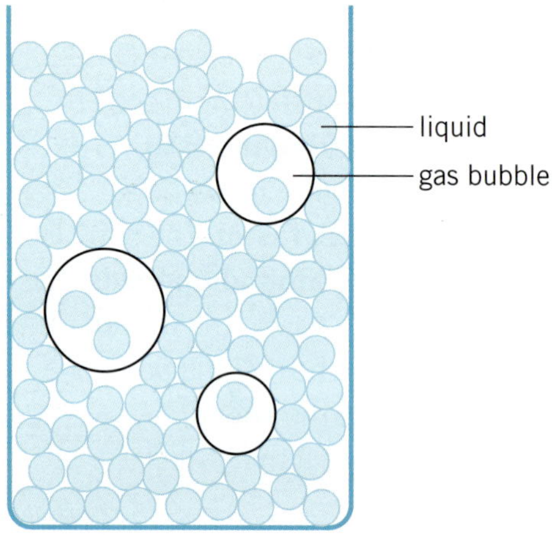

▲ Boiling water.

Fantastic Fact!

The boiling point of a substance depends how high above the Earth's surface you are. At Mount Everest Base Camp (5364 m above sea level), water boils at 82 °C.

Close your eyes. Imagine water boiling. What can you hear? What can you see? When a substance is boiling it is changing from the liquid state to the gas state.

Explaining boiling

When water boils, bubbles of steam form all through the liquid. In the liquid, water particles touch their neighbours. Inside the bubbles, the water particles are spread out.

As water boils, the steam bubbles rise to the surface of the liquid. They escape into the air. The total mass of steam and water is the same as the mass of water at the start. Scientists say that mass is **conserved** in **boiling**.

A Name the substance in the bubbles in boiling water.

What is a boiling point?

Boiling happens if enough energy is transferred to the particles. Different substances need different amounts of energy to boil. This means that different substances boil at different temperatures. The temperature a substance boils at is its **boiling point**.

Measuring boiling point

You can measure the boiling point of a substance like this:

- Pour the liquid into a beaker.
- Heat the liquid, and measure the temperature every minute.
- Plot the results on a graph.

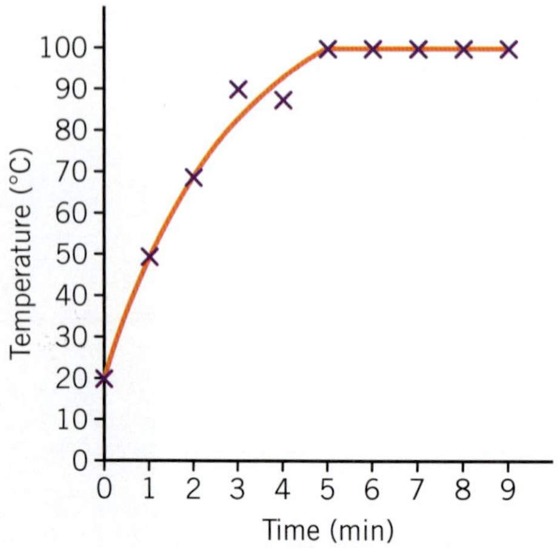

▲ A temperature–time graph for heating water.

A student heated liquid water and plotted the graph shown on the opposite page. At first, the temperature increased. At 100 °C, the water bubbled vigorously. It was boiling. The temperature remained at 100 °C. This is the boiling point of water.

B State what is meant by the term boiling point.

Using boiling points

Identifying substances

You can use data about boiling points to help identify substances. Lucy has a colourless liquid. Her teacher tells her it could be water, ethanol, or propanol. Lucy notes the boiling points of these substances in the table below.

Substance	Boiling point (°C)
water	100
ethanol	78
propanol	97

Lucy heats her liquid on an electric heater. She measures its temperature every minute. At 78 °C the liquid bubbles vigorously. It remains at 78 °C for several minutes. Lucy concludes that the liquid is ethanol.

Predicting states

If you know the melting point and the boiling point of a substance, you can predict its state at different temperatures. The melting and boiling points of silver are shown below.

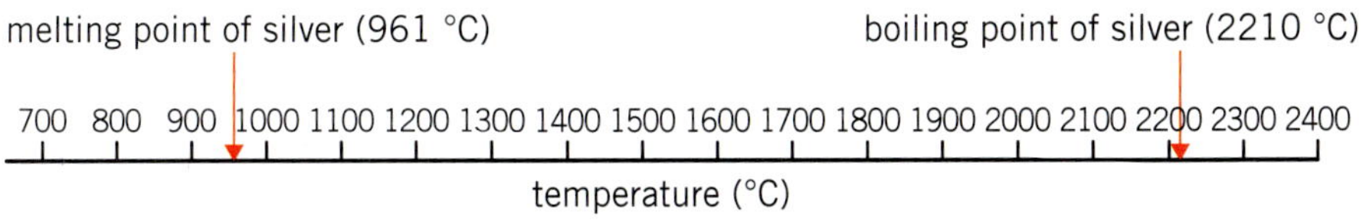

At room temperature (20 °C), silver is in the solid state. At 961 °C, the melting point, silver exists as both a solid and a liquid. Between 961 °C and 2210 °C silver is a liquid. At 2210 °C, the boiling point, silver exists as both a liquid and a gas. Above 2210 °C silver exists in the gas state.

C Predict the state of silver at 1000 °C.

Mystery liquid

Sarah has a liquid. It could be water, ethanol, or propanol. Sarah heats the liquid. It bubbles vigorously at 97 °C. Use data from this page to suggest what the liquid might be.

Key Words

conserve, boiling, boiling point

Summary Questions

1 Copy the sentences below, choosing the correct bold words.

When a substance boils, it changes state from **liquid/gas** to **liquid/gas**. Bubbles form **at the top of/all the way through** the liquid. A certain substance boils at **any/a certain** temperature.

(4 marks)

2 Use the data to predict the state of copper at 2000 °C.

Data for copper:

melting point = 1083 °C

boiling point = 2595 °C

(1 mark)

3 Design a particle model that can explain why different substances boil at different temperatures. Use the data on this page to compare two substances using your particle model. Identify the strengths and weaknesses of your model.

(6 marks)

1.5 More changes of state

Learning objectives

After this topic you will be able to:

- describe changes of state involving gases
- use the particle model to explain evaporation, condensation, and sublimation.

What happens to the water when you use a hairdryer to dry your hair? It changes state from liquid to gas without boiling. This is called evaporation.

Explaining evaporation

In a liquid, some particles have more energy than others. The particles with most energy leave the liquid surface. Then they move away from the liquid. The particles spread out, forming a gas. They mix with air particles. This is **evaporation**.

A substance can change from the liquid to the gas state by evaporating or boiling. The table below shows some differences between these two processes.

Process	How particles leave the liquid	Temperature	Does the mass change?
evaporation	Particles escape from the liquid surface.	happens at any temperature	no
boiling	Bubbles of the substance in the gas state form throughout the liquid. They rise to the surface and escape.	happens only at the boiling point	no

A State two differences between evaporation and boiling.

Key Words

evaporation, condensation, sublimation

How is evaporation useful?

Why do you sweat? Sweating cools you down by evaporation. Sweat comes out of pores in your skin. Water from the sweat evaporates. The water particles need energy to move away as a gas. They take this energy from your skin. This cools you down.

◀ Sweat helps to cool you down by evaporation.

Evaluating evaporation

Eva is investigating evaporation. She puts a small, damp tissue in a cold place. She puts a big, wet towel above a heater. The tissue dries first. Eva concludes that cold conditions speed up evaporation. Evaluate Eva's investigation: How could she improve it? Does the evidence support the conclusion?

Why is it quicker to dry your hair with a hairdryer? The hairdryer speeds up evaporation in two ways. It transfers energy to help particles leave the liquid surface. It also moves just-evaporated water particles away from your hair.

B Identify two ways that a hairdryer speeds up evaporation.

▲ Stage smoke comes from solid carbon dioxide. The solid is also known as dry ice.

What is condensation?

Is the inside of your bedroom window ever wet after a cold night? At bedtime, water particles were mixed with air particles. They were spread out, as a gas. During the night, water particles hit the cold glass of the window. They moved closer to other water particles, until they were touching. This formed liquid water. The change of state from gas to liquid is called **condensation**. It can happen at any temperature below the boiling point.

C Identify the state formed when a substance condenses.

What is sublimation?

Where does stage smoke come from? It comes from solid carbon dioxide. Carbon dioxide is solid at temperatures below –78.5 °C. At this temperature and above, solid carbon dioxide changes state to become a gas. It does not normally exist as a liquid. The change of state from solid to gas is called **sublimation**.

At first, the carbon dioxide gas is very cold. Water particles condense around carbon dioxide particles. Tiny drops of liquid water form. It is this liquid water that makes stage smoke.

Solid grey iodine sublimes to form purple iodine gas. ▶

D Name the change of state that occurs when a substance in the solid state changes into a gas.

Summary Questions

1 Write **five** correct sentences from the sentence starters and enders below.

Sentence starters

In boiling...
In condensing...
In evaporating...

Sentence enders

...particles leave from the surface of the liquid.
...substances change from the liquid to the gas state.
...particles leave from all parts of the liquid.
...substances change from the gas to the liquid state.

(5 marks)

2 Describe the changes in behaviour of the particles when a substance condenses.

(2 marks)

3 Compare the processes of evaporation, boiling, and condensation.

(6 marks)

1.6 Diffusion

Learning objectives

After this topic you will be able to:

- use the particle model to explain diffusion
- describe evidence for diffusion.

▲ Coloured ink particles diffuse through water. There is no need to stir.

Do you wear perfume or deodorant? How does the smell reach your nose?

Perfume particles evaporate from your skin. The particles move around randomly. They mix with the air. As the perfume particles spread out, some enter your nose. Your nose detects the smell. The random moving and mixing of particles is called **diffusion**.

Why do substances diffuse?

Particles diffuse because they are moving. Perfume particles move randomly in the air, even if the air seems completely still. Ink particles spread through water by themselves. You do not need to shake or stir.

A State what is meant by diffusion.

What factors affect diffusion speed?

Diffusion does not always happen at the same speed. Three factors affect the speed of diffusion:

- temperature
- particle size
- the state of the diffusing substance.

Temperature

At higher temperatures, particles are moving more quickly. Perfume particles leaving warm skin travel faster than perfume particles leaving a cold bottle.

B Explain why particles diffuse more quickly at higher temperatures.

Fantastic Fact!

At room temperature, particles in liquid water move at an average speed of 1600 km/h (444 m/s).

Key Words

diffusion

Link

You can learn more about diffusion in B1 1.4 Movement of substances

Particle size

A teacher sets up the apparatus below to demonstrate diffusion.

Hydrogen chloride particles evaporate from the piece of cotton wool at the left side of the test tube. Ammonia particles evaporate from the piece of cotton wool at the right. The particles diffuse along the tube. The two types of particle meet, and form a ring of white solid. The solid is closer to the hydrogen chloride end. This shows that the hydrogen chloride particles diffuse more slowly. Hydrogen chloride particles are bigger and heavier than ammonia particles. Big, heavy particles diffuse more slowly than small, light ones.

State

Diffusion happens quickly in gases. This is because the particles are far apart. A particle in a gas travels a long way before hitting another particle.

In the liquid state, particles are closer than in the gas state. This is why diffusion is slower in liquids.

Diffusion does not happen in solids. The particles cannot move from place to place.

Fair's fair

Raj investigates how temperature affects diffusion speed. He puts purple crystals into five test tubes. He adds water of a different temperature to each test tube. He watches the purple colour spread through the water. Identify the variables Raj should change, measure, and control to make it a fair test.

▲ Particles of potassium manganate(VII) diffuse through the water.

Summary Questions

1. Copy and complete the sentences below.

   When food cooks, you can smell it because some ______ leave the food. The particles move ______ and mix with the ______. This is called ______. Particles diffuse because ______ is transferred. The higher the temperature, the ______ the diffusion.

   (6 marks)

2. Describe **three** pieces of evidence for diffusion.

   (3 marks)

3. The air contains particles of argon, nitrogen, and other substances. Use the data below to predict which type of particle diffuses faster. Give a reason for your choice.

   Relative masses of particles: nitrogen = 28 and argon = 40

   (2 marks)

4. Explain in detail the different diffusion speeds through substances in the solid, liquid, and gas states.

   (6 marks)

1.7 Gas pressure

Learning objectives

After this topic you will be able to:

- use the particle model to explain gas pressure
- describe the factors that affect gas pressure.

Fantastic Fact!

Racing-car tyres reach 100 °C. Before a race, technicians pump tyres to a lower pressure than they need in the race. The air pressure in the tyre increases as it heats up.

▲ The air pressure in racing-car tyres increases during a race.

Particle performance

Read the Fantastic Fact before you do this task.

Racing-car tyres are pumped full of air. Write a script for particles in a racing-car tyre. What do they say as the car goes faster and the air gets hotter? Then perform your script.

Why do balloons get bigger as you blow them up? When you blow up a balloon, you are filling it with air particles. The more air particles you add, the bigger the balloon.

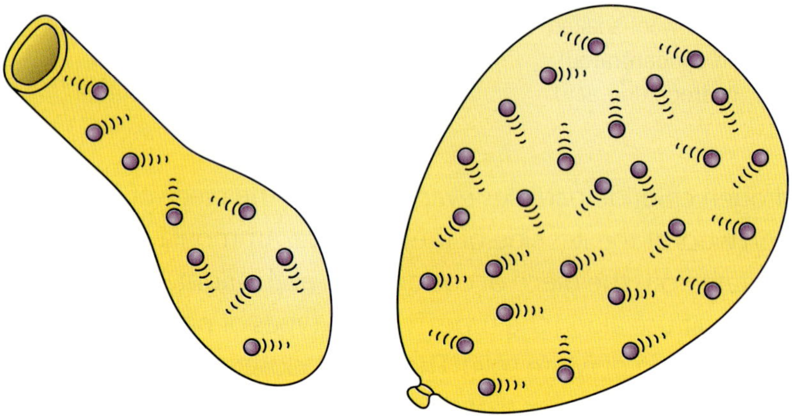

▲ The more particles you blow into a balloon, the bigger the balloon.

Inside the balloon, the air particles move quickly from place to place. They bump into, or collide with, each other. They also **collide** with the rubber the balloon is made from. The collisions exert a force on the rubber. The force per unit area (every square metre) is the **gas pressure**.

Gas particles always exert pressure on the walls of their container, whatever the container is made from.

A State what is meant by gas pressure.

How does the number of particles affect pressure?

Rubber is stretchy. So when you blow more particles into a balloon, the balloon expands.

But some containers cannot expand. Adding more particles causes more frequent collisions with the walls. The pressure inside the container increases.

B Explain why adding more air increases the pressure inside a container.

How does temperature affect pressure?

Hotter and hotter

Balloons sometimes burst on hot days. Why does this happen?

As the air in a balloon gets warmer, more energy is transferred to the particles. The particles move faster. They collide with the rubber more often. The pressure inside the balloon increases.

The higher the temperature, the higher the air pressure. At first the rubber stretches. As the temperature gets even higher, the rubber cannot withstand the greater pressure. Eventually, it cannot stretch any further and the balloon bursts.

Cooling down

Imagine a plastic bottle of air in a freezer. The particles transfer energy to the freezer, and the air cools down. The particles move more slowly. They collide with the plastic less often. The pressure in the bottle decreases. The particles outside exert a higher pressure than the particles inside. The bottle collapses.

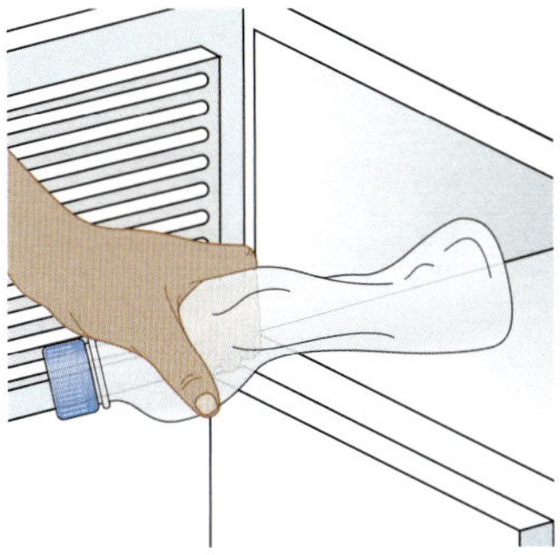

◀ In the freezer, the air pressure inside the bottle decreases.

Now imagine taking the bottle out of the freezer. The air inside the bottle warms up. Soon, the air particles inside and outside the bottle exert the same pressure. The bottle returns to its normal shape.

C Explain why a bottle collapses in the freezer.

Key Words

collide, gas pressure

Summary Questions

1 Copy the true sentences below. Write corrected versions of the false sentences.

Gas particles collide with the walls of their container.

Colliding gas particles exert pressure on the inside of the container.

The more particles in a container, the lower the pressure.

The higher the temperature, the lower the pressure.

(4 marks)

2 Jack was camping. He put a can of baked beans on his camp fire, without opening the lid. The can exploded. Use ideas about particles to explain why.

(3 marks)

3 Plan a talk that you could give to another class to explain what happens to an inflated balloon when you put it in a warm room and when you put it in a fridge.

(6 marks)

C1 Chapter 1 Summary

Key Points

- Materials are made up of tiny particles.
- A substance is made up of just one type of material.
- The properties of a substance describe what it looks like and how it behaves.
- The properties of a substance depend on what its particles are like, and how they are arranged.
- There are three states of matter – solid, liquid, and gas. For a certain substance, the particles never change. But in different states, the particles move differently, and have different arrangements.
- In the solid state, you cannot compress a substance, or make it flow.
- In the liquid state, you cannot compress a substance, but you can make it flow.
- In the gas state, you can compress a substance, and make it flow.
- The change of state from solid to liquid is melting. A substance melts at its melting point. Pure substances have sharp melting points.
- A substance changes from the liquid to the gas state by evaporating or boiling. A substance boils at its boiling point.
- The change of state from gas to liquid is condensing.
- The change of state from liquid to solid is freezing.
- Some substances change directly from the solid state to the gas state. This is subliming.
- Diffusion is the random moving and mixing of particles.
- Gas particles collide with the walls of their container. The collisions cause gas pressure.

Maths Challenge

Up in the air

The air is a mixture of substances. The table shows the percentages of the substances in the air.

Substance	Percentage of substance in dry air
nitrogen	78.08
oxygen	20.95
argon	0.93
others, including carbon dioxide	0.04

Task

Draw a graph or chart to represent the data in the table. Decide which type of chart is best, and explain why.

Key Words

material, particle, mixture, substance, property, solid, liquid, gas, states of matter, melting, change of state, freezing, melting point, boiling, boiling point, conserve, evaporation, condensation, sublimation, diffusion, collide, gas pressure

End-of-chapter questions

1 The diagram shows some particles in solid gold. Draw another diagram to show particles of gold in the gas state.

(**2 marks**)

2 Describe the arrangement and movement of particles in the liquid state.

(**2 marks**)

3 The table shows the melting points and boiling points of six substances.

Substance	Melting point (°C)	Boiling point (°C)
bromine	–7	59
krypton	–157	–152
mercury	–39	357
neon	–249	–246
platinum	1769	4530
silver	961	2210

a Write down the name of the substance with the highest boiling point.

(1 mark)

b Write down the names of the substances in order of increasing melting point, starting with the lowest.

(5 marks)

c Name **one** substance in the table that is in the gas state at 20 °C.

(1 mark)

d Name **two** substances in the table that are in the liquid state at 20 °C

(2 marks)

e Name **one** substance in the table that is in the liquid state at 100 °C.

(1 mark)

(**10 marks**)

4 Read the statements about particles in a substance in the solid state.

A The particles touch other particles.

B The particles are in a pattern.

C The particles do not move around from place to place.

D The particles vibrate.

a Write down the letter of the statement that best explains why you cannot pour a solid.

(1 mark)

b Choose one of the other statements and explain why it does not explain why you cannot pour a solid.

(1 mark)

(**2 marks**)

5 Olivia says that gas pressure is the result of particles colliding with each other. Is Olivia correct? Explain your answer.

(**2 marks**)

6 Compare the processes of boiling and evaporating.

(**6 marks**)

2.1 Elements

Learning objectives

After this topic you will be able to:

- state what an element is
- recall the chemical symbols of six elements.

Fantastic Fact!

You are made up of elements. A 50 kg person is 32.5 kg oxygen, 9 kg carbon, 5 kg hydrogen, 1.5 kg nitrogen, 0.5 kg phosphorus, and 1.5 kg other elements.

Look at the pictures. What do the objects have in common?

▲ Jewellery.

▲ A catalytic converter. This changes harmful car exhaust gases into less harmful ones.

▲ A hard disk. This stores data on a computer.

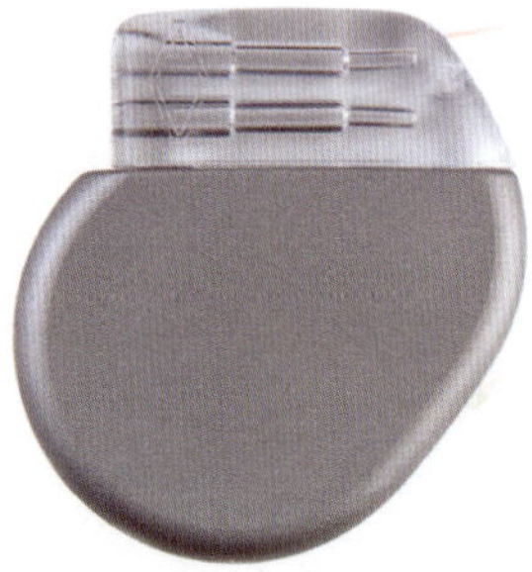

▲ A heart pacemaker. This helps the heart to beat regularly.

All of these objects contain platinum. Platinum is a shiny substance. It is not damaged by air or water. It is easy to make platinum into different shapes.

Platinum is an example of an **element**. An element is a substance that cannot be broken down into other substances. You've probably heard of some elements: gold, silver, oxygen, chlorine, and helium are all examples of elements.

A State what an element is.

Platinum propaganda

Platinum is useful. But it is very rare. It is also expensive. In March 2013, 1 g of platinum cost £33. Write the text for a leaflet to persuade car scrapyard owners to recycle platinum used in car exhausts.

How many elements?

There are millions of materials. They are all made up of one or more elements. There are 92 elements that exist naturally. Scientists have made a few more.

The **Periodic Table** lists the elements. In the Periodic Table, elements with similar properties are grouped together.

Group

Key: relative atomic mass / chemical symbol / name / atomic (proton) number

1.0 H hydrogen 1

1	2											3	4	5	6	7	8
																	4 He helium 2
7 Li lithium 3	9 Be beryllium 4											11 B boron 5	12 C carbon 6	14 N nitrogen 7	16 O oxygen 8	19 F fluorine 9	20 Ne neon 10
23 Na sodium 11	24 Mg magnesium 12											27 Al aluminium 13	28 Si silicon 14	31 P phosphorus 15	32 S sulfur 16	35.5 Cl chlorine 17	40 Ar argon 18
39 K potassium 19	40 Ca calcium 20	45 Sc scandium 21	48 Ti titanium 22	51 V vanadium 23	52 Cr chromium 24	55 Mn manganese 25	56 Fe iron 26	59 Co cobalt 27	59 Ni nickel 28	63.5 Cu copper 29	65 Zn zinc 30	70 Ga gallium 31	73 Ge germanium 32	75 As arsenic 33	79 Se selenium 34	80 Br bromine 35	84 Kr krypton 36
85.5 Rb rubidium 37	88 Sr strontium 38	89 Y yttrium 39	91 Zr zirconium 40	93 Nb niobium 41	96 Mo molybdenum 42	(98) Tc technetium 43	101 Ru ruthenium 44	103 Rh rhodium 45	106 Pd palladium 46	108 Ag silver 47	112 Cd cadmium 48	115 In indium 49	119 Sn tin 50	122 Sb antimony 51	128 Te tellurium 52	127 I iodine 53	131 Xe xenon 54
133 Cs caesium 55	137 Ba barium 56	139 La lanthanum 57	178.5 Hf hafnium 72	181 Ta tantalum 73	184 W tungsten 74	186 Re rhenium 75	190 Os osmium 76	192 Ir iridium 77	195 Pt platinum 78	197 Au gold 79	201 Hg mercury 80	204 Tl thallium 81	207 Pb lead 82	209 Bi bismuth 83	210 Po polonium 84	(210) At astatine 85	222 Rn radon 86
(223) Fr francium 87	(226) Ra radium 88	(227) Ac actinium 89	(261) Rf rutherfordium 104	(262) Db dubnium 105	(266) Sg seaborgium 106	(264) Bh bohrium 107	(277) Hs hassium 108	(268) Mt meitnerium 109	(271) Ds darmstadtium 110	(272) Rg roentgenium 111	Elements with atomic numbers 112–116 have been reported but not fully authenticated						

140 Ce cerium 58	141 Pr praseodymium 59	144 Nd neodymium 60	(145) Pm promethium 61	150 Sm samarium 62	152 Eu europium 63	157 Gd gadolinium 64	159 Tb terbium 65	163 Dy dysprosium 66	165 Ho holmium 67	167 Er erbium 68	169 Tm thulium 69	173 Yb ytterbium 70	175 Lu lutetium 71
232 Th thorium 90	231 Pa protactinium 91	238 U uranium 92	237 Np neptunium 93	239 Pu plutonium 94	243 Am americium 95	247 Cm curium 96	247 Bk berkelium 97	252 Cf californium 98	(252) Es einsteinium 99	(257) Fm fermium 100	(258) Md mendelevium 101	(259) No nobelium 102	(260) Lr lawrencium 103

▲ The Periodic Table lists the elements.

B State what the Periodic Table is.

What are chemical symbols?

Every element has its own **chemical symbol**. This is a one- or two-letter code for the element. Scientists all over the world use the same chemical symbols.

The table shows some chemical symbols.

Name of element	Chemical symbol
carbon	C
nitrogen	N
nickel	Ni
chlorine	Cl
gold	Au
iron	Fe
tungsten	W

For some elements, the chemical symbol is the first letter of its English name. For others, the chemical symbol is the first and second, or first and third, letters of its name. The chemical symbols of some elements come from their Latin names, for example, *aurum* for gold and *ferrum* for iron. The chemical symbol of tungsten comes from its German name, *Wolfram*.

C Write down the chemical symbols of the elements carbon, chlorine, gold, and iron.

Key Words

element, Periodic Table, chemical symbol

Link

You can learn more about the Periodic Table in C2 1.2 Groups and periods

When you write a chemical symbol, make sure the first letter is a capital letter. The second letter is lowercase.

Summary Questions

1 Write down the names of **10** elements.

(10 marks)

2 Use the Periodic Table to write the names and chemical symbols of six elements whose names begin with the letter C.

(6 marks)

3 Write a paragraph describing some uses of platinum. Choose two of these uses, and explain why the properties of platinum make it suitable for these two uses.

(6 marks)

2.2 Atoms

Learning objectives

After this topic you will be able to:

- state what atoms are
- compare the properties of one atom of an element to the properties of many atoms.

Look at the picture below. What do you think it shows?

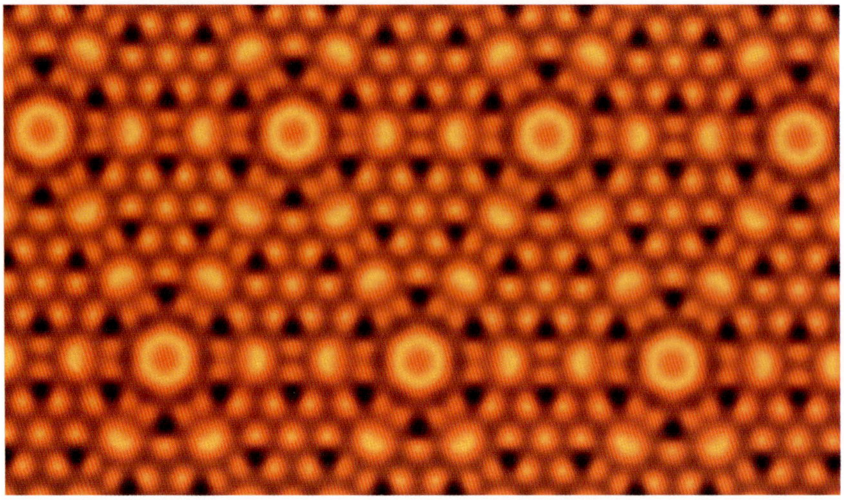

The picture shows the surface of a silicon crystal. Silicon is an element. Every computer, calculator, and mobile phone has silicon crystals inside. The crystals are called silicon chips. They contain millions of tiny electronic parts. These make the computers, calculators, and phones work.

▲ A silicon chip. This photograph was taken with a normal camera.

Atoms

The picture shows atoms of silicon. An **atom** is the smallest part of an element that can exist.

The picture above was not taken with a normal camera. It was taken with a special type of microscope that can detect things as small as an atom.

A State what an atom is.

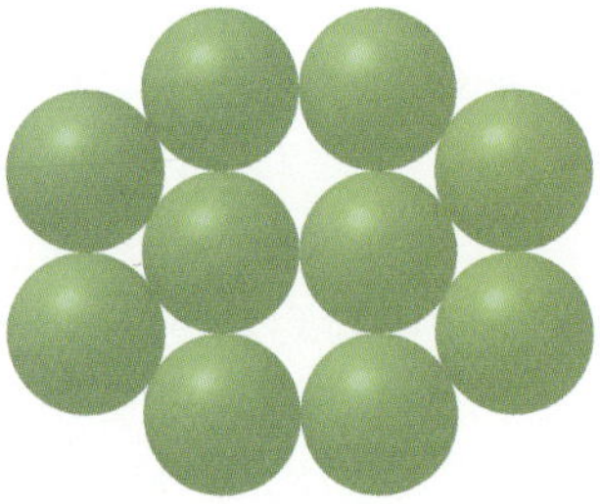

▲ This diagram shows silicon atoms in solid silicon.

How many types of atom are there?

Every element is made up of one type of atom. All the atoms of an element are the same as each other. The atoms of one element are different to the atoms of all other elements. There are 92 elements that exist naturally, so there are 92 types of atom.

All silicon atoms are the same. But silicon atoms are different to gold atoms. For example, gold atoms are bigger.

Gold atoms are heavier than silicon atoms. This explains the data in the table on the next page.

Key Words

atom

Element	Mass of 1 cm^3 of the element (g)
gold	19.3
silicon	2.33

B Describe two differences between gold and silicon atoms.

▲ This diagram shows gold atoms in solid gold.

Just one atom?

One atom on its own does not have the properties of the element. A gold atom is not yellow. It is not shiny. It is not in the solid, liquid, or gas state.

◀ The atoms in this piece of gold are all the same.

The properties of an element are the properties of very many atoms joined together. The piece of gold in the picture has a mass of 1000 g. It is made up of about 3 000 000 000 000 000 000 000 000 atoms. Together, these atoms make the gold yellow and shiny.

The atoms are touching each other in rows. They vibrate on the spot. The gold in the picture is in the solid state. If you heat gold to 1063 °C its atoms start moving around. The gold is melting. One atom of gold cannot melt. Only a group of many atoms can melt.

Going for gold?

A gold ring has a mass of 10 g. Choose data from the paragraphs above to estimate the number of atoms in the ring.

Fantastic Fact!

The 2012 Olympic gold medals are only 1% gold by mass. There are 170 times more silver atoms than gold atoms in a gold medal.

Summary Questions

1 Copy and complete the sentences below.

The smallest part of an element that can exist is called an __________. All the atoms of an element are the __________. The atoms of one element are __________ to the atoms of all other elements.

(3 marks)

2 An Olympic bronze medal is made up of three elements – copper, zinc, and tin. State the number of types of atom in the medal. Explain your answer.

(2 marks)

3 Create and illustrate a visual summary to summarise and organise the information on this spread.

(6 marks)

2.3 Compounds

Learning objectives

After this topic you will be able to:

- state what a compound is
- explain why a compound has different properties to the elements in it.

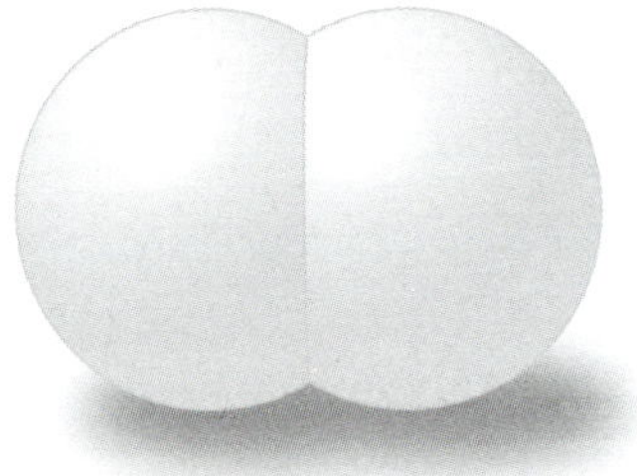

▲ A hydrogen molecule consists of two hydrogen atoms.

▲ An oxygen molecule consists of two oxygen atoms.

▲ A water molecule has one oxygen atom joined to two hydrogen atoms.

Key Words

compound, molecule

How much water have you used today?

Water is vital for survival. But what is water? Water is made up of atoms of two elements, hydrogen and oxygen. This means that water is a **compound**. A compound is a substance made up of atoms of two or more elements. The atoms are strongly joined together.

The properties of a compound are different to the properties of the elements it is made up of.

A State what a compound is.

Why is water different to its elements?

Hydrogen is a gas at room temperature. Mixed with air, and ignited with a spark, it explodes. Hydrogen atoms go round in pairs. These are **molecules** of hydrogen. A molecule is a group of two or more atoms strongly joined together.

Oxygen is a gas at room temperature. You cannot see or smell it. Oxygen exists as molecules. Each molecule is made up of two oxygen atoms. In the air, oxygen molecules mix with atoms and molecules of other substances.

Water exists as molecules. The molecules are made up of atoms of two elements. This means that water is a compound.

Water molecules are different to hydrogen molecules and oxygen molecules. This is why water has different properties to hydrogen and oxygen. For example, water has a higher boiling point than hydrogen.

Weak forces hold molecules close to each other in liquid hydrogen. Stronger forces hold molecules close together in liquid water. It takes more energy to separate water molecules from each other than to separate hydrogen molecules from each other. Water has a higher boiling point than hydrogen.

B State which has a higher boiling point, water or hydrogen.

What is salt?

Do you add salt to your food? Salt is a compound. Its scientific name is sodium chloride. It contains atoms of two elements, sodium and chlorine.

- Sodium is a shiny metal. It fizzes in water.
- Chlorine is a smelly green poisonous gas.

So why doesn't salt smell? Or poison you? Or fizz in your mouth?

In salt, the atoms of sodium and chlorine are not just mixed up. They are joined together to make one substance – sodium chloride. This compound has different properties to the elements in it.

C Describe one difference in properties between sodium chloride and sodium.

Fantastic Fact!

Tooth enamel is a compound of calcium (a shiny metal that fizzes in water), phosphorus (a poisonous solid that catches fire easily), and oxygen (a gas that helps things burn).

Link

You can learn more about boiling points in C1 1.4 Boiling

Organising ideas

Make a table showing properties of sodium, chlorine, and sodium chloride. Use the table to help you plan and then write some paragraphs comparing the properties of the three substances.

Summary Questions

1 Copy the sentences below, choosing the correct bold words.

A compound is a substance made up of atoms of **one/two** or more elements. The properties of a compound are **the same as/ different to** the properties of its elements. A molecule is a group of **two/three** or more atoms **weakly/ strongly** joined together.

(4 marks)

2 Suggest an explanation for this boiling-point data:
oxygen = -183 °C; water = 100 °C

(3 marks)

3 Write a paragraph to compare the properties of hydrogen, oxygen, and water.

(6 marks)

2.4 Chemical formulae

Learning objectives

After this topic you will be able to:

- write the chemical names for some simple compounds
- write and interpret chemical formulae.

Link

You can learn more about the property differences between compounds and elements in C1 2.3 Compounds

Are the windows closed? If so, there is probably more carbon dioxide in the room now than there was 10 minutes ago. Every cell in your body makes carbon dioxide. You breathe it out. Carbon dioxide is a compound. It is made up of two elements – carbon and oxygen.

Carbon monoxide is another compound. It also consists of atoms of carbon and oxygen. But carbon monoxide is poisonous. It can be deadly if you breathe it in.

Why are carbon compounds different?

You already know that the properties of a compound depend on the elements in it. The numbers of atoms of each element also make a difference.

A carbon dioxide molecule has one carbon atom and two oxygen atoms.

A carbon monoxide molecule has one carbon atom and one oxygen atom.

Carbon dioxide always has 12 g of carbon for every 32 g of oxygen. The amounts of carbon and oxygen in carbon monoxide are different. Carbon monoxide has 12 g of carbon for every 16 g of oxygen.

A State the number and types of atoms that make up one carbon dioxide molecule.

What's water?

Water contains 2 g of hydrogen for every 16 g of oxygen. Nitrogen dioxide contains 14 g of nitrogen for every 32 g of oxygen. Which compound has the higher proportion of oxygen? Show your working.

How do we name compounds?

Compounds made up of oxygen and another element have two-word names. The second word is *oxide*.

Elements in compound	Name of compound
aluminium and oxygen	aluminium oxide
zinc and oxygen	zinc oxide

Some elements form more than one type of oxide.

Molecule of compound made up of…	Name of compound
1 carbon atom and 1 oxygen atom	carbon **mon**oxide
1 carbon atom and 2 oxygen atoms	carbon **di**oxide

The compound of sodium and chlorine is called sodium chloride. Chlori***n***e becomes chlori***d***e.

B Name the compound of sodium and chlorine.

What is a chemical formula?

A **chemical formula** shows the relative number of atoms of each element in a compound – 'relative number' means how many of one type of atom there are compared to another. For example:

- The chemical formula of carbon dioxide is CO_2. This shows that there is one carbon atom for every two oxygen atoms.
- The chemical formula of carbon monoxide is CO. This shows that there is one carbon atom for every oxygen atom.

When you are writing chemical formulae, the numbers should be:

- to the right of their chemical symbol, just below the line
- smaller than the chemical symbols.

Key Words

chemical formula

Summary Questions

1 Copy and complete the sentences below.

The formula of carbon dioxide is __________. This shows that a molecule of carbon dioxide is made up of __________ carbon atom and __________ atoms of __________. The relative masses of carbon and oxygen in carbon dioxide are __________.

(5 marks)

2 The chemical formula of water is H_2O. State the number of atoms of each element in a water molecule.

(2 marks)

3 Draw and label diagrams to show how you could make models of the molecules on this spread. If possible, make the models.

(6 marks)

C1 Chapter 2 Summary

Key Points

- All materials are made up of one or more elements.
- Elements are substances that cannot be broken down.
- There are 92 elements that exist naturally.
- The Periodic Table lists all the elements.
- Every element has its own chemical symbol.
- An atom is the smallest part of an element that can exist.
- Every element is made up of one type of atom. All the atoms of an element are the same.
- The atoms of one element are different to the atoms of all other elements.
- The properties of a substance are the properties of many atoms, not just a single atom.
- A compound is a substance made up of atoms of two or more elements, strongly joined together.
- The properties of a compound are different to the properties of the elements that it is made from.
- A molecule is a group of two or more atoms that are strongly joined together.
- A chemical formula shows the relative number of atoms of each element in a compound.

BIG Write

Science web

You work for a company that makes on-line revision resources for school students. Your boss wants you to write some new webpages for Key Stage 3 science.

Task

Write the text for the revision pages about elements, atoms, compounds, and chemical formulae.

Tips

- Before you start writing, decide what to include on each web page. Work out how many pages you will need. Do not try to include too much information on a page.
- Include diagrams and examples to help students understand the text.
- Highlight key words and explain their meanings.

Key Words

element, Periodic Table, chemical symbol, atom, compound, molecule, chemical formula

End-of-chapter questions

1 Carbon dioxide is a compound made up of two elements.

a State what is meant by the word element. *(1 mark)*

b State the number of types of atom in the element carbon. *(1 mark)*

c One of the elements in carbon dioxide is carbon. Name the other element. *(1 mark)*

d State the number of types of atom in carbon dioxide. *(1 mark)*

e Copy and complete the sentences below. The formula of carbon dioxide is CO_2. There is __________ atom of carbon for every two atoms of __________. *(2 marks)*

(6 marks)

2 The diagram below shows a molecule of sulfur dioxide. Each sphere represents one atom. Different-coloured spheres represent atoms of different elements.

a State the total number of atoms in the molecule. *(1 mark)*

b State the number of different types of atom in the molecule. *(1 mark)*

c State whether sulfur dioxide is an element or a compound. Explain your decision. *(2 marks)*

d Copy and complete the table below. *(2 marks)*

Name of element	Number of atoms of this element in one sulfur dioxide molecule
sulfur	
	2

e Write the formula of sulfur dioxide. *(2 marks)*

(8 marks)

3 Describe **two** differences between elements and compounds.

(2 marks)

4 The table below shows data for six elements. The diagram shows their positions in the Periodic Table.

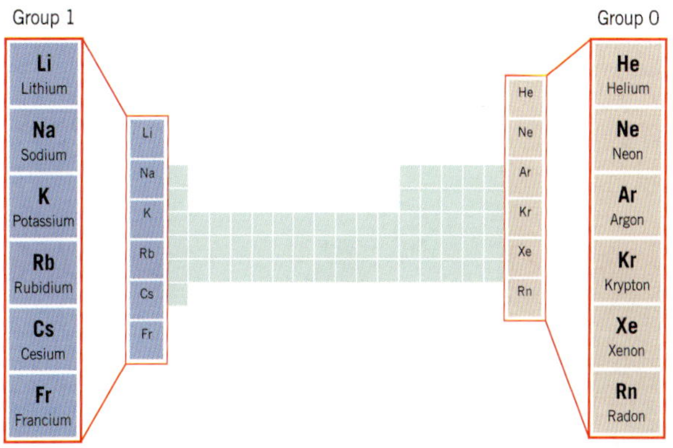

Name of element	Chemical symbol	Melting point (°C)
lithium	Li	180
sodium	Na	98
potassium	K	64
neon	Ne	–249
argon	Ar	–189
krypton	Kr	–157

Compare the melting point patterns for the Group 1 and Group 0 elements.

(6 marks)

3.1 Chemical reactions

Learning objectives

After this topic you will be able to:

- describe what happens to atoms in chemical reactions
- explain why chemical reactions are useful
- compare chemical reactions to physical changes.

▲ Chemical reactions mean you can fry an egg.

Reaction, reaction, reaction

'Chemical reactions?' says Rick. 'They're all bangs and bad smells.' Is he right? Read over the examples from this page to help you decide. Make a visual summary to help you organise your ideas, and then write down what you plan to say to Rick.

Key Words

chemical reaction, reversible, catalyst, physical change

What did you have for breakfast today?

Chemical reactions make food and drink. Chemical reactions in cows produce milk from grass. Chemical reactions in plants produce maize, for cornflakes. Chemical reactions convert raw egg to fried egg. Burning gas for cooking is another chemical reaction.

What are chemical reactions?

A **chemical reaction** is a change in which atoms are rearranged to create new substances. The atoms are joined together in one way before the reaction and in a different way after the reaction.

All chemical reactions:

- make new substances.
- transfer energy to or from the surroundings.

Most chemical reactions are not easily **reversible**. At the end of the reaction it is very difficult to get back the substances you started with.

A State what happens to the atoms in a chemical reaction.

How do you know if it's a chemical reaction?

You do an experiment in the lab. How do you know if it involved chemical reactions? There are many clues to look out for. You might:

- see huge flames … or tiny sparks

- notice a sweet smell … or a foul stink

- feel the chemicals getting hotter … or colder

- hear a loud bang … or gentle fizzing.

B State three pieces of evidence that may suggest that a chemical reaction is happening.

Why are chemical reactions useful?

Chemical reactions are very useful. They make many useful substances. These include:

- medicines, such as paracetamol
- fabrics, such as polyester
- building materials, such as cement.

Chemical reactions also transfer energy. This transfer can be useful. Burning petrol makes vehicles go. Burning coal heats water to produce steam to generate electricity.

Some chemical reactions are not useful. Rusting is a chemical reaction. It may damage cars, boats, and bridges. Chemical reactions make food rot.

C State three examples of useful products made in chemical reactions.

Are all chemical reactions fast?

Some reactions happen quickly. Others are much slower. Chemists use **catalysts** to speed up slow reactions if they want to make a product more quickly. Different reactions need different catalysts. A catalyst is not used up in a reaction.

Are all changes chemical reactions?

Not all changes involve chemical reactions. If you warm chocolate, it melts. But you still have chocolate. Changes of state, and dissolving, are reversible. This means you can get back what you started with. This is called a **physical change**.

D Give examples of two types of physical change.

▲ This car burns methane gas instead of petrol. Chemical reactions make methane from human waste at a sewage works.

Summary Questions

1 Copy the sentences below, choosing the correct bold words.

Chemical reactions involve re-arranging **atoms/states**. Chemical reactions **always/sometimes** make new substances. They **are/are not** easily reversible. They **always/never** involve energy transfers. Physical changes include changes of **substance/state**. They **are/are not** reversible.

(6 marks)

2 State which of the changes listed below are chemical changes, and which are physical changes.

a burning diesel to make carbon dioxide and water *(1 mark)*

b dissolving sugar in tea to make it taste sweet *(1 mark)*

c boiling water to make steam *(1 mark)*

d baking raw cake to make cooked cake *(1 mark)*

3 Compare chemical changes with physical changes. Include examples to illustrate your answer.

(6 marks)

3.2 Word equations

Learning objectives

After this topic you will be able to:

- identify reactants and products in word equations
- write word equations to represent chemical reactions.

▲ Charcoal is a form of carbon. It reacts with oxygen from the air to make carbon dioxide.

Risky reaction

Many reactions have **hazards**. A hazard is a possible source of danger. You must control the **risks** from hazards. Risk is the chance of damage or injury from a hazard. Burning magnesium has two hazards:

- The bright flame could be harmful to eyesight.
- The flame is difficult to put out.

Suggest how to control the risks from these hazards.

Do you like barbeques? What happens when charcoal burns?

Charcoal is a form of carbon. In the burning reaction, carbon reacts with oxygen from the air. The reaction makes a new substance, carbon dioxide. It forms as an invisible gas. In this reaction, two elements join together to make a compound.

A Name the two elements that react to make carbon dioxide.

Representing reactions

Many other pairs of elements join together in chemical reactions. You can mix iron filings and sulfur powder. They do not react. But if you heat them, the mixture glows red. A chemical reaction happens, and a new substance forms. The new substance looks different to the substances you started with. It has different properties. The new substance is iron sulfide.

▲ A mixture of iron and sulfur has different properties to iron sulfide.

In chemical reactions, the starting substances are called **reactants**. The substances made in the reaction are called **products**. In the reaction of iron with sulfur, the reactants are iron and sulfur. There is one product – iron sulfide.

B Name the reactants and products in the reaction of carbon with oxygen to make carbon dioxide.

Key Words

reactant, product, word equation, hazard, risk

Word equations represent reactions in a simple way.

A word equation shows:

- reactants on the left
- products on the right.

The arrow means *reacts to make*. It is different to an equals sign (=) in a maths equation.

The word equation for the reaction of iron and sulfur is:

iron + sulfur → iron sulphide

C Write a word equation for the reaction of iron and sulfur to make iron sulfide.

Re-arranging atoms

Magnesium burns in air. It reacts with oxygen. The product is magnesium oxide.

magnesium + oxygen → magnesium oxide

In this reaction there are many signs that a chemical reaction is taking place. There is a bright white flame, transferring energy to the surroundings.

The reactants and products look different.

- reactants – shiny magnesium and invisible oxygen gas
- product – white magnesium oxide powder

In every chemical reaction, the atoms get re-arranged. The diagrams show how the atoms are arranged in magnesium, oxygen, and magnesium oxide.

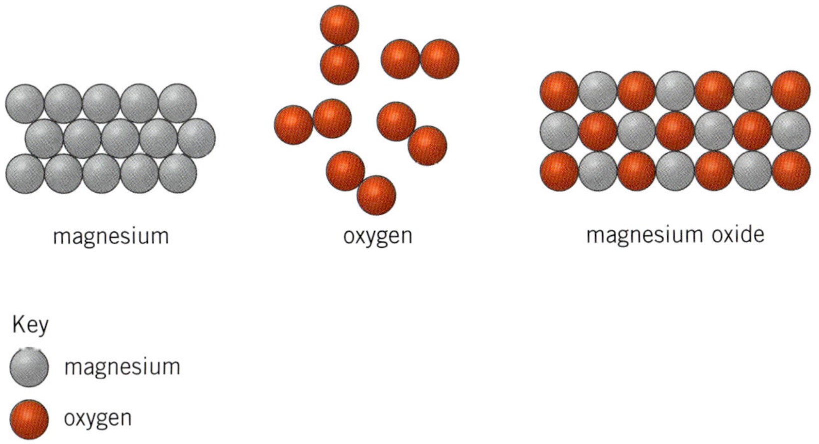

Summary Questions

1 Match the sentence starters and endings.

Sentence starters

Reactants are...

Products are...

Hazards are...

Risks are...

Sentence endings

...possible sources of danger.

...the chances of damage or injury from hazards.

...the starting substances in chemical reactions.

...the substances made in chemical reactions.

(4 marks)

2 Name the reactants and products in each reaction below.

a aluminium + iodine → aluminium iodide *(2 marks)*

b sodium + chlorine → sodium chloride *(2 marks)*

c lithium + bromine → lithium bromide *(2 marks)*

3 Write word equations for the reactions below.

a sulfur and oxygen producing sulfur dioxide *(2 marks)*

b potassium and chlorine *(2 marks)*

4 Use information from this page to compare the burning reactions of carbon and magnesium. Include word equations in your answer. *(6 marks)*

3.3 Burning fuels

Learning objectives

After this topic you will be able to:

- predict products of combustion reactions
- categorise oxidation reactions as useful or not.

How do you heat your home? Many central-heating systems burn methane gas. Methane comes from under the ground, or under the sea. It was formed from tiny plants and animals that lived millions of years ago.

If you live in Poundbury, Dorset, your methane might come from another source. Waste from chocolate and cereal factories produces methane in just a few weeks.

▲ This apparatus makes methane from waste.

What are fuels?

Methane is a **fuel**. A fuel is a material that burns to transfer energy by heating. Fuels include petrol, diesel, coal, hydrogen, and waste cooking oil.

▲ This vehicle burns waste cooking oil.

A State the meaning of the word fuel.

What happens when fuels burn?

Fuels burn in chemical reactions. Burning is also called **combustion**. Methane is a compound of carbon and hydrogen. Its chemical formula is CH_4. When it burns, it reacts with oxygen from the air. The reaction makes two products, carbon dioxide and water:

methane + oxygen → carbon dioxide + water

Petrol is a mixture of compounds. Most of its compounds consist of atoms of hydrogen and carbon. Petrol makes mainly carbon dioxide and water when it burns in car engines.

Key Words

fuel, combustion, fossil fuel, non-renewable, oxidation

Foul Fact!

In Cirencester, Gloucestershire, methane made from chicken poo burns in a power station to generate electricity.

B Name the two elements that methane is made up of.

Petrol, diesel, coal, and methane from under the ground or sea, are **fossil fuels**. They are **non-renewable**. This means that they cannot be replaced once they have been used. They will run out one day.

▲ North Sea oil and methane gas are fossil fuels.

Hydrogen – future fuel?

A few types of car burn hydrogen in their engines. In this reaction, hydrogen joins with oxygen. There is one product.

hydrogen + oxygen → water

Some people think that hydrogen should be used to fuel more cars. This is because the only product of its combustion is harmless water. Burning methane, petrol, and diesel produce carbon dioxide and water. Extra carbon dioxide in the air is harmful to the environment. It is a cause of climate change.

But where does the hydrogen to fuel cars come from? Companies make hydrogen from methane, or water. The processes they use to make the hydrogen also produce harmful gases.

C Name the two reactants when hydrogen burns in air.

What are oxidation reactions?

Burning reactions are **oxidation** reactions. In oxidation reactions, substances react with oxygen. Rusting is another oxidation reaction. In rusting, iron reacts with oxygen and water.

D State one example of an oxidation reaction.

Fuels for the future

Should we fuel cars with petrol and diesel or find other fuels, such as hydrogen or waste cooking oil? Organise your ideas in a table, then write a few paragraphs to explain your decision.

Link

You can learn more about climate change in C2 4.6 Climate change

Summary Questions

1 Copy the sentences below, choosing the correct bold words.

- **a** Fuels burn to transfer **useless/useful** energy. *(1 mark)*
- **b** Combustion is another word for **burning/melting**. *(1 mark)*
- **c** When a substance burns it reacts with **nitrogen/oxygen** from the air. *(1 mark)*
- **d** Methane is a **compound/element** of carbon and hydrogen. It burns to make carbon dioxide and **water/hydrogen**. *(2 marks)*

2 Cooking oil contains compounds of carbon, hydrogen, and oxygen. Predict two products of its combustion. *(2 marks)*

3 Nathan says that burning any fuel contributes to climate change. Riana thinks Nathan is wrong. Use cartoon pictures and speech bubbles to show them having a conversation about burning fuels. *(6 marks)*

3.4 Thermal decomposition

Learning objectives

After this topic you will be able to:

- identify decomposition reactions from word equations
- use a pattern to predict products of decomposition reactions.

▲ Copper carbonate.

Key Words

decomposition, thermal decomposition, discrete

▲ Copper oxide and carbon dioxide form when copper carbonate decomposes.

What made this man's hair so blond?

He put hydrogen peroxide in his hair. Hydrogen peroxide is a compound. It has atoms of two elements, hydrogen and oxygen. Its formula is H_2O_2.

You cannot bleach hair with old hydrogen peroxide. This is because hydrogen peroxide molecules break up. When this happens there are two products – water and oxygen.

hydrogen peroxide → water + oxygen

This is a **decomposition** reaction. In decomposition reactions, a compound breaks down into simpler compounds or elements.

A State what a decomposition reaction is.

Decomposition reactions

Copper carbonate is a green compound. It is made up of atoms of three elements – copper, carbon, and oxygen.

If you heat copper carbonate, it breaks down. The reaction makes copper oxide and carbon dioxide. Copper oxide is black. It remains in the test tube. Carbon dioxide forms as a gas.

copper carbonate → copper oxide + carbon dioxide

You can show that the gas is carbon dioxide by bubbling it through limewater. The limewater goes cloudy.

Other types of carbonate decompose on heating:

lead carbonate → lead oxide + carbon dioxide

zinc carbonate → zinc oxide + carbon dioxide

When a substance breaks down on heating, the reaction is a **thermal decomposition** reaction.

B Name the products of the thermal decomposition reaction of lead carbonate.

Comparing reactions

Edward compares thermal decomposition reactions. He heats different carbonates. He measures the time for the limewater to start looking milky.

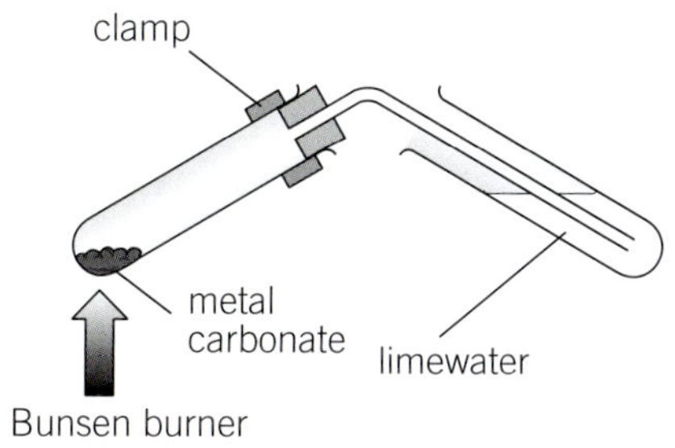

Edward's apparatus.

Edward writes his results in a table.

Compound	Time for limewater to start looking milky (min)
copper carbonate	0.5
zinc carbonate	2.5
lead carbonate	1.0

He presents his results on a bar chart. This is because the variable he changes is **discrete**. A discrete variable is described by words, or by numbers that can only have certain values, such as shoe sizes.

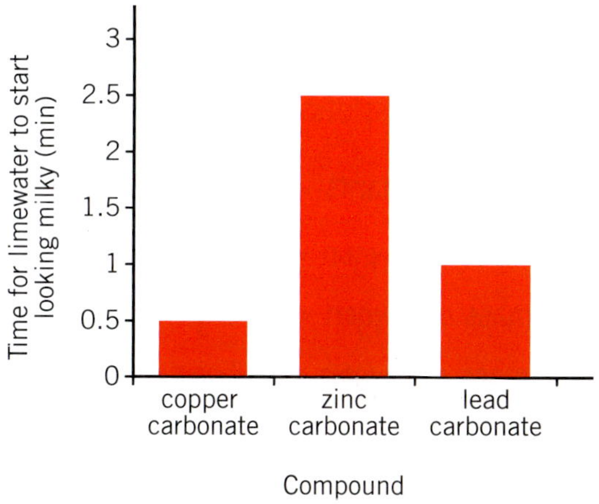

This bar chart shows the time for carbonate compounds to start decomposing.

C State what a discrete variable is.

All's fair?

Think about Edward's investigation. Discuss the variables with a partner. Which variable does he change and which does he measure? Which should he keep the same to make the investigation fair? What does the bar chart show? What conclusion could Edward make?

Summary Questions

1 Copy and complete the sentences below.

In a decomposition reaction, a ______ breaks down to make ______ compounds and elements. Copper carbonate decomposes to make ______ oxide and ______ dioxide gas. You can use ______ to test for the gas.

(5 marks)

2 Choose the reactions below that are decomposition reactions. Explain each choice.

a calcium + oxygen → calcium oxide *(1 mark)*

b zinc carbonate → zinc oxide + carbon dioxide *(1 mark)*

c hydrogen peroxide → water + oxygen *(1 mark)*

d aluminium + iodine → aluminium iodide *(1 mark)*

3 Compare combustion reactions with decomposition reactions. Include examples to illustrate your answer.

(6 marks)

3.5 Conservation of mass

Learning objectives

After this topic you will be able to:

- explain conservation of mass in chemical reactions
- calculate masses of reactants and products.

▲ When it is burnt the substances in wood react with oxygen.

▲ Burning magnesium.

What happens to wood in campfires?

Wood is a mixture of many substances. On burning, the substances react with oxygen.

The reactions make many products, including ash and carbon dioxide. The total mass of reactants is equal to the total mass of products.

mass of wood + mass of oxygen = total mass of all products

In any chemical reaction, the total mass of reactants is equal to the total mass of products. This is called **conservation of mass**. Mass is also conserved in physical changes.

A State what conservation of mass means.

Calculating masses

Samindee has some magnesium. She finds its mass. She burns the magnesium. She finds the mass of the product.

mass of magnesium = 0.24 g
mass of product = 0.80 g

Samindee writes a word equation. She adds the masses she knows.

magnesium + oxygen → magnesium oxide
0.24 g   0.80 g

Samindee calculates the mass of oxygen that reacted:

total mass of reactants = total mass of products
0.24 g + mass of oxygen = 0.80 g
mass of oxygen = 0.80 g − 0.24 g
mass of oxygen = 0.56 g

Writing balanced equations

Word equations show reactants and products in reactions. **Balanced symbol equations** also show:

- the formulae of reactants and products
- how the atoms are rearranged
- the relative amounts of reactants and products.

Burning carbon

- First, write a word equation:

carbon + oxygen → carbon dioxide

- Write chemical symbols or formulae for each reactant and product. You cannot guess these.

$$C + O_2 \rightarrow CO_2$$

- Now balance the equation. There must be the same number of atoms of each element on each side of the equation. The equation shows one atom of carbon on each side of the arrow, and two atoms of oxygen. It is balanced.

B State what balanced symbol equations show.

Burning magnesium

- Write a word equation and add symbols and formulae:

magnesium + oxygen → magnesium oxide

$$Mg + O_2 \rightarrow MgO$$

- Balance the amounts of oxygen. There are two atoms on the left of the arrow, and one on the right. Add a big 2 to the left of the MgO. Do not add or change any little numbers:

$$Mg + O_2 \rightarrow 2MgO$$

The big 2 applies to both Mg and O in magnesium oxide.

- Now balance the amounts of magnesium. There is one atom on the left, and two on the right.
Add a big 2 to the left of the Mg. The equation is balanced.

$$2Mg + O_2 \rightarrow 2MgO$$

Mass matters

Look at Samindee's calculation. Calculate the masses of reactants and products if she started with 0.48 g of magnesium.

Key Words

conservation of mass, balanced symbol equation

Summary Questions

1 Copy and complete the sentences below.

In chemical reactions, the total mass of reactants ______ the total mass of products. This is called ______ of mass.

(2 marks)

2 Kezi heats 12.5 g of zinc carbonate. It decomposes to make 8.1 g of zinc oxide. Calculate the mass of carbon dioxide made.

(2 marks)

3 Copper carbonate ($CuCO_3$) decomposes to make copper oxide (CuO) and carbon dioxide (CO_2). Write a balanced equation for the reaction.

(3 marks)

4 Draw diagrams to show how you could make models to represent the equations on this page. If possible, make the models.

(6 marks)

3.6 Exothermic and endothermic

Learning objectives

After this topic you will be able to:

- describe the characteristics of exothermic and endothermic changes
- classify changes as exothermic or endothermic.

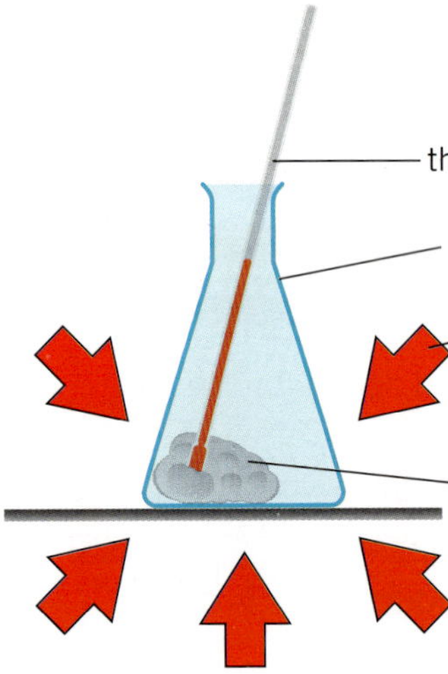

▲ The reaction of citric acid with sodium hydrogen carbonate is endothermic.

Have you ever used a cold pack on an injury? How did the pack get cold?

One type of cold pack includes two substances. An outer bag contains liquid water. An inner bag contains solid ammonium nitrate. When you break the inner bag, the water and ammonium nitrate mix. The solid dissolves in the water, and the mixture cools. The injury transfers energy to the mixture. The mixture slowly returns to the temperature of the surroundings.

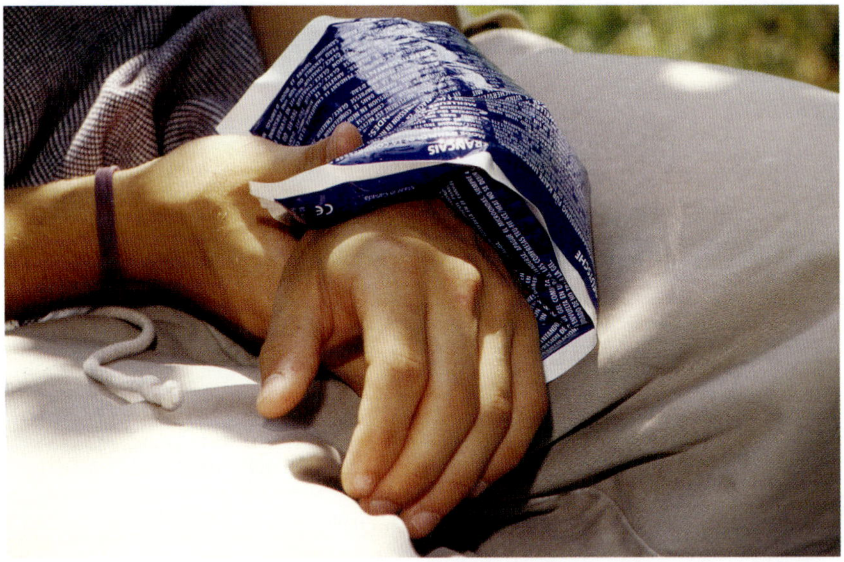

▲ A cold pack on a sports injury.

What is an endothermic change?

The process in the cold pack is an **endothermic change**. The surroundings transfer energy to substances in an endothermic change. Some chemical reactions are endothermic. Melting and boiling are also endothermic. So is the formation of some solutions.

Tom has some citric acid crystals. Their temperature is 20 °C. He adds sodium hydrogen carbonate powder. There is a chemical reaction. The reacting mixture feels cold. Its temperature goes down to 10 °C. The temperature decrease shows that the reaction is endothermic.

Once the reaction is complete, Tom leaves his mixture of products in the lab. After a while its temperature returns to 20 °C.

A State what an endothermic change is.

Foul Fact!

You can get frostbite from cold packs if you don't use them properly. Never leave them on your skin for longer than the pack says.

What is an exothermic change?

Some changes transfer energy to the surroundings. These are **exothermic changes**. Burning wax warms up the surroundings. All burning reactions do the same. They are exothermic.

▲ Burning reactions transfer energy to the surroundings. They are exothermic.

Zoe has some dilute sulfuric acid. She also has some sodium hydroxide solution. The temperature of both solutions is 20 °C. Zoe mixes them. There is a chemical reaction. She measures the temperature again. It is 30 °C. The temperature increase shows that the reaction is exothermic.

Once the reaction is complete, Zoe leaves the mixture of products in the lab. After a while its temperature returns to 20 °C. Some changes of state are examples of exothermic changes, for example, condensing and freezing.

Literacy

Here's an easy way to remember the difference between exothermic and endothermic reactions:

Exothermic reactions transfer energy out. You go out through an **ex**it.

Endothermic reactions transfer energy in. You go in through an **en**trance.

Key Words

endothermic change, exothermic change

Summary Questions

1 Copy the sentences below, choosing the correct bold words.

All chemical reactions involve **colour/energy** transfers. If the temperature increases, the change is **exothermic/endothermic**. If the temperature decreases, the change is **exothermic/endothermic**. Boiling and melting are **exothermic/endothermic** changes.

(4 marks)

2 The table shows the temperature changes when some substances dissolve in water. Write down the names of the substances that dissolve exothermically. Explain your choices.

(3 marks)

Name of substance	Temperature before dissolving (°C)	Temperature after dissolving (°C)
potassium chloride	20	10
calcium chloride	20	35
sodium hydrogen carbonate	20	15
sodium carbonate	20	24

3 Write a paragraph to compare exothermic and endothermic changes. Include examples to illustrate your answer.

(6 marks)

C1 Chapter 3 Summary

Key Points

- Physical changes are reversible. They include changes of state and dissolving.
- Chemical reactions are not reversible.
- In a chemical reaction, atoms are re-arranged to make new substances.
- In a chemical reaction, the total mass of reactants is equal to the total mass of products. This is conservation of mass.
- In a chemical reaction, the starting substances are called reactants. The substances that are made in the reaction are called products.
- Word equations represent reactions simply. They show reactants on the left and products on the right. The arrow means *reacts to make*.
- In a balanced symbol equation, chemical formulae represent the reactants and products. The equation shows how atoms are re-arranged. It gives the relative amounts of reactants and products.
- Chemical reactions can make useful products and transfer energy.
- In oxidation reactions, substances join with oxygen to form oxides.
- Oxidation reactions include burning and rusting. Burning is also called combustion.
- In a thermal decomposition reaction, a compound breaks down when it is heated. The products are simpler compounds, and elements.
- Exothermic changes transfer energy to the surroundings.
- Endothermic changes transfer energy from the surroundings.
- A hazard is a possible source of danger.
- A risk is the chance of damage or injury from a hazard.

BIG Write

Tune in

Radio 99 makes exciting discussion programmes. And you will be on next week! A listener has sent in this text: "Rusting, explosions, making drugs… They are all chemical reactions. Chemistry should be banned."

Task

Plan what to say to convince listeners that chemical reactions are very important, and that chemistry must not be banned.

Tips

- Give examples of useful chemical reactions, and ask listeners to imagine a world without chemistry. What would they miss?

Key Words

chemical reaction, physical change, catalyst, reactant, product, word equation, hazard, risk, fuel, combustion, fossil fuel, non-renewable, oxidation, decomposition, thermal decomposition, discrete, conservation of mass, balanced symbol equation, endothermic change, exothermic change

End-of-chapter questions

1 Izzy heats some magnesium in a Bunsen burner. It burns with a bright flame. A white ash forms.

a Describe **two** observations that show this is a chemical reaction. *(2 marks)*

b State what happens to the atoms in a chemical reaction. *(1 mark)*

(3 marks)

2 Marcus plans an investigation to find out which fuel makes water hotter, ethanol or propanol.Marcus burns each fuel in turn to heat water. He measures how hot the water gets.

a State whether the burning reactions are exothermic or endothermic. Explain your decision. *(2 marks)*

b Name the independent variable in the investigation. *(1 mark)*

c Name **two** variables that Marcus must keep the same. *(2 marks)*

d Explain why he must keep these variables the same. *(1 mark)*

(6 marks)

3 Sze-Kie heats some calcium carbonate in a test tube. There is a chemical reaction:

calcium carbonate →
calcium oxide + carbon dioxide

a State what type of reaction the word equation shows. Choose from the list below. *(1 mark)*

combustion
oxidation
thermal decomposition
exothermic

b Name the product(s) of the reaction. *(1 mark)*

c Sze-Kie started with 100 g of calcium carbonate. At the end of the reaction, there was 56 g of calcium oxide in the test tube. Calculate the mass of carbon dioxide made. Show your working. *(2 marks)*

(4 marks)

4 Burning methane is a chemical reaction. Here are some ways of representing this reaction.

Equation X

methane + oxygen → carbon dioxide + water

Equation Y

$CH_4 + 2O_2 \rightarrow CO_2 + 2H_2O$

Diagram Z

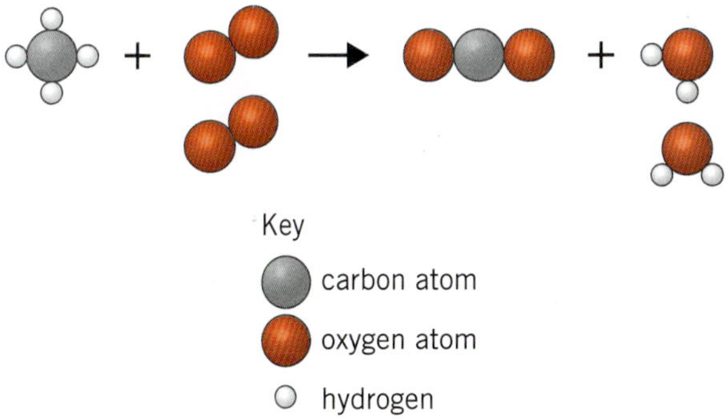

a Explain how Equation X, Equation Y, and Diagram Z all show that burning methane is a chemical reaction. *(2 marks)*

b Compare the advantages and disadvantages of representing the reaction with Equation X, Equation Y, and Diagram Z. *(6 marks)*

(8 marks)

4.1 Acids and alkalis

Learning objectives

After this topic you will be able to:

- compare the properties of acids and alkalis
- describe differences between concentrated and dilute solutions of an acid.

▲ These solutions are corrosive.

▲ Vinegar contains ethanoic acid.

What do vomit, vinegar, and lemons have in common?

They all taste sour. This is because they contain **acids**. Vomit includes an acid from the stomach, hydrochloric acid. This acid helps digest foods. Vinegar is a solution of ethanoic acid and other substances. Lemons contain citric acid.

Alkalis are the chemical opposite of acids. Soap solution is an alkali, and so is toothpaste. Most alkalis feel soapy.

A List the chemical names of three acids.

Using acids and alkalis safely

It is safe to eat the acid in lemons, and to use alkaline soap. But there are hazards linked to some acids and alkalis.

The bottle opposite has a hazard symbol. The symbol shows that the solution in the bottle is **corrosive**. It could burn your skin and eyes.

You can control risks from corrosive solutions by:

- wearing eye protection
- keeping the solution off your skin.

If a solution is very corrosive, a teacher might wear protective gloves when using it.

B State two hazards of using a corrosive solution.

Concentrated or dilute?

Pure ethanoic acid causes severe burns. It catches fire easily.

Vinegar contains ethanoic acid. It is safe to eat, and does not catch fire. Why is there a difference? Pure ethanoic acid contains no water. Dissolving in water changes some properties.

The amount of water makes a difference, too. Both the bottles at the top of the next page contain hydrochloric acid. Hydrochloric acid is a solution of hydrogen chloride in water.

Bottle A Bottle B

- Acid A has 370 g of hydrogen chloride in 1 litre of solution.
- Acid B has 3.70 g of hydrogen chloride in 1 litre of solution.

Acid A has more hydrogen chloride per litre than acid B. Acid A is **concentrated**. Acid B is **dilute**. The concentrated solution burns skin and eyes. The dilute solution hurts if it gets into a cut but has no other hazards.

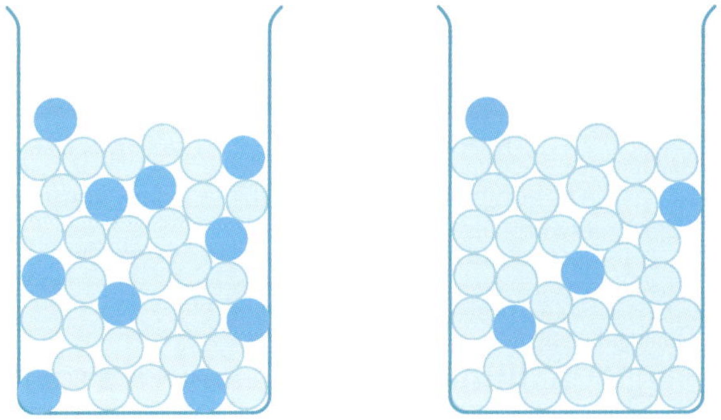

▲ The solution on the left is more concentrated. It has more acid particles per litre. Not to scale.

The hazards of using acids and alkalis depend on:

- the acid or alkali you are using
- whether the solution is concentrated or dilute.

C State one difference between a concentrated solution of an acid and a dilute solution of the same acid.

Safe handling

A teacher has a solution of an alkali. The solution is corrosive – it causes severe burns and is dangerous to the eyes. Describe how to control the risks from these hazards. Do you think the teacher should allow your class to use the alkali? Explain your decision.

Foul Fact!

William Beaumont discovered stomach acid when treating a shooting victim. Beaumont removed stomach juices through holes in the skin and stomach. He tested the juices with different foods.

Key Words

acid, alkali, corrosive, concentrated, dilute

Summary Questions

1 Copy the sentences below, choosing the correct bold words.

Acids **taste sour/feel soapy**.
Some acidic and alkaline solutions are **corrosive/correlated**.
A concentrated solution of an acid is **more/less** corrosive than a dilute solution. A concentrated solution has **fewer/more** acid particles per litre than a dilute solution.

(4 marks)

2 Calculate which is more concentrated – 20 g of alkali in 250 cm^3 of solution or 10 g of the same alkali in 500 cm^3 of solution. Show your working.

(3 marks)

3 Use the information on this spread to compare the properties of acids and alkalis.

(6 marks)

4.2 Indicators and pH

Learning objectives

After this topic you will be able to:

- use the pH scale to measure acidity and alkalinity
- describe how indicators categorise solutions as acidic, alkaline, or neutral.

A student has two beakers. One contains an acid and the other contains an alkaline solution. How can he find out which is which?

You can use an **indicator** to find out whether a solution is acidic or alkaline. An indicator contains a dye. The dye turns a different colour in acidic and alkaline solutions.

A State what an indicator is.

Which plants make good indicators?

You can make indicators from plants. The table shows the colours of some plant indicators in acidic and alkaline solutions.

Juice extracted from…	Colour in dilute hydrochloric acid	Colour in dilute sodium hydroxide solution (an alkali)
red cabbage	red	yellow/green
hibiscus flower	dark pink/red	dark green
beetroot	red/purple	yellow

At school, you might use **litmus** indicator. Litmus is a solution of dyes from lichens.

- Red litmus paper turns blue on adding alkali.
- Blue litmus paper turns red on adding acid.

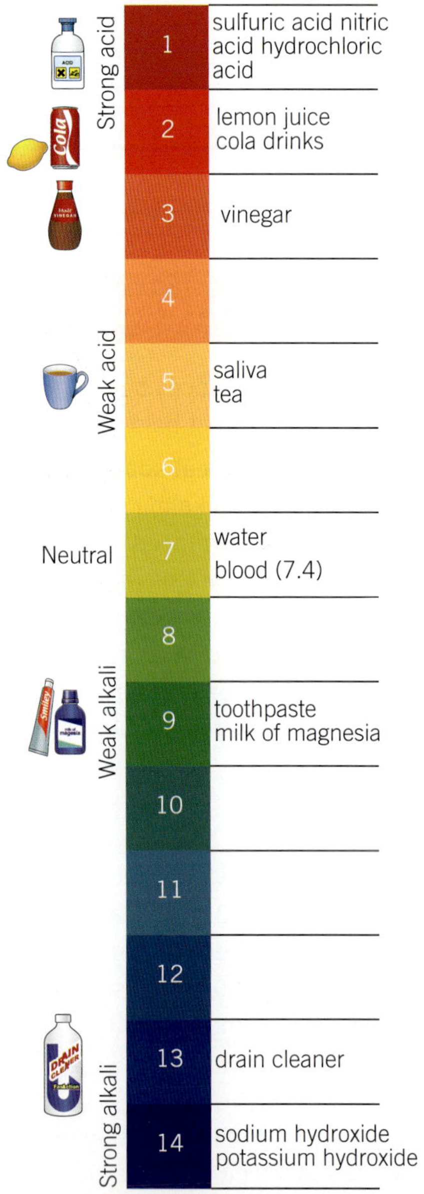

▲ Universal indicator changes colour depending on the pH.

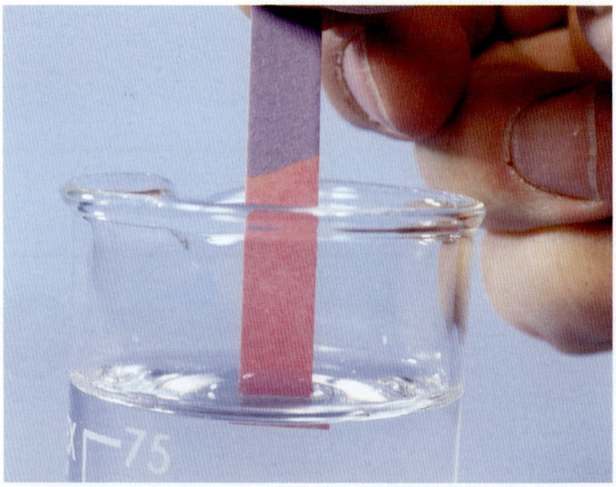

◀ Using litmus paper.

B State the colour change when a student adds an acid to blue litmus paper.

How acidic? How alkaline?

Which is more acidic, vinegar or stomach acid? How can you find out? You cannot use blue litmus paper. Both acids would make it red.

Instead, you need **universal indicator**. Universal indicator is a mixture of dyes. It changes colour to show how acidic or alkaline a solution is.

What is the pH scale?

The **pH scale** is a measure of how acidic or alkaline a solution is. On the pH scale:

- An acid has a pH of less than 7. The lower the pH, the more acidic the solution.
- An alkaline solution has a pH of more than 7. The higher the pH, the more alkaline the solution.

Some solutions are **neutral**. This means they are neither acidic nor alkaline. The pH of a neutral solution is exactly 7.

Universal indicator is a different colour at each pH. The scale shows the colours of universal indicator in solutions of different pH.

Acidity

Amie collected the data in the table. Use the data to list the names of the solutions in order of increasing acidity, starting with the least acidic.

Solution	pH
milk	6.6
urine	6.1
orange juice	3.2
black coffee	5.5
lemon juice	2.3
vinegar	2.8

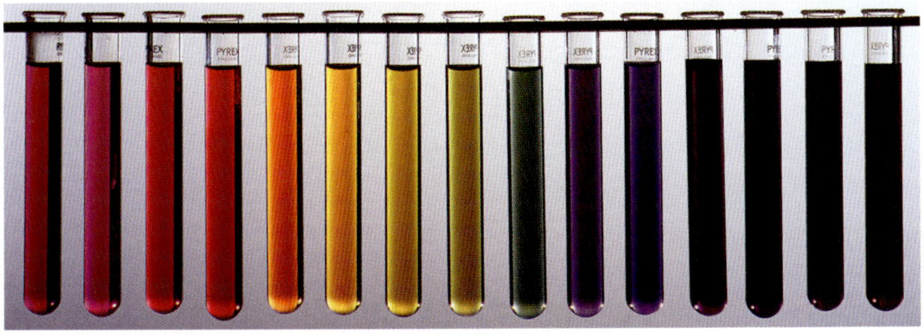

▲ Universal indicator turns orange in vinegar. It turns red in stomach acid.

C State the pH of a neutral solution.

Foul Fact!

Murderer John Haig, also known as the Acid Bath Murderer, disposed of the bodies of his victims in baths of concentrated sulfuric acid. The acid pH was between 0 and 1.

Key Words

indicator, litmus, universal indicator, pH scale, neutral

Summary Questions

1 Copy the sentences below, choosing the correct bold words.

Adding an acid to red litmus paper makes the litmus paper go **red/blue**. On the pH scale, acids have a pH of **less than/more than** 7. The higher the pH, the **more/less** acidic the solution. A solution is alkaline if its pH is **more than/less than** 7. A solution of pH of **7/0** is neutral.

(5 marks)

2 John has a solution. It turns yellow when he adds red-cabbage juice. Predict what colour the solution would turn if he added hibiscus-flower juice. Explain your answer.

(2 marks)

3 Using information from this page, create a chart to show the colours of dilute hydrochloric acid and dilute sodium hydroxide solution in five different indicators.

(6 marks)

4.3 Neutralisation

Learning objectives

After this topic you will be able to:

- describe how pH changes in neutralisation reactions
- state examples of useful neutralisation reactions.

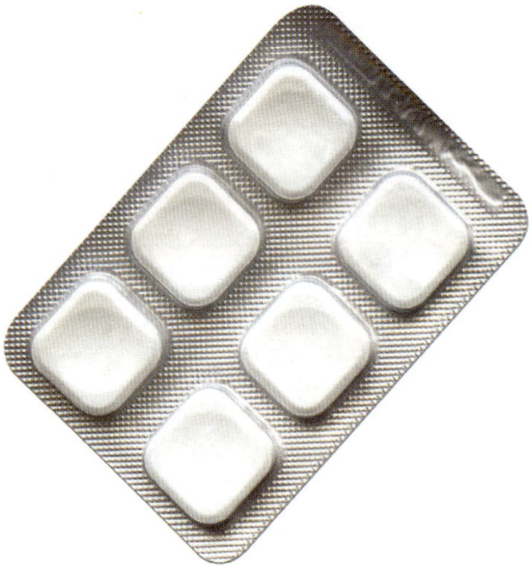

▲ Indigestion tablets neutralise stomach acid.

Volume of sodium hydroxide added (cm^3)	pH
0	1
1	2
2	2
3	2
4	3
5	4
6	5
7	7

Key Words

neutralisation, base

Have you ever had stomach ache? Did you take an indigestion tablet?

Extra stomach acid makes your stomach hurt. An indigestion tablet reacts with this acid in a **neutralisation** reaction. In a neutralisation reaction an acid reacts with a substance that cancels it out. The pH gets closer to 7.

Which substances neutralise acids?

A **base** is a substance that neutralises an acid. Bases include sodium hydroxide, calcium oxide, and copper oxide. Some bases are soluble in water. A soluble base is an alkali.

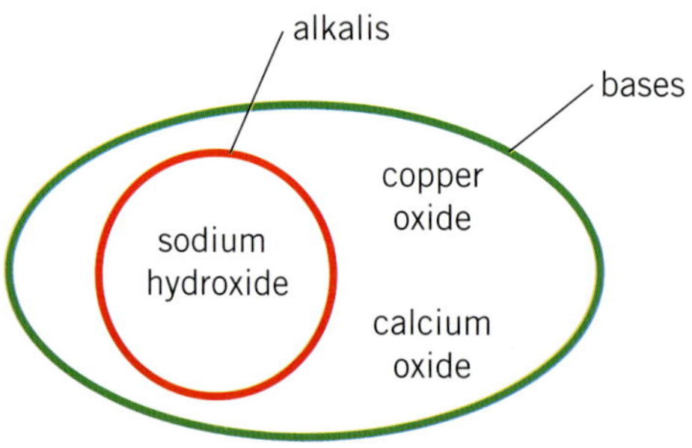

◀ Alkalis are bases that dissolve in water.

A State one difference between a base and an alkali.

pH changes in neutralisation reactions

Gwil has 10 cm^3 of acid. He adds universal indicator. He looks at the colour of the mixture, and compares it to the indicator colour chart. He records the pH.

Then Gwil adds 1 cm^3 of sodium hydroxide solution. The pH increases. Gwil writes down the new pH. He continues to add sodium hydroxide solution. The pH gets closer to 7. The alkali is neutralising the acid. Gwil stops adding alkali when the pH is 7. His mixture is neutral.

B State what volume of sodium hydroxide solution was needed to neutralise the acid.

How is neutralisation useful?

Soil for crops

Some soils are more acidic than others. Every plant has its favourite soil pH.

Deepa lives in India. She has a farm. She wants to grow tea. She tests the soil. Its pH is 4.5. The soil is too acidic to grow tea.

Plant	Soil pH range that the plant grows best in
apple tree	5.0–6.8
cabbage	6.0–7.0
onion	6.0–6.5
tea	5.0–6.0
tomato	5.5–7.0

▲ Tea plants grow best in soil of pH 5.0 to 6.0.

Deepa adds a base to the soil. The base neutralises some of the soil acid. The soil pH increases to pH 5.0. It is now suitable for growing tea.

Data logger details

Ralph has a solution. He adds acid to the solution. A pH probe reads the pH. The probe is attached to a data logger, which sends the data to a computer. The computer draws a graph of the data. Describe in detail what the graph shows.

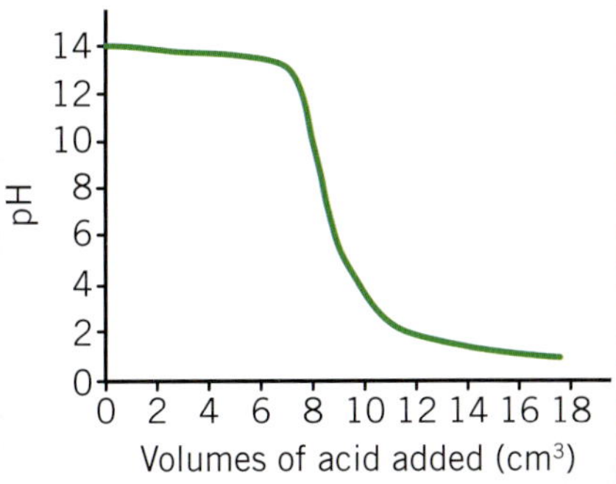

Acidic lakes

◀ Adding a base to an acidic lake.

In some places, gases from burning coal make sulfur dioxide gas. The gas dissolves in rainwater to make acid rain. The rain falls in lakes, making lakes more acidic. Some water animals and plants cannot live in these lakes.

Environment organisations may add bases to acid lakes. The pH of the lake water increases.

C Describe two situations in which neutralisation reactions are useful.

Summary Questions

1 Copy and complete the sentences below.

A base cancels out an acid in a _______ reaction. An alkali is a soluble _______. You can measure pH with an _______ or a pH probe attached to a _______ logger.

(4 marks)

2 The soil in Freya's farm is pH 7.0. Use data from this page to suggest three crops she could try growing. Explain your choices.

(2 marks)

3 Explain to gardeners why they should measure soil pH, and how they can change soil pH.

(6 marks)

4.4 Making salts

Learning objectives

After this topic you will be able to:

- describe what a salt is
- predict the salts that form when acids react with metals or bases.

▲ Sodium chloride.

▲ Copper sulfate.

▲ Bolivian salt flats.

Here are the formulae of three acids. What do they have in common?

- HCl – hydrochloric acid
- HNO_3 – nitric acid
- H_2SO_4 – sulfuric acid

The formulae show that the acids are compounds. They all include hydrogen atoms.

What are salts?

A **salt** is a compound that forms when an acid reacts with a metal element or compound. The hydrogen atoms of the acid are replaced by atoms of the metal element. The pictures on the left show two salts.

Sodium chloride is the salt you may add to food. Its formula is NaCl. A sodium atom has replaced the hydrogen of hydrochloric acid.

Farmers use copper sulfate to kill fungus. Its formula is $CuSO_4$. Copper atoms have replaced the hydrogen atoms of sulfuric acid.

A Describe what a salt is.

Which reactions make salts?

Many salts exist naturally. Sodium chloride makes the sea salty. It also exists underground. There are huge amounts of salts in Bolivian salt flats.

You can also make salts in chemical reactions.

Acids and metals

Reacting an acid with a metal makes two products – a salt, and hydrogen. For example:

magnesium + hydrochloric acid → magnesium chloride + hydrogen

zinc + sulfuric acid → zinc sulfate + hydrogen

Key Words

salt

Acids and bases

Reacting an acid with a base also makes a salt. The products are a salt, and water. For example:

sodium hydroxide + hydrochloric acid → sodium chloride + water

copper oxide + nitric acid → copper nitrate + water

The reactions show that:

- hydrochloric acid is a chloride maker
- sulfuric acid is a sulfate maker
- nitric acid is a nitrate maker.

B Name the salt made when sodium hydroxide reacts with hydrochloric acid.

How can you make salt crystals?

The reactions of acids with metal or bases make salt solutions. Removing water makes salt crystals. The diagrams show how to make copper sulfate crystals.

1

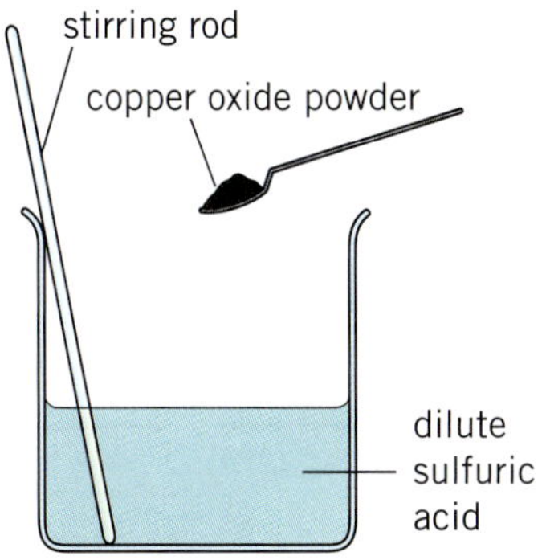

▲ Add copper oxide powder (a base) to dilute sulfuric acid. Keep adding until some copper oxide is left over. All the acid has now reacted.

2

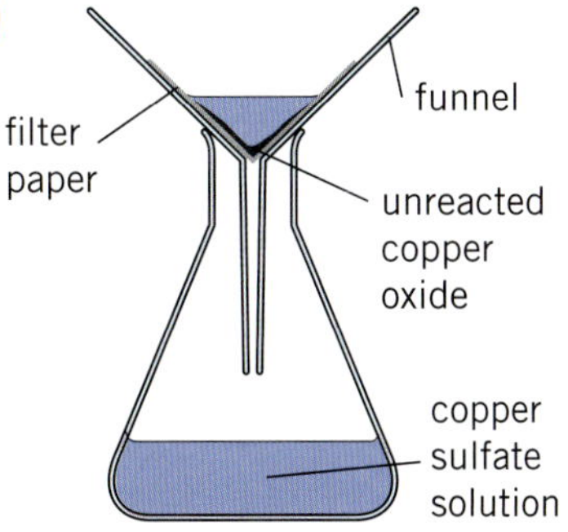

▲ Filter to remove the extra copper oxide.

3

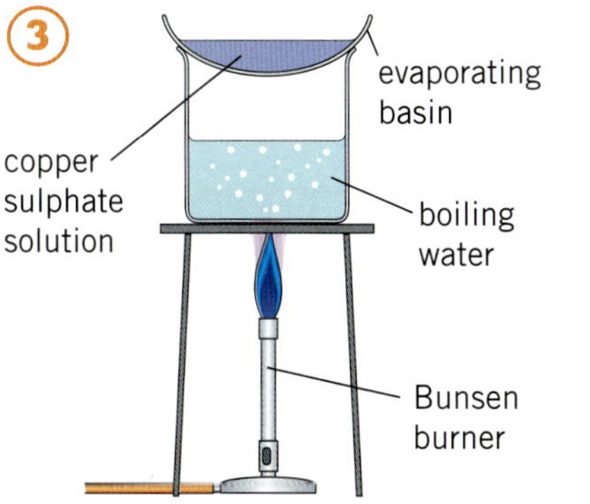

▲ Heat the copper sulfate solution in an evaporating basin until most of the water evaporates.

4

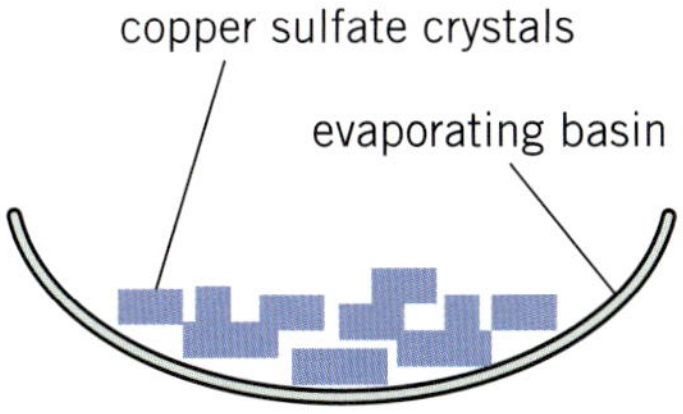

▲ Leave the evaporating basin in a warm place. The rest of the water evaporates. Copper sulfate crystals remain.

Making magnesium salts

You can make magnesium chloride crystals from magnesium and hydrochloric acid. The method is similar to that for making copper sulphate. The only difference is that magnesium, not copper oxide, is left over in the first stage. Write clear and detailed instructions for making magnesium chloride.

Summary Questions

1 Copy the sentences below, choosing the correct bold words.

A salt is **an element/a compound**. In a salt, the **hydrogen/oxygen** atoms of an acid are replaced by metal atoms. When an acid reacts with a metal, the products are a salt and **water/hydrogen**. When a base reacts with an acid, the products are a salt and **water/hydrogen**.

(4 marks)

2 Predict the products of the reaction of magnesium with sulfuric acid.

(2 marks)

3 Predict the products of the reaction of zinc oxide with nitric acid.

(2 marks)

4 Describe and explain the stages in making copper chloride crystals from an insoluble base and an acid.

(6 marks)

C1 Chapter 4 Summary

Key Points

- The pH scale shows how acidic or alkaline a solution is.
- Acids have pH values below 7. The lower the pH, the more acidic the solution.
- Alkaline solutions have pH values above 7. The higher the pH, the more alkaline the solution.
- Neutral solutions are neither acidic nor alkaline. Their pH is exactly 7.
- Indicators change colour to show whether a solution is acidic or alkaline.
- Universal indicator changes colour to show the pH of a solution.
- Litmus is an indicator. Blue litmus paper turns red on adding acid. Red litmus paper turns blue on adding an alkaline solution.
- In a neutralisation reaction, an acid cancels out a base, or a base cancels out an acid.
- A base is a substance that neutralises an acid.
- An alkali is a soluble base.
- Adding bases or acids to soil can change its pH, making it suitable for different crops.
- Adding a base to an acidic lake increases the lake pH, making it suitable for different plants and animals.
- If an acid reacts with a base, there are two products – a salt, and water.
- If an acid reacts with a metal, there are two products – a salt, and hydrogen.
- Sulfuric acid makes sulfate salts, hydrochloric acid makes chloride salts, and nitric acid makes nitrate salts.

Case study

Useful neutral

Neutralisation happens when an acid cancels out a base or when a base cancels out an acid.

Task

Prepare a piece of writing that explains how neutralisation reactions are useful.

Tips

- Start by drawing a visual summary to help you organise your ideas.
- Make sure your paragraphs are in a sensible order.
- Swap your work with another student and discuss improvements.

Key Words

acid, alkali, alkaline solution, acidic solution, corrosive, concentrated, dilute, indicator, litmus, universal indicator, pH scale, neutral, neutralisation, base, salt

End-of-chapter questions

1 A scientist measures the pH of samples of sweat, blood, and urine from one person. Copy the table. Write down whether each sample is acidic, alkaline, or neutral.

Name of mixture	pH	Acidic, alkaline, or neutral?
sweat	5.3	
blood	7.4	
urine	6.8	

(***3 marks***)

2 Joe wants to make a red-cabbage indicator. He has the apparatus below.

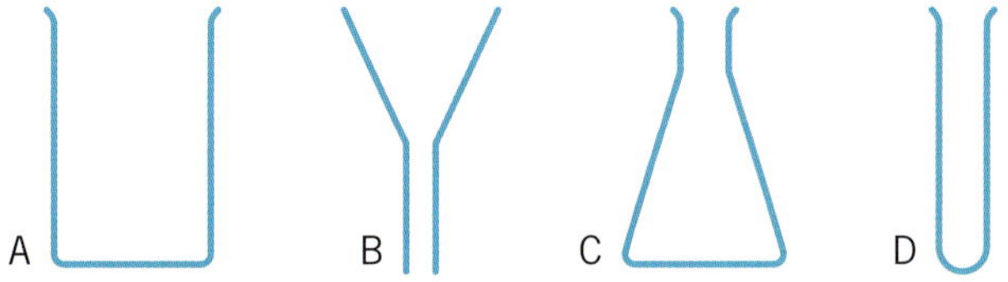

a First, Joe heats a mixture of chopped red cabbage and water. Write the letter of the best apparatus for this. *(1 mark)*

b Next, Joe filters the mixture. He keeps the solution. Write the letters of the best **two** pieces of apparatus for this. *(2 marks)*

c Lastly, Joe adds the red-cabbage solution to acidic and alkaline solutions. Write the letter of the best apparatus for this. *(1 mark)*

(***4 marks***)

3 The table below gives the preferred soil pH of some fruit plants.

Fruit plant	Preferred soil pH
blueberry	4.0–5.0
sweet cherry	6.0–7.5
cranberry	4.2–5.0
pineapple	5.0–6.0
strawberry	5.0–6.5

a Name the plant in the table that can grow well in alkaline soil. *(1 mark)*

b Name the plant in the table that can grow in the most acidic soil. *(1 mark)*

c The soil pH in Andy's garden is 6.0. Name **three** fruit plants that might grow well in this soil. *(3 marks)*

d The soil pH in Clare's garden is 8.0. She wants to grow strawberry plants. State the type of substance she should add to the soil so that the pH is suitable. Explain your answer. *(2 marks)*

(***7 marks***)

4 Describe and explain the stages in making magnesium chloride crystals from an acid and a metal. Include the names of the acid and the metal.

(***6 marks***)

Physics 1

The first astronaut to walk on the Moon, Neil Armstrong, looked back and saw the Earth as no-one had ever seen it before. In P1 you will learn about how you see, and how light and sound waves behave. You will learn about the place of the Earth in the Universe. You will also learn about the forces that keep you from falling through the floor and allow astronauts to stand on the Moon.

You already know

- The force of gravity pulls objects to the Earth.
- Friction, air resistance, and water resistance slow down moving objects.
- You see things because light reflects off them.
- Light travels in straight lines, which explains the size and shape of shadows.
- Vibrating objects make sound, which varies in pitch and loudness, and gets fainter as you move away.
- The Earth orbits the Sun and the Moon orbits the Earth.
- The length of a day and the temperature change during the year.
- Day and night and the Sun's movement across the sky happen because the Earth spins on its axis.

Q

What happens to the length of a day during the year?

BIG Questions

- Where do forces come from?
- How do we hear and see things?
- What is outside the Solar System?

Picture Puzzler
Key Words

Can you solve this Picture Puzzler?

The first letter of each of these images spells out a science word that you will come across in this book.

Picture Puzzler
Close Up

Can you tell what this zoomed-in picture is?

***Clue**: The person floating in the sea is reading one.*

Making connections

In **P1** you will learn about the Earth and our place in the Solar System.

In **C1** you will learn about how everything is made up of atoms and elements.

In **B1** you will learn about what makes up living things and how they reproduce.

1 Introduction to forces

Learning objectives

After this topic you will be able to:

- explain what forces do
- describe what is meant by an interaction pair.

▲ This rocket took a rover to Mars.

What does a rocket have in common with you? There are forces acting on you and on the rocket.

What do forces do?

A rocket going to Mars moves away from the surface of the Earth very quickly. There is a force pushing the rocket up and forces pulling it down. A force can be a **push** or a **pull**.

Forces explain *why* objects move in the way that they do, or why they don't move at all. That's not all. Forces can change the direction that objects are moving in, and change their shape.

A List three things that forces do.

Describing forces

You can't see forces but you can see the effect of them. When you draw a diagram you add arrows to show the forces that are acting. 'Force arrows' show the direction *and* the size of the force. Forces act on objects so the arrow must touch the object in the diagram.

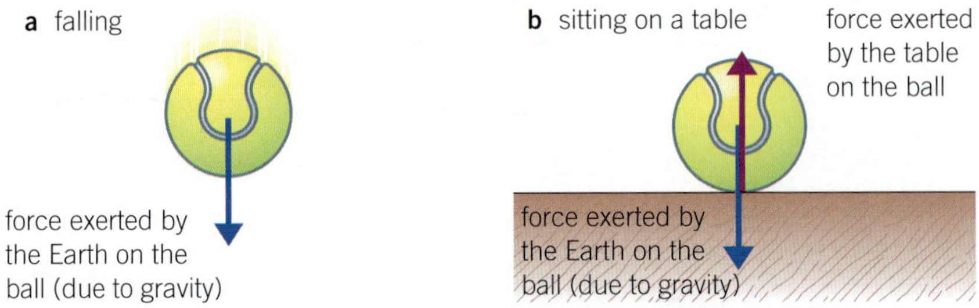

▲ These force arrows show the forces acting on a tennis ball.

Different types of force

Some forces act when you are touching something. This is a **contact force**. **Friction** and **air resistance** are contact forces. Support forces, like upthrust, are also contact forces.

The force of **gravity** acts on a tennis ball travelling through the air. The Earth pulls the ball down even though it is not touching it. Gravity is a **non-contact force**. The force between magnets is another non-contact force.

B Describe the difference between a contact force and a non-contact force.

Foul Fact!

Astronauts on the International Space Station cannot burp. The gas and liquid does not separate in their stomachs while they are in orbit.

Pairing up

A girl and her sister are hanging from a bar in a playground. Think about the forces acting on the girls.

▲ Forces act on the girls hanging from a bar.

- Gravity pulls the girls down. *This is the force of the Earth on the girls.*
- The girls pull the Earth up. *This is the force of the girls on the Earth.*

Forces always come in pairs. The pairs are called **interaction pairs**.

There is another interaction pair of forces acting on the girls.

- The bar supports the girls. *This is the force of the bar on the girls.*
- The girls pull on the bar. *This is the force of the girls on the bar.*

How do you measure forces?

You can measure force with a **newtonmeter** (sometimes called a spring balance). All forces are measured in **newtons** (N).

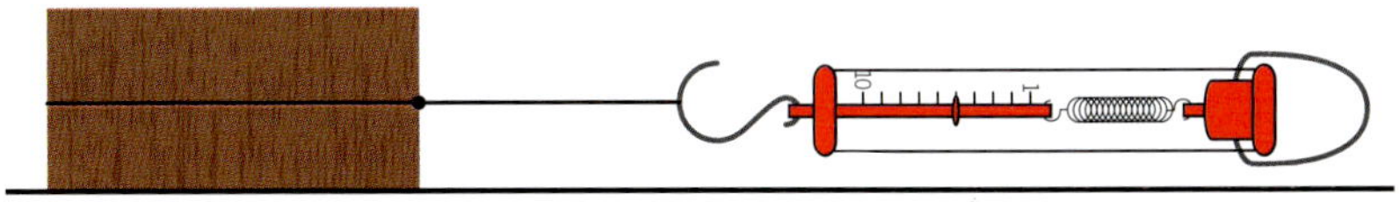

▲ A student is pulling the block with a force of 5 N.

C State the unit of force.

Newton predicts...

In the 1600s, Isaac Newton first explained how gravity affects objects. Scientists later used his ideas to predict that there was a planet beyond Uranus. In 1846 they discovered Neptune. A good explanation means that you can make predictions and test them.

▲ Upthrust supports you when you float.

Link

You can learn more about non-contact forces in P1 1.4 Forces at a distance

Key Words

push, pull, contact force, friction, air resistance, gravity, non-contact force, interaction pair, newtonmeter, newton (N)

Summary Questions

1 Copy and complete the sentences below.

A force is a ______ or a ______.
We can show the forces acting on an object using force ______.
Forces come in pairs, called ______ pairs. To measure forces you use a ______.

(5 marks)

2 Describe one of the interaction pairs for an apple hanging from the branch of a tree.

(2 marks)

3 You are probably sitting on a chair as you read this book. Explain in detail why the two forces acting on you are not two forces in the same interaction pair.

(6 marks)

1.2 Squashing and stretching

Learning objectives

After this topic you will be able to:

- describe how forces deform objects
- explain how solid surfaces provide a support force
- use Hooke's Law.

▲ Even a solid golf ball changes shape when you hit it.

Foul Fact!

When a footballer heads a ball the forces deform both the ball and the footballer's head.

Link

You can learn more about particles in solids, liquids, and gases in C1 1.1 The particle model

Key Words

deform, compress, stretch, reaction, extension, tension, elastic limit, Hooke's Law, linear

Why don't you fall through the chair you're sitting on? The chair changes shape, or deforms, when you sit on it. This produces the force that pushes you up.

Changing shape

When a ball hits the floor the ball **deforms**. Forces can **compress** (squash) or **stretch** objects. When you exert a force you can deform an object. You can compress it or you can stretch it.

A Describe what happens to a tennis ball when it hits the ground.

How can the floor push you up?

The floor pushes up on you when you stand on it. It seems strange to talk about the floor exerting a force on you. You can't see anything happening.

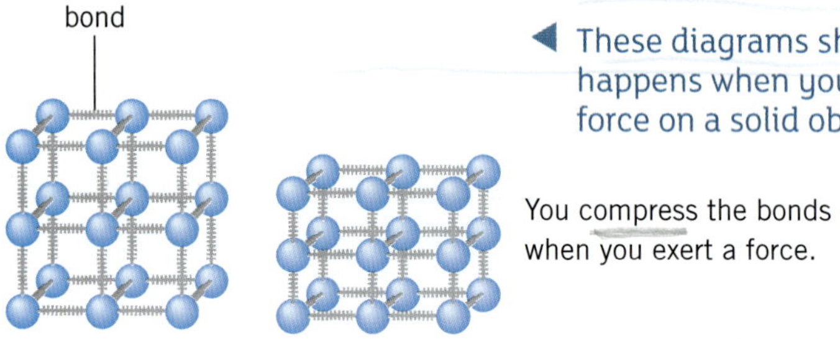

bond
You compress the bonds when you exert a force.

◀ These diagrams show what happens when you exert a force on a solid object.

The floor is a solid; solids are made up of particles arranged in a regular pattern. The particles are joined strongly together by bonds. This is what happens when you stand on the floor:

- Your weight pushes the particles together.
- The bonds are compressed.
- They push back and support you.

Solid materials are only compressed a very small amount when you apply a force to them. A support force from a chair or the floor is called the **reaction** force.

Stretching

Bungee cords, springs, and even lift cables all stretch when you exert a force on them. The amount that they stretch is called the **extension**.

A bungee cord stretches as the jumper falls. When the bungee cord has stretched as far as it will go, it pulls her back up. This force is called **tension**.

What happens when you stretch a spring?

Springs are special. If you ***double*** the force on the spring the extension will ***double***. You can use the length of the spring to measure the size of a force. When you remove the force the spring goes back to its original length.

What's the limit?

At some point the spring will not go back to its original length when you remove the force. This is the **elastic limit**. Trampoline springs are designed to never go past their elastic limit.

◀ The shape of a bungee cord changes when you stretch it.

Tension

Hooke's Law

If the extension doubles when you double the force then the object obeys **Hooke's Law**. The graph of force against extension is a straight line, or **linear**. Hooke's Law is a special case. Not everything behaves like a spring when you stretch it. If you double the force on an elastic band the extension may not double.

B State Hooke's Law.

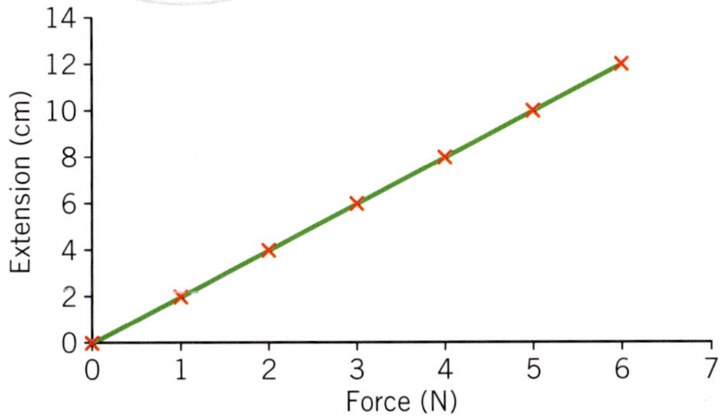

▲ This graph shows how the extension of a spring changes as you pull it.

A straight-line graph

Using the graph below, find the extension when the force is 3 N and again when it is 6 N. Does this spring obey Hooke's Law? Explain your answer.

How long?

You have a spring that is 4 cm long. When you exert a force of 3 N it stretches to a length of 6 cm. What is the extension? What would the extension be if you doubled the force?

3N = 2cm (6-4)
6N =

Summary Questions

1 Copy and complete the sentences below.

Forces can change the shape of objects or ______ them. Solid surfaces are made of ______. The bonds between particles are compressed when you apply a force. They ______ back on you. This provides a ______ force called the ______ force.

(5 marks)

2 Describe how your chair pushes you up.

(2 marks)

3 Design a new style of trampoline that would make trampolining more fun. Use the ideas on this page to explain how it works.

(6 marks)

1.3 Drag forces and friction

Learning objectives

After this topic you will be able to:

- describe the effect of drag forces and friction
- explain why drag forces and friction arise.

Fantastic Fact!

Which material has the lowest friction? BAM is a material that contains aluminium, magnesium, and boron. It is twice as slippery as ice.

▲ You need friction to move across surfaces.

Fantastic Fact!

In 1995 Fred Rompelberg travelled at 167 mph.... on a bicycle! He did it by cycling behind a lorry where there was very little air resistance.

Slide your finger along the desk. Does the surface feel smooth or rough? Even really smooth surfaces exert a force.

What is friction?

A surface such as a metal slide in a playground looks and feels really smooth. Now imagine zooming in on it; you will see that it is actually rough.

When a book is resting on the table you can push on it but it may not move. **Friction** grips objects. As you increase the force by pushing harder the book will start to move. If you remove the force the book slows down and stops. This is because the rough surfaces can no longer move past each other.

A State two things that friction does.

Is friction useful?

Friction can be a good thing. You need friction to walk, as the friction between your foot and the road produces the force to move you forward. The brakes on your bike and in a car work because of friction.

B Describe how friction helps you to walk.

How can you reduce friction?

One way to reduce friction is by using oil or grease. This is called **lubrication**. When you oil the chain of your bike the surfaces move past each other more easily. Snowboarders wax their boards to reduce the friction between the board and the snow.

C Suggest why the hinges of a door need to be lubricated.

What are drag forces?

A dolphin swimming through the water and a surfer paddling through water will both experience **water resistance**. As a snowboarder jumps through the air he will experience **air resistance**. Water resistance and air resistance are **drag forces**.

▲ When you move through water you experience water resistance.

To understand drag forces you need to think about the particles in the air and the water.

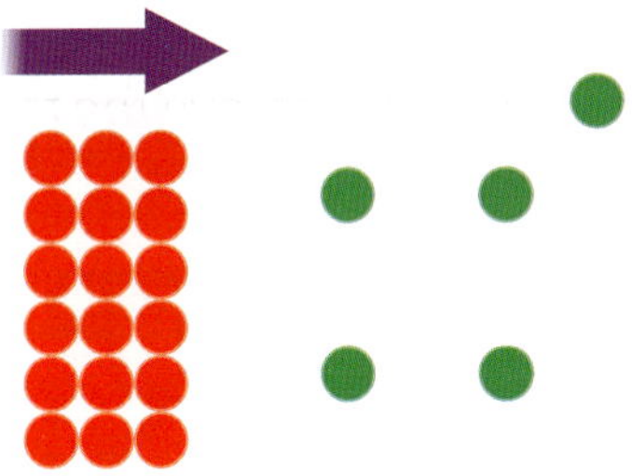

A solid moves through a gas.

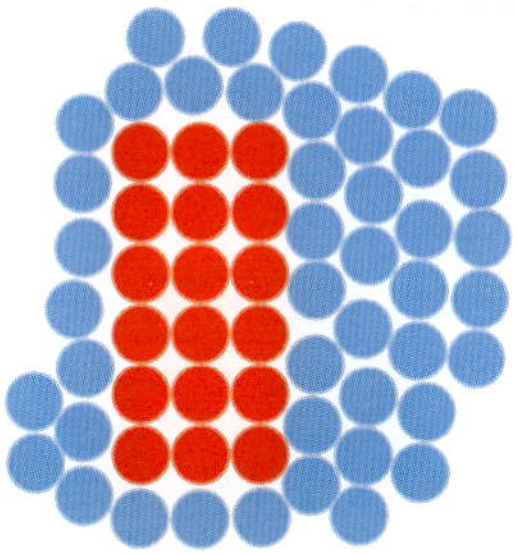

A solid moves through a liquid.

▲ A moving object is in contact with air or water particles.

As a dolphin moves through the water it pushes the water particles out of the way. This produces a drag force, which slows it down.

D Name the drag force acting on an aeroplane in flight.

How can you use drag forces?

Parachutes are used to slow down drag-racing cars and skydivers. The contact with the air produces a drag force.

How can you reduce drag forces?

An Olympic cyclist will tuck her arms in close to her body as she cycles. She will even make sure that her thumbs are as close to the handlebars as possible. This makes her more **streamlined**, which reduces the force of air resistance.

Testing a parachute

A company wants to compare different materials for making parachutes. Name **three** ways that they could make it a fair test.

Key Words

friction, lubrication, water resistance, air resistance, drag force, streamlined

Summary Questions

1 Copy and complete the sentences below.

The force of ______ acts between two solid surfaces in contact that are sliding across each other. The surfaces are ______ and will grip each other. This is why you need to exert a ______ to make something move. There are two drag forces: ______ and ______. When a moving object is in contact with ______ or ______ particles it has to push them out of the way.

(7 marks)

2 Describe the effect of water resistance acting on a bird diving into a lake to catch a fish.

(1 mark)

3 Suggest and explain a reason why the brake blocks on a bicycle need to be replaced from time to time.

(2 marks)

4 A dragster is a car that uses a parachute as a brake. Use the ideas on this page to compare the drag force due to the parachute acting on cars travelling at different speeds, or using parachutes of different sizes.

(6 marks)

1.4 Forces at a distance

Learning objectives

After this topic you will be able to:

- describe the effects of a field
- describe the effect of gravitational forces on Earth and in space.

Link

You can learn more about electrostatic forces in P2 1.1 Charging up

Foul Fact!

The strongest gravitational field in the Universe is made by a black hole. It is called a 'black' hole because even light cannot escape from its gravitational field. If you stood close to a black hole, the force of gravity on your feet would be much bigger than the force of gravity on your head. You'd be stretched. This is called 'spaghettification'.

Key Words

magnetic force, electrostatic force, field, weight, mass, kilogram (kg), gravitational field strength

If you let go of your pen and it moved upwards you'd be very surprised. We are so familiar with the force of gravity that sometimes we don't even think of it as a force.

Gravitational forces

A gravitational force acts on a diver jumping off a diving board. It is a non-contact force. There are other types of non-contact force.

Magnets exert a **magnetic force** on magnetic materials or other magnets without touching them. If you rub a balloon you can pick up bits of paper with it. This is an electric or **electrostatic force**. Magnetic and electrostatic forces are non-contact forces.

▲ A magnet picks up filings.

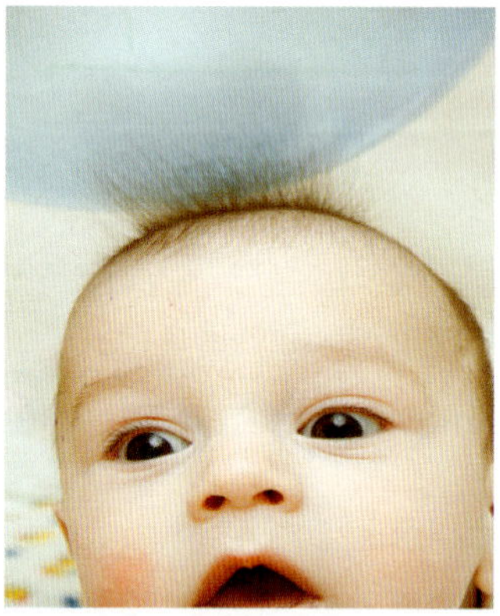

▲ A balloon rubbed on your jumper attracts a baby's hair.

A Identify three forces that act at a distance.

Force fields

In physics a **field** is a special region where something experiences a force. There is a magnetic field around a magnet where magnetic materials experience a force. There are gravitational fields where things with mass experience a force.

Gravitational, magnetic, and electrostatic fields have something in common. As you get further away from the mass, magnet, or charge, the field gets weaker. Contact forces only act when the objects are touching each other. Non-contact forces act at any distance, even if the objects are not touching.

B Describe what is meant by a field.

What do I weigh?

You can use a newtonmeter to find the **weight** of an apple. The Earth pulls the apple downwards. Measuring the weight of the apple means measuring the force of the Earth on it.

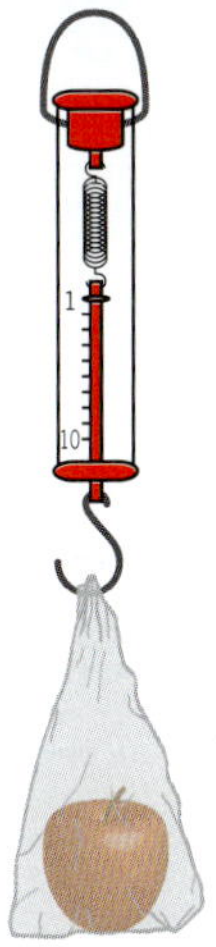

An apple has a weight of about 1 N.

What is the difference between weight and mass?

Weight is a force so it is measured in newtons (N). **Mass** is the amount of 'stuff' something is made up of. It is a measure of how hard it is to get something to move. Mass is measured in **kilograms** (kg).

> **Units of mass**
>
> Smaller masses are measured in grams (g).
>
> There are 1000 g in 1 kilogram (kg).
>
> Convert these masses into grams: **a** 2 kg **b** 3.5 kg **c** 0.4 kg
>
> Convert these masses into kilograms: **d** 4700 g **e** 250 g

You can calculate weight using an equation.

weight (N) = mass (kg) x **gravitational field strength**, g (N/kg)

On Earth gravitational field strength is about 10 N/kg.

This means that, if your mass is 50 kg, for example, then your weight on Earth is:

$$\text{weight} = 50\text{ kg} \times 10\text{ N/kg}$$
$$= 500\text{ N}$$

Gravitational field strength is different on other planets and stars. Your weight would be different on different planets because g would be different.

The Apollo astronauts could jump much higher on the Moon because g on the Moon is about one sixth of g on Earth.

C State the unit of mass and the unit of weight.

What would happen to my weight in space?

Imagine blasting off from the Earth in a spacecraft. As you move away from the Earth the gravitational field gets weaker. If you stood on scales in the spacecraft the reading would be less than it would be on Earth.

The amount of 'you' would not change. Your mass stays the same. It is the force of the Earth on you, your weight, that is less.

Summary Questions

1 Copy and complete the sentences below.

Some forces act a distance. The force of gravity acts on things that have ______. A balloon has an ______ force when you rub it. You can feel a ______ force between two magnets. Your weight is a ______ and is measured in ______. Your ______ is the amount of stuff you are made up of and is measured in ______.

(7 marks)

2 Explain one reason why your weight on Jupiter is 2.7 times your weight on Earth.

(3 marks)

3 Describe what happens to the force of gravity as you move away from the Earth.

(1 mark)

4 Imagine the first Olympic Games conducted on the Moon in a specially designed dome. Use the ideas on this page to state and explain which sports would produce new records, and which would not.

(6 marks)

1.5 Balanced and unbalanced

Learning objectives

After this topic you will be able to:

- describe the difference between balanced and unbalanced forces
- describe situations that are in equilibrium
- explain why the speed or direction of motion of objects can change.

▲ When the teams pull with the same force the forces are balanced.

Equal and opposite...?

Isaac Newton said, 'For every action there is an equal and opposite reaction'. The forces in an interaction pair are equal and opposite. Is lying in bed an example of this law? No, it is not. Each of the forces acting on you comes from a *different* interaction pair.

Key Words

balanced, equilibrium, unbalanced, driving force, resistive force

To get out of bed in the morning you need a force to get you moving.

What are balanced forces?

When the forces acting on an object are the same size but in opposite directions we say that they are **balanced**. You can think of balanced forces like two teams in a tug of war. If each team pulls with the same force the rope doesn't move. The forces cancel out. The object is in **equilibrium**.

A State what equilibrium means.

All stationary objects are in equilibrium. There has to be a support force acting on them to balance out their weight.

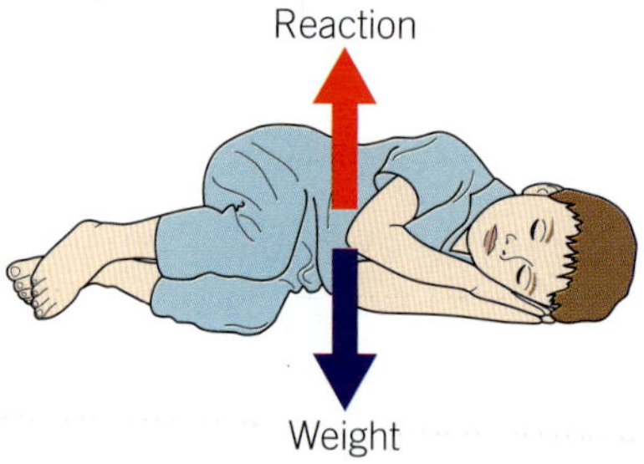

◀ You are in equilibrium when lying in bed.

B Draw a diagram showing the forces acting on a stationary mass hanging on a spring.

What are unbalanced forces?

The forces acting on this rocket-powered car are **unbalanced**. They are not the same size so they do not cancel out.

The **driving force** from the engine is much, much bigger than the **resistive forces** from air resistance and friction.

▲ The Thrust SSC was the first car to travel faster than sound.

C State the difference between balanced forces and unbalanced forces.

How do unbalanced forces change speed?

When the car's rocket-powered engine starts up the driving force will become very big very quickly. When the driver wants to stop he will fire a parachute to slow the car down. In both cases the forces on the car are unbalanced.

The driver uses a parachute because this gives a much bigger resistive force on the car than just using the brakes. The speed of the car will change much more quickly. The car will stop in a much shorter time.

	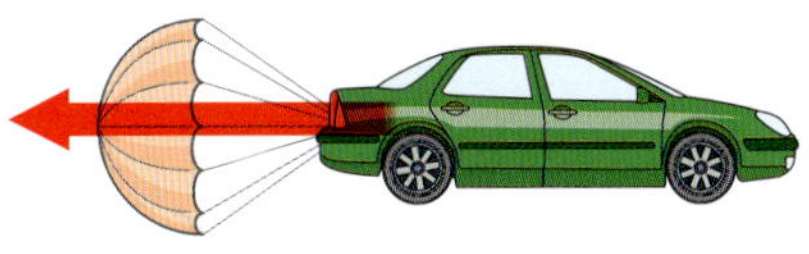
The driving force is bigger than the resistive forces acting on the car.	The only forces acting on the car are resistive forces.
The speed of the car increases.	The speed of the car decreases.

How do unbalanced forces change direction?

Isaac Newton worked out that the Earth exerts a force on the Moon. The force of gravity acting on the Moon keeps the Moon in orbit around the Earth. It is this same force that acts on an apple and pulls it to the ground. It changes the *direction* of motion, not the speed.

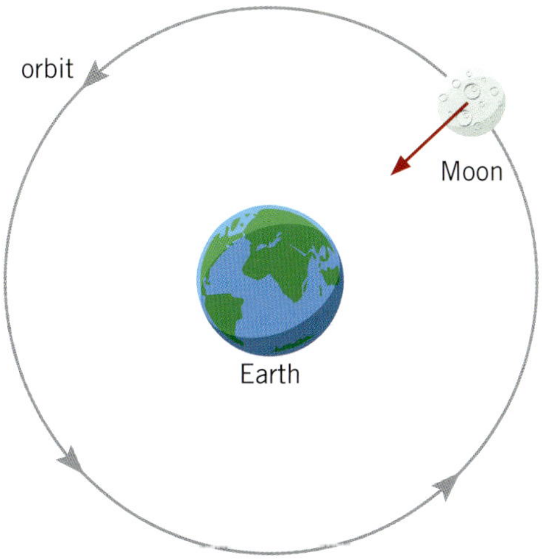

The force of gravity keeps the Moon in orbit.

Every time you go around a corner in a car the friction between the tyres and the road changes the direction of the car.

Link

You can learn more about speed in P2 3.1 Speed

Friction changes the direction of a motorbike.

Summary Questions

1 Copy and complete the sentences below.

If the forces on an object are the same_______ but act in _______ directions they are balanced. This is called _______. The forces acting on any stationary object are _______. If the forces on an object are unbalanced the _______ will change. If the _______ force is bigger than the _______ force it speeds up. If the _______ force is bigger than the _______ force it slows down.

(9 marks)

2 A cyclist is slowing down as she is cycling along a road.

a Draw a diagram to show the forces acting on the cyclist. *(1 mark)*

b Label the forces using the words 'resistive' and 'driving'. *(1 mark)*

c Explain why her speed is decreasing. *(1 mark)*

3 Design a new ride for a theme park. Describe and explain the motion of people who go on the ride using the ideas on this page.

(6 marks)

P1 Chapter 1 Summary

Key Points

- Forces are pushes or pulls, measured in newtons (N) using a newtonmeter.
- Forces exist when objects interact – this produces an interaction pair.
- Forces can deform objects, change their speed, or the direction of motion.
- Contact forces occur when objects are touching.
- Friction, air resistance, and water resistance are contact forces.
- Friction can be reduced by lubrication. Air resistance and water resistance can be reduced by streamlining.
- Non-contact forces occur when objects are not touching.
- Gravitational, electrostatic, and magnetic forces are non-contact forces.
- Solid surfaces provide a support force when they are compressed.
- Springs or ropes extend when you apply a force.
- For some objects if you double the force the extension doubles. This is Hooke's Law.
- A field is a region where something feels a force, for example, a mass in a gravitational field.
- Mass is the amount of stuff an object is made up of, measured in kilograms.
- Weight is the force of the Earth on an object, measured in newtons.
  Weight (N) = mass (kg) x g (N/kg)
- When the forces acting on an object are equal in size and acting in opposite directions they are balanced. The object is in equilibrium.
- If the forces are not balanced the object will speed up, slow down, or change direction.

BIG Write

Mission to Mars

NASA's Curiosity rover landed on Mars in August 2012. Imagine that the first astronauts have just returned from Mars in the year 2034.

Task

You were one of the astronauts on the mission. Write a blog that covers the whole mission. Start from when you take off from the Earth and finish with splash down when you return home.

Tips

- Explain the motion of the rocket during each stage of the journey to and from Mars.
- Use what you have learnt about where forces come from and how they affect motion.

Key Words

push, pull, contact, non-contact, interaction pair, newtonmeter, weight, newton (N), deform, compress, stretch, reaction, extension, tension, elastic limit, Hooke's Law, linear, friction, lubrication, water resistance, air resistance, drag forces, streamlined, gravity, magnetic, electrostatic, field, mass, weight, kilograms (kg), gravitational field strength, balanced, equilibrium, unbalanced, driving force, resistive force

End-of-chapter questions

1 State which of the forces below are contact forces and which are non-contact forces.

magnetic force, friction, air resistance, gravitational force, electrostatic force, upthrust

*(**6 marks**)*

2 For each object below state whether the forces on it are balanced or unbalanced.

a a boat that is speeding up *(1 mark)*

b a boy who is floating in a swimming pool *(1 mark)*

c a cyclist who is slowing down *(1 mark)*

*(**3 marks**)*

3 A student is investigating friction. She puts a block of wood on a ramp and lifts the ramp until the block starts to move. She repeats the experiment with different types of surface on the ramp.

a State the variable that she is changing (the independent variable). *(1 mark)*

b State the variable that she is measuring (the dependent variable). *(1 mark)*

c State the variable or variables that she should control. *(1 mark)*

d Explain why she will need to plot a bar chart in this investigation. *(2 marks)*

*(**5 marks**)*

4 A cyclist is sitting on her bicycle at the start of a race.

a Draw a diagram of the cyclist and label the forces acting on her. *(2 marks)*

b Explain how the bicycle seat exerts a force on the cyclist. *(2 marks)*

c The race begins. State whether the forces on her when she goes around a corner are balanced or unbalanced. *(1 mark)*

*(**5 marks**)*

5 A student wants to make a newtonmeter. He coils a piece of wire around his pencil to make a spring. He puts a 100 g mass on the spring. A 100 g mass has a weight of 1 N. He measures the extension.

a Describe how to measure the extension of a spring. *(3 marks)*

b Explain the difference between a mass of 100 g and a weight of 1 N. *(2 marks)*

The student measures the extension for different forces and plots his results on a graph. The line on the graph is a straight line.

c Use the shape of the graph to explain why the spring obeys Hooke's Law. *(2 marks)*

*(**7 marks**)*

6 Another student decides to use an elastic band as a newtonmeter and plots these results.

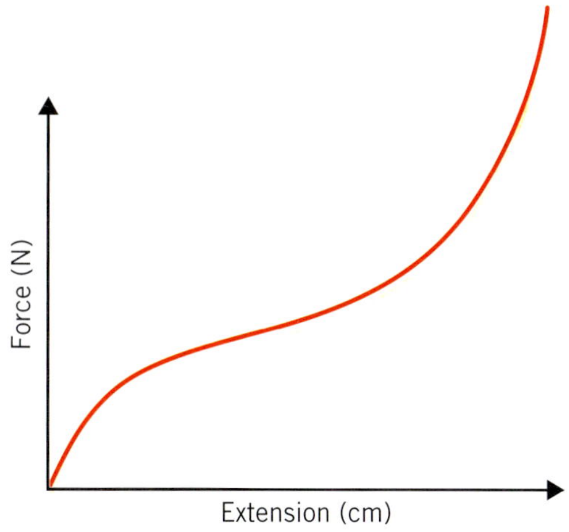

Explain in detail why the elastic band cannot be used as a newtonmeter but a spring can.

*(**6 marks**)*

2.1 Waves

Learning objectives

After this topic you will be able to:

- describe the different types of wave and their features
- describe what happens when water waves hit a barrier
- describe what happens when waves superpose.

Key Words

oscillation, vibration, energy, undulation, sound, amplitude, frequency, wavelength, peak, crest, trough, transverse, longitudinal, compression, rarefaction, reflection, incident wave, reflected wave, superpose

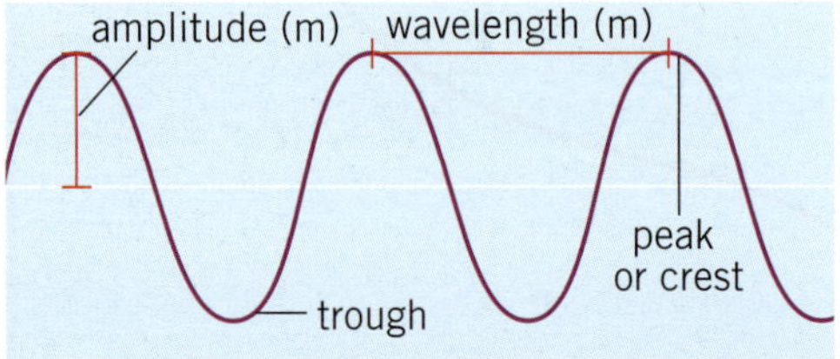

▲ This diagram shows the amplitude and wavelength of a wave.

▲ You can make a transverse wave on a slinky.

Mexican waves are very popular at concerts and sporting events. But what is a wave?

What is a wave?

In science a wave is an **oscillation** or **vibration** that transfers **energy** or information. A wave can also be an **undulation** on the surface of water. Matter does not get transferred. Waves have many uses, for example, microwaves cook food, and **sound** waves help you communicate.

Features of a wave

All waves have three important features:

- an **amplitude**, which is the distance from the middle to the top or bottom of a wave
- a **frequency**, which is the number of waves that go past a particular point per second
- a **wavelength**, which is the distance from one point on a wave to the same point on the next wave.

The top of a wave is called a **peak** or **crest**, and the bottom of a wave is called a **trough**.

A Name three properties of a wave.

Transverse or longitudinal?

You can send pulses down a slinky spring. You can make the pulses in two ways.

You can move your hand at right angles to the spring. This produces a **transverse** wave on the slinky. In a transverse wave the oscillation is at 90° to the direction of the wave.

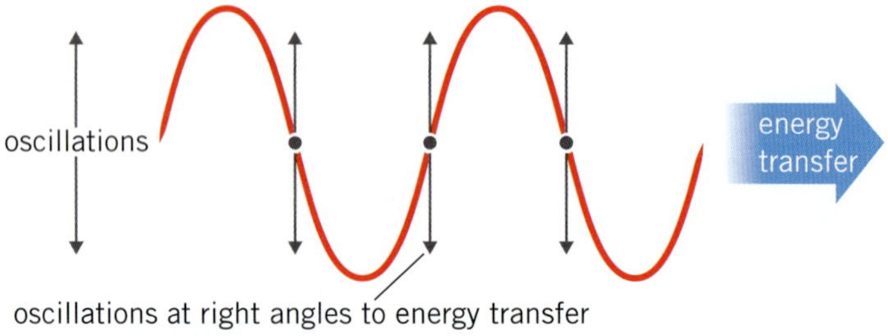

▲ In a transverse wave the oscillation is at 90° to the direction of the wave.

You can also push and pull the spring. This produces a **longitudinal** wave on the slinky. The oscillation is parallel to the direction of the wave – it is in the same direction as the spring itself.

In a **compression** the coils of the spring are close together. In a **rarefaction** the coils are further apart. Sound is a longitudinal wave and light is a transverse wave.

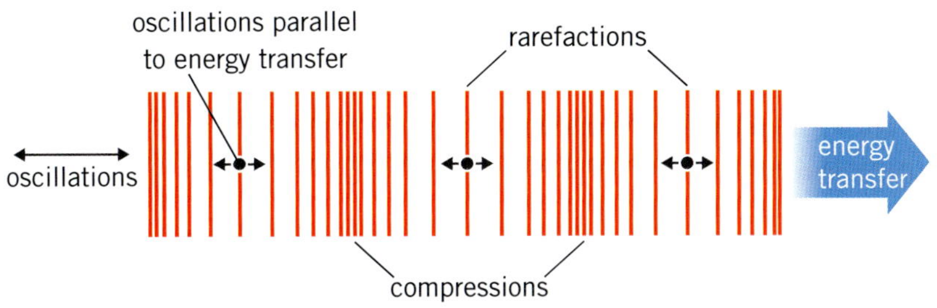

▲ In a longitudinal wave the oscillation is parallel to the direction of the wave.

B State the direction of the oscillation of a longitudinal wave.

Reflecting waves

Waves bounce off surfaces and barriers, just like a football bounces off a wall. This is called **reflection**.

The wave coming into the barrier is called the **incident wave**. The wave bouncing off is called the **reflected wave**.

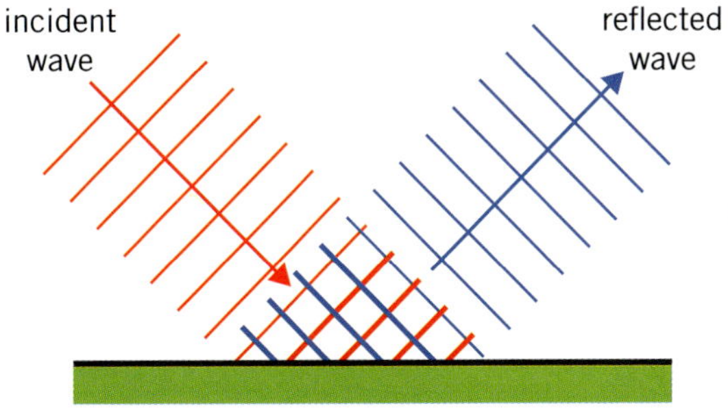

◄ A wave reflects off a barrier.

C State the name of the wave that hits the barrier.

Adding waves

When waves are put together they **superpose**. This means that they add up or they cancel out.

If the waves are in step they will add up. You get more than you had before. If they are not in step then they cancel out and you get less than you had before.

Spot the word

Write the word from each of these definitions:

a the distance from the top to the bottom of a wave

b where the links of a spring are squashed together

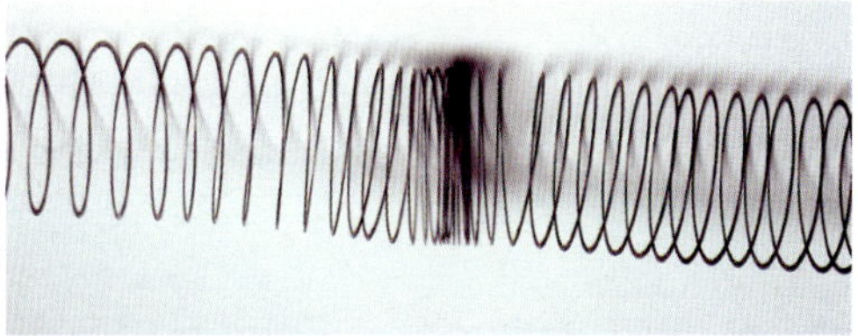

▲ You can make a longitudinal wave on a slinky.

Summary Questions

1 Copy the sentences below, choosing the correct bold words.

A wave is an oscillation or vibration that transfers **energy/matter**. The distance from the centre to the top of the wave is the **amplitude/wavelength**. The distance from one crest to the next crest is the **amplitude/wavelength**. Waves can **reflect/superpose** when they hit a barrier, and cancel out or add up when they **reflect/superpose**.

(5 marks)

2 Describe the difference between a compression and a rarefaction in a longitudinal wave on a spring.

(2 marks)

3 Explain the similarities and differences between longitudinal and transverse waves.

(6 marks)

2.2 Sound and energy transfer

Learning objectives

After this topic you will be able to:

- describe how sound is produced and travels
- explain why the speed of sound is different in different materials
- contrast the speed of sound and the speed of light.

▲ The ends of a tuning fork are vibrating.

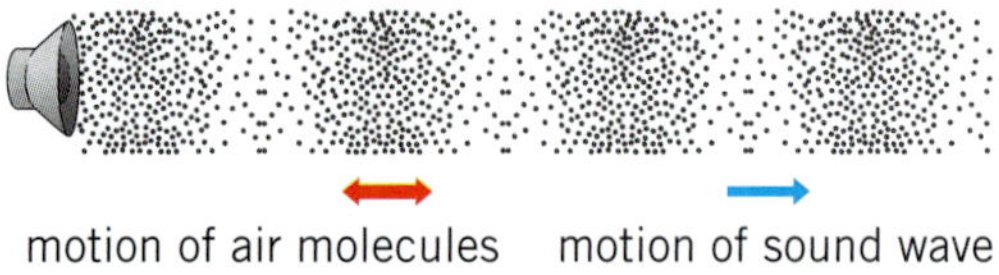

▲ Air molecules move backwards and forwards.

▲ Dolphins communicate underwater.

If you very gently press the front of your throat while you are talking you will feel a vibration. This is your vocal chords vibrating. The vibration produces the sound waves that travel through the air from your mouth.

What is a sound wave?

A **vibration** produces a sound wave. All speakers, like the ones in your headphones, have something that moves backwards and forwards, or vibrates. This makes the air molecules move backwards and forwards, which produces a sound wave.

Some people think that sound just 'dies away'. It doesn't. It spreads out as it moves away from the source.

A State what produces a sound wave.

What does sound travel through?

Dolphins and whales use sound waves to communicate underwater. Elephants stamp their feet when a predator comes near – the warning travels through the ground to other elephants. Sound needs a **medium** like a solid, liquid, or gas to travel through. It cannot travel through empty space, a **vacuum**, because there are no air molecules to vibrate.

How fast does sound travel?

Sound travels at 340 m/s in air. Sound travels much faster in liquids, about 1500 m/s. Sound travels fastest in solids. In metals like steel it can travel at 5000 m/s. You can explain why a sound wave travels faster in a solid than in a gas if you think about particles. The particles in a solid are very close together, so the vibration is passed along more quickly than in a gas.

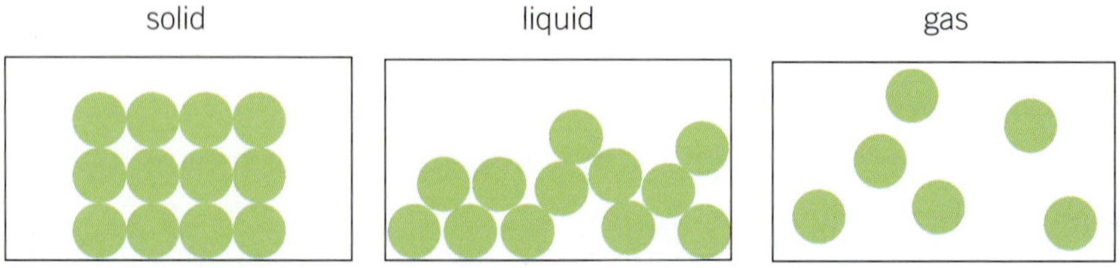

▲ The arrangement of particles explains the speed of sound in different materials.

Some people talk about the 'sound barrier'. There is no difference between travelling at or beyond the **speed of sound**.

Chuck Yeager broke the sound barrier first in 1947, and many others have since. Felix Baumgartner jumped from a balloon 24 miles above the Earth and broke the sound barrier in free fall.

Felix Baumgartner travelled faster than sound.

B State the speed of sound.

How fast?

A student uses some secondary sources of information to make a list of the speed of sound in different materials.

a Draw a suitable table that she could use to record the data.

b State and explain which type of graph she could plot to show the data.

C Name the three types of medium that sound can travel through.

Which is faster: sound or light?

Light travels much faster than sound. The **speed of light** is 300 000 000 m/s, so it is almost a million times faster than sound. You notice this difference during a thunderstorm. The thunder and lightning are produced at the same time. You see the lightning immediately but it takes time for the sound of thunder to reach you.

Light can travel through a vacuum. It doesn't need a medium to travel through.

Key Words

vibration, medium, vacuum, speed of sound, speed of light

Stormy night

A girl sees a flash of lightning and then hears the thunder four seconds later.

a How far away is the storm? State your answer in kilometres.

b What would she notice about the thunder and lightning when the storm is directly overhead?

Summary Questions

1 Copy and complete the sentences below.

Sound is produced by objects that are ________________.
This makes the air molecules __________ and produces a sound wave. Sound travels fastest in ________ and slowest in _______, and it cannot travel through a ________.

(5 marks)

2 Explain why sound travels slower in a gas compared to a liquid.

(2 marks)

3 Compare the time it takes the light to travel from your teacher to your eye with the time it takes sound to travel the same distance.

(6 marks)

2.3 Loudness and pitch

Learning objectives

After this topic you will be able to:

- describe the link between loudness and amplitude
- describe the link between frequency and pitch
- state the range of human hearing and describe how it differs from the range of hearing in animals.

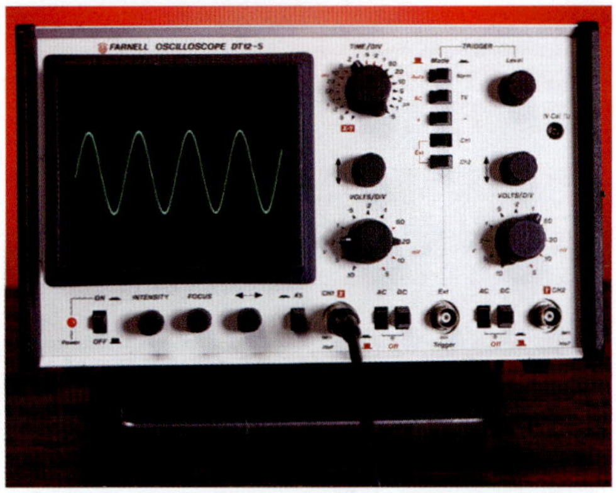

▲ An oscilloscope shows a representation of a sound wave made, for example, by a tuning fork.

If you play a loud note of exactly the right pitch then you can shatter a glass. What's the difference between loudness and pitch?

Seeing sound

You can plug a **microphone** into an **oscilloscope** to see what the sound of your voice looks like. The wave on the screen is transverse but the wave that you are making when you talk is longitudinal. The microphone produces a signal that represents the sound wave.

What affects the loudness of a sound?

If a drummer hits the drum harder the sound is louder.

▲ A drum produces a sound with a large amplitude.

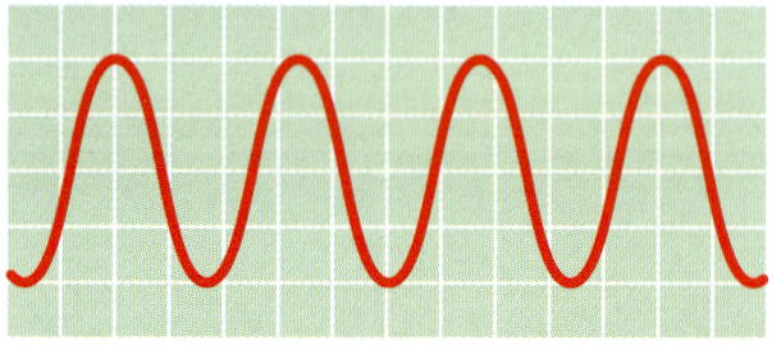

loud

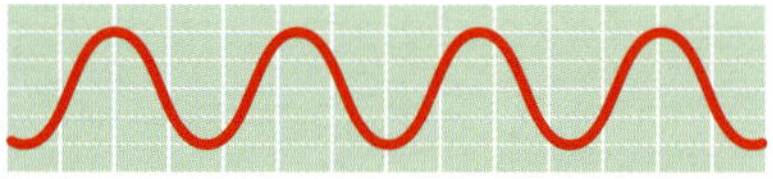

soft

▲ A loud sound has a bigger amplitude than a soft sound.

You bang a drum harder or pull a guitar string more to produce a louder sound. A loud sound has a bigger amplitude than a soft sound. It transfers more energy than a soft sound. To make a louder sound you need to make the vibration bigger.

A State the property of a sound wave that affects the loudness of the sound.

What affects the pitch of a sound?

Some singers can sing higher-pitched notes than others. The **pitch** of a note depends on the frequency. High-pitched sounds have a high frequency and low-pitched sounds have a low frequency. Frequency is measured in **hertz** (Hz) or **kilohertz** (kHz).

1 kHz = 1000 Hz. To make a higher-pitched sound you need to make something vibrate faster, so that there are more waves per second.

Key Words

pitch, loudness, microphone, oscilloscope, hertz, kilohertz, audible range, infrasound, ultrasound

Fantastic Fact!

Grasshoppers make sounds that they cannot even hear.

▲ A whistle produces a sound with a high frequency.

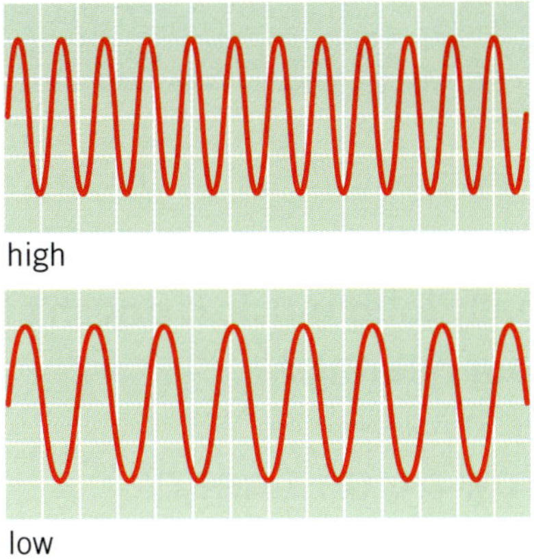

▲ A high sound has a higher frequency than a low sound.

You can have a loud, high-pitched sound or a loud, low-pitched sound. Changing the frequency does not affect the amplitude.

B State the property of a sound wave that affects the pitch of the sound.

What frequencies can you hear?

You can only hear a particular range of frequencies, called the **audible range**. You have the biggest audible range when you are young: 20–20 000 Hz. Your audible range changes as you get older. You will find it more difficult to hear high-frequency sounds.

What frequencies can other animals hear?

Bats, dolphins, and grasshoppers have a completely different audible range to humans. Lots of animals can hear frequencies that are much higher than the frequencies we can hear. Frequencies below 20 Hz are called **infrasound**. Frequencies above 20 000 Hz are called **ultrasound**.

Species	Audible range (Hz)
bat	2000–110 000
cat	45–64 000
dog	67–45 000
dolphin	1000–100 000
goldfish	20–3000
hedgehog	250–45 000
whale	1000–123 000

Conversions

a Convert the audible range for humans into kilohertz.

b Convert the audible range of the whale into kilohertz.

Link

You can learn more about ultrasound in P1 2.5 Echoes and ultrasound

Summary Questions

1 Copy the sentences below, choosing the correct bold words.

The loudness of a sound depends on the **amplitude/frequency** and the pitch of the sound depends on the **amplitude/frequency**. Frequency is measured in **hertz/metres**. The range of frequencies you can hear is called the **audible/visible** range.

(4 marks)

2 State the range of human hearing and compare it to the range of dolphin hearing.

(2 marks)

3 A singer produces sounds that vary in pitch and loudness. Use the ideas above to suggest and explain in detail what her vocal chords do to produce different types of sound wave.

(6 marks)

2.4 Detecting sound

Learning objectives

After this topic you will be able to:

- describe how the ear works
- describe how your hearing can be damaged
- describe how a microphone detects sound.

Link

You can learn more about specialised cells B1 1.3 Specialised cells

Key Words

ear, pinna, auditory canal, eardrum, outer ear, ossicle, middle ear, amplify, oval window, cochlea, auditory nerve, inner ear, decibel, diaphragm, amplifier

Foul Fact!

Your ossicles don't grow. They are the correct size when you are born. They are the smallest bones in your body.

Your ear is your body's microphone. If you listen to really loud music it doesn't hurt but can it damage your hearing?

How do you hear?

Your **ear** detects sound waves. The part of your ear that you can see, called the **pinna**, directs the sound wave into your auditory canal towards your ear drum. The pinna, **auditory canal**, and **eardrum** make up your **outer ear**.

Your eardrum vibrates and passes the vibration on to the **ossicles**. The ossicles make up your **middle ear**. They are tiny bones that **amplify** the sound. They make the **oval window** vibrate.

This passes the vibration on to liquid in the **cochlea**. This contains thousands of tiny hairs. As the liquid moves the hairs move. Specialised cells at the base of the hairs convert the movement to an electrical signal. The signal travels down the **auditory nerve** to your brain. You hear the music.

The cochlea and the semi-circular canals make up your **inner ear**. The semi-circular canals help you to balance.

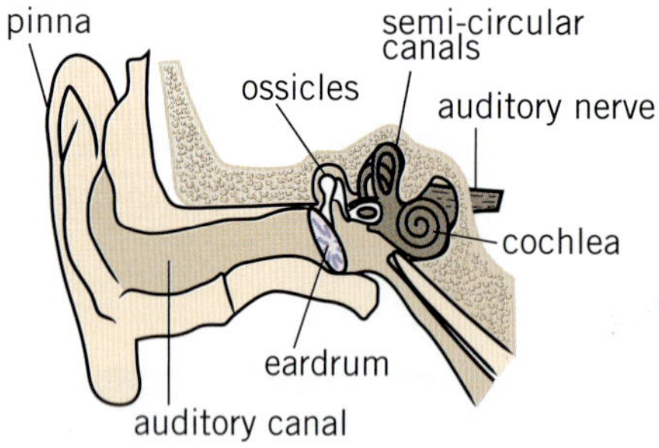

▲ Structure of the ear.

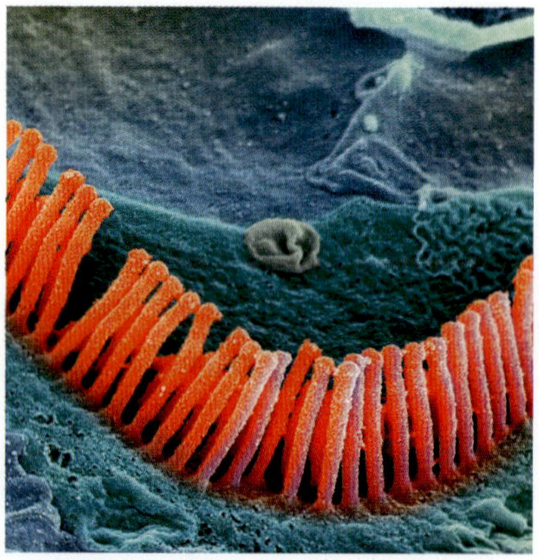

▲ Without these tiny hairs inside your cochlea you would not be able to hear.

A Name the first part of the ear that vibrates when a sound wave enters it.

How do you measure loudness?

In the 2010 World Cup in South Africa the crowd used vuvuzelas to make very loud sounds. Vuvuzelas can be so loud that they are painful.

You measure sound intensity in **decibels** (dB). The decibel scale is not like a ruler. Each increase of 10 dB increases the sound intensity by 10 times. A 40 dB sound is 100 times more intense than a 20 dB sound.

0 dB	20 dB	40 dB	60 dB	80 dB	100 dB	120 dB	140 dB
cannot be heard	leaves rustling	talking quietly	normal speech	heavy traffic	jet taking off	pain threshold	gun shot

How can you damage your hearing?

Your hearing can be damaged if a sharp object makes a hole in your eardrum but your eardrum will grow back. A build-up of ear wax can also be damaging. Very loud sounds or head injuries can permanently damage your hearing.

You can reduce the risk of damage by turning down the volume or using ear defenders.

B Describe one way that your hearing can be damaged.

How does a microphone work?

When a singer sings into a microphone the sound wave hits a flexible plate called a **diaphragm**. The diaphragm vibrates, like your eardrum. It produces an electrical signal, just like the cells in your cochlea. The signal carries the information that the sound wave carried.

You can use an **amplifier** to make the sound louder. Loudspeakers convert the electrical signal back into sound when they vibrate.

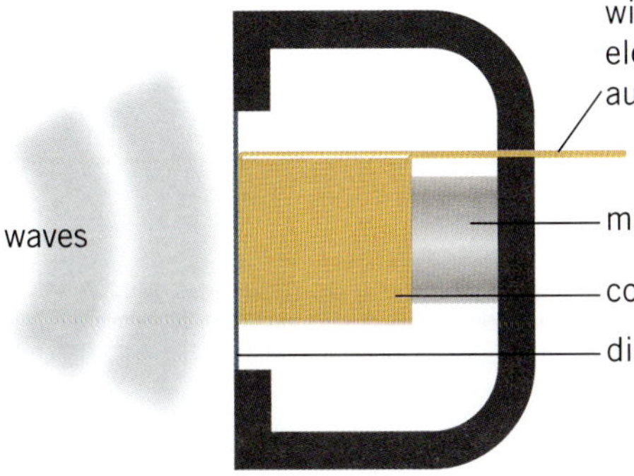

▲ A microphone detects sound in a similar way to your ear.

What protection?

Two companies make ear defenders. Plan an experiment to find out which pair is best at reducing sound intensity.

Summary Questions

1 Copy and complete the sentences below.

When a sound wave enters your ear it makes the ____________ vibrate. This makes the ____________ vibrate. The ____________ vibrates and this makes the liquid inside your ____________ vibrate. Cells at the base of ____________ inside your ____________ produce an electrical signal that travels up your ____________ to your brain. Sound intensity is measured in ____________. Your hearing can be ____________ by loud sounds. In a microphone a ____________ vibrates, which produces an electrical signal.

(10 marks)

2 Describe one way that your hearing can be damaged that is not permanent, and one way that it can be permanently damaged.

(2 marks)

3 Compare the ear and the microphone.

(6 marks)

2.5 Echoes and ultrasound

Learning objectives

After this topic you will be able to:

- describe what ultrasound is
- describe some uses of ultrasound.

Where is the quietest place in the world? Scientists have designed a room where it is so quiet you can hear your own heartbeat. The surfaces are designed to absorb sounds. There are no echoes.

▲ This room is designed to produce no echoes.

What is an echo?

When sound reflects off a surface it produces an **echo**. Sound takes time to travel. There is a time delay between making a sound and hearing an echo.

Measuring distances

Imagine that you are standing a long way from the school sports hall. You clap and you hear an echo one second later. How far away is the wall?

The speed of sound in air is 340 m/s. The sound travels a total distance of 340 m in one second. The distance to the wall is 165 m because the sound has travelled there and back. You can use the time taken to hear the echo to work out distance.

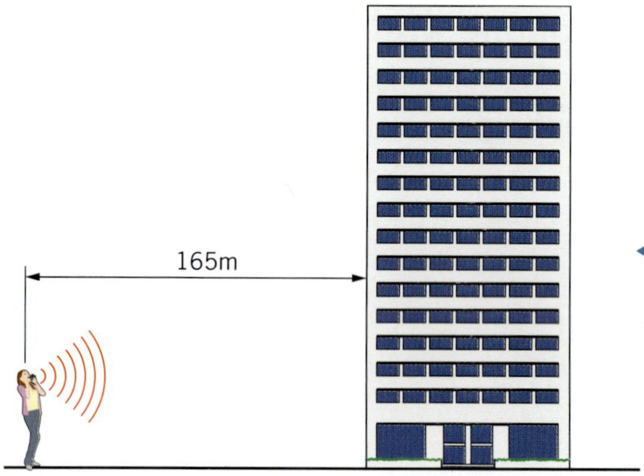

◀ You can work out how far away a wall is using echoes.

A State what an echo is.

How do you reduce echoes?

If lots of echoes join together to produce a longer sound this is called a **reverberation**. Reverberations can be a nuisance in concert halls or cinemas. You can reduce the effect of echoes by covering the walls with soft materials and putting carpet on the floor.

Key Words

echo, reverberation, transmitter, receiver

Fantastic Fact!

People used to think that a duck's quack and a wolf's howl don't echo. They do. Sometimes the echo gets mixed in with noise so you don't hear it.

What is ultrasound?

Bats use ultrasound to find their food. Doctors use ultrasound to make images of unborn babies. Ultrasound is sound with a frequency above 20 000 Hz.

B State the frequency of ultrasound.

When doctors make images of unborn babies, the ultrasound wave travels through the woman and reflects off the fetus. The machine detects the echo. It uses the time taken for the echo to build up an image of the fetus.

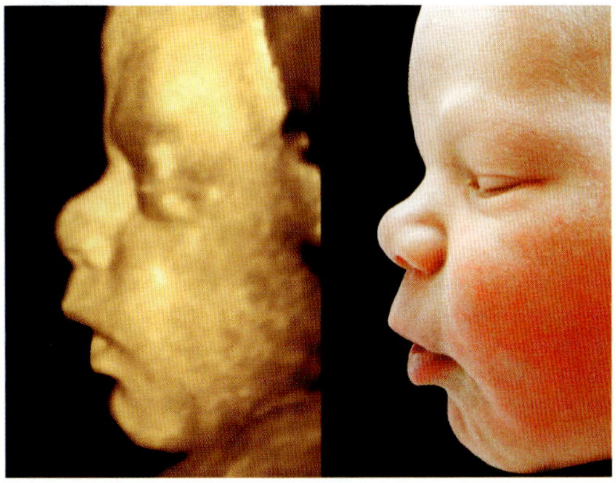

◀ This shows an ultrasound image of a baby and a photograph of the same baby after he was born.

Doctors also use ultrasound in physiotherapy. For example, ultrasound reduces the pain and swelling of a damaged tendon. They can also look for cancer..

Another use of ultrasound is sonar, used on ships. A **transmitter** under the ship sends out a beam of ultrasound. It travels through the water and reflects off the seabed. A **receiver** detects the reflection and uses the time taken to work out the depth of the water.

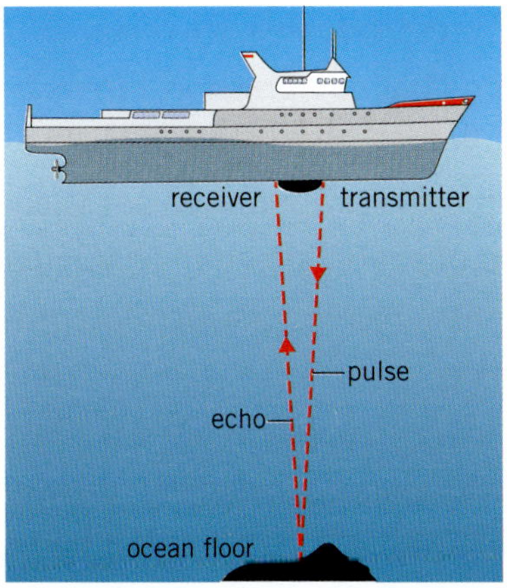

◀ Ships use ultrasound to work out the depth of the ocean.

Literacy

The word "sonar" is an acronym. It comes from the term "Sound Navigation And Ranging'.

C State a use of ultrasound.

How deep?

A ship's sonar detects an echo 1.6 s after it sends the pulse. The speed of sound in water is 1500 m/s. Work out how deep the water is.

Summary Questions

1 Copy and complete the sentences below.

An echo is a ______________ of sound. You can use the ________ between making a sound and hearing an echo from a surface to calculate the ____________ to it. Soft materials ____________ sound and reduce echoes. Animals use ultrasound to ______________ and ______________.
Ultrasound is used to make an ________ of a fetus, or break down ______________ .
Fishermen can use ultrasound to find the __________ of the ocean.

(9 marks)

2 Describe one way that a doctor might use ultrasound.

(2 marks)

3 Imagine that you are the captain of a fishing boat. Write a detailed presentation that you will show to the fishermen, explaining how to use sonar to detect shoals of fish.

(6 marks)

P1 Chapter 2 Summary

Key Points

- Waves are oscillations or vibrations that have an amplitude, wavelength, and frequency. The top of a wave is a crest and the bottom is a trough.
- In a transverse wave the oscillation is at 90° to the wave direction, and in a longitudinal wave it is parallel to the wave direction.
- Waves can reflect from barriers and add up or cancel out.
- A sound wave is produced by vibrating objects and is longitudinal.
- Sound travels at 340 m/s. Sound travels fastest in solids and slowest in gases and cannot travel through a vacuum.
- The loudness of a sound depends on its amplitude, and the pitch depends on its frequency. Frequency is measured in hertz (Hz).
- A human's audible range is from 20–20 000 Hz.
- Your outer ear consists of the pinna, auditory canal, and eardrum. Your middle ear contains your ossicles. Your inner ear contains your cochlea and semi-circular canals.
- Vibrations travel from your eardrum to the hairs in your cochlea. This produces a signal that is sent to your brain.
- Loudness is measured in decibels (dB).
- An echo is a reflection of sound that you can use to work out distance. Soft materials absorb sound and don't produce echoes.
- Ultrasound is sound with a frequency of more than 20 000 Hz. Humans use ultrasound to produce images of inside the body, and to find the depths of water.

Big Write

Sound campaign

You are a scientific advisor to a council. There are several issues to do with sound in the area:

- Shopkeepers want to install high-frequency speakers to put-off young people hanging around outside their shops.
- People who live near a busy road are concerned about the traffic noise.

Task

Produce an information pack that includes:

- what a sound wave is, its properties, and how it behaves
- how you hear, and how hearing can be damaged.

Key Words

oscillation, vibration, energy, undulation, sound, amplitude, frequency, wavelength, peak, crest, trough, transverse, longitudinal, compression, rarefaction, reflection, incident wave, reflected wave, superpose, vibration, medium, vacuum, speed of sound, speed of light, pitch, loudness, microphone, oscilloscope, hertz, kilohertz, audible range, infrasound, ultrasound, ear, pinna, auditory canal, eardrum, outer ear, ossicles, middle ear, amplify, oval window, cochlea, auditory nerve, inner ear, decibels, diaphragm, amplifier, echo, reverberation, transmitter, receiver

End-of-chapter questions

1 Draw a wave and label the amplitude and the wavelength.

(2 marks)

2 A tuning fork produces this wave on an oscilloscope:

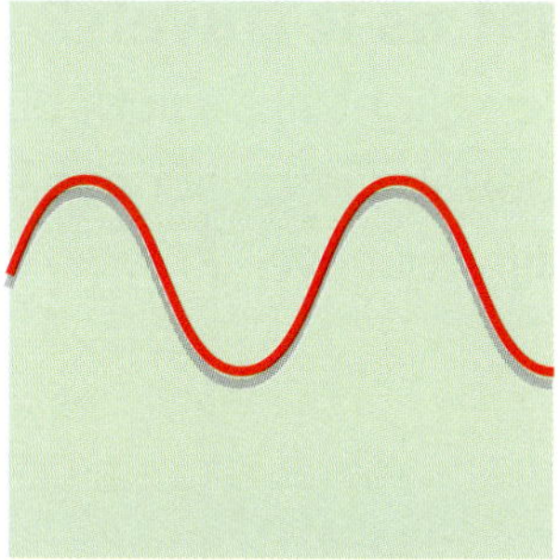

a Draw the wave you would see if the sound was louder. *(1 mark)*

b Draw the wave you would see if the sound had a higher pitch. *(1 mark)*

(2 marks)

3 A note has a frequency of 400 Hz. State how many sound waves pass a point per second.

(1 mark)

4

a Describe what happens when a wave hits a barrier. *(1 mark)*

b Describe what happens when waves superpose. *(2 marks)*

(3 marks)

5

a Explain why a Mexican wave is transverse. *(1 mark)*

b Explain why sound is a longitudinal wave. *(1 mark)*

(2 marks)

6 Suggest a situation where you might need to use ear defenders.

(1 mark)

7 Here is a table showing the speed of sound in three different materials: A, B, and C.

Material	Speed (m/s)
A	1250
B	300
C	5000

a State which material, A, B or C, is probably a solid. *(1 mark)*

b State which material, A, B or C, is probably a gas. *(1 mark)*

c Suggest a reason why the three speeds are different. *(3 marks)*

(5 marks)

8 A student is measuring sound intensity with a meter. He wonders if there is a link between the loudness of a sound and how far away you are from the source.

a Suggest a question that the student could investigate based on this idea. *(1 mark)*

b Name the independent, dependent, and control variables in the investigation. *(1 mark)*

c State the type of graph that he could plot with the results of this investigation. *(1 mark)*

(3 marks)

9 A loudspeaker produces a sound wave that you can hear. Describe in detail how the sound is produced, travels, and is detected by your ear.

(6 marks)

3.1 Light

Learning objectives

After this topic you will be able to:

- describe what happens when light interacts with materials
- state the speed of light.

▲ You can see a starfish through water.

▲ Frosted glass is translucent.

How long? How far?

It takes light eight minutes to travel here from the Sun. Sound is about a million times slower. Calculate how long it would take sound to travel the same distance. Convert your answer to years.

As you go deeper and deeper into an ocean it gets darker and darker until you can hardly see a thing. Some fish that live there make their own light. Why is it so dark?

What happens to light as it travels?

You look at a book. A **source** of light, like a light bulb, **emits** light. This light **reflects** off the book and into your **eye**. You see the book when the light is **absorbed** in your eye.

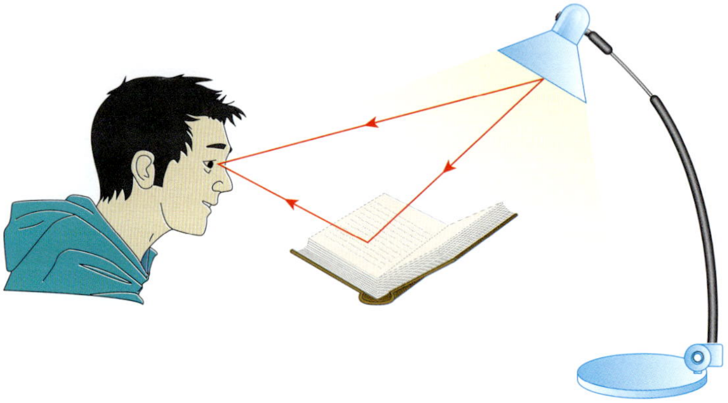

▲ You see objects because light reflects off them.

Something that gives out light is **luminous**. Most objects that you look at are **non-luminous**. You see them because they reflect light into your eyes. Light spreads out, just like sound.

When you look through a window, light travels through the glass and into your eye. The glass **transmits** the light. When light travels through glass, Perspex, or shallow water most of the light goes through but a small amount is absorbed. They are **transparent** and you can see through them. In very deep water most of the light is absorbed.

A State the difference between 'emit' and 'transmit'.

Materials like frosted glass or tissue paper are **translucent**. Light can travel through them but it is scattered so you cannot see clearly. Materials that do not transmit light are **opaque**.

Opaque materials produce shadows. You can predict the size and shape of shadows. This is because light travels in straight lines.

B State the difference between a translucent and a transparent material.

What can light travel through?

Light can travel through gases like the air, some liquids like water, and some solids like glass. It can even travel through completely empty space, which is called a **vacuum**. It does not need a medium to travel in. Light travels as a **wave**.

How fast does light travel?

It takes light about eight minutes to reach the Earth from the Sun, a distance of 150 million km. The speed of light is about 300 000 km/s. Sound travels about a million times slower than light. Astronomers use '**light-time**' to measure distances in space. A light-minute is the distance that light travels in one minute. A light-year is how far it travels in a year. Light-time is a measure of distance, not time.

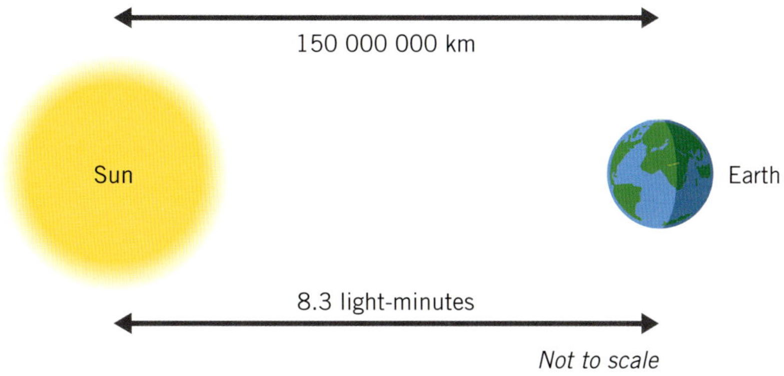

▲ There are two ways of showing the distance to the Sun.

C State what is meant by a light-year.

Sort those words

Use the words below to make up three sentences involving a light bulb and a flower in a vase of water. The words can be used more than once but try to use them only once if you can.

emit transmit reflect absorb luminous non-luminous transparent opaque

Key Words

source, emit, reflect, eye, absorb, luminous, non-luminous, transmit, transparent, translucent, opaque, vacuum, wave, light-time

Link

You can learn more about the properties of waves in P1 2.1 Waves

Fantastic Fact!

If light from the Sun travelled at 100 mph it would take 100 000 years to reach Earth.

Summary Questions

1 Copy these sentences, choosing the correct bold words.

The Sun is **luminous/non-luminous** because it **emits/transmits** light. The light **reflects/transmits** off an object that is **luminous/non-luminous** into your eye so that you see it. Most objects do not transmit light; they are **translucent/opaque**.

(5 marks)

2 Explain why it is so dark at the bottom of the ocean even though water is transparent.

(2 marks)

3 Describe the journey that light takes from the Sun to your eye when you are looking at fish in a pond.

(6 marks)

3.2 Reflection

Learning objectives

After this topic you will be able to:

- explain how images are formed in a plane mirror
- explain the difference between specular reflection and diffuse scattering.

There are lots of places that you see your reflection every day. Shop windows, saucepans, car doors . . . but why do you see your image in some surfaces but not others?

Why do I see an image in the mirror?

When you look in the mirror it appears that there is someone who looks just like you behind the mirror. The **image** is a **virtual** image. Your brain uses the fact that light travels in straight lines to work out where the light appears to come from. This is where you see the image.

When you look at your mirror image in a flat, or **plane**, mirror, it is the same shape and size as you are. It appears to be as far behind the mirror as you are in front of the mirror. Left and right appear swapped.

▲ You see a reflection in a window.

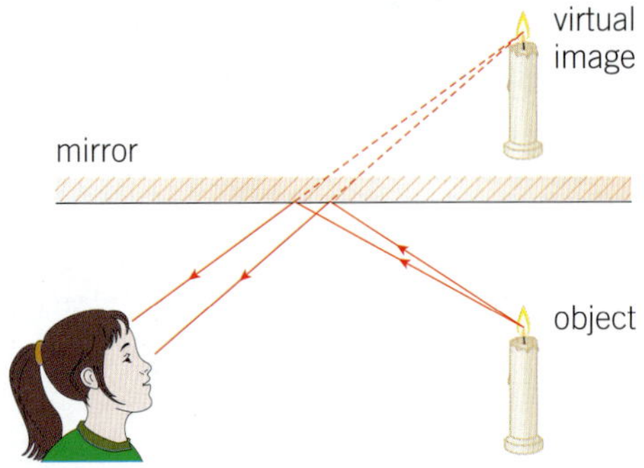

▲ You see an image in a mirror.

The law of reflection

You know that you need light to reflect from an object for you to see it. Light reflects off a mirror in the same way that a wave reflects off a barrier.

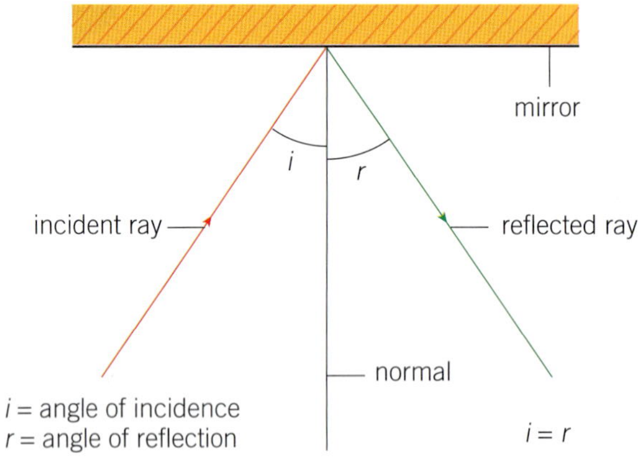

▲ Light is reflected at equal angles.

The ray that hits the mirror from your ray box is called the **incident ray**. The ray that reflects off the mirror is called the **reflected ray**.

There is an imaginary line at 90° to the mirror called the **normal**. You measure angles from the normal to the rays of light. The angle between the incident ray and the normal is the **angle of incidence**. The angle between the normal and the reflected ray is the **angle of reflection**.

Fantastic Fact!

The Salar de Uyuni in Bolivia, South America is a huge dry salt lake that acts like a mirror. It is so big that you can see it from space.

When light is reflected from a mirror, the angle of incidence is equal to the angle of reflection. This is the **law of reflection**.

A State the law of reflection.

Rough surfaces

Every surface reflects at least some light. You can only see your image in surfaces that reflect light in a regular way.

Reflection from a smooth surface is called **specular reflection**. Reflection from a rough surface is called **diffuse scattering**.

To form an image, the rays from each part of the object have to reflect off a surface in the same way. If two rays that are parallel are reflected at different angles you won't see an image.

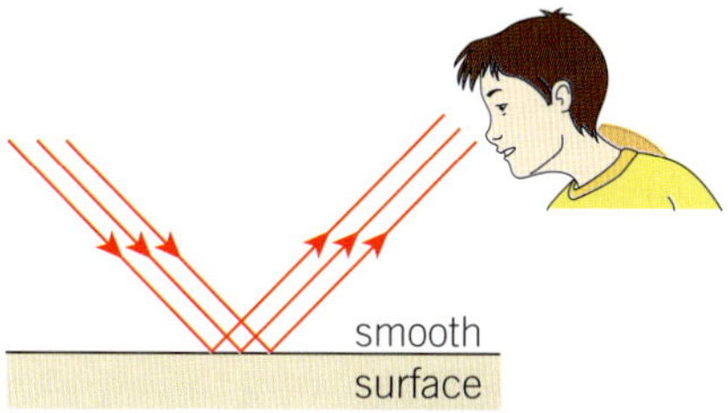

▲ Reflection from a smooth surface (specular reflection).

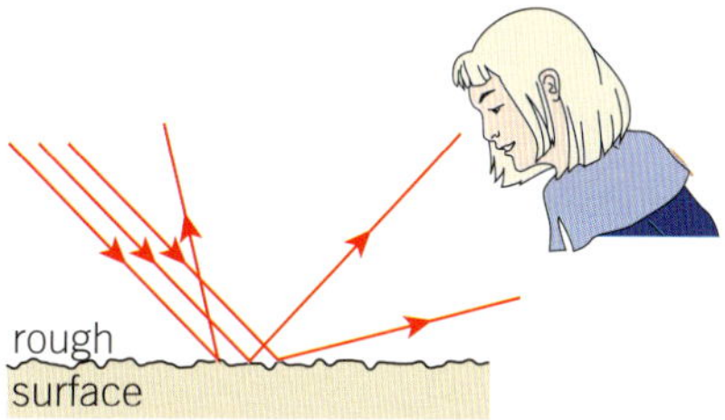

▲ Reflection from a rough surface (diffuse scattering).

B State the type of reflection when light hits a mirror.

Bouncing light

A student wants to investigate the light that is reflected from different types of material using a light meter.

a Explain why the student should repeat the experiment several times.

b State and explain which type of graph she should plot from the data that she collects.

Key Words

image, virtual, plane, incident ray, reflected ray, normal, angle of incidence, angle of reflection, law of reflection, specular reflection, diffuse scattering

Angular problem

A student makes a mistake and measures the angle between the mirror and the incident ray. It is 40°.

a What is the angle of incidence?

b What is the angle of reflection?

c He says the angle of incidence and the angle of reflection always add up to 90°. Is he correct? Explain your answer.

Summary Questions

1 Copy and complete the sentences below.

When you look in a mirror you see a ________ image of yourself. The image is the same ________, ________, and ________ from the mirror. When you close your left eye the image appears to close their ________ eye. The image is formed because light reflects off the mirror so that the angle of ________ is equal to the angle of ________.

(7 marks)

2 Explain why you cannot see an image of your face when you look at a white wall, even though most of the light hitting it is reflected.

(2 marks)

3 Design a model to demonstrate how light can be diffusely scattered but still obey the law of reflection. Use marbles and footballs instead of light in your model. Explain how it works.

(6 marks)

3.3 Refraction

Learning objectives

After this topic you will be able to:

- describe and explain what happens when light is refracted
- describe what happens when light travels through a lens.

▲ A pencil looks bent when you put it in a glass of water.

You can bend a pencil without touching it. Put it in a glass and fill it with water. It looks bent but it isn't. Why?

Optical illusions

The pencil reflects light and the light travels from the pencil through the water. It then travels through the air into your eye. As the light leaves the water, the direction it is travelling in changes. This is called **refraction**.

Refraction happens whenever light travels from one **medium** (material) to another.

The change in direction explains why the pencil appears to be bent. Your brain thinks that the light has travelled in a straight line. You see the end of the pencil in a different place to where it actually is. The pencil looks bent. Refraction also explains why a swimming pool looks shallower than it actually is.

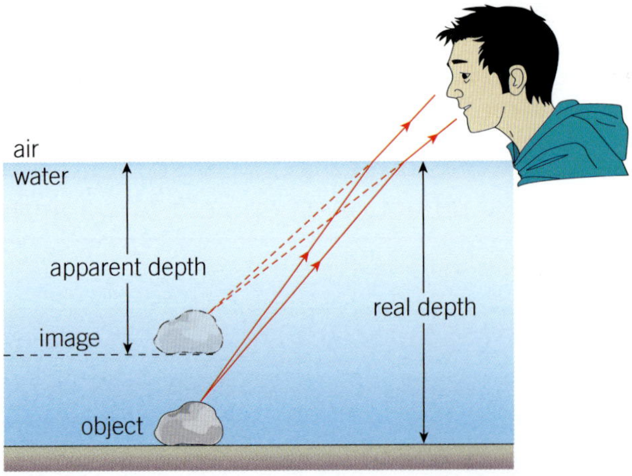

▲ A rock at the bottom of a pool looks closer to the surface than it actually is.

A State the difference between reflection and refraction.

Fantastic Fact!

Stars twinkle because light is refracted as it travels through the atmosphere.

Why does light change direction?

Imagine a truck driving from a road onto mud. When the first wheel of the truck hits the mud it slows down. The other wheels keep going – this pushes the truck in another direction. This is similar to what happens when light travels from air into water or glass, or when water waves go from deep to shallow.

Key Words

refraction, medium, lens, convex, converging, focus, focal point

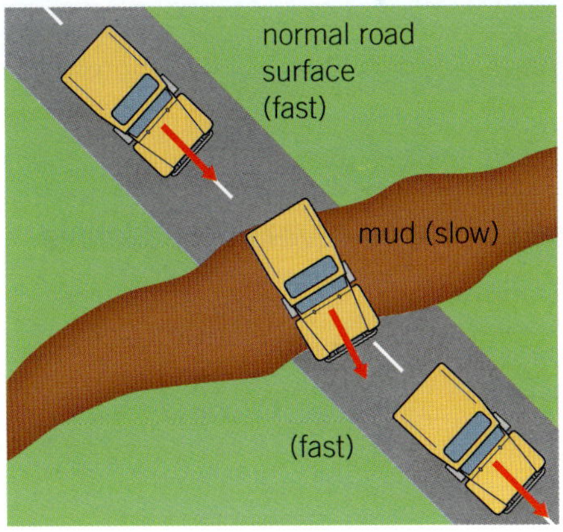

▲ A truck changes direction as it slows down.

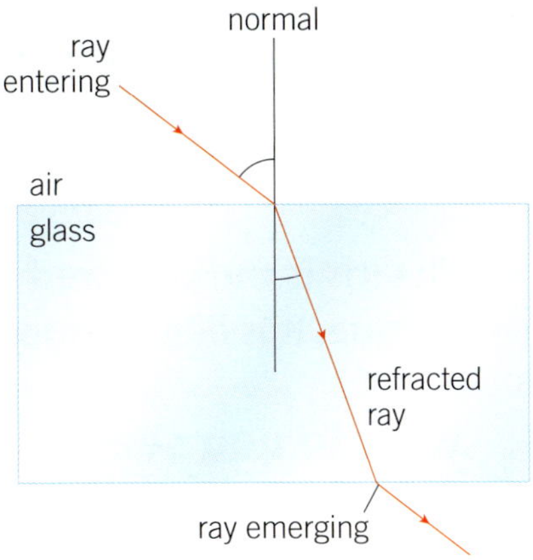

▲ Light is refracted when it slows down.

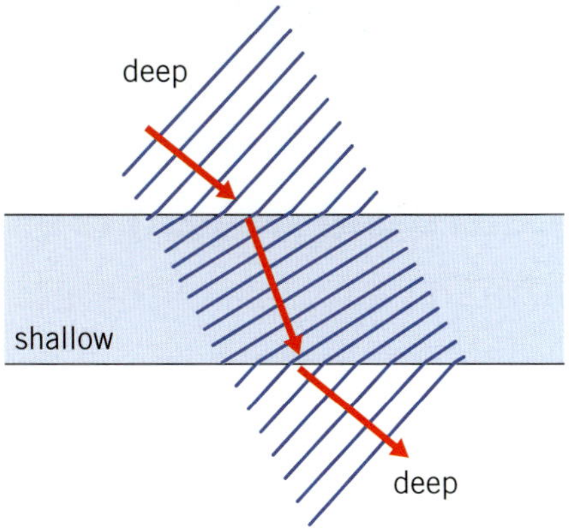

▲ Waves are refracted when they slow down.

When light travels through a glass block it slows down when it goes in, and speeds up again when it comes back out. The direction changes twice. Light bends towards the normal when it goes into glass. It bends away from the normal when it comes out. The two rays outside the block are parallel.

What does a lens do?

There are two lenses in your body. The **lens** in each of your eyes is a **convex** or **converging** lens. It focuses the light and enables you to see. The point where the rays cross is called the **focus** or **focal point**. The light is refracted as it goes into the lens and as it comes back out.

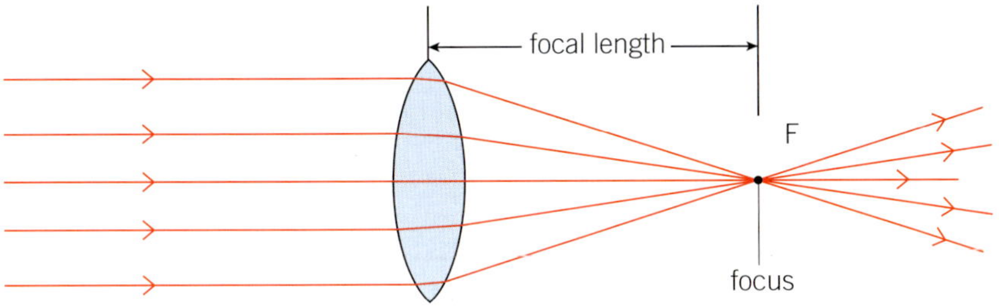

▲ A piece of glass shaped like a lens focuses light.

B Describe what a lens does to light.

Watch that spelling!

In each list below, choose the correct spelling of the word. Make up a rule that will help you to remember the spelling.

a lense, lenz, lens

b parallel, parrallel, paralell

Summary Questions

1 Copy the sentences below, choosing the correct bold words.

When you look at a rock in the bottom of a swimming pool it appears **above/below** where it actually is. That is because the light **reflects/refracts** when it travels from water into air. It bends **towards/away from** the normal as it goes into the air. This is because it **slows down/speeds up**.

(4 marks)

2 Explain what would happen to:

a the speed and direction of water waves if they went straight into the area of shallow water rather than at an angle *(2 marks)*

b the speed and direction of light waves if they went straight into the glass block rather than at an angle. *(2 marks)*

3 Describe in detail how you could use the idea of marching soldiers to make a model of light refracting as it goes through a glass block.

(6 marks)

3.4 The eye and the camera

Learning objectives

After this topic you will be able to:

- describe how the eye works
- describe how a simple camera forms an image.

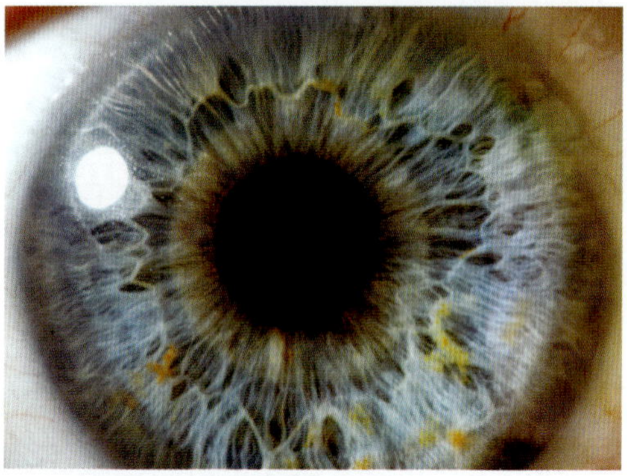

▲ No-one has the same pattern in their iris as you.

Key Words

retina, pupil, iris, cornea, inverted, photoreceptor, optic nerve, brain, pinhole camera, real (image), pixel, charge-coupled device (CCD)

Foul Fact!

The pupil is a hole in the front of your eye. If you dissect a cow's eye you can put your finger through it.

Link

You can learn more about specialised cells in B1 1.3 Specialised cells

The iris is the coloured part of your eye. Everyone's iris is unique. It is like a fingerprint.

How do you see?

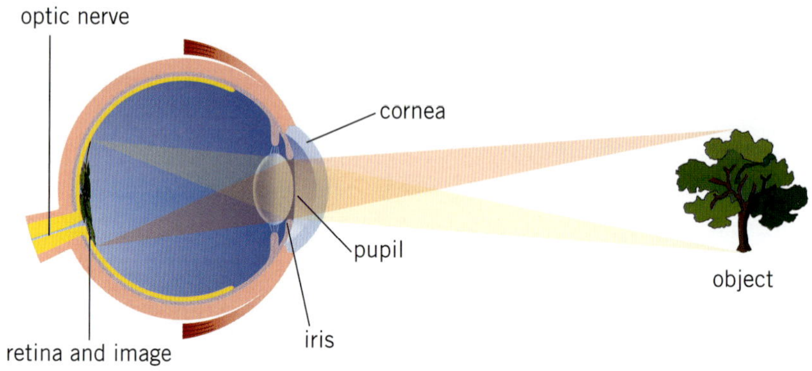

▲ How an image is formed in your eye.

When you look at your friend, an image of your friend is formed on the **retina** of your eye. Light reflected from your friend goes through the **pupil** of your eye. The **iris** is a muscle that controls the size of the pupil. The **cornea** (the transparent outer part of your eye) and the lens focus the light onto the retina. This forms an image. The image is **inverted** (upside down) but your brain sorts it out so you see an image of your friend that is the right way up.

A State which parts of the eye focus the light.

What happens in the retina?

The retina is a photosensitive material that contains cells that respond to light. They are called photoreceptors. There are two types of **photoreceptor**: rods and cones. Rods are sensitive to movement and dim light. Cones are sensitive to bright light and colour. When light hits the rods and cones, chemical reactions produce an electrical impulse that travels up the **optic nerve** to your **brain**.

B State the type of reaction that takes place in the retina.

How is the eye like a camera?

A camera produces an image, just like your eye. One of the simplest cameras is a **pinhole camera**.

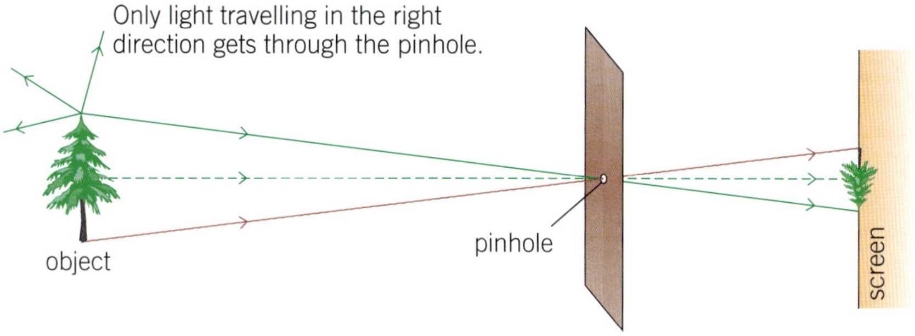

▲ An image is formed in a pinhole camera.

Light enters the camera through the pinhole, just like it does through your pupil. An image is formed on the screen, just like it is on your retina. The image is a **real** image, not like your image in a mirror. Any image that you can make on a screen is a real image.

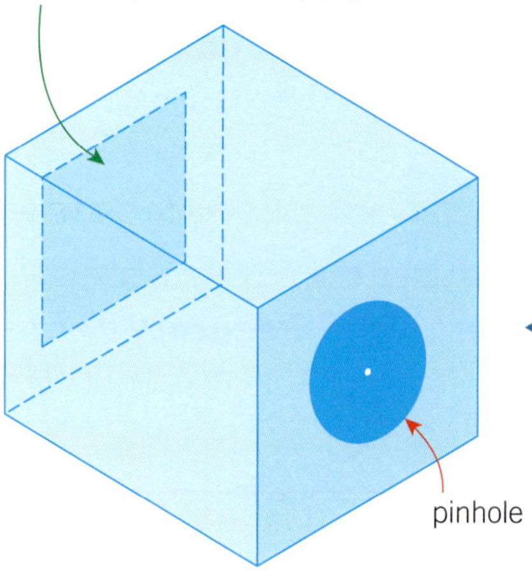

◀ This is a simple pinhole camera.

Cameras used to contain photographic film, which was photosensitive. When light hit the film there was a chemical reaction that changed the chemicals in the film. When you processed the film you saw the image.

At the back of a digital camera there is a grid of photosensitive picture elements, or **pixels**. This is called a **charge-coupled device** (CCD). When light hits each pixel it produces charge. The light produces an electrical, not chemical, effect. When you take a picture, this charge is moved off each of the pixels and stored. That is why there is a slight delay before you can take another picture.

C Name the photosensitive grid at the back of a digital camera.

Real or virtual?

Here are some words that describe real and virtual images. Use these words to explain the difference between the two types of image.

screen **virtual** **real** **mirror**

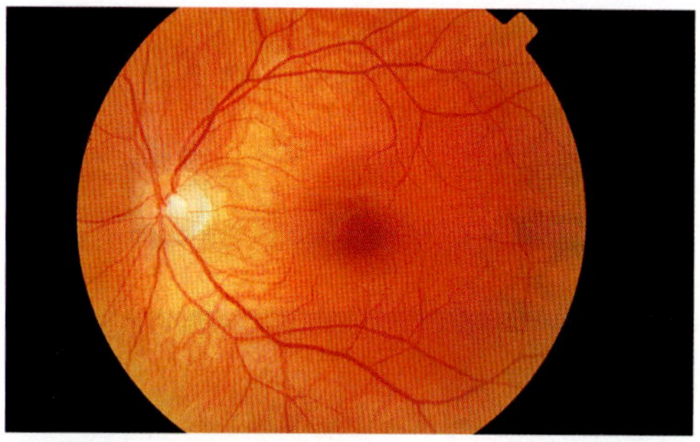

▲ This is the view of your retina that an optician would see.

Summary Questions

1. Copy and complete the sentences below.
   When you look at an apple, light ________ off the apple into your eye. The light enters your eye through the ________ . The ________ and the ________ focus the light onto the ________ . The light forms a ________ image. A chemical reaction produces an ________ signal that is sent down your ________ ________ to your brain.
   (9 marks)
2. Describe how the camera in your phone is different to a pinhole camera.
   (2 marks)
3. Compare the eye and the pinhole camera.
   (6 marks)

3.5 Colour

Learning objectives

After this topic you will be able to:

- explain what happens when light passes through a prism
- describe how primary colours add to make secondary colours
- explain how filters and coloured materials subtract light.

▲ A prism splits white light into a spectrum.

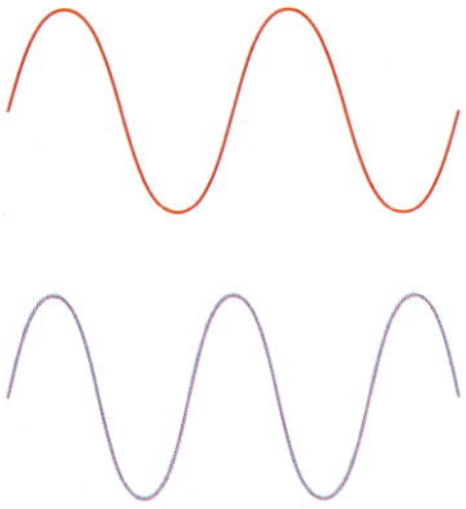

▲ Red light has a lower frequency than blue light.

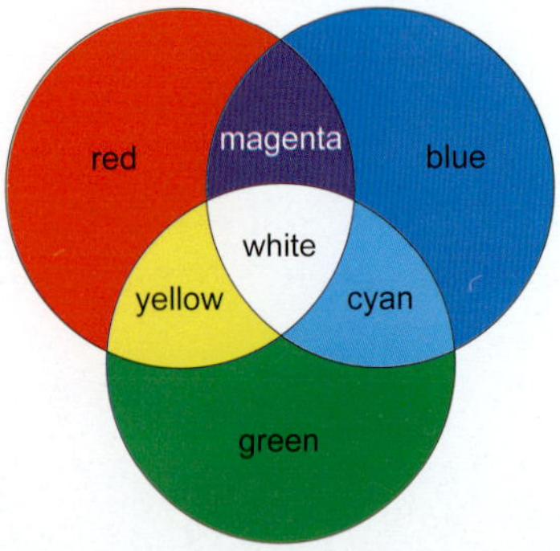

▲ This Venn diagram shows the primary and secondary colours of light.

Have you ever seen really big bubbles? There are colours on the bubbles just like the colours in a rainbow or on a CD or DVD.

◀ Where do the colours come from?

Splitting white light

White light is made up of seven different colours of light. You can use a **prism** to split white light into a **spectrum**. This is called **dispersion**. The spectrum of white light is **continuous**. There are no gaps between the colours. Sir Isaac Newton first did this experiment in about 1666.

Dispersion happens because different colours of light are refracted by different amounts. Violet is refracted the most and red is refracted the least. Violet light has a higher **frequency** than red. Light with a higher frequency is refracted more than light with a lower frequency.

A State what a prism does to light.

Adding colours

You can make all the colours of light from just three colours: red, green, and blue. These are called the **primary colours** of light. Your eye detects these three colours. You can make any colour from different amounts of red, green, and blue. When you mix two primary colours you get **secondary colours** of light: cyan, yellow, and magenta. You get white light when you mix all three colours of light.

B Name the secondary colours of light.

Subtracting colours

Coloured lights on a stage can make a spectacular display. White light contains all the colours of light so if you want blue light you need to get rid of all the other colours.

What do filters do to light?

A red **filter** subtracts colours from white light. It transmits red light and absorbs the rest. It does not change the colour of light. If you put a red and a green filter together no light would get through them.

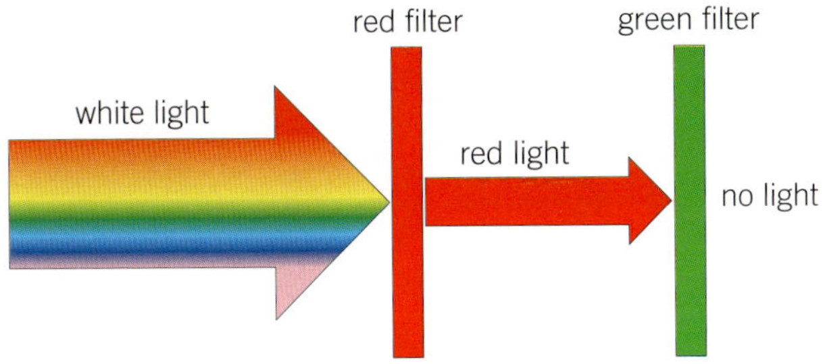

▲ Filters transmit the colours that they are and absorb the rest.

Why are objects different colours?

A red car reflects red light into your eyes. When the white light from the Sun hits the car, the paint absorbs all the other colours except red. Any coloured object reflects the colour that it is and absorbs the rest. Black objects absorb all the colours. White objects absorb no colours and reflect all the light.

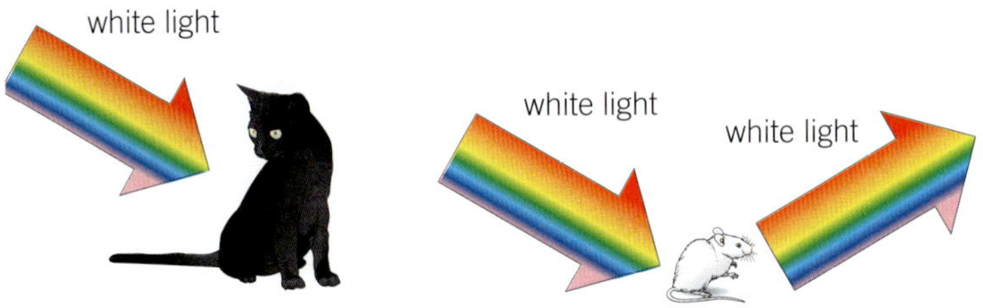

▲ Black objects absorb all the colours of light and white objects reflect all the colours of light.

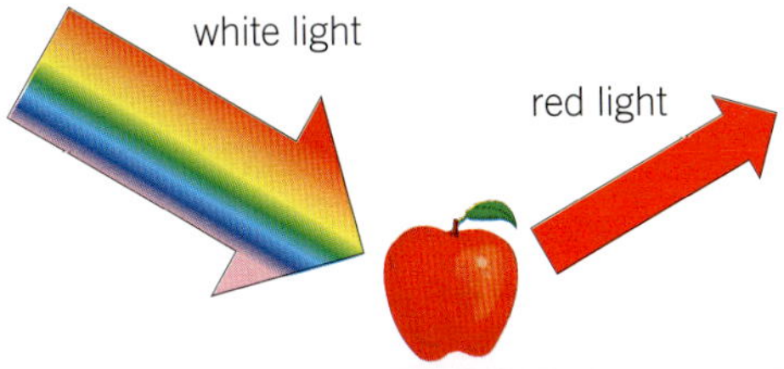

◀ An apple reflects red light and absorbs the other colours.

What table?

A student wants to record data in an experiment where she is shining all the primary and secondary colours of light onto pieces of coloured material. Draw a table to show how she could record her results.

C State what a black object does to white light.

Fantastic Fact!

You can never see a rainbow when the Sun is in front of you.

Key Words

prism, spectrum, dispersion, continuous, frequency, primary colour, secondary colour, filter

Summary Questions

1 Copy the sentences below, choosing the correct bold words.

When white light goes through a prism, red light is **reflected/refracted** the **most/least** and violet light is refracted the **most/least**. This is called **dispersion/refraction**. A green filter **absorbs/transmits** green light and **absorbs/transmits** the rest. A cyan object **absorbs/reflects** red light, **absorbs/reflects** blue light, and **absorbs/reflects** green light. A magenta object would look black in **blue/green** light.

(10 marks)

2 Explain why a green shirt looks black in red light.

(2 marks)

3 Explain in detail why you cannot have a white filter or a black filter.

(6 marks)

P1 Chapter 3 Summary

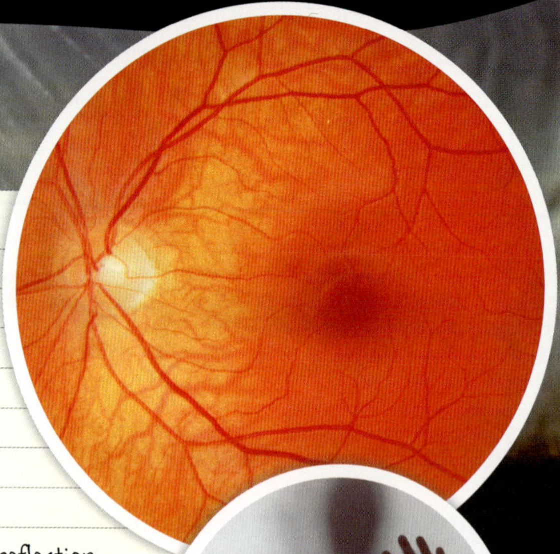

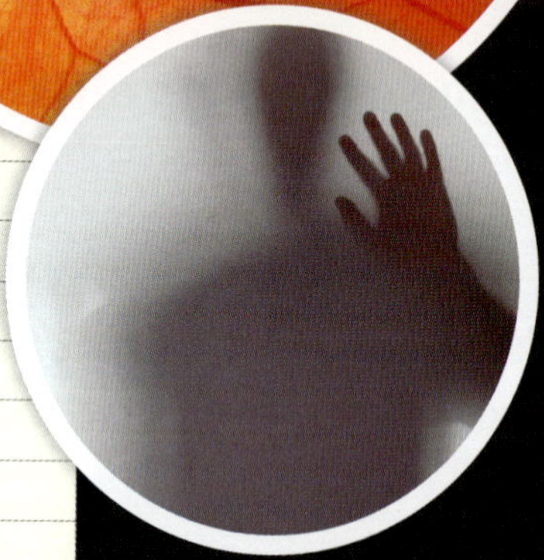

Key Points

- Light is emitted from luminous sources. It can be transmitted through, reflected, or absorbed by non-luminous objects.
- Objects are transparent, translucent, or opaque.
- Light travels through a vacuum at 300 000 km/s.
- A light-year is the distance light travels in one year. Light-years are used to measure very large distances.
- Your brain uses the fact that light travels in straight lines and you see a virtual image when you look in the mirror.
- The law of reflection says that the angle of incidence equals the angle of reflection.
- Images are formed when reflection is specular but not when there is diffuse scattering from a surface.
- When light slows down it is refracted towards the normal.
- A lens can focus light to a focal point.
- Light enters your eye through the pupil. The cornea and lens focus light to produce a real image on your retina. A chemical reaction in the photoreceptors in your eye produces an electrical signal. The signal travels down the optic nerve to your brain.
- Light forms an image in a camera in the same way. Digital cameras store images produced when light hits a charge-coupled device (CCD).
- Prisms disperse white light to produce a continuous spectrum. Primary colours of light add up to make secondary colours. All three colours add to make white light.
- Filters and coloured objects subtract colours from white light by transmitting or reflecting the colour that they are and absorbing the rest.

Key Words

source, emit, reflect, eye, absorb, luminous, non-luminous, transmit, transparent, translucent, opaque, umbra, penumbra, vacuum, wave, light-time, image, virtual, plane, incident ray, reflected ray, normal, angle of incidence, angle of reflection, law of reflection, specular reflection, diffuse scattering, refraction, medium, lens, convex, converging, focus, focal point, retina, iris, pupil, cornea, inverted, photoreceptor, optic nerve, brain, pinhole camera, real (image), pixel, charge-coupled device (CCD), prism, spectrum, dispersion, continuous, frequency, primary colour, secondary colour, filter

Big write

The big production

A theatre has asked you to come up with some ideas for a play about ghost hunters.

Task

Write a plan for your team to do some investigations to produce special effects. The effects could include reflection in mirrors and glass and different-coloured lights and materials.

Tips

- As well as what happens on the stage, you could design posters and programmes that look different in different-coloured lights.

End-of-chapter questions

1 Mirrors reflect light. State which capital letters of the alphabet would look the same if you saw them in a mirror.

(1 mark)

2 An actor is wearing a uniform that has a blue jacket and red trousers. Suggest and explain what the audience would see if he stood on stage in:

a white light *(2 marks)*

b green light *(2 marks)*

(4 marks)

3 A hunter is trying to spear a fish.

a Explain why he aims above where he sees the fish. *(2 marks)*

b Explain why diving birds dive straight down to catch fish. *(2 marks)*

(4 marks)

4 A student has collected data about different types of plastic block. He measured the mass and the angle of refraction of a ray of light going into the block. Each block is the same size.

Here are his results:

Mass of block (g)	Angle of refraction (°)
250	27
220	32
275	24
300	21

a State **one** variable that the student must keep the same during this investigation.

(1 mark)

b State the name of the independent variable.

(1 mark)

c State the name of the dependent variable.

(1 mark)

d Describe the relationship between the mass and the angle of refraction. *(1 mark)*

e Describe **one** way that the student could improve the way that the results are presented in the table *(1 mark)*

(5 marks)

5 Copy and complete the diagram below to show what happens when light goes through a lens.

(4 marks)

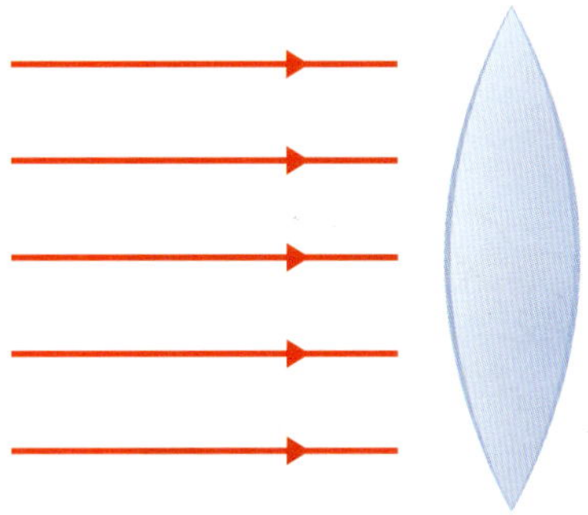

6 Light slows down from 300 000 km/s to 200 000 km/s in glass and to 226 000 km/s in water. A ray of light enters each medium with an angle of incidence of 40°. State and explain whether the angle of refraction would be bigger or smaller in water than in glass.

(2 marks)

7 Here is some information about the speed of light in different materials. Describe and explain what you would see if you shone rays of light through a lens made of each material.

Material	Speed of light in the material (million m/s)
diamond	125
glass	200
plastic	187

(6 marks)

4.1 The night sky

Learning objectives

After this topic you will be able to:

- describe the objects that you can see in the night sky
- describe the structure of the Universe.

▲ An astronaut on a spacewalk is building part of the ISS.

Foul Fact!

The odds of being killed by falling space debris are one in five billion.

Key Words

artificial satellite, orbit, Earth, Moon, natural satellite, planet, Sun, Solar System, comet, meteor, meteorite, star, galaxy, Milky Way, Universe, astronomer

When you look at the stars in the night sky you do not see them as they are today. The light from them has taken years to get here. You are looking back in time.

Satellites

The nearest objects that you can see without a telescope are **artificial satellites**. They **orbit** the **Earth**. You can see the International Space Station (ISS) with the naked eye (without using binoculars or a telescope). The light reflected from the ISS reaches us in a fraction of a second.

Light reflected from the **Moon** reaches us in just over a second. The Moon orbits the Earth. It is the Earth's only **natural satellite**.

A Name the natural satellite that orbits the Earth.

What is wandering across the sky?

There are five **planets** that most people can see with the naked eye: Mercury, Venus, Mars, Jupiter, and Saturn. Like the Earth they orbit the **Sun**. Venus gets closest to the Earth, about two light-minutes away. Light from Saturn takes about 1.5 hours. The planets form part of the **Solar System**.

B Name the planets that are visible to the naked eye.

Comets and meteors

A **comet** is one of the most spectacular sights in the night sky. They are huge snowballs that orbit the Sun.

Meteors are bits of dust or rock that burn up as they move through the Earth's atmosphere and produce streaks of light. Any meteor that makes it to the ground is called a **meteorite**.

C Describe how the appearance of a comet is different to the appearance of a meteor.

Lights in the sky

Most of the dots of light that we see are **stars** in our **galaxy**, the **Milky Way**. A galaxy is a collection of stars and there are billions of stars in the Milky Way.

Light takes about eight minutes to get to us from the Sun, our nearest star. Our next nearest star is over four light-years away.

This shows our Sun in our galaxy, the Milky Way.

Some of the dots of light in the night sky are other galaxies. A galaxy contains billions of stars. The Milky Way is just one of billions of galaxies that make up the **Universe**. Our nearest large galaxy is Andromeda, which you can see with the naked eye. Light from Andromeda takes 2 million years to get to Earth.

The Andromeda galaxy is the nearest large galaxy to us.

D State what is meant by a 'galaxy'.

How do we know?

Astronomers have learned about the objects that we see in the night sky from the observations they have made. You cannot do experiments in astronomy. Astronomers use models to work out what makes up the Solar System, the Milky Way, and the Universe.

Comet Hale–Bopp was visible in the night sky in 1997.

Fantastic Fact!

All the elements that you are made of were made in the centre of stars in galaxies.

Summary Questions

1. Copy the sentences below, choosing the correct bold words.

   There are thousands of satellites in orbit around the **Sun**/**Earth**. The Moon is a natural satellite of the **Sun**/**Earth**. Comets are huge snowballs that orbit the **Sun**/**Earth**. Planets orbit the **Sun**/**Earth**.

   (4 marks)

2. Describe the difference between a meteor and a meteorite.

   (2 marks)

3. When you look up at the night sky you see dots of light that don't appear to move. List what the dots of light could be.

   (2 marks)

4. Compare the time it takes light to reach us from the different objects that you can see in the night sky.

   (6 marks)

4.2 The Solar System

Learning objectives

After this topic you will be able to:

- name the objects in the Solar System
- describe some similarities and differences between the planets of the Solar System.

▲ These are NASA images of the planets of the Solar System.

Remember that order!

Before Pluto was renamed a dwarf planet, people used to remember the order of the planets using this mnemonic:
My Very Easy Method Just Speeds Up Naming Planets. A mnemonic uses first letters to make up a sentence. Make up your own mnemonic for the planets as they are now: M, V, E, M, J, S, U, N.

Key Words

ellipse, asteroid, Mercury, Venus, Mars, terrestrial, gas giant, dwarf planet, gravity

No-one has ever seen all of the Solar System at once because it is too big. Scientists have used observations to build a model of the Solar System.

What's in our Solar System?

Starting from the Sun and moving outwards the Solar System contains four inner planets and four outer planets. All of the planets orbit the Sun. Each orbit is a slightly squashed circle called an **ellipse**. Between the orbits of Mars and Jupiter there is an **asteroid** belt.

A State the number of planets in the Solar System.

The planets

The inner planets, **Mercury**, **Venus**, Earth, and **Mars**, are all **terrestrial** planets; they are made of rock. The conditions on the planets are very different. Mercury does not have an atmosphere. At night the temperature drops to –170 °C and during the day it can reach 430 °C. Venus has an atmosphere of carbon dioxide that traps energy from the Sun.

◄ The Curiosity rover on Mars takes a picture of itself.

The outer planets are called **gas giants**; they are made mainly of gases such as hydrogen and helium. All of the gas giants are very cold and are much bigger than the inner planets.

Many of the planets have moons in orbit around them. Saturn has 60 moons but Earth has only one.

Planet	Diameter (km)	Distance from Sun (million km)	Distance from Sun	Temperature (°C)
Sun	1 391 000	–	–	–
Mercury	4879	58	3.2 light-minutes	–180 to 430
Venus	12 104	108	6.0 light-minutes	465
Earth	12 756	150	8.3 light-minutes	–89 to 58
Mars	6787	228	12.7 light-minutes	–82 to 0
Jupiter	142 800	778	43.3 light-minutes	–150
Saturn	120 660	1427	1 light-hour 19 light-minutes	–170
Uranus	51 118	2871	2 light-hours 39 light-minutes	–200
Neptune	49 528	4498	4 light-hours 10 light-minutes	–210

B List the planets in size order, starting with the smallest.

The asteroid belt

There are thousands of pieces of rock in the asteroid belt. Some are tiny specs of dust but one is large enough to be called a **dwarf planet**. Ceres is the only dwarf planet inside the orbit of Neptune.

Outside the Solar System

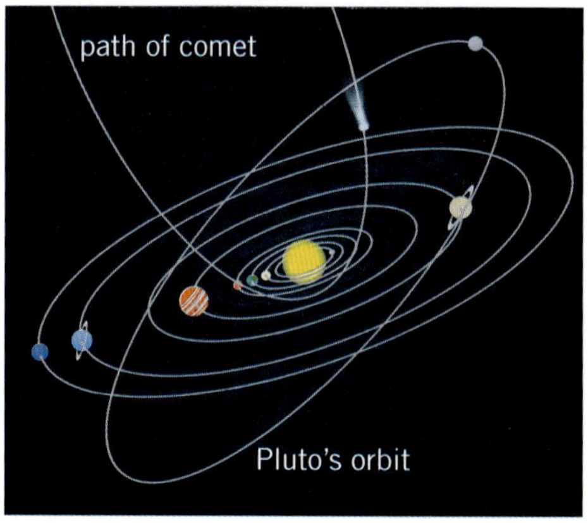

This diagram shows how the orbits of Pluto and a comet are different to the orbits of the planets.

Pluto used to be called a planet but in 2006 it was renamed a dwarf planet. Beyond Pluto's orbit is a region called the Kuiper Belt. Astronomers think that most comets come from outside our Solar System in a region called the Oort Cloud, beyond the Kuiper Belt.

How did our Solar System form?

Scientists think that **gravity** pulled the gas and dust together to form our Sun about 5 billion years ago. They think planets formed from a disc of gas and dust surrounding the Sun. Astronomers are looking for evidence from observations of other clouds of gas and dust to see if they can detect planets forming.

Fantastic Fact!

Venus spins in the opposite direction to all the other planets in the Solar System.

Summary Questions

1 Copy and complete the sentences below.

There are ______ inner and ______ outer planets in the Solar System. The band of dust and rocks between Jupiter and Mars is called the ______ ______. Pluto is a ______ planet. Scientists think that most comets come from a region outside the Solar System called the ______ ______.

(5 marks)

2 State one similarity and one difference between the inner and outer planets.

(2 marks)

3 Compare planets and asteroids.

(2 marks)

4 Describe and explain the link between distance from the Sun and temperature of the planets. Explain why Venus is the odd planet out.

(6 marks)

4.3 The Earth

Learning objectives

After this topic you will be able to:

- explain the motion of the Sun, stars, and Moon across the sky
- explain why seasonal changes happen

▲ This photograph of the night sky was taken over 10.5 hours.

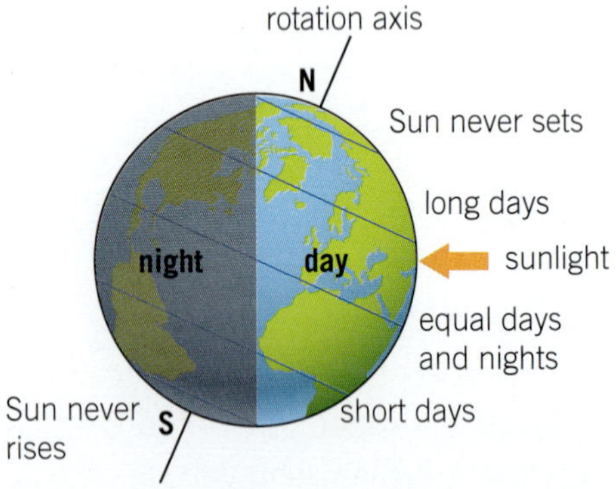

▲ When the Earth spins, half the Earth is in the light and half is in the dark.

Is the Earth special? Astronomers have discovered hundreds of planets orbiting other stars. They call these exoplanets. So far Earth is the only planet known to contain life.

The spinning Earth

The Earth spins on its **axis**. If you take a photograph over a long time the stars appear to move in circles. This shows that the Earth is spinning.

A Describe how you can demonstrate that the Earth is spinning.

There is **day** and **night** on Earth because Earth spins on its axis. It takes 24 hours to complete one full spin.

The Sun rises in the east each morning, reaches its highest point at noon, and then sets in the west in the evening. The Sun isn't moving. You are.

B State the direction in which the Sun rises.

The orbiting Earth

The Earth moves around the Sun once each **year**. The Earth takes 365.2422 days to orbit the Sun. There is an extra day in a leap year every four years.

Spin and orbit

Write the shortest sentence that you can to explain day length and year length using these words:

spin, day, night, orbit, year

Over the year the height of the Sun at noon, average daily temperature, and stars that you see at night all change during the different **seasons**.

The Earth's axis is tilted by 23.4°.

It is hotter in the summer than the winter because the tilt of the Earth's axis means that the Sun's rays spread over a smaller area and the days are longer.

In the summer in the North Pole the tilt of the axis means that the Sun doesn't set. This is called the 'Land of the Midnight Sun'. In the winter the Sun does not rise, giving a 'polar night'. This also happens at the South Pole.

Key Words

exoplanet, axis, day, night, year, season, constellation

▲ The Sun never sets – this shows the Sun in the Arctic over a 24-hour period in the summer.

February 29th?

It takes 21 600 seconds longer to orbit the Sun than just the 365 days you use for one year. Show that in 4 years these extra seconds add up to one whole day.

The groups of stars, or **constellations**, that we see in the summer at night are different to the stars that we see in the winter. This is because the Earth is moving around the Sun. The side of the Earth that has night is facing different stars at different times of the year.

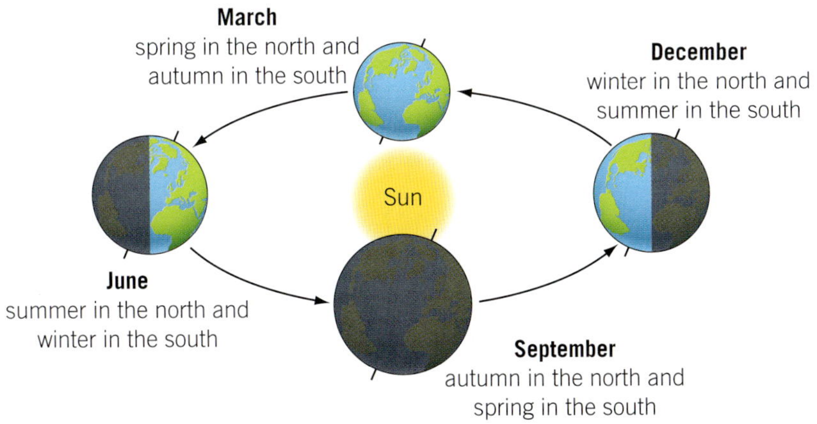

▲ The Sun's light is spread out over a bigger area in the winter.

Summary Questions

1 Copy the sentences below, choosing the correct bold word.

You see the Sun rise in the **east/west** and set in the **east/west** because the Earth **spins/orbits**. A **month/year** lasts approximately 365 days. This is the time that it takes the Earth to **orbit the Sun/spin once**. The days are **longer/shorter** in the summer and the Sun is **higher/lower** in the sky at noon.

(7 marks)

2

a Explain why it is hotter in the summer than it is in the winter. *(2 marks)*

b Explain why the shadow of a fence post is longer in the winter than in the summer. *(1 mark)*

3 Explain in detail what you would experience throughout the year if the axis of the Earth was not tilted. *(6 marks)*

4.4 The Moon

Learning objectives

After this topic you will be able to:

- describe the phases of the Moon
- explain why you see phases of the Moon
- explain why eclipses happen.

▲ There is a side of the Moon that you never see from Earth.

Many years ago, people used to have different ideas about space. The Ancient Chinese thought a solar eclipse was a demon eating the Sun. In other civilisations, people linked the changing appearance of the Moon with strange changes in behaviour.

Why does the Moon look different?

The Moon takes 27 days and 7 hours to orbit the Earth once.

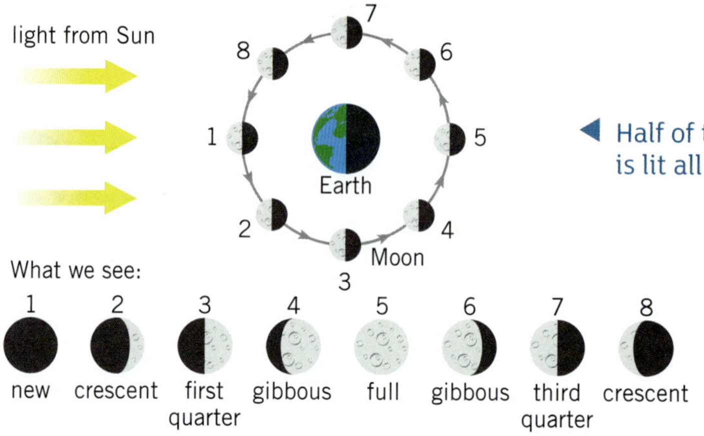

◀ Half of the Moon is lit all the time.

A List the phases of the Moon, starting with a full moon.

Half the Moon is lit up by the Sun all the time. As the Moon moves around the Earth it looks different from the Earth. The changing shapes are called **phases of the Moon**. When the Moon is in position 1 you see a 'new' moon. You see the side of the Moon that is in shadow. The Moon moves around the Earth to position 2 and you see a crescent moon. In position 5, the Sun lights up the whole of the side that you can see from the Earth and you see a full moon.

A lunar month is the period of time from one new moon to the next new moon.

B State how much of the Moon's surface is lit up by the Sun during a new moon.

Farewell, Moon

The Moon is 38 000 000 000 cm away and is moving away from the Earth at a rate of about 3.8 cm per year. Work out how much closer to the Earth it was when you were born.

Fantastic Fact!

A 'blue' moon happens when there are two full moons in one calendar month. It happens quite often, about once every three years.

Why do we see eclipses?

Solar eclipses

When the Moon comes between the Sun and the Earth it makes a shadow on the Earth's surface. If you are standing in the **umbra**, the Moon completely blocks the light from the Sun and you see a **total solar eclipse**. If you are standing where only part of the Sun's light is blocked (the **penumbra**) you will see a **partial solar eclipse**.

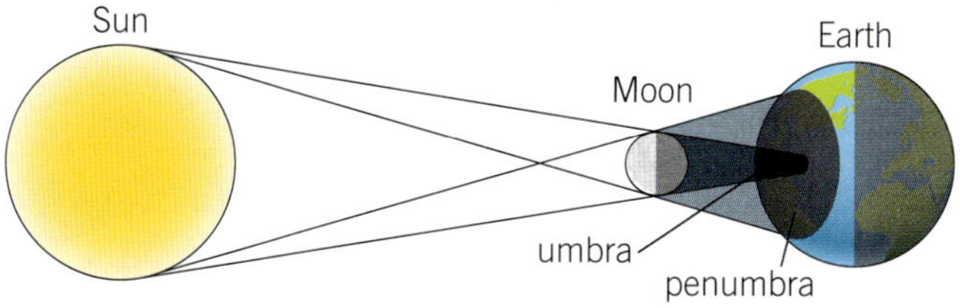

▲ A solar eclipse happens when the Moon blocks the light from the Sun.

c State the name of the deep shadow that produces a total solar eclipse.

Lunar eclipses

A **lunar eclipse** happens when the Earth comes between the Sun and the Moon.

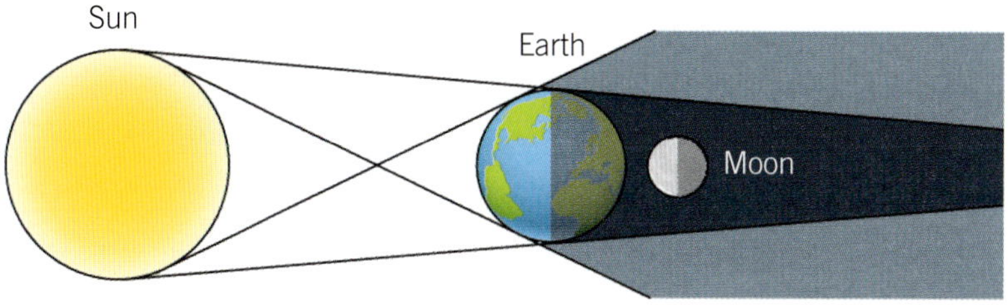

Far side of the Moon

The Moon spins on its axis but the time it takes to spin all the way around is the same time that it takes to orbit the Earth. This means that the same side of the Moon always faces the Earth. There is a side that you never see.

This doesn't mean there is a side of the Moon that is always in the dark. When you are looking at a new moon the Sun is lighting up the side of the Moon that you can't see.

▲ You can see a total eclipse of the Sun.

Key Words

phases of the Moon, umbra, total solar eclipse, penumbra, partial solar eclipse, lunar eclipse

Summary Questions

1 Copy and complete the sentences below.

You see a ______ moon when the Sun lights up the whole of the side that you can see. When the side of the Moon that you can see is in shadow you see a ______ moon. A solar eclipse happens when the ______ comes between the Sun and the ______. A lunar eclipse happens when the ______ comes between the Sun and the ______.

(6 marks)

2 Explain why you would see an eclipse on some of the planets in the Solar System but not others.

(1 mark)

3 Describe how you could use a torch, a beach ball, and a tennis ball to demonstrate the difference between a solar eclipse and a lunar eclipse.

(6 marks)

P1 Chapter 4 Summary

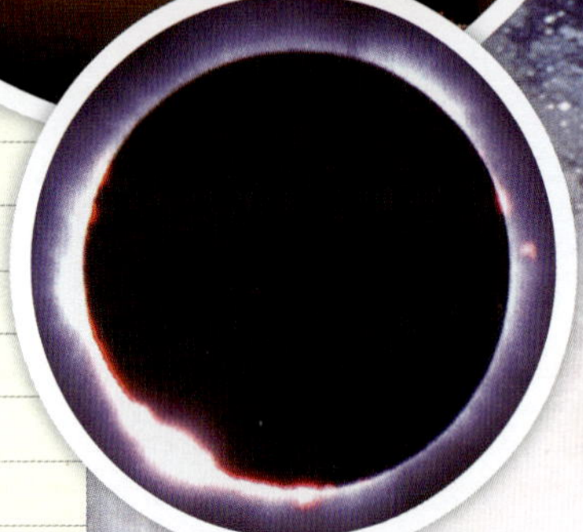

Key Points

- You can see satellites, the International Space Station, the Moon, comets, meteors, planets, stars, and galaxies in the night sky.
- The distances to objects in the night sky can be measured in light-time (light-seconds, light-minutes, light-hours, and light-years).
- The natural objects that you see are made of mixtures of gas, dust, rock, and ice.
- The Universe consists of millions of galaxies. Each galaxy contains billions of stars. Each star may have planets, asteroids, and comets in orbit around them. Each planet may have moons in orbit around them.
- There are four rocky inner planets (Mercury, Venus, Earth, and Mars), an asteroid belt, and four outer planets (Jupiter, Saturn, Uranus, and Neptune), made of gas.
- Planets further from the Sun are colder. Venus is hotter than Mercury, even though it is further from the Sun. This is because Mercury does not have an atmosphere to trap energy.
- The Earth spins on its axis once a day. This is why we have day and night, and why the Sun and stars appear to move across the sky.
- The Earth orbits the Sun in one year. The axis of the Earth is tilted and this explains the height of the Sun at noon, day length, temperature, and constellations that you see change during the year.
- You see phases of the Moon because the Moon is orbiting the Earth. Half of the Moon is always lit by the Sun.
- A solar eclipse happens when the Moon is between the Sun and the Earth. A lunar eclipse happens when the Earth is between the Sun and the Moon.

Key Words

star, artificial satellite, orbit, Earth, Moon, natural satellite, planet, Sun, Solar System, comet, meteor, meteorite, star, galaxy, Milky Way, Universe, astronomer, ellipse, asteroid, Mercury, Venus, Mars, terrestrial, gas giant, dwarf planet, gravity, exoplanet, axis, day, night, year, season, constellation, phases of the Moon, umbra, total solar eclipse, penumbra, partial solar eclipse, lunar eclipse

BIG Write

A new Earth...?

The table shows some information about the planet Pegasi b and Earth.

	51 Pegasi b	Earth
Distance from the star (million km)	7.7	150
Time to orbit the Sun (days)	4	365
Time to spin once on its axis (days)	4	1
Tilt of the axis (degrees)	79	23.5

Task

Write a guide to the new planet, comparing it to Earth and other planets in the Solar System.

Tips

- Could there be life on Pegasi b?

End-of-chapter questions

1 Here is a list of objects that you can see in the night sky. Sort the objects into those that are in orbit around the Sun and those that are in orbit around the Earth.

comet planet Moon satellite asteroid International Space Station

(***2 marks***)

2 The diagram shows the Earth in orbit around the Sun:

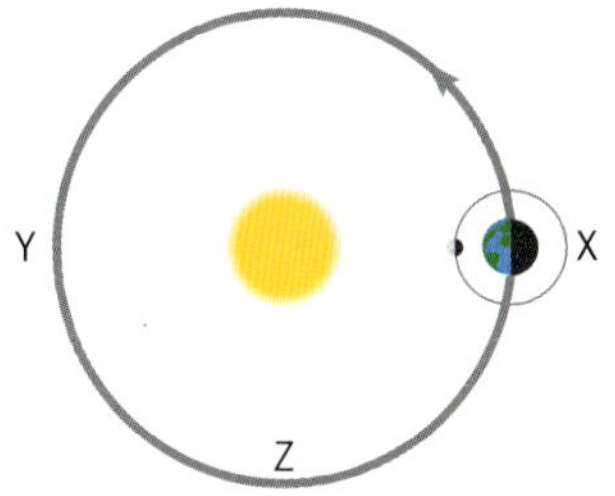

a Copy the diagram and label the Sun, the Earth, and the Moon. *(3 marks)*

b It is summer in the southern hemisphere when the Earth is at position X. State which season it would be when the Earth is at position Y. *(1 mark)*

c State how many months it would take the Earth to move between X and Z. *(1 mark)*

(***5 marks***)

3 This diagram shows how the Sun moves across the sky during the day in summer:

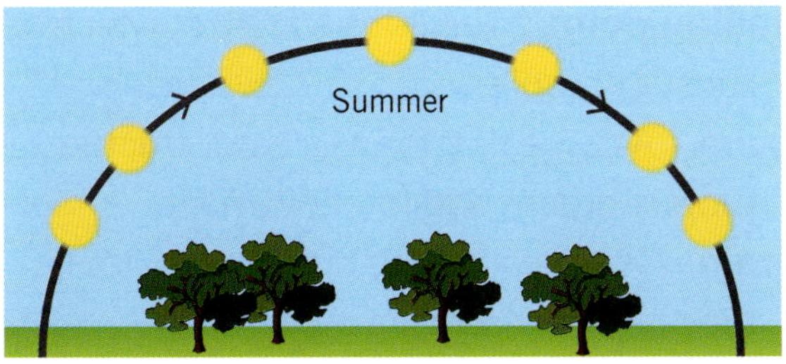

a Copy the diagram and add these labels: east, west, sunrise, sunset, noon

(2 marks)

b On the diagram sketch the path of the Sun in winter. *(2 marks)*

c Explain why the path of the Sun in the sky is different in autumn and in winter.

(2 marks)

(***6 marks***)

4 Here are some objects in the Universe:

Sun inner planet outer planet galaxy our nearest star Moon

a State which object or objects are a distance of light-seconds away and which are light-years away. *(2 marks)*

b Describe a problem with communicating with people on a spacecraft travelling through the Solar System. *(2 marks)*

(***4 marks***)

5 The table below shows the angle of tilt of the axes of all the planets in the Solar System.

Use the information in the table and your scientific knowledge to describe the seasonal changes on each of the planets and compare them to conditions on Earth.

(***6 marks***)

Planet	Angle of tilt (o)	Planet	Angle of tilt (o)
Mercury	0	Jupiter	3
Venus	177	Saturn	27
Earth	23.5	Uranus	98
Mars	25	Neptune	30

Glossary

absorb Taken into a material.

accurate Close to the true value of what you are measuring.

acid An acid is a solution with a pH value less than 7.

acidic solution An acidic solution has a pH less than 7.

adolescence The period of time when a child changes into an adult.

air resistance The force on an object moving through the air that causes it to slow down (also known as drag).

alkali An alkali is a soluble base.

alkaline solution An alkaline solution has a pH greater than 7.

alveolus (air sac) A structure inside the lungs where gas exchange takes place with the blood.

amoeba A unicellular organism.

amplifier A device for making a sound louder.

amplify To increase the amplitude of a sound so that it sounds louder.

amplitude The distance from the middle to the top or bottom of a wave.

analyse The process of looking at data and writing about what you have found out.

angle of incidence The angle between the incident ray and the normal line.

angle of reflection The angle between the reflected ray and the normal line.

antagonistic muscles A pair of muscles that work together to control movement at a joint – as one muscle contracts, the other relaxes.

anther The part of a flower that produces pollen.

artificial satellite A manmade spacecraft.

asteroid Lumps of rock orbiting the Sun left over from when the Solar System formed.

astronomer A scientist who studies space.

atom The smallest part of an element that can exist.

audible range The range of frequencies that you can hear.

auditory canal The passage in the ear from the outer ear to the eardrum.

auditory nerve An electrical signal travels along the auditory nerve to the brain.

axis (Earth) The imaginary line that the Earth spins around.

balanced (forces) Forces acting on an object that are the same size but act in opposite directions.

balanced symbol equation In a balanced symbol equation, chemical formulae represent the reactants and products. The equation shows how atoms are rearranged, and gives the relative amounts of reactants and products.

bar chart A way of presenting data when one variable is discrete or categoric and the other is continuous.

base A base is a substance that neutralises an acid.

boiling The change of state from liquid to gas that occurs when bubbles of the substance in its gas state form throughout the liquid.

boiling point The temperature at which a substance boils.

bone A tissue that forms a hard structure, used to protect organs and for movement.

brain The organ in the human body that processes signals from receptors

carpel The female reproductive part of the flower.

cartilage The strong, smooth tissue that covers the end of bones to prevent them rubbing together.

categoric A variable that has values that are words.

cell The smallest functional unit in an organism – the building block of life.

cell membrane The cell component that controls which substances can move into and out of the cell.

cell wall The plant cell component that surrounds the cell, providing support.

cervix The ring of muscle at the entrance to the uterus. It keeps the baby in place while the woman is pregnant.

change of state The process by which a substance changes from one state to another.

charge-coupled device (CCD) A grid of pixels at the back of a digital camera that absorbs light and produces an image.

chemical formula A formula that shows the relative number of atoms of each element in a compound.

chemical reaction A change in which atoms are rearranged to create new substances.

chemical symbol A one- or two-letter code for an element that is used by scientists in all countries.

chloroplast The plant cell component where photosynthesis takes place.

cilia Tiny hairs on the surface of cells.

cochlea Snail-shaped tube in the inner ear with the sensory cells that detect sound.

collide To bump into, or hit, a particle or surface.

combustion A chemical reaction in which a subsance reacts quickly with oxygen and gives out light and heat. Also called burning.

comet Dust particles frozen in ice that orbit the Sun.

compound A substance made up of atoms of two or more elements, strongly joined together.

compress To squash into a smaller space.

compression The part of a longitudinal wave where the air particles are close together.

concentrated A solution is concentrated if it has a large number of solute particles per unit volume (litre or cubic metre).

concentration A measure of the number of particles of a substance in a given volume.

conclusion What you write down to say what you have found out during an investigation.

condense The change of state from gas to liquid.

condom A barrier method of contraception, which prevents semen being released into the vagina.

confidence (in a conclusion) How sure you are of your conclusion based on the data.

conservation of mass In a chemical reaction, the total mass of reactants is equal to the total mass of products. This is conservation of mass. Mass is conserved in chemical reactions and in physical changes.

constellation A collection of stars that make a pattern in the sky.

contact force A force that acts when an object is in contact with a surface, air, or water.

continuous A variable that has values that can be any number.

contraception A method of preventing pregnancy.

contraceptive pill A chemical method of contraception.

control variable A variable that you have to keep the same in an investigation.

converging (lens) Bringing rays of light together.

convex (lens) A lens that produces converging rays of light.

cornea The transparent layer at the front of the eye.

corrosive A substance is corrosive if it can burn your skin or eyes.

crest The top of a wave.

cytoplasm A 'jelly-like' substance found in cells, where all the chemical reactions take place.

data Words or numbers that you obtain when you make observations or measurements.

day The time it takes a planet to make one full spin on its axis.

decibel A commonly used unit of sound intensity or loudness (dB).

decomposition A chemical reaction in which a compound breaks down to form simpler compounds and/or elements.

deform To change shape.

dependent variable A variable that changes when you change the independent variable.

diaphragm (breathing) The sheet of muscle used in breathing.

diaphragm (microphone) The part of the microphone that vibrates when a sound wave hits it.

diffuse reflection Reflection from a rough surface.

diffusion The movement of liquid or gas particles from a place of high concentration to a place of low concentration.

dilute A solution is dilute if it has a small number of solute particles per unit volume (litre or cubic metre).

discrete A variable that can only have whole-number values.

dispersion The splitting up of a ray of light of mixed wavelengths by refraction into its components.

drag force The force acting on an object moving through air or water that causes it to slow down.

driving force The force that is pushing or pulling something.

dwarf planet A small lump of rock in orbit around the Sun.

ear The organ of the body that detects sound.

eardrum A membrane that transmits sound vibrations from the outer ear to the middle ear.

Earth A rocky inner planet, third from the Sun in the Solar System.

echo A reflection of a sound wave by an object.

ejaculation When semen is released from the penis.

elastic limit The point beyond which a spring will not return to its original length when the force is removed.

electrostatic force The force acting between two charged objects.

element A substance that cannot be broken down into other substances.

ellipse A squashed circle or oval shape.

embryo A ball of cells that forms when the fertilised egg divides.

emit To give out.

endoscope A medical instrument for seeing inside the human body.

endothermic change An endothermic change transfers energy from the surroundings.

energy Energy is needed to make things happen.

equilibrium Balanced.

euglena Unicellular organism that performs photosynthesis.

evaluate To discuss the quality of data collected during an investigation and suggest improvements to the method.

evaporate The change of state from liquid to gas that occurs when particles leave the surface of the liquid only. It can happen at any temperature.

evidence Observations and measurements that support or disprove a scientific theory.

exhale Breathing out, to remove carbon dioxide.

exoplanets A planet in orbit around a star other than our Sun.

exothermic change An exothermic change transfers energy to the surroundings.
extension The amount by which an object gets longer when a force is applied.
eye Organ of sight, which focuses and detects light.

fertilisation The process where the nucleus of a sperm cell joins with the nucleus of an egg cell.
fetus The name given to an unborn baby from eight weeks of development.
field A region where something feels a force.
filament The part of a flower that holds up the anther.
filter A piece of material that allows some radiation (colours) through but absorbs the rest.
flagellum A tail-like structure that allows euglenas to move.
fluid sac Contains fluid. This acts as a shock absorber, protecting the fetus from bumps.
focal point The point at which the rays refracted by a convex lens cross over.
focus Another name for the focal point.
fossil fuel A fuel made from the remains of animals and plants that died millions of years ago. Fossil fuels include coal, oil, and natural gas.
freezing The change of state from liquid to solid.
frequency The number of complete waves or vibrations produced in one second (measured in hertz).
friction The force that resists movement because of contact between surfaces.
fruit The part of a plant that contains seeds.
fuel A material that burns to transfer useful energy.

galaxy A number of stars and the solar systems around them grouped together.
gametes Reproductive cells. The male gamete is a sperm cell and the female gamete is an egg cell.
gas In the gas state, a substance can flow and can also be compressed.
gas exchange The transfer of gases between an organism and its environment.
gas giant An outer planet in the Solar System, made mainly from gas.
gas pressure The force exerted by gas particles per unit area of a surface.
germination The period of time when a seed starts to grow.
gravity A non-contact force that acts between two masses.

hazard A possible source of danger.
hertz The unit of frequency (Hz).
Hooke's Law A law that says that if you double the force on an object the extension will double.
hormones Chemical messengers that travel around the body in the blood.

image The point from which rays of light entering the eye appear to have originated.
implantation The process where an embryo attaches to the lining of the uterus.
incident ray The ray coming from a source of light.
incident wave The wave coming from a source.
independent variable A variable you change that changes the dependent variable.
indicator A substance that changes colour to show whether a solution is acidic or alkaline.
infrasound Sound below a frequency of 20 Hz.
inhale Breathing in, to take in oxygen.
inner ear The semi-circular canals that help you to balance, and your cochlea.
interaction pair When two objects interact there is a force on each one that is the same size but in opposing directions.
inverted Upside down.
investigation An experiment or set of experiments designed to produce data to answer a scientific question or test a theory.
iris The coloured part of your eye.

joint A part of the skeleton where two bones join together.

kilogram "A unit of mass, symbol kg.

kilohertz 1 kilohertz (kHz) = 1000 hertz (Hz)

law of reflection The angle of incidence is equal to the angle of reflection.

leaf cell The plant cells that contain chloroplasts, where photosynthesis takes place.

lens A device made of shaped glass that focuses light rays from objects to form an image.

ligament Joins two bones together.

light-time Distance measured in terms of how far light travels in a given time.

line graph A way of presenting results when there are two numerical variables.

line of best fit A smooth line on a graph that travels through or very close to as many of the points plotted as possible.

liquid In the liquid state, a substance can flow but cannot be compressed.

litmus An indicator. Blue litmus paper goes red on adding acid. Red litmus paper goes blue on adding alkali.

longitudinal A wave where the vibrations are in the same direction as the direction the wave moves.

loudness How loud you perceive a sound of a certain intensity to be.

lubrication A substance that reduces friction between surfaces when they rub together.

luminous Gives out light.

lunar eclipse An eclipse that happens when the Earth comes between the Sun and the Moon.

lungs The organ in which gas exchange takes place.

magnetic force The force between two magnets, or a magnet and a magnetic material.

Mars A rocky inner planet, fourth from the Sun in the Solar System.

mass The amount of matter (stuff) a thing is made up of.

material The different types of stuff that things are made from.

mean An average of a set of data, found by adding together all the values in the set and dividing by the number of values in the set.

medium The material that affects light or sound by slowing it down or transferring the wave.

melting The change of state from solid to liquid.

melting point The temperature at which a substance melts.

menstrual cycle The monthly cycle during which the uterus lining thickens, and then breaks down and leaves the body if an egg is not fertilised.

Mercury A rocky inner planet, closest to the Sun in the Solar System.

meteor A piece of rock or dust that makes a streak of light in the night sky.

meteorite A stony or metallic object that has fallen to Earth from outer space.

microphone A device for converting sound into an electrical signal.

microscope An optical instrument used to magnify objects, so small details can be seen clearly.

middle ear The ossicles (small bones) that transfer vibrations from the outer ear to the inner ear.

Milky Way The galaxy containing our Sun and Solar System.

mitochondria The cell component where respiration takes place.

mixture A material whose properties are not the same all the way through.

molecule A group of two or more atoms, strongly joined together.

Moon A rocky body orbiting Earth; it is Earth's only natural satellite.

multicellular Made of many cells.

multicellular organism An organism made up of many cells.

natural satellite A moon in orbit around a planet.

nerve cell An animal cell that transmits electrical impulses around the body.

neutral A solution that is neither alkaline nor acidic. Its pH is 7.

neutralisation In a neutralisation reaction, an acid cancels out a base or a base cancels out an acid.

newton The unit of force, symbol N.

newtonmeter A piece of equipment used to measure weight in newtons.

night The period on one section of the Earth or other planet when it is facing away from the Sun.

non-contact force A magnetic, electrostatic, or gravitational force that acts between objects not in contact.

non-luminous Objects that produce no light.

non-renewable Some fuels are non-renewable. They form over millions of years, and will one day run out.

normal An imaginary line at right angles to a surface where a light ray strikes it.

nucleus The cell component that controls the cell and contains genetic material.

observation Carefully looking at an object or process.

opaque Objects that absorb, scatter, or reflect light and do not allow any light to pass through.

optic nerve A paired sensory nerve that runs from each eye to the brain.

orbit The path taken by one body in space around another.

organ A group of tissues working together to perform a function.

organ systen A group of organs working together to perform a function.

organism A living thing.

oscillation Something that moves backwards and forwards.

oscilloscope A device that enables you to see electrical signals, like those made by a microphone.

ossicles The small bones of the middle ear (hammer, anvil, and stirrup) that transfer vibrations from the eardrum to the oval window.

outer ear The pinna, auditory canal, and eardrum.

outlier A result that is very different from the other measurements in a data set.

oval window The membrane that connects the ossicles to the cochlea.

ovary (human) Contains egg cells.

ovary (plant) The part of a flower that contains ovules.

oviduct Tube that carries an egg to the uterus.

ovulation The release of an egg from an ovary.

ovule The female gamete of a plant.

oxidation A chemical reaction in which substances react with oxygen to form oxides.

partial eclipse A solar eclipse where only part of the Sun is covered by the Moon.

particle The tiny things that materials are made from.

peak The top of a wave.

penis The structure that carries sperm and semen out of the body.

penumbra The area of blurred or fuzzy shadow around the edges of the umbra.

period Loss of uterus lining through the vagina.

Periodic Table A table of all the elements, in which elements with similar properties are grouped together.

petal The brightly coloured part of a flower that attracts insects.

pH scale The pH scale shows whether a substance is acidic, alkaline, or neutral. An acid has a pH below 7. An alkaline solution has a pH above 7. A solution of pH 7 is neutral.

phases of the Moon Shape of the Moon as we see it from Earth.

photoreceptor A specialised cell that is sensitive to light.

photosynthesis A chemical reaction where carbon dioxide and water are converted into oxygen and glucose.

physical change A change that is reversible, in which new substances are not made. Examples of physical changes include changes of state, and dissolving.

pie chart A way of presenting data when one variable is discrete or categoric and the other is continuous.

pinhole camera A simple camera made of a box with a small hole at the front and a screen at the back.

pinna The outside part of the ear that we can see.

pitch A property of sound determined by its frequency.

pixel A picture element found at the back of a digital camera.

placenta The organ where substances pass between the mother's and the fetus's blood. It acts as a barrier, stopping infections and harmful substances reaching the fetus.

plan A description of how you will use equipment to collect valid data to answer a scientific question.

plane A mirror with a flat, reflective surface.

planet Any large body that orbits a star in a Solar System.

pollen The male gamete of a plant.

pollination The transfer of pollen from the anther to the stigma.

precise This describes a set of repeat measurements that are close together.

prediction A statement that says what you think will happen.

pregnant When a baby is growing inside a woman she is pregnant.

primary colour The colours red, blue, and green.

prism A triangular-shaped piece of glass used to produce a spectrum of light.

product A substance that is made in a chemical reaction.

property A quality of a substance or material that describes its appearance, or how it behaves.

puberty The physical changes that take place during adolescence.

pull A type of force.

pupil The hole in the front of your eye where light goes in.

push A type of force.

random (error) A error that causes there to be a random difference between a measurement and the true value each time you measure it.

range The difference between the lowest and highest values a variable can have.

rarefaction The part of a longitudinal wave where the air particles are spread out.

reactant A starting substance in a chemical reaction.

reaction The support force provided by a solid surface like a floor.

real (image) An image that you can put on a screen; the image formed in your eyes.

receiver The device that absorbs the sound waves.

red blood cell An animal cell that transports oxygen around the body.

reflect Bounce off.
reflected ray The ray that is reflected from a surface.
reflected wave The wave that is reflected from a surface.
reflection The change in direction of a ray or wave after it hits a surface and bounces off.
refraction The change in direction of a ray or wave as a result of its change in speed.
repeatable (results) When you repeat measurements in an investigation and get similar results they are repeatable.
reproducible (results) When other people carry out an investigation and get similar results to the orginal investigation the results are repeatable.
resistive force Any force that acts to slow down a moving object.
respiration A chemical reaction where food and oxygen are converted into energy, water, and carbon dioxide.
respiratory system The organs involved in gas exchange.
retina The layer of light sensitive cells at the back of the eye.
reverberation The persistence of a sound for a longer period than normal.
ribcage The bones that protect the lungs.
risk The chance of damage or injury from a hazard.
risk assessment A description of how you will make it less likely that people will be injured, or equipment damaged, and what to do if this happens.
root hair cell A plant cell that takes in water and minerals from the soil.

salt A salt is a compound in which the hydrogen atoms of an acid are replaced by atoms of a metal element.
scrotum The bag of skin that holds the testes.
season Changes in the temperature during the year as the Earth moves around its orbit.
secondary colour Colours that can be obtained by mixing two primary colours.
seed The structure that develops into a new plant.
seed dispersal The movement of seeds away from the parent plant.
semen Fluid containing sperm.
sepal The special leaves found under the flower, which protect unopened buds.
sexual intercourse The process where the penis releases semen into the vagina.
skeleton All the bones in an organism.
solar eclipse An eclipse where the Moon comes between the Sun and the Earth.
Solar System The Sun and the planets and other bodies in orbit around it.
solid In the solid state, a substance cannot be compressed and it cannot flow.
sound A series of compressions and rarefactions that move through a medium.
source (light or sound) Things that emit (give out) light or sound.
specialised cell A cell whose shape and structure enable it to perform a particular function.
spectrum A band of colours produced when light is spread out by a prism.
specular reflection Reflection from a smooth surface.
speed of light The distance light travels in one second (300 million m/s).
speed of sound The distance sound travels in one second (330 m/s).
sperm cell A cell containing male genetic material.
sperm duct Tube that carries sperm from the testes to the penis.
spread The difference between the highest and lowest measurements of a set of repeat measurements.
stamen The male reproductive part of the flower.
star A body in space that gives out its own light.
states of matter The three forms in which a substance can exist – solid, liquid, and gas.

stigma The part of a flower that is sticky to catch grains of pollen.

streamlined Shaped to reduce resistance to motion from air or water.

stretch An object can be stretched if you exert a force on it.

style The part of a flower that holds up the stigma.

sublime The change of state from solid to gas.

substance A material that is not a mixture. It has the same properties all the way through.

Sun The star at the centre of our Solar System.

superpose When waves join together so that they add up or cancel out.

systematic (error) An error that causes there to be the same difference between a measurement and the true value each time you measure it.

tendon Joins a muscle to a bone.

tension A stretching force.

terrestrial Made of rock.

tertiary colour A colour made by mixing three primary colours.

testes The testes produce sperm and the male sex hormones.

tissue A group of similar cells working together to perform a function.

total eclipse An eclipse where all of the Sun is covered by the Moon.

translucent Objects that transmit light but diffusing (scattering) the light as it passes through.

transmit When light or other radiation passes through an object.

transmitter (light or sound) A device that gives out light or sound.

transparent Objects that transmit light and you can see through them.

transverse The vibrations are at right angles to the direction the wave moves.

trough The bottom of a wave.

ultrasound Sound at a frequency greater than 20 000 Hz, beyond the range of human hearing.

umbilical cord Connects the fetus to the placenta.

umbra The area of total shadow behind an opaque object where no light has reached.

unbalanced (forces) Opposing forces on an object that are unequal.

uncertainty The doubt in the result because of the way that a measurement is made.

unicellular Consisting of just one cell.

universal indicator An indicator that changes colour to show the pH of a solution. It is a mixture of dyes.

Universe Everything that exists.

upthrust The force on an object in a liquid or gas that pushes it up.

urethra Tube that carries urine or sperm out of the body.

uterus Where a baby develops until its birth.

vacuole The plant cell component that contains cell sap and helps to keep the cell firm.

vacuum A space in which there is no matter.

vagina Receives sperm during sexual intercourse. This is where the male's penis enters the female's body.

variable A quantity that can change, for example, time, temperature, length, mass.

Venus A rocky inner planet, second from the Sun in the our Solar System.

vibration Backwards and forwards motion of the parts of a liquid or solid.

virtual An image that cannot be focused onto a screen.

vocal chords The pieces of skin that vibrate to produce sound.

water resistance The force on an object moving through water that causes it to slow down (also known as drag).

wave A vibration that transfers energy.

wavelength The distance between two identical points on the wave.

weight The force of the Earth on an object due to its mass.

windpipe (trachea) The structure through which air travels from the mouth to the lungs.

word equation A way of representing a chemical reaction simply. The reactants are on the left of an arrow, and the products are on the right. The arrow means *reacts to make*.

year The length of time it takes for a planet to orbit the Sun.

Index

The Periodic Table

Times of discovery

- before 1800
- 1800–1849
- 1849–1899
- 1900–1949
- 1949–1999

Key: relative atomic mass / chemical symbol / name / atomic (proton) number

1.0 H hydrogen 1

Period	Group 1	Group 2											Group 3	Group 4	Group 5	Group 6	Group 7	Group 8
																		4 He helium 2
2	7 Li lithium 3	9 Be beryllium 4											11 B boron 5	12 C carbon 6	14 N nitrogen 7	16 O oxygen 8	19 F fluorine 9	20 Ne neon 10
3	23 Na sodium 11	24 Mg magnesium 12											27 Al aluminium 13	28 Si silicon 14	31 P phosphorus 15	32 S sulfur 16	35.5 Cl chlorine 17	40 Ar argon 18
4	39 K potassium 19	40 Ca calcium 20	45 Sc scandium 21	48 Ti titanium 22	51 V vanadium 23	52 Cr chromium 24	55 Mn manganese 25	56 Fe iron 26	59 Co cobalt 27	59 Ni nickel 28	63.5 Cu copper 29	65 Zn zinc 30	70 Ga gallium 31	73 Ge germanium 32	75 As arsenic 33	79 Se selenium 34	80 Br bromine 35	84 Kr krypton 36
5	85.5 Rb rubidium 37	88 Sr strontium 38	89 Y yttrium 39	91 Zr zirconium 40	93 Nb niobium 41	96 Mo molybdenum 42	(98) Tc technetium 43	101 Ru ruthenium 44	103 Rh rhodium 45	106 Pd palladium 46	108 Ag silver 47	112 Cd cadmium 48	115 In indium 49	119 Sn tin 50	122 Sb antimony 51	128 Te tellurium 52	127 I iodine 53	131 Xe xenon 54
6	133 Cs caesium 55	137 Ba barium 56	139 * La lanthanum 57	178.5 Hf hafnium 72	181 Ta tantalum 73	184 W tungsten 74	186 Re rhenium 75	190 Os osmium 76	192 Ir iridium 77	195 Pt platinum 78	197 Au gold 79	201 Hg mercury 80	204 Tl thallium 81	207 Pb lead 82	209 Bi bismuth 83	210 Po polonium 84	(210) At astatine 85	222 Rn radon 86
7	(223) Fr francium 87	(226) Ra radium 88	(227) # Ac actinium 89	(261) Rf rutherfordium 104	(262) Db dubnium 105	(266) Sg seaborgium 106	(264) Bh bohrium 107	(277) Hs hassium 108	(268) Mt meitnerium 109	(271) Ds darmstadtium 110	(272) Rg roentgenium 111	Elements with atomic numbers 112–116 have been reported but not fully authenticated						

*58–71 Lanthanides	140 Ce cerium 58	141 Pr praseodymium 59	144 Nd neodymium 60	(145) Pm promethium 61	150 Sm samarium 62	152 Eu europium 63	157 Gd gadolinium 64	159 Tb terbium 65	163 Dy dysprosium 66	165 Ho holmium 67	167 Er erbium 68	169 Tm thulium 69	173 Yb ytterbium 70	175 Lu lutetium 71
#90–103 Actinides	232 Th thorium 90	231 Pa protactinium 91	238 U uranium 92	237 Np neptunium 93	239 Pu plutonium 94	243 Am americium 95	247 Cm curium 96	247 Bk berkelium 97	252 Cf californium 98	(252) Es einsteinium 99	(257) Fm fermium 100	(258) Md mendelevium 101	(259) No nobelium 102	(260) Lr lawrencium 103

OXFORD
UNIVERSITY PRESS

Great Clarendon Street, Oxford, OX2 6DP, United Kingdom

Oxford University Press is a department of the University of Oxford. It furthers the University's objective of excellence in research, scholarship, and education by publishing worldwide. Oxford is a registered trade mark of Oxford University Press in the UK and in certain other countries

First published in 2013

British Library Cataloguing in Publication Data
Data available

978-0-19-839256-9

20 19 18 17 16 15

Paper used in the production of this book is a natural, recyclable product made from wood grown in sustainable forests.
The manufacturing process conforms to the environmental regulations of the country of origin.

Printed in China by Shanghai Offset Printing Product Ltd.

Acknowledgements
The publisher and the authors would like to thank the following for permissions to use their photographs:

Cover image: Sebastian Tomus/Shutterstock; **p2**: Rido/Shutterstock; **p2**: Rex Features; **p10**: Arcady/Shutterstock; **p12**: Andrew Syred/Science Photo Library; **p12**: Dr Jeremy Burgess/Science Photo Library; **p12-13**: Dr Gopal Murti/Science Photo Library; **p13**: Olga Sapegina/Shutterstock; **p13**: rangizzz/Shutterstock; **p13**: hddigital/Shutterstock; **p13**: Steex/iStockphoto; **p13**: Astrid & Hanns Frieder Michler/Science Photo Library; **p12**: R-Studio/Shutterstock; **p14**: Dr Gopal Murti/Science Photo Library; **p14**: Dr Jeremy Burgess/Science Photo Library; **p16**: Dr Gopal Murti/Science Photo Library; **p17**: J.C.Revi/ISM/Science Photo Library; **p24**: J.C.Revi/ISM/Science Photo Library; **p24**: Dr Gopal Murti/Science Photo Library; **p24-25**: Dr Gopal Murti/Science Photo Library; **p28**: yumiyum/iStockphoto; **p29**: Daniel Täger/Flux/Glow Images; **p32**: muratseyit/iStockphoto; **p34**: itsmejust/iStockphoto; **p38**: itsmejust/iStockphoto; **p38-39**: yumiyum/iStockphoto; **p39**: muratseyit/iStockphoto; **p41**: ZIG8/iStockphoto; **p40**: Dawn Poland/iStockphoto; **p44**: Eye of Science/Science Photo Library; **p47**: Keith/Custom Medical Stock Photo/Science Photo Library; **p48**: Matka Wariatka/iStockphoto; **p49**: energyy/iStockphoto; **p49**: AJ Photo/Science Photo Library; **p50**: Nnehring/iStockphoto; **p51**: guhl/iStockphoto; **p51**: Noppharat05081977/iStockphoto; **p52**: adlifemarketing/iStockphoto; **p54**: vithib/iStockphoto; **p55**: kiorio/iStockphoto; **p55**: Clark and Company/iStockphoto; **p56**: guhl/iStockphoto; **p56**: Noppharat05081977/iStockphoto; **p56-57**: vithib/iStockphoto; **p58**: Andrew Lambert Photography/Science Photo Library; **p58**: tankbmb/iStockphoto; **p58-59**: Christian Degroote/Dreamstime; **p59**: Mark Evans/iStockphoto; **p59**: Jeffrey Smith/iStockphoto; **p59**: catnap72/iStockphoto; **p59**: Stepan Popov/iStockphoto; **p59**: Pekka Parviainen /Science Photo Library; **p60**: Christian Degroote/Dreamstime; **p60**: Maciej Laska/E+/Getty Images; **p62**: jml5571/iStockphoto; **p64**: Charles D.Winter/Science Photo Library; **p64**: tankbmb/iStockphoto; **p65**: Martyn F. Chillmaid/Science Photo Library; **p68**: Ridofranz/iStockphoto; **p69**: Ariturk/Dreamstime; **p69**: Andrew Lambert Photography/Science Photo Library; **p70**: Stefaanh/Dreamstime; **p71**: Andrew Lambert Photography/Science Photo Library; **p72**: Mark Evans/iStockphoto; **p74**: Mark Evans/iStockphoto; **p74**: Ridofranz/iStockphoto; **p74-75**: Charles D.Winter/Science Photo Library; **p76**: Damian Palus/iStockphoto; **p76**: Science Photo Library; **p76**: sqback/iStockphoto; **p76**: Carolina Smith/iStockphoto; **p78**: Northwestern University/Science Photo Library; **p78**: Tek Image/Science Photo Library; **p79**: t_kimura/iStockphoto; **p80**: grandriver/iStockphoto; **p81**: Fertnig/iStockphoto; **p84**: grandriver/iStockphoto; **p84**: Fertnig/iStockphoto; **p84-85**: Tek Image/Science Photo Library; **p86**: Ulga/iStockphoto; **p87**: Wessex Water/ GENeco; **p88**: ZekaG/iStockphoto; **p88**: Martyn F. Chillmaid/Science Photo Library; **p88**: Martyn F. Chillmaid/Science Photo Library; **p90**: Rex Features; **p90**: Martin Bond/Science Photo Library; **p91**: Rob_Ellis/iStockphoto; **p92**: Quirex/iStockphoto; **p92**: Bonzodog/Dreamstime; **p92**: Andrew Lambert Photography/Science Photo Library; **p94**: wolv/iStockphoto; **p94**: Andrew Lambert Photography/Science Photo Library; **p96**: Carolyn A.Mckeone/Science Photo Library; **p97**: messenjah/iStockphoto; **p98**: ZekaG/iStockphoto; **p98**: wolv/iStockphoto; **p98-99**: Bonzodog/Dreamstime; **p100**: Mark Evans/iStockphoto; **p100**: Rbozuk/iStockphoto; **p102**: Andrew Lambert Photography/Science Photo Library; **p103**: Andrew Lambert Photography/Science Photo Library; **p104**: jpa1999/iStockphoto; **p105**: Robert Churchill/istockphoto; **p105**: Universal Images Group/Getty Images; **p106**: 4kodiak/iStockphoto; **p106**: JulieVMac/iStockphoto; **p106**: Hanis/iStockphoto; **p108**: Andrew Lambert Photography/Science Photo Library; **p108**: 4kodiak/iStockphoto; **p108-109**: JulieVMac/iStockphoto; p110: 262276/Shutterstock; **p110**: ProfStocker/Shutterstock; **p110-111**: Diego Cervo/Shutterstock; **p111**: Elke Meitzel/Science Photo Library; **p111**: Michael Dunning/Photographer's Choice/Getty Images; **p111**: svetlana55/Shutterstock; **p111**: bkindler/iStockphoto; **p111**: Tish1/Shutterstock; **p111**: Susumu Nishinaga/Science Photo Library; **p112**: Terry Renna/AP Images; **p113**: ProfStocker/Shutterstock; **p113**: MichaelHitoshi/Photodisc/Getty Images; **p114**: Brave Rabbit/Shutterstock; **p115**: Elina/Shutterstock; **p116**: Velychko/Shutterstock; **p117**: Gallo Images/Vetta/Getty Images; **p118**: Tommounsey/iStockphoto; **p118**: 262276/Shutterstock; **p120**: Diego Cervo/Shutterstock; **p120**: Yousef Allan/AP images; **p121**: Racefotos2008/Shutterstock; **p122-123**: Brave Rabbit/Shutterstock; **p122**: Racefotos2008/Shutterstock; **p122**: Velychko/Shutterstock; **p124**: Andrew Lambert Photography/Science Photo Library; **p125**: science photos/alamy; **p126**: Steve Allen/ Science Photo Library; **p126**: Stuart Westmorland/Corbis; **p127**: Jay Nemeth/Red Bull/Associated Press; **p128**: Andrew Lambert Photography/Science Photo Library; **p128**: Image Source/Getty Images; **p129**: Elke Meitzel/Science Photo Library; **p130**: Steve Gschmeissner/Science Photo Library; **p132**: Henrik Sorensen/The Image Bank/Henrik Sorensen; **p133**: Thierry Berrod, Mona Lisa Production/Science Photo Library; **p134**: Jay Nemeth/Red Bull/Associated Press; **p134**: Steve Allen/Science Photo Library; **p134-135**: Stuart Westmorland/Corbis; **p136**: Efired/Shutterstock; **p136**: auremar/Shutterstock; **p138**: gabczi/Shutterstock; **p140**: Martyn F. Chillmaid/Science Photo Library; **p142**: Tatiana Makotra/Shutterstock; **p143**: Paul Parker/Science Photo Library; **p144**: Atlantide Phototravel/Corbis; **p144**: Andrzej Wojcick/Science Photo Library; **p146**: Tatiana Makotra/Shutterstock; **p146**: Paul Parker/Science Photo Library; **p146**: auremar/Shutterstock; **p148**: NASA/Science Photo Library; **p149**: Marcel Clemens/Shutterstock; **p149**: Celestial Image Picture Co./Science Photo Library; **p150**: Marcel Clemens/Shutterstock; **p150**: NASA/Science Photo Library; **p152**: David Parker/Science Photo Library; **p153**: Dr Juerg Alean/Science Photo Library; **p154**: NASA/Science Photo Library; **p155**: bkindler/iStockphoto; **p156**: David Parker/Science Photo Library; **p156**: bkindler/iStockphoto; **p156-157**: Celestial Image Picture Co./Science Photo Library; **pii**: Albert Klein/Oxford Scientific/Getty Images; **contents**: pixelparticle/shutterstock

Artwork by Phoenix Photosetting and Q2A Media